PSYCHOLOGY LIBRARY EDITIONS:
PERCEPTION

I0125951

Volume 9

THE DEVELOPMENT
OF PERCEPTION, COGNITION
AND LANGUAGE

THE DEVELOPMENT OF PERCEPTION, COGNITION AND LANGUAGE

A theoretical approach

PAUL VAN GEERT

Routledge
Taylor & Francis Group

LONDON AND NEW YORK

First published in 1983 by Routledge & Kegan Paul plc

This edition first published in 2017
by Routledge
2 Park Square, Milton Park, Abingdon, Oxon OX14 4RN

and by Routledge
711 Third Avenue, New York, NY 10017

Routledge is an imprint of the Taylor & Francis Group, an informa business

© 1983 Paul van Geert

British Library Cataloguing in Publication Data
A catalogue record for this book is available from the British Library

ISBN: 978-1-138-68824-7 (Set)
ISBN: 978-1-315-22895-2 (Set) (ebk)
ISBN: 978-1-138-69443-9 (Volume 9) (hbk)
ISBN: 978-1-138-69449-1 (Volume 9) (pbk)
ISBN: 978-1-315-52813-7 (Volume 9) (ebk)

Publisher's Note
The publisher has gone to great lengths to ensure the quality of this reprint but points out that some imperfections in the original copies may be apparent.

Disclaimer
The publisher has made every effort to trace copyright holders and would welcome correspondence from those they have been unable to trace.

The development of perception, cognition and language

A theoretical approach

Paul van Geert

Routledge & Kegan Paul
London, Boston, Melbourne and Henley

First published in 1983
by Routledge & Kegan Paul plc
39 Store Street, London WC1E 7DD,
9 Park Street, Boston, Mass. 02108, USA,
296 Beaconsfield Parade, Middle Park,
Melbourne, 3206, Australia, and
Broadway House, Newtown Road,
Henley-on-Thames, Oxon RG9 1EN
Printed in Great Britain by
Redwood Burn Ltd, Trowbridge, Wiltshire

Library of Congress Cataloging in Publication Data

Geert, Paul van.
The development of perception, cognition, and
language.
(International library of psychology)
Bibliography: p.
Includes index.
1. Perception. 2. Cognition. 3. Psycholinguistics.
4. Developmental psychology. I. Title. II. Series.

BF311.G38   1983   153   83-9753

ISBN 0-7100-9420-5

Contents

Preface

The aim of this book is to discuss some fundamental problems
of cognitive developmental psychology. The theme which underlies the discussion is that scientific knowledge of the cognitive
characteristics of other people starts from the cognitive instruments that we psychologists employ, viz. our theories, models,
assumptions, methods of inquiry, etc. Thus, our scientific
cognitive equipment not only provides the format in which
cognition in other people is expressed, it also exemplifies, in
some abstract sense, this cognition. The fundamental similarity
between the object, means, and outcome of investigation is a
distinctive property of psychological science. The first part of
the book deals with the concept of development in relation to
the structure of developmental theories. It is argued that
theories originate from (implicit) conceptual analyses of (implicit)
final state definitions.

Starting from this specific view on the nature of developmental theories, the second part of the book discusses perception and perceptual development. The process of perception is
defined formally as a transformational relationship between a
perceived, external world and the physical energies acting
upon the senses. From this definition, a specific model of
perceptual development is inferred. In the chapters on sensory
integration, space perception, and perception of form and pattern, a comparison is made between the theoretical model and
present empirical findings. The present account of perception
and perceptual development is of the 'classical' type, which
views perception as a matter of relationships between proximal
stimuli and perceived distal qualities and objects. The argument
does not go so far, however, as to claim that perception is a
matter of internal scenes or images in the head. Rather, it is a
basic property of perception, from its beginnings in early
development, that it presents the perceiver with an external,
qualitatively present, objective world.

The Gibsonian, ecological viewpoint, which is an attractive
alternative of much promise, is nevertheless incompatible with
this stimulus-perceived object-approach. This book holds to the
more or less classical view, however, for two reasons. The
first of these is to demonstrate how a specific view on the
nature of perceptions shapes the structure of a developmental
theory. This approach avoids the need to argue that one specific model of perception should be preferred to another. Thus,
the classical view is chosen simply because it is the view with

which many people are acquainted, and because it is tacitly taken as the 'standard' theory of perception. The second reason is more personal. It stems from the author's advocacy of conceptual pluralism in psychology, the acceptation that paradigmatically distinct psychological theories are comparable with distinct viewpoints in visual perception. Just as our perception of an object becomes more veridical by orderly changing viewpoints during (loco)motion, our scientific knowledge becomes more 'objective' by changing paradigmatical viewpoints in a long and complicated act of 'epistemic (loco)motion'. The general acceptance and critical, empirical refinement of one viewpoint does not imply that other viewpoints are taken to be basically false. Just as in actual, mobile visual exploration viewpoints cannot literally become integrated, the plea for conceptual pluralism does not equal an attempt towards eclecticism. The first chapters of part two present a picture of the various aspects of perceptual development. The following chapter outlines the rudiments of a theory that views attention as explanation of the internal dynamics of perceptual development. The final chapter in this section provides a metatheoretical reflection on description and explanation of developmental phenomena. Part three of the book deals with the development of cognition and language viewed as systems of (re)presentation. The first chapter discusses the attributed character of knowledge. The following chapters explore respectively, representation in general, the relation between knowledge and meaning and syntactic aspects of language and perception. The final chapter discusses aspects of the conceptual spaces in which theoretical models of mind, behaviour and development are formulated.

It would not be appropriate to conclude without making some form of personal statement. First, I would like to express my gratitude to the Netherlands Institute for Advanced studies in Wassenaar, the Netherlands, for giving me the opportunity to spend the academic year 1978-9 in the company of distinguished psychologists and linguists, viz. M. and W.R. Bowerman, J.S. Bruner, R.N. Campbell, M.S. van Ierland, D.R. Olson, H.D.K. Parret, M. Schegloff, and M.L. Ryan. Special thanks go to Bea de Gelder, with whom I discussed in detail many of the problems explored in the present book. Our common interest in knowledge and representation resulted in a conference, held at NIAS in March 1979 (the proceedings edited by De Gelder have been published in the ILP-series).

Finally, I would like to thank my colleagues of the Department of Developmental Psychology in Groningen. Despite differences in interests and skills, they have been responsible for the friendly and co-operative atmosphere without which the writing of this book would have been impossible. At the end of the day, however, the most enjoyable and inspiring environment for writing was to be found in the little village of Sint Annen, with my wife, Leen, and my children Liesbet and David.

Part I

A framework for thinking about development

1 The concept of development

1.1 INTRODUCTORY REMARKS

The study of psychological development is concerned with general long-term changes in what can be described as the person's mind, behaviour, abilities, skills, etc.

Traditionally, the basic variable of developmental studies has been age, a person's chronological position in the life-cycle.

Life-span and age are not the only variables that can explain a person's mind or behaviour. It is a speculative even ideological question whether the long-term changes one assumes to be attributable to age alone are more essential to development than the changes attributable to such factors as schooling, social environment, material conditions, etc. Is there enough uniformity between babies or between adults to enable us to make valid and reliable statements about what happens in general between birth and adulthood (or between birth and death)?

It may also be questioned whether psychological development is a kind of physicalistic, i.e. natural science property of a human being. On the one hand, we may safely assume that the structure of human digestion or the way in which the brain works is anthropologically universal and can be conceived of as involving physicalistic, natural science properties. Digestion and the working of the brain are independent of one's knowledge about the existence of a digestive system, or a brain, or how they work. On the other hand, it is probable that psychological development must be dealt with not as a physicalistic but as a social science property of a human being. It might be that discussion related to psychological development is relevant only in cultures or groups which already, either explicitly or implicitly, employ this concept (for instance, the structure of the schooling system, child-rearing, the regulation of transitions into new stages and so forth). I certainly do not deny that the concept of development can be imposed upon cultures which do not employ it (given that such cultures exist) but I may question whether such imposition is theoretically relevant and valid.

The study of development is concerned with more than the construction and empirical testing of explanatory models. Developmental psychologists are also confronted with the problem of finding appropriate limitations and definitions for their basic concept. In this chapter I shall outline a formal approach and try to show the deductive basis of models of development. In the second chapter, I shall discuss the impact of social, historical and cultural factors on a definition of the concept of development and show how they relate to the questions of relevance and validity.

1.2   A FORMAL APPROACH TO THE CONCEPT OF DEVELOP-MENT

Basically, the concept of development is concerned with transitions between states, with particular emphasis on the transition from an initial to a final state. Development can therefore be defined as a set of temporally ordered states and transitions. In everyday usage, for instance, development is viewed as what happens between birth and adulthood. From the state 'neonate' to the state 'adult' there are a number of temporally ordered intermediate states, described as toddler, school-child and adolescent. In Piaget's model, cognitive development begins with the sensori-motor and ends with the formal operational stage, via the pre-operational and concrete operational stages. Bruner's criterion for distinguishing the states of cognitive development is the mode of representation applied by the subject. Representation starts with the enactive mode (representation of knowledge in the form of action-patterns), then proceeds to the iconic mode (representation-rules adopted from perception) and ends with the mastery of the symbolic mode of representation by the age of seven.

In principle, developmental states do not need to have the stage-like character of the foregoing examples. In a continuous developmental process the states are defined simply as points on the developmental continuum. Furthermore, the temporal span of a developmental process does not necessarily cover large parts of the life. It is also possible to study the development of a particular skill, e.g. the ability to use the notion of volume (Gagné, 1968), or a particular set of skills, e.g. the development of concepts (Klausmeier, 1976).

In Ariès' study of the historical development of childhood and family, the first chapter is devoted to the medieval conception of the ages of life (Ariès, 1962). The author refers to a popular thirteenth-century text that describes the ages or periods of life as follows. The first age is childhood, from birth until seven years. It is the age in which the teeth are planted, a fact which explains why the child cannot talk well. The second age is 'pueritia' and lasts till fourteen. The third age is adolescence. The medieval scholars disagree on the age at which it ends, either twenty-one or thirty-five. 'This age is called adolescence because the person is big enough to beget children.... In this age, the limbs are soft and able to grow and receive strength....' (Ariès, 1962, page 21).

The fourth age is youth, lasting until forty-five. The fifth stage is called senectitude, the sixth is old age, followed by the age called 'senies'. Human life counts seven ages because of its correspondence with the then known seven planets. Ariès states that the medieval conception of development must be seen within the framework of medieval thinking with correspondencies (e.g. between life and the planets). The ages of life are a system for classifying people. There is no notion of causal or conditional antecedent-consequent relationships between stages of development.

From the foregoing examples we may infer some basic properties of the concept of development.

First, every account of development uses a particular kind of 'language' or vocabulary to specify and describe its developmental states. In the colloquial model we use the concepts of baby, toddler, adolescent and so forth. Piaget speaks about sensori-motor, pre-operational and operational stages. Obviously, the language of development contains more than names of states: it must also be capable of defining the nature and content of these states, i.e. criteria which determine their properties and mutual differences. In a developmental model, two states are particularly important, namely the initial state and the final state.

Second, every account of development implicitly or explicitly limits and specifies the nature of the transitions that may take place. In some cases, the logical structure of the developmental stages prescribes one transitional step at a time and in a fixed order (e.g. the common sense and Piagetian model). Some models may also accept regression (partial reversibility of the transition, such as in the Freudian model or in some Piagetian approaches to the effects of ageing on cognition). Other models may be relatively free: they may allow the occurrence of more than one stage at a time. They may also permit a certain degree of freedom in the order of attainment of the stages (such as in Gagné's partly branched model for the development of conservation skills). Within each theory, however, the developmental system must proceed from the initial to the final state within the limitations set by the transition rules.

The transition rules do not only regulate the order of occurrence of developmental states, they also describe the nature of the parameters that determine why and when state-transitions take place. This particular aspect of the transition rules might be called the stability rules. Stability rules may be distinguished on the basis of two relatively independent criteria: they define states as either internally stable or unstable and as either open or closed, that is, susceptible or not to changes due to external factors. Maturational theories, for instance, are characterized by largely closed and internally unstable states. Learning theories of development are characterized by states that are internally unstable and open. According to Piaget, the instability of the states is explained as a search for equilibrium (see, for instance Piaget, 1959). When a particular equilibrium is reached, the system is ready for a confrontation with reality that annihilates the existent equilibrium and sets into motion a process towards a new equilibrium. The process stops when a final equilibrium, formal operational thinking, has been reached.

Third, the models of development claim to have empirical applicability. Consequently, they require an appropriate empirical operationalization of the concepts they employ. The theory must permit its user to decide what kind of state or transition can be ascribed to an individual at a certain point of time. In Piaget's theory, for instance, the inability to solve a conservation problem is an empirical criterion for belonging to the pre-operational stage, whereas, in Bruner's theory, it is a criterion for the state of iconic representations. The empirical criteria must be decisive and determinable. Decisiveness means that one and only one developmental state answers the criterion (e.g. the appearance of a specific type of behaviour which is found at one developmental stage but not at another). Being determinable implies that it must be possible to decide in an unambiguous way whether or not a given empirical state of affairs is an instance of the criterion. The empirical operationalization of the theoretical concepts and hypotheses is determined by a set of rules that regulate the relationship between the theory and the world of observation, experiment, application and so forth. We shall call these rules the empirical mapping rules. These rules do not only regulate the mapping of theoretical expressions on empirical facts (operationalization) but also the translation of observable events in terms of the theory (diagnosis).

It is clear that the properties we have distinguished constitute a formal description of a developmental theory. In practice, a theory consists of a model which is a particular exemplification of the formal components. The theory describes a model of development which allows the theoretical psychologist to infer the 'grammar' (i.e. the state language, the transition rules and the mapping rules) that underlies it. Further, theories are not only exemplifications, but also specifications. That is, a theory might reflect only one of the many possible models that might be based on its underlying grammar (the theory might present itself in the form of a particular empirical mapping, for instance – see Figure 1.1).

The first and second property of a developmental model make it comparable with a finite state automaton. The concept of finite state automaton stems from systems-theory. It has proved its merits in cybernetic approaches to behaviour (Ashby, 1952) as well as in transformational linguistics (Chomsky, 1957). A two-dimensional matrix consisting of two co-ordinates containing the first ten natural numbers can be used to demonstrate such an automaton. Every point in the matrix is characterized by an ordered set of two natural numbers. These points constitute the possible states. As transitional rules, i.e. rules which regulate the transition from one point to another, we might take the following examples: first, a transition is only allowed from one point to an adjacent point; second, transitions must be horizontal or vertical; third, transitions take place at arbitrary moments.

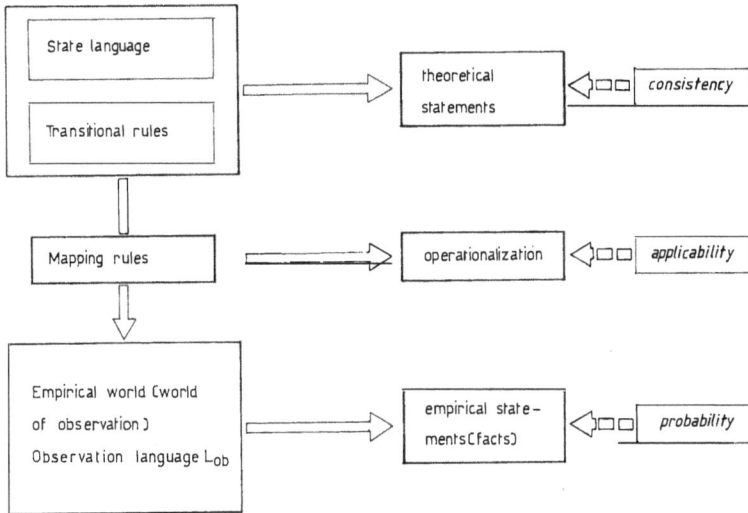

Figure 1.1 The formal components of a developmental theory

In Figure 1.2, two developmental lines have been drawn, connecting the initial point (1,1) and the final point (5,5). Both lines represent a set of developmental steps which are permitted by the transitional rules and each set represents a possible model of development within the formal framework.

It is very important to state that the set of possible developmental lines may be determined deductively. The set of possible lines is obviously determined by the properties of the framework, such as the two-dimensional matrix, on the one hand, and the transitional rules, on the other. The set of lines, then, can be deduced by rigorously applying the rules to the framework.

I shall give a very brief overview of two theories, Piaget's stage theory and Klausmeier's theory of conceptual development, and try to show how the succession of developmental states in both theories reflects a deductive structure. Klausmeier's theory will be discussed in the light of the relationship between empirical investigations and theoretical statements, which will be dealt with in the next section.

Before I proceed to a very sketchy analysis of Piaget's

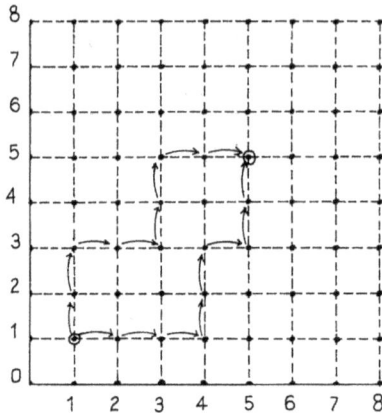

Figure 1.2   An example of a finite state automaton. A state
is characterized by two integers. The arrows indicate two
possible paths between an initial state (1,1) and a final
state (5,5). The transition rules are explained in the text

and Klausmeier's theories I must caution against two possible
misunderstandings. First, the analysis is based on a very rudimentary image of the theories and I do not pretend that they
can be reduced to this elementary form. Second, the assumption that the kernel of these theories is of a deductive nature
is not intended to devalue them (see section 1.3 for further
discussion, see also Smedslund, 1978).

In Piaget's stage theory, the final state of cognitive development is called the stage of formal operational thinking (see
Brainerd, 1978, for an excellent overview). The basic property of this stage is that thinking is an internal process,
consisting of operations that are carried out upon formal,
abstract contents. Operations are mental actions. They can be
compared with physical actions but they differ from the latter
in a number of points. The basic difference is that operations
are a sort of abstract actions. Unlike concrete actions, they
can go back to their starting-point, i.e. they are reversible.
In the formal operational stage, the subject is able to think
about the operations themselves, for instance, and he or she
no longer depends on the spatiotemporal limitations of the
concrete objects and events.

The description of the final state provides a particular
point of view from which we may interpret the meaning of
the behaviours and abilities of the initial state-child. For
Piaget, the neonate's and infant's behaviour does not yet
reflect the intellectual properties ascribed to the final state.
A large number of complex reasons, which we shall not discuss here, can be brought forward to support the assumption
that the infant's intellectual life is completely determined by

external actions. 'External' does not exclude mental events such as perception and feeling, however, but implies that the entire process of thinking does not take place internally. The infant's thinking is not internal and not operational but 'actional'. It is limited, therefore, to the material and spatiotemporal properties of the concrete objects and events.

The order in which internalization, the transition from action to operation and from concrete to abstract contents, is acquired is determined by the meaning of these concepts. Since operations are defined as 'abstract', mental actions, it is necessary that internalization occurs before the transition from concrete action to operation. Actions as well as operations can be carried out with concrete contents, but abstract contents require operational activity and cannot be dealt with on the action-level. The emergence of abstract, formal contents, therefore, depends on the presence of operations.

In principle, the transition from external to internal, from action to operation and from concrete to abstract content may occur quasi-simultaneously, i.e. they might succeed each other with such short intervals that the successive stages are almost unobservable. For the theory, it does not matter however, how much time it takes for proceeding from the initial to the final state. The mapping of a deductive theoretical kernel upon empirical variables, such as a specific course of time, belongs to the empirical aspect of the theory.

If we summarize the orders in which the various acquisitions must take place we find the following theoretical states of development. If the final state is characterized by thinking as an internal process of operations carried out upon abstract contents, the initial state must be characterized by non-internal (external), non-operational (actional) and non-abstract (concrete) thinking. The initial state has been given the name of sensori-motor stage of development. The first developmental acquisition, which makes all the others possible, consists of the emergence of internal thinking processes. The second developmental state, in which action with concrete contents has become internalized, is called the pre-operational stage. This stage is characterized by a number of particular properties that are due to the fact that thinking is still actional, i.e. that it is not reversible. Interiorization of the thinking process is a necessary condition for the emergence of the next acquisition, namely operational thinking. The actions have become reversible and organized in logical systems. Thinking is still carried out with the kind of content employed in the foregoing state, namely concrete contents. Piaget calls this state the concrete operational stage. The final step in the developmental process concerns the transition from concrete to abstract contents. This transition cannot be made before thinking has become operational. Summarizing, the definitions of the concepts employed in the description of the final state tolerate no other succession of developmental states than the one described in Piaget's theory.

The fact that the order of the Piagetian stages, namely from sensori-motor to formal operational thinking via pre-operational and concrete operational thinking, represents a deductive necessity does not imply that the actual Piagetian theory is also deductively true. In the actual theory the formal, deductive kernel that we have sketched has been mapped upon a number of empirical variables. Piaget assumes, for instance, that the developmental process lasts roughly until the middle of the second decade of life, that the transition from pre-operational to concrete-operational thinking occurs at the age of seven, and so forth. It is clear that the truth of this empirical mapping can only be decided on empirical grounds. The relationship between deductive and empirical aspects of a developmental theory will be the topic of the next section.

simultaneous conditions of occurrence of state–properties

INTERNAL ———→ OPERATIONAL ———→ FORMAL

e.g. if at t_n S: operational, then at t_n S: internal

successive conditions of occurrence of state–properties

EXTERNAL ———→ INTERNAL

ACTIONAL ———→ OPERATIONAL

CONCRETE ———→ FORMAL

e.g. if at t_n S: operational, then at t_m before t_n S: actional

(a)

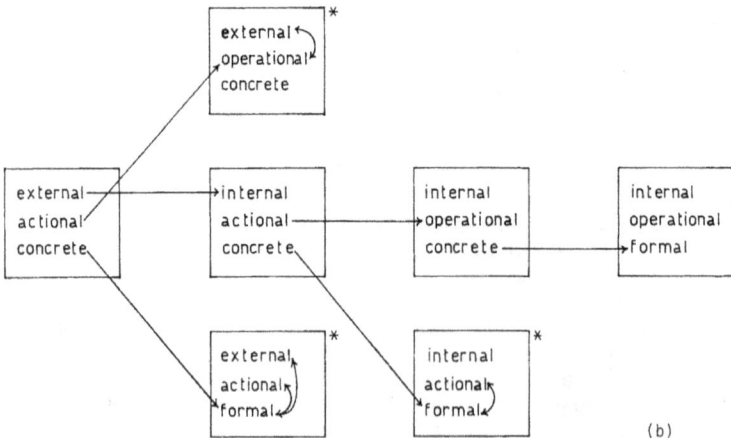

(b)

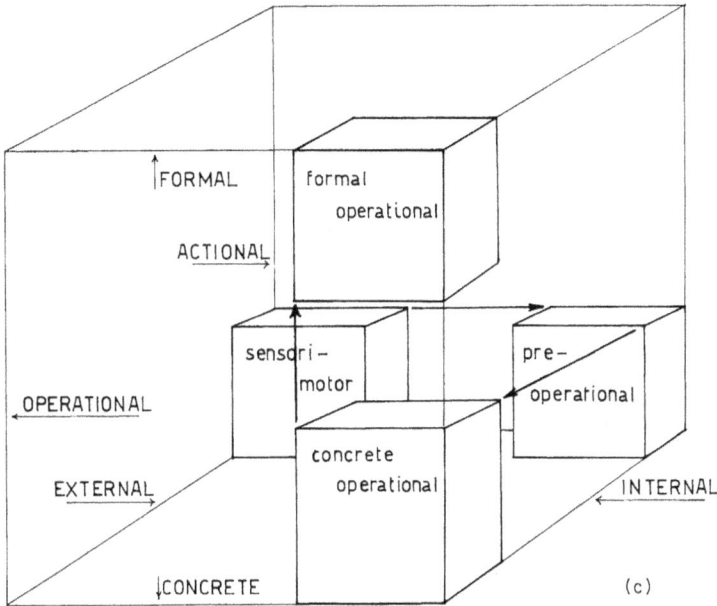

Figure 1.3 A proposed conceptual deep structure of Piaget's stage theory.
(a) shows the state transition rules consist of simultaneous and successive conditions of occurrence of state-properties
(b) shows the state-transition rules determine the conceptually permitted succession of developmental states; the change of one state-property corresponds with a developmental state-transition; double arrows indicate conceptually incompatible state-properties, the resulting states – indicated by an asterisk – are inexistent
(c) shows the basic state properties can be mapped onto spatial axes: external versus internal on the horizontal axis, operational versus actional on the depth axis, concrete versus formal on the vertical axis

1.3 DEDUCTIVE AND EMPIRICAL TRUTH OF DEVELOPMENTAL STATEMENTS

A theory of development is provided with mapping rules necessary to 'translate' theoretical statements into empirical statements, i.e. statements about observable states of affairs. These rules have a purely instrumental function: they simply tell how to apply a theoretical term or statement to an empirical data base. The mapping rules must be distinguished from the actual empirical mappings of the theoretical statements. These mappings explicitate the empirical variables with which the theoretical statements are assumed to be associated, such as particular ages, social classes, persons and so forth (see, for instance, the mapping of Piagetian stages upon ages). In order to find out whether these mappings upon empirical variables are true, we must employ the mapping rules in order to set up decisive experiments.

In the following discussion, I shall try to make clear how the deductive nature of the developmental statements is related to empirical research. I shall give an example of a theory on the development of concepts put forward by Klausmeier (1976). Klausmeier describes the development of concepts as a four-stage process. The initial one constitutes the concrete level. The individual is capable of recognizing an object that has been encountered on a prior occasion in an identical form. Prerequisites for attaining the initial level are: being capable of attending to an object; discriminating it from other objects; representing it internally; and maintaining the representation (Klausmeier, 1976, p. 7). The second stage, the identity level, is reached when the individual is capable of recognizing an object from a different spatiotemporal perspective or sensed in a different modality. The third, classificatory, level is reached when the individual can treat different objects as members of one class without however being capable of making explicit the basis of the classification. The formal level is attained when 'the individual can define the concept in terms of its defining attributes and can evaluate actual or verbally described examples and non-examples of the particular concept in terms of the presence or absence of the defining attributes ...' (Klausmeier, 1976, p. 10).

It is clear that Klausmeier's stages of development are ordered in a logically incontestable way. The final state is characterized as the ability to make the rule of classification explicit. Conditional to this is the ability to classify, i.e. make classes of objects, events, etc. Classification is based on the ability to recognize (at least) one common property in arbitrary pairs of objects (or events ...), which, in turn, implies the ability to recognize objects which have everything in common except their place or time of appearance. It is also clear that Klausmeier's theory is based on a particular definition of 'concept' which is reflected in the description of the final state of development. Vygotsky, for instance, has pointed out that scientific and formal concepts, which are of basic importance for cognitive development, start with the teaching of a (preliminary) definition of the concept, which is then applied to various fields of concrete phenomena. In a way, the development of Vygotsky's concepts is the reverse of the development of Klausmeier's concepts.

However, what if we find empirical evidence against the deductive and descriptive (or definitory) model of concept-development put forward by Klausmeier? Is it possible that such empirical evidence could be found? In order to answer these questions, I shall briefly discuss a case which seems incompatible with Klausmeier's theory.

There is sufficient empirical evidence for the statement that the infant's perceptual apparatus executes operations of information-abstraction which make him perceive the world in a highly classified way (see Chapter 6 on perception of form and pattern). The infant is just not capable of recognizing individual objects: objects are represented in terms of some salient perceptual or functional features, which implies that in fact classes or sets of different objects are represented, viz. all the objects which are characterized by these features. At a later point of development the infant's representation of singular objects will become less iconic and abstracted, which will allow him to recognize an object in a way described by Klausmeier as 'concrete' and logically antecedent to the classificatory mode of perception with which the infant actually starts. We have thus found empirical evidence against a logically deduced model of conceptual development. What implications has this finding for such a model?

Three standpoints are arguable.

According to the first one, the model's concepts of developmental states and state-properties are less firmly defined than might seem at first sight, and as a result no compelling deductions can be made. Thus, the critique is directed towards the model's conceptual qualities and its seeming deductive character. Put differently, the empirical evidence has illustrated the conceptual shortcomings of the model.

According to the second standpoint, the theoretical concepts have been defined appropriately but the theory has not exhaustively dealt with all the theoretically possible lines of development. One explanation of this incompleteness is based on the fact that the model's transition rules have been applied incompletely. In this case, the empirical evidence illustrates a possible model of development that has not yet been inferred from the underlying grammar of the original model (i.e. the original model is only one of many possible exemplifications of the grammar). The second explanation of the incompleteness of the theory is that it has been mapped prematurely upon a number of empirical variables. This might be the case with Piaget's theory of development. Piagetian predictions are often empirically contradicted, for instance, with regard to formal operational thinking. Adults are supposed to solve problems in a formal and logical way whereas their actual problem-solving strategies are frequently pre-operational (Wason and Johnson-Laird, 1972; Van Geert, 1979). But, on the other hand, children from two to six years of age, though still in their pre-operational period, are sometimes capable of thinking according to rules which fulfil the formal operational requirements, for instance when they have to convey information about an object belonging to a set of objects varying according to several dimensions, such

as colour, size, form, etc (Sinclair, 1979). What the empirical
findings prove thus far is that Piaget's original idea about a
connection between age and the emergence of the various
forms of thinking might be not completely true. The findings do
not affect the descriptive adequacy and relevance of notions
such as 'pre-operational' and 'formal operational thinking'.
Nor do they affect the deductive truth of the thesis that if
formal operational thinking arises from more primitive forms of
thinking, these forms must be sensori-motor, pre-operational
and concrete operational.

   According to the third standpoint, the evidence against a
deductively based developmental model falsifies only apparently
the model's predictions. It is possible that the investigator who
has found the falsifying evidence has applied the theoretical
concepts and relationships in an erroneous way. In Klausmeier's theory, for instance, the concrete level of concept-
attainment is defined as the ability to recognize an object as
being the same as a formerly encountered object given that the
points of perspective are equal. The definition should be
restricted in such a way, however, that the identity amongst
the points of perspective is defined as being viewed from the
infant's point of view. If the infant's perceptual apparatus is
such that he sees empirically different objects as being identical,
then these objects are identical for him and, thus, will be
recognized on the concrete level. If the investigator employs
his adult concept of 'object', he will apply Klausmeier's theory
on a wrong basis (see, for instance, Figure 1.4).

Figure 1.4 Two fathers plus two sons do not necessarily equal
four persons. This example could be used as an empirical proof
of the inaccuracy of the statement that two plus two equals
four. It can be objected, however, that the 'proof' is based on
an inaccurate operationalization of the number concept

   The foregoing point makes clear that a theory should be as
clear as possible in specifying the empirical conditions for its
falsification and verification (De Groot, 1961, pp. 96 ff.). In
practice, however, the specification of these empirical conditions - i.e. the mapping rules - is never fully worked out by
the time the theory gives rise to its first serious empirical
attacks. One of the functions that empirical research might have

is that it contributes to a further elaboration of the mapping rules. New theories in particular are characterized by incomplete mapping rules, which frequently consist of a number of paradigmatical operationalizations of concepts and theoretical statements. In Piaget's earlier work, for instance, the concept of 'conservation' and its theoretical relationship with concrete operational thinking was represented by a number of empirical examples that served as a rule of guidance for further research. Attempts to attack empirically Piaget's theory of conservation and concrete operational thinking have often led to a revision of the original concepts and their mapping upon empirical facts. The reader of Piagetian research often gets the impression that his theory is elusive and wrapped up in continuous revision, that it palters with the normal, methodological, agreement to specify unambiguously the conditions of verification and falsification. I do not know whether this accusation is tenable, since the further elaboration of the operationalizations, i.e. the empirical mapping rules, is one of the permitted functions that falsifying evidence may fulfil.

The fact that falsifying evidence is not necessarily an argument against the deductive nature of statements about development seems incompatible with the current tradition in research methodology, which claims that theories should contain 'falsificators', i.e. elements which make them falsifiable. The points of criticism that can be made against the deductive kernel-hypothesis are as follows.

The main criticism states that if developmental theories are deductive, they cannot be falsified empirically, which makes them unfit for true scientific use. A distinction must be made, however, between the theory as a descriptive and definitorial framework, on the one hand, and hypotheses derived from the framework, claiming explicitly to be empirically determinable (De Groot, 1961, p. 62). The descriptive and deductive part of a theory cannot be subject to the falsifiability rule. The specific part of the theory which defines and specifies the concepts one is going to use in order to describe the field of inquiry and to formulate (falsifiable) hypotheses and statements cannot be evaluated on the basis of truth and falsity but only on the basis of applicability, descriptive adequacy, and so forth. Another argument which I might raise is that an ideal deductive theory can exhaustively describe the set of all theoretically possible lines of development but cannot decide which one will appear in reality. At the end of this section I shall go deeper into this relationship between empirical findings and theoretical statements.

A second argument against the thesis that developmental theories are essentially deductive is that no existing theory has actually been developed in a deductive way but always on the basis of empirical research and theoretical speculation. A theory such as the Piagetian one has evolved over the course of some fifty years of observation and experiment and includes many corrections and extensions to the original theory. We must make a distinction, however, between the actual process by which a theory evolves and the nature of the final product of such growth. (Normally, a theory never reaches completion, thus we will have to view a theory in an ideal form that will not necessarily be achieved in practice.) Take, for instance, the way in which mathematical proofs or theorems are constructed. It may take years or even centuries of patient search, empirical trial and experience to find the proof of a theorem, whereas the proof or theorem itself is a purely deductive construction which does not at all reflect its laborious inductive history.

A third more serious criticism against the hypothesis of a deductive developmental theory holds that the concepts we use in developmental theories are rather vaguely defined, i.e. that their content is not accurately specified. Further, psychologists are also quite unconscious of the kind of 'logic' they apply, i.e. of the exact nature of the transitional rules used to deduce the theoretically possible lines of development. This criticism sounds more serious than it actually is. Again, the history of mathematics may help us to understand that the lack of formal preciseness is not incompatible with developing a deductive science: until the nineteenth century most of the branches of mathematics, such as Euclidean geometry, showed a considerable lack of insight into the precise meaning of their concepts and the nature of the rules employed to deduce theorems from axioms.

A fourth and final point of criticism holds that the empirical as well as the theoretical value of a theory depends on its ability to provide guidelines for influencing and facilitating development. The main problem with this pragmatic criterion, however, is that there is no universal final state of development. Every theory employs its own particular definition of the abilities, knowledge and behaviours that will be acquired by the end of the developmental process. The pragmatic criterion, therefore, must be reformulated. The best theory, then, is the theory that is most successful in influencing and facilitating the course of development that it has defined itself. Unfortunately, even the reformulated version of the pragmatic criterion will give rise to difficulties. The first is that the evaluation of the developmental goals itself escapes the pragmatic criterion and should be decided on the basis of theoretical or ideological grounds. The second difficulty is that developmental theories might abstract from the external factors that influence development and define it as the process that takes place 'within' the subject, taking for granted that the adequate external conditions are present. In Piaget's theory, for instance, the process of development concerns exclusively the organization of internal structures. The activity of the environment creates the conditions but does not cause the organization to take place. Although a more detailed discussion would lead us too far, it is important to note that Piaget's relative lack of interest in education does not necessarily imply that he believes that education does not matter or that the child develops without the help of other people. It is simply a consequence of Piaget's particular definition of development that the educational and external interference is not taken into account (see also Chapter 2, section 2.4).

Besides the criterion of practical effectivity, also predictivity, which is another frequently used pragmatic criterion, is not applicable beyond the limits of a particular theory. The statement that the best theory is the one that predicts best holds only for theories that agree on the nature and relevance of developmental properties that constitute the object of prediction.

2 Meaning and relevance of developmental statements

2.1 LANGUAGES OF DEVELOPMENT

We shall now deal with the question of how we are going to define the developmental states and transitions, i.e. what kind of 'language' we are going to employ.

One might say that finding the initial and final state of development is merely an empirical question: observe their properties and there will be no problem about how to describe them. But what, for instance, are we going to take as a final state? The state we call adulthood, old age, the time at which the maximal level of social success has been reached?

It is clear that our choice of the state at which the highest point of development is reached will depend entirely on how we have defined development, i.e. on what we have chosen as a criterion for development: age, social success, experience, cognitive development as defined in western society, magical power, happiness .... Our choice is determined by our hierarchy of values which in turn depends largely on the social and cultural context in which we live. In an industrialized, western community, magical powers, that is to say, behaviours and skills that are embedded in the complex domain of magical meanings, will not be taken into consideration as a criterion of development. Magical powers and actions do however play a considerable role in many non-western cultures. In these cultures obtaining magical competence is a legitimate and relevant goal in life. If we want to describe the cognitive development of people living in these cultures, we have to analyse what kind of abilities are required to carry out magical actions. First, we need a very profound insight into the nature and place of magic in the overall cognitive and meaning systems of these cultures. Second, we must understand what kind of differences are ascribed to people with and without knowledge and mastery of magic. Thus, we have to know the difference between what is conceived of as the final and as the initial state of the development of magic. Third, we have to investigate what kind of transitional steps the cultures allow between the initial and final state. The transitional steps will not necessarily follow our western 'developmental logic', since they are related to the meaning that is attached to the cultures' concept of 'magic' (see also, Figure 2.1).

The question regarding the kind of 'language' we are going to employ for describing the states of development can be answered tentatively by stating that the 'language' must be inferred from a profound conceptual analysis of the meaningful environment in which development must take place.

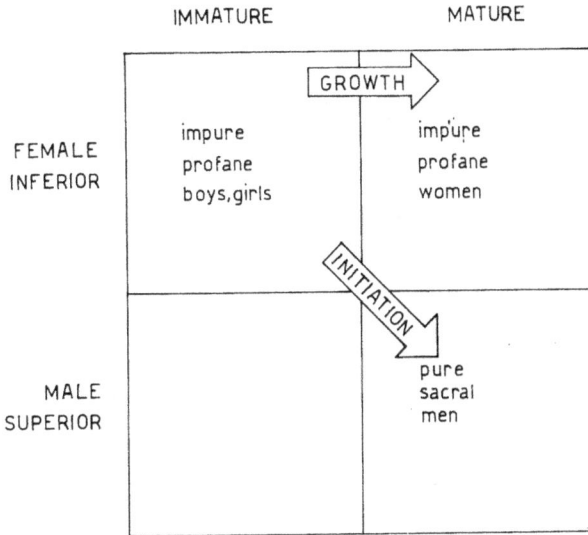

IMMATURE   MATURE

GROWTH

FEMALE
INFERIOR

impure
profane
boys,girls

impure
profane
women

INITIATION

pure
sacral
men

MALE
SUPERIOR

Figure 2.1 A hypothetical developmental space of the Murngin of northern Australia. The model is based on Levi-Strauss analyses of characteristic conceptual distinctions in Murngin culture. State-transition principles consist of bodily and social growth on the one hand and initiation on the other hand

A comparable point of view has been put forward in a book written by Michael Cole and a number of co-authors on the cultural context of learning and thinking (Cole et al., 1971, pp. 213 ff.). The authors state that they 'make ethnographic analysis prior to experimentation in order to identify the kinds of activities that people often engage in and hence ought to be skillful at dealing with' (p. 217). The authors discuss aspects of learning and thinking in a group of Liberian people, the Kpelle. The investigators did not employ the standard western but the original Kpelle concepts, questions and problems.

It might be questioned, however, whether the work carried out by Cole and his collaborators proves that Kpelle subjects follow different lines of development, only because the concepts and problems they have to deal with in everyday life differ from the ones faced by western subjects. What is wrong with describing Kpelle cognition in terms of a scientifically accepted theory of development and then investigate how the subjects acquire the level ascribed to them by this theory? If Kpelle cognition would occupy a rather low level on our developmental

scale, we might assume that their endo- and exogenous environments provide less developmental opportunities than – for
instance – the western environment. This is the kind of conclusion that is often drawn, or at least questioned, in many
accounts of non-western cognitive development (see Cole et al.,
1971, p. 28 for discussion).

Basically, the problem we just touched upon concerns the
applicability of developmental models. Determining the anthropological validity, i.e. worldwide applicability, of developmental models has long been one of the underlying motives of
cross-cultural research. Piaget's theory of cognitive development is one of the most frequently studied issues (probably
together with Freudian psychology) (Dasen, 1972; Berry and
Dasen, 1974, pp. 295 ff.), and in particular whether cognitive
development in 'primitive' cultures goes beyond the 'pre-
operational stage', a stage at which the western child employs
a magical conception of causality and a system of classification
which does not operate on the basis of independent classificatory variables. According to the Durkheimian tradition, the
latter properties also characterize the thinking of primitive
cultures.

The cognitive system which goes one step beyond the pre-
operational mode of thinking is called concrete operational and
answers the rules and structures of a concrete and practical
logic. The criterion which is generally considered as determining the transition from the pre-operational to the concrete
operational stage is conservation, i.e. succeeding in a conservation task. The subject is shown a beaker filled with water
or sand, for instance, that is then poured into a beaker of
different form and size. The water or sand will now occupy a
different spatial extension: let us assume that height will have
increased, whereas width has decreased.

Subjects capable of employing a concrete logic will be capable
of inferring that the actual and the original amount of water
are the same in spite of the observable and obvious spatial
difference between the original and actual form of the water
or sand column. Conservation research has been carried out
in many different cultures. Some peoples, such as the Woloff
of Senegal (Greenfield, 1966; Irvine, 1978) or people living in
New Guinea (see Price, 1978 for an overview) have been shown
not to attain conservation even at an adult age or were at
least well below the western standard.

In some cultures, conservation of mass is very easily attained
because it is embedded in particular, culture-specific pottery-
technologies which facilitate the discovery of conservation
(Price-Williams et al., 1969; Steinberg and Dunn, 1976). In
these cultures, the attainment of a concrete operational level of
intellectual functioning is conditional to the kind of technological
abilities they impose upon their members.

Thus, cross-cultural research seems to provide a definite
proof for the applicability of the Piagetian framework of develop-

ment. It enables us, for instance, to make distinctions between cultures that achieve concrete operational and even formal operational thinking or stagnate intellectually at the pre-operational stage (see Dasen, 1972, for a research overview).

It may be asked whether this empirical test of applicability is anything more than a triviality. It is trivial that the con-servation experiment can be done in any culture since it deals with contents such as water, sand and beakers, and operations such as pouring and comparing, which are universally known and relevant. The heart of the matter is, however, whether the criterion-function of the conservation experiment is uni-versally valid, i.e. whether notions such as 'pre-operational' or 'concrete operational' are applicable just because of the trivial fact that the conservation experiment can be executed. In our present western culture in which people have to work with abstract systems, logic and hypotheses, the Piagetian notions clearly make sense. Consequently, it also makes sense to consider the child's success with a conservation task as an index for his having climbed one step of the Piagetian develop-mental ladder, namely, the step called concrete operational thinking. Put differently, it is only within the perspective of a developmental process that has formal operational thinking as its highest level that the conservation experiment gets its particular meaning as a criterion for concrete operational think-ing. It may be questioned, however, whether conservation has the same meaning in a culture in which the final state of devel-opment cannot be characterized in terms of one of the Piagetian stages, such as cultures in which the notions of 'formal opera-tional' and 'concrete operational' do not sufficiently describe the cognitive competence of their mature members. Differences in the conceptual framework necessary to describe development will have direct consequences for the developmental (criterial) meaning of concrete instances of behaviour, e.g. the child's responses in a conservation experiment.

2.2 CONTEXT AND MEANING OF DEVELOPMENTAL STATE-MENTS

I shall try to make the previous claims more clear by examining what happens actually when I apply a label, description or specification to a denotatum, for instance, a colour name, 'red' to an object, 'x'.

The meaning of the label does not only depend on its referent - the actual colour of x - but on its relationship with other terms. Berlin and Kay (1969) have studied colour vocabularies of various languages and found that each vocabulary divides the colour field in a specific way. This implies, for instance, that the referential extension, as well as the conceptual mean-ing of 'red' depends on the extension of the colour vocabulary, e.g. whether it contains four or eleven colour terms. Consequently, when I apply a label, 'red' for instance, to an object, 'x', the label can be assigned meaning only if I specify, either implicitly or explicitly, to which particular colour vocabulary the term belongs. In 1931 the German linguist Trier introduced the notion of 'semantic field' in order to refer to a particular way of dividing a field of denotata (Bierwisch, 1970). The notion is based on de Saussure's assumption that words not only have signification but also value, i.e. a relationship with other words (de Saussure, 1974, pp. 144 ff.). In accordance with our previous reasoning, the use of a particular label implies the introduction of a particular semantic field. In modern semantics (see for instance Leech, 1974) the notion of semantic field has been replaced by the idea of structures of semantic features, such as 'animate'-'inanimate' and 'human'-'non-human'. The meaning of a lexical item depends on its constituent features. The features determine the way in which the item and its related terms will divide and specify a field of denotata to which they are applicable. Actually, structures of features represent the 'logic' according to which a field of denotata is dissociated into constituent fields. Each logic of dissociation reflects a particular perspective on a semantic field. Sometimes, the various perspectives are determined by universal properties. This is the case, for instance, with colour terms, which are based on physical and physiological aspects of colour perception, and kinship-terms, which are based on biological lines of descent. In other cases, however, the logic of constructing fields is based on complex ideological and cultural schemata which lead to largely incompatible classifications and conceptual structures, such as in the various scientific and ethnic systems of plant classification, cosmology and so forth.

Formally, developmental theories can be conceived of as semantic fields which represent particular views on sets of denotata that consist of behavioural events in a specific temporal order. In some cases it is possible to make the underlying logic, the grammar of the theory, explicit, although our insight into most of the theories does not go beyond a speculative analysis of their basic conceptual constituents. If I assign a theoretical label or description to a behavioural event, I imply a specific theory, i.e. a network of labels to which the label belongs and from which it borrows its meaning. If I say, for instance, that a subject shows formal operational thinking, it should be clear whether this term is situated within a learning-theoretical or a Piagetian conceptual framework, since both theories assign different meanings to this term. We have seen that the semantic features that constitute the kernel of Piaget's theory of stages are 'actional'-'operational', 'abstract'-'concrete' and 'external'-'internal'. Learning-theoretical approaches might subscribe that these features are important, but they will not agree on the fact that these features are necessary and sufficient. Probably they will attach considerable importance to the fact that cognitive activities are content-bound, which implies that content-specifying features are more important than features such as 'actional' or 'operational'.

In the present context, the most important conclusion that may be drawn from our comparison of a theory with a semantic field is that a label is meaningful only if the semantic field – the theory – to which the label belongs can be applied meaningfully to the structure of events to which the referent of the label belongs. If I imply the label 'concrete operational thinking' to the cognitive activities of Kpelle and Woloff subjects, I imply that the theory in which the label is embedded, i.e. Piaget's theory, is meaningful with regard to Kpelle or Woloff cognition in general. Piaget's theory, however, reflects a particular view on the nature of thinking which is expressed by the choice of formal operational thinking as the final state of development. It may be questioned whether this perspective is adequate with regard to Kpelle or Woloff thinking, irrespective of the fact that some forms of this thinking answer the empirical definitions of concepts such as 'pre-operational' or 'concrete operational thinking'.

A crucial aspect of social reality, within which all developmental events take place, is that it imposes a particular kind of reality upon itself (see Mead, 1934; Berger and Luckmann, 1966; and Mehan and Wood, 1975). Social reality is characterized by a structure of rules, meanings and values that are reflexive: they define the kind of reality in which they function. A culture, social class or particular group of people has its own, specific definitions of the nature of interaction, of knowledge, how knowledge functions, how it is acquired and so forth. In western culture, with its strong emphasis on rational and controlled reflection, most of the implicit 'definitions' are made explicit, in the form of scientific theories or explicit ideologies, which, however, remain based upon a complex substrate of tacit knowledge (Polanyi, 1967, and Smedslund, 1978, with regard to psychological theories). This tacit knowledge may be described as a set of rules for how to interact with other people, how to talk, how to acquire and use knowledge and how to determine the presence or absence of a specific item of knowledge and so forth. These rules provide a theoretical description of the interactions on the social level; they need not be explicitly represented within the individual (see for instance Cicourel, 1973). Thus, a culture or society is characterized by a particular, overall cognitive system, a system for making sense of what happens, for determining 'what is the case', and so forth. This system need not be verbally or discursively represented: it is implicitly present in the way in which people interact, talk, plan their actions or in what they want or fear. Consequently the meaning of what people actually do or avoid is not an implicit property of this action; it depends entirely on the position that this action occupies in the framework of the overall cognitive system. That is to say, materially or objectively identical

actions and interactions can have totally different meanings
when they function in different symbolic or cognitive social
structures. Identical requests for action – such as in psychological experimentation – may cause totally different responses
and call for totally different abilities when the function and
meaning of the request differs, i.e. when the request has
different meanings in different symbolic and cognitive social
structures (see for instance Cole et al., 1971; Cole and
Bruner, 1971; and also Labov, 1970). Slowness in carrying out
instructions may be the expression of either smartness or
dullness, dependent on the meaning of slowness within a particular culture (see Goodenough, 1976).

We have seen that the application of a theoretical label to a
behavioural event implies a particular structure of labels, a
theory, which takes the form of a semantic field. The application of the label to the behavioural event is meaningful only
if the theory is meaningful with regard to the structure of
behavioural events, which, in the case of developmental theories,
is represented by a particular temporal order. Since developmental theories make statements about events embedded in
social reality, and since social reality imposes a 'theory of
reality' upon itself, the validity of a developmental theory
depends on its relationship with this reality of society. The
developmental theory might consist of a critical – or uncritical –
paraphrase of the implicit theory of development of society,
it may consist of a useful meta-theory, and so forth. The
criterion by means of which we shall measure the relationship
between a developmental theory and the meaningful social
framework in which development takes place is called 'descriptive adequacy'.

2.3 DESCRIPTIVE ADEQUACY OF DEVELOPMENTAL STATE-
MENTS

I shall try to show that an analysis of the concepts and skills,
such as they are defined and understood within the framework
of culture, must contain an analysis of the culture's conceptions of what it means 'to know the concept', 'to possess the
skill' and also of how they are acquired. In speaking about the
culture's conceptions I do not only mean the explicit verbally
explicable conceptions. More important are the 'implicit' conceptions, i.e. those that may be attributed to the way in which
people interact, the structure of their institutions and so
forth. Bruner (1966, pp. 59 ff.), for instance, observed that
Kung bushmen – and probably also people of many other cultures – never teach concepts and skills explicitly, and never
explain things out of the context of concrete action. The lack
of formal teaching practices reveals the nature of the skill or
concept itself. The concept or skill is action- and situation-
determined and is not structured along explicit, verbally

mediated rules. Such a skill differs from the skill which covers a resembling ability but which is acquired outside a directly functional context and mediated by means of separate, verbally communicable rules. The skill acquired in this case is situation-independent and rule-structured. It consists partly of the ability to make its rules explicit and to apply it separated from its natural context.

Bruner (see for instance Bruner et al., 1966) has also suggested that certain cognitive skills, such as the one referred to by the term 'formal operational thinking', cannot be acquired other than by virtue of specific teaching and education. Thus, the suggested relationship between these cognitive skills and education is conditional: without education, these skills can never be acquired. However, I assume that the relationship between these cognitive skills and education is largely a matter of definition. The skills are defined in such a way that it is an integral part of their meaning that they cannot be acquired other than through a particular educational and interactional process. These skills are based on rules that the subject must be able to make explicit. They are strongly connected with processes of argumentation and legitimation and operate with contents that are not concrete but 'abstract', that is, that only exist by virtue of a socially shared and conventionalized knowledge. If the skill or concept is defined in this way, it is implied that it must be acquired by means of explicit social practices we call education. Put differently, if formal operational thinking is defined as the interiorization of complex, social ways of dealing with particular kinds of information, its relationship with schooling and education becomes a matter of definition. Consequently, the discussion among developmental psychologists about formal operational thinking may not in the first place be a discussion about acquisition but rather about definition.

Ariès' study of the structure of medieval schools shows that they did not employ a conception of a gradual and age-bound, stage-like increase in the qualitative capacities of the individual. In fact, there was no concept of a correspondence between age and studies (Ariès, 1962, p. 152).

The structure of the medieval school of the twelfth and thirteenth centuries reveals not only a very particular concept of intellectual development but also of the kind of knowledge or skills that constituted its final point. The first characteristic Ariès has observed is that the schools showed a lack of gradation (p. 145): 'Nobody thought of having a graduated system of education in which the subjects for study would be distributed according to difficulty, beginning with the easiest'. Second, the courses - grammar, logic, rhetoric, geometry and so forth - were taught simultaneously. In 1215, a reform of the University of Paris was announced. The courses were divided into a first cycle containing basic knowledge and a second one containing complementary subjects. These courses, however, were spread over the week in such a way that all the

pupils followed them both (p. 150). Third, the ages were
mixed. That is, the same course was attended by pupils of
variable ages (from eight to twenty). 'The older students were
distinguished from the new not by the subjects they studied –
they were the same – but by the number of times they had
repeated them' (p. 150). Naturally, the structure of the school
was not inspired by an explicit pedagogy or conception of intellectual development but rather by a number of practical matters,
such as the scarcity of manuscripts. Nevertheless, the school
system forms the reflection of an implicit view of intellectual
development that is entirely different from the current one. In
our view, the medieval conception is completely a- – or even
anti- – developmental. There is not the slightest reference to
qualitative stages. The school system reveals also a particular
conception of the nature of what has to be acquired as a result
of the schooling process. Personal understanding and processing of information, critical reflection upon the content being
taught, understanding the structure of the skills and contents,
none of these are taken into consideration. Memory is heavily
emphasized, the mind being seen as a thesaurus. The schooled
intellect is the one that is able to reproduce knowledge as
precisely and reliably as possible. In this respect it is quite
understandable that the basic principle of medieval pedagogy
was mere repetition (Ariès, p. 142).

The partly analytical relationship between a 'theory' about a
concept or skill, i.e. a definition of them, and a 'theory' about
how they must develop, does not only hold for 'overt' developmental processes, such as formal schooling and education, but
also for 'covert' processes. Take for instance a theory of the
number concept in which it is stated that it must be acquired
in two steps, acquisition of conservation and acquisition of
classification (such a simple theory is inexistent but I employ
it for the sake of the argument). The two developmental steps
are 'covert', that is, they are not seen as resulting from
instructions given by a tutor, but rather as individually evolv-
ing cognitive abilities. Now, any behavioural expression related
to a number concept, such as counting, that emerges along
crucially different lines of development, such as modelling
processes, will not be accepted as the expression of the 'real'
number concept. At best, it will be classified as the expression
of a pseudo-concept unless the modelling process may be conceived of as a disguised form of classification – and conservation – development. That is to say, the hypothesized developmental process does not contain a purely empirical but rather
an analytical statement, namely defining the nature of the
number concept as a particular form of knowledge that develops
according to both above-mentioned steps. It may be questioned,
for instance, whether the Piagetian theory of development
would subscribe to my assumptions about the analytic nature
of statements about developmental processes. The fact that
Piaget's primary point of interest lies in genetic epistemology –

a theory about the nature of knowledge seen from a developmental viewpoint - suggests that the foregoing question may be answered positively.

The previous examples illustrate that the nature and content of skills or abilities contain a developmental theory: the relationship between an ability and its development is a matter of definition. If the ability has been acquired, development - as implied by the definition of this ability - has finished. Descriptive adequacy implies that we should examine the relationship between the course of development implied by the nature of the developing ability and the theory of development that we employ. I shall try to illustrate the problem with the help of some questions raised by Piaget's theory of cognitive development.

In Piaget's theory, the final state of development is described as the ability to exempt from the direct influence of the perceptual world and to manipulate abstract contents in a logical way. Consequently the initial and transitory states will be defined in terms which make sense with regard to this description. The initial state is described as sensomotoric, i.e. determined by the perceptual world, infra-logical and entirely concrete. It is a matter of empirical research whether infants are indeed characterized by such a lack of logical, abstract thinking, whereas, on the other hand, it is a non-empirical, conceptual decision whether the first state will be described within the framework of notions such as 'logic', 'operatory system', 'concrete contents', 'abstract contents', etc.

What I want to make clear now is that the question of whether the Piagetian developmental stages are universally applicable must be separated from the question of whether Piaget's developmental theory is universally descriptively adequate. What do we mean, for instance, when we state that the Woloff and a number of Papua cultures never reach concrete operational thinking? What do we say about the structure of their knowledge and actions, their practical, theoretical and religious habits when we characterize them as being of a pre-operational nature?

Irvine (1978) replicated and extended Greenfield's research on conservation with unschooled Woloff adults (Greenfield, 1966). Greenfield found that many Woloff adolescents showed a high incidence of non-conservation, probably based upon their lack of distinction between 'appearance' and 'reality' and their lack of vocabulary for distinguishing equal level from equal amount. Irvine's observation of Woloff everyday activity, however, did give no ground to the assumption that their daily handling with water, which is a scarce resource for them, or with grain and peanuts, expresses the tacit belief that equal level and equal amount are identical. We may 'map' this finding upon Piagetian terminology and say that the Woloff have a sensori-motor concept of conservation (comparable with the kind of sensori-motor conservation of weight that Mounoud and Bower (1975) found with babies). What we are interested in, however, is

whether the Woloff have a concrete-operational concept of
conservation, i.e. the understanding of conservation at the
level of explicit decision and justification. Irvine found that
a number of Woloff adults showed conservation when they were
treated as linguistic informants and when the beaker experiment
was used as a help in a discussion about the meaning of words.
Irvine's most important finding, however, is that Woloff attitudes towards talk are largely incompatible with the kind of
experiment that is necessary to determine whether a subject
possesses a genuinely concrete operational understanding of
conservation. The expression of a concrete operational conservation concept is embedded in a specific argumentational
structure, consisting of specific attitudes towards talk, motives,
personal thought processes and so forth. When this particular
embedding structure is lacking, the existence of concrete
operational conservation becomes indeterminable (or at least
very difficult to determine). In this case, statements about the
presence or absence of concrete operational conservation lose
a good deal of the meaning they have when the appropriate
argumentational context is present. The main conclusion that
may be drawn from the foregoing discussion is that the descriptive adequacy of a theory that operates with distinctions
between sensori-motor and concrete operational intelligence
depends on the presence of a social and communicative framework within which the expression of this difference is possible
and meaningful.

Anthropological and cross-cultural research has shown that
there exist considerable differences in the demands which cultures make on their members. These demands not only cover
the field of practical, perceptual, manual and physical skills,
but also of social relations, personality and cognition. We
seldom realize that the belief in a universe in which man-
directed magical powers play a primordial role requires particular cognitive systems and skills. These structures are only
slightly comparable with and tremendously more complex than
the kind of childish thinking to which we have also given the
predicate 'magical', simply on the basis of some superficial
resemblances. The same holds for so called 'primitive' systems
of classification which probably have some properties in common with the classification-habits of five-year-old western
children but also have a structure that is incredibly more complex and of an entirely different nature.

When we are confronted with a culture in which adults employ
a particular form of magical 'unlogical' thinking, employ classificatory principles which we would interpret as very unsystem-
atic and wrongly structured, it is not enough to ascribe the
predicate 'pre-operational' to their cognitive system and thereby
deny that they have gone through a process of development
which eventually has as many transitory states as the corresponding process of development in a western culture.

Maccoby and Modiano's research provides an example of a

final state of cognitive development that is – at least partly – different from the final state we are accustomed to (Maccoby and Modiano, 1966). In their research on conceptual development in a rural Mexican culture it was found that the final state could not be described as the ability to abstract from perceptual information, but rather as the ability to use and discriminate perceptual information in a very complex way. Naturally, the investigators could have described the final state of conceptual development as the inability to abstract from perceptual information, but it would have been unjust with respect to what these Mexican people are actually capable of doing. Consequently, it would have made little sense to characterize the initial state of conceptual development in terms of an inability to abstract from perceptual information. This characterization contains not so much an untruth as a completely irrelevant statement, since the final state is characterized by the same kind of inability to abstract. The initial state must be characterized in terms which make clear to what extent and how the initial ability to discriminate perceptual information differs from the final one. Thus, it may be stated that, as far as the present data are concerned, Piagetian theory is applicable to but not descriptively adequate for the cognitive development of the people studied by Maccoby and Modiano.

An interesting point of view is offered in Price's review of conservation studies in Papua-New Guinea (Price, 1978). Price states that the finding that Papua subjects are years below European children in conservation is not a sign of intellectual inferiority. The author assumes that conservation experiments typically fit our western conception of cognitive development that is closely related with the function and content of the western educational system. However, since the western educational system is also imported in Papua-New Guinea, it becomes necessary to know in how far 'Papua-cognition' fits the requirements set forth by this educational system. Thus, although conservation is rather inadequate as an indication of genuine 'Papua-cognition', it is quite useful as an indication of the distance between 'Papua-cognition' and the cognitive requirements necessary to attain the western type of schooling system.

If we overview the various examples we have discussed, it could be easily concluded that the descriptive adequacy of Piaget's developmental definition of cognition is questionable. It should be clear, however, that these examples are mere illustrations of how the adequacy problem can be formulated and investigated. A reliable statement about the descriptive adequacy of a theory can only be made after a thorough analysis of the proper symbolic and cognitive system that characterizes a particular culture. At present, we are still very far from such an analysis. The descriptive adequacy of the theory also depends on the level of formality and abstractness of the concepts it employs. In principle, the concepts may be so abstract and formal that they are descriptively adequate with regard to any culture, in spite of the tremendous structural and content differences that may exist between the cognitive systems of various cultures.

The latter point leads us to the problem of how we can arrive at a description of the overall cognitive system of a culture, that is, the domain within which our understanding of individual development within that culture will have to take place. In fact, we are confronted with a second-order problem of descriptive adequacy. The first-order problem concerned the descriptive adequacy of developmental concepts with regard to different cultures and contexts of development. Now, the second-order problem consists of the descriptive adequacy of the language for describing cognitive contents of various cultures and of the descriptions in front of which the descriptive adequacy of developmental theories is evaluated. At present we are far from solving the problem of how to describe the underlying features of cognitive and belief systems different from our own.

Even the analysis of the basic features of different modes of thinking without our own culture has led to considerable difficulties. At this moment we do not yet possess a satisfactory formal description of the axioms and principles underlying schizophrenic thinking, colloquial thinking, religious thinking, rational argumentation and so forth. Nevertheless, these forms of thought constitute a considerable part of the final states of many individual lines of cognitive development.

A 'language' for describing the cognitive contents and structures of different cultures and times must be maximally descriptively powerful. In searching for such a language, we might profit from the work that has been done in disciplines such as linguistics and logic. Propositional logic or the logic of sets, for instance, may be employed to describe the internal structure of different systems of knowledge. Piaget employs logic as a descriptive means to specify the nature of knowledge at different developmental stages. Lévi-Strauss (1966) has developed a logic of oppositions to describe cognitive systems of different cultures. It may be questioned, however, whether descriptive devices such as propositional or dialectical logic are indeed descriptively adequate or whether they impose their own axioms deceptively upon the axioms underlying the cognitive contents they describe. In this connection, Pinxten's detailed analysis of the languages of space of the Dogon and the Navajo Indians are worth mentioning (see Pinxten 1975, 1980). The author developed a system of concepts that has to function as a universal frame of reference for dealing with any possible spatial differentiation. The concepts of which this 'UFOR' consists are based on praxeological, i.e. action-logical, grounds. It is quite plausible indeed that concepts based on the structure and possibilities of our actions in space are more universally relevant than concepts based on a highly culture-specific view of space - Euclidean geometry, for instance.

In practice, however, students of development will rarely be faced with the investigation of development in general. Normally, the research topics are quite limited, such that a study of the framework within which a particular kind of development takes place is not impossible.

Probably the best example of a field of inquiry within which the principles put forward in this chapter are most obviously present is the field of language development. It is clear that language development cannot be studied without a knowledge of the language the child has to acquire. Language is a very typical example of a cognitive structure that exists at the social level. It will be discussed in the third part of this book.

2.4 DEVELOPMENT, LEARNING AND CHANGE

We may now come to a tentative answer to the question: what is (psychological) development. Firstly, I shall outline some of the 'naive' semantic connotations of the concept of development. I shall therefore concentrate upon the resemblances with and the differences between 'development' and the concepts of 'change' and 'learning'. Then I shall try to point out how these conceptual properties can be related to the formal theory of development put forward in this chapter.

The basic relationship between 'development' and 'change' is that every process of development implies change, whereas not every process of change implies development. Both development and change imply that the states (either of change or of development) be described in terms of one coherent semantic field, such that the descriptions of the states are mutually exclusive. The main difference between 'development' and 'change' is that the states are conceptualized differently. Developmental states are defined in terms of specific antecedent and consequent relationships with other states. The basic antecedent-consequent relationship exists between the initial and final state. We have seen that the initial state is defined in a way that makes clear that it is the opening state of a process of change that ends with a particular closing, i.e. final, state. Processes of change do not normally imply a strict logic of state succession.

The basic resemblance between 'development' and 'learning' is, first, that both imply processes of change and, second, that both are described in terms of states that show clear antecedent-consequent relationships, among which the initial-final relationship is most essential. The difference between development and learning is not that development is a long-term process whereas learning is a short-term process (see for instance Gagnè, 1968), nor that learning is concerned with specific contents of skills whereas development is an overall process (see the development of the number concept, for instance). I assume that the basic difference between learning and develop-

ment is that development takes place 'within' the subject,
whereas learning takes place 'between' the subject and an
objective or objectivized content. 'Learning' and 'development',
therefore, are just two different points from which one phenomenal process is viewed. If I take the content into account,
the process is characterized as learning; if I only take the
internal effects into account, the process is characterized as
development. Contents can be described at various levels of
abstraction. The more I withdraw from the actual phenomenal
properties of the content, the closer I come to abstractions
such as concepts that I employ as building blocks for my model
of the described subject's mind. At a particular level of abstraction, the learning statements will turn into statements of development, because the external aspects are defined in terms of
internal variables.

The resemblances between 'development', 'learning' and
'change' can be defined not only in terms of state properties,
but also in terms of characteristic properties of the state-
transition rules. When the developmental states are defined in
such a way that the definition of one state conceptually implies
the nature and order of the others, the transition rules become
strongly constrained. In such a case we can no longer speak of
'change' but of 'development' or 'learning'. The further distinction between 'development' and 'learning' can be made clear by
specifying the nature of the stability rules. The stability rules
define states either as open or closed or as unstable or stable.
It is plausible that a typical property of states in a learning
model is that they are maximally open, i.e. determinable by
external influences, in connection with relative internal stability,
i.e. the transitional process tends to immobility or equilibrium
if external influences on the process are lacking (learning
depends on either explicit or implicit forms of teaching).

Since we have defined a developmental state in terms of
internal variables and made the subjective existence of external
factors depend on the latter (assimilation), we are obliged to
ascribe relative closeness and internal instability to developmental states. That is, if the states determine the meaning and
content of the external factors, the latter have only a very
limited capacity for directing the state transitions, which have
to be explained, then, on the basis of a particular form of
internal instability, e.g. a striving after equilibration (the
smaller the external pull, the greater the internal push).

One consequence of the formal framework is that the differences between change, development and learning cease to
be categorical and become gradual and exemplary. That is,
the processes need no longer to be conceived of as intrinsically
different, but rather as three examples of the types of processes that may be formulated within the formal framework.

A second consequence of the formal framework is that development is defined formally, i.e. as a process of transitions
between states. Consequently, the concept of development may

be applied to any process to which these formal properties can be attributed. Development is not exclusively the process that takes place between birth and adulthood. It is possible to take any state of the subject as a final state in which development one is interested. Gerontologists, for instance, may try to explain cognition in old age as the final state of a process that takes adult cognition as its starting point. Moreover, development needs not to be conceived of as a process that necessarily leads to 'higher' or to 'superior' states or as a process that is limited to human behaviour. It is possible, for instance to study the development of social or mental deviance. When microprocessor technology proceeds according to current expectations, it will not be long until self-adapting processors will be used in the management of complex systems, the expenses of a family for instance. It is probable that a minimally complex self-adapting process will go through a series of developmental states that might be understood with the aid of a formal theory of development.

Finally, development need not be exclusively concerned with long-term changes (which however was the assumption with which we started this chapter). It is possible to study short-term changes, for instance changes occurring during a series of repeated tasks or changes during one task, by applying the formal structure of development to these processes (see for instance Karmiloff-Smith and Inhelder, 1975).

The final conclusion that may be associated with the preceding remarks and speculations is that developmental psychology should abandon its still-existing image of child or, at best, life-span studies. Developmental psychology must become the science of psychological development, starting from an elaborated theory that specifies the formal structure of the conceptual framework within which concrete processes of development are described and studied.

Part II

The development of perception

3 Perception and perceptual development

3.1 THE CONCEPT OF PERCEPTION

Every language contains a group of words that are used to refer
to a particular sort of cognitive relation between man and the
world, namely the words referring to perception. 'See', 'hear',
'taste', 'feel' and 'smell' express the existence of a sensory
relationship between an organism and the universe that is
different from conceptual relations expressed by words such as
'think', 'know', 'assume' and affective relationships such as
'love', 'like', 'dislike'. Unfortunately, these words, along with
many other natural language terms, share a considerable degree
of vagueness and ambiguity in the way they are used. Vagueness, which is necessary in natural language, hinders the
technical investigations of the dispositions and processes denoted
by them. That is, it is difficult to study how the process of
seeing and hearing comes about if it is unclear what kind of
processes these terms exactly refer to. If, for instance, it is
unclear what is exactly meant by the noun 'cat', it will be very
difficult to investigate the characteristics of cats. It is clear
that the conceptual boundary between cat and no-cat will not
become clear, however much we observe and empirically study
animals, since it remains unclear for a number of animals,
whether they are cats or not. In fact, we need to start from
the vague definition which is at our disposal and then decide
theoretically which kind of characteristics will be necessary
and sufficient in order to call an animal a cat or not. The
adequacy of our theoretical decision about what is a cat and
what is not a cat depends on theoretical and empirical criteria:
conceptual consistency, empirical applicability, the extension
of the empirical class, the existence of prototypes, and so
forth.

Assuming that the concepts of perception expressed by terms
like 'see', 'hear' and so forth suffer from the same kind of
vagueness as the concept of 'cat' in our example, then the same
kind of theoretical decision about their definitive boundaries
will be required.

One of the main difficulties in the precise definition of perception lies in the specification of what human subjects actually
perceive. In order to answer this question we must rely, at least
initially, on our intuition of what we experience perceptually.
Take for instance Figure 3.1(a). It may be questioned whether
we see this figure as a two-dimensional configuration which we

know represents a three-dimensional Necker cube, or whether we see it as a three-dimensional, though not stereoscopic Necker cube which we know is represented by the two-dimensional configuration of lines on the paper. According to my intuition (which in this case I rarely find in conflict with the intuition of others) the latter description comes closer to my experience than the former.

I shall try to demonstrate this with Figure 3.1(b). Try to see this figure as a Necker cube which is tilted slightly differently to the first one. You will presumably see the figure in a three-dimensional, though not stereoscopic way (it may take some time before one sees the figure as a variant of 3.1(a). Then look at Figure 3.1(c), which represents an octagon with the opposite angles connected. Next try to see Figure 3.1(b) as a variant of 3.1(c), viz. as a hexagon with interconnected opposite angles. I expect that your perceptual experience of Figure 3.1(b) will now be different than if you saw 3.1(b) as a variant of 3.1(a).

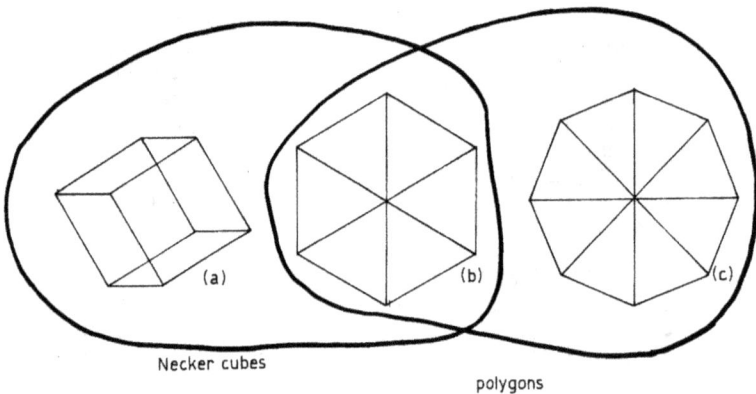

Figure 3.1 Necker cube(a), polygon(c) and ambiguous figure (b). The ambiguous figure can be seen either as a Necker cube or as a polygon. Although the two- or three-dimensional organization of the figure is based on a conceptual decision, the result is of a perceptual nature

This little experiment shows that perception is not the mere reception of a sensory stimulus, but a particular way of experiencing and organizing the stimulus, for instance as a hexagon or a drawing of a three-dimensional Necker cube. The fact that our perception of the figures has been determined by conceptual dispositions does not alter the fact that different perceptual experiences were present. The same principle can be demonstrated by means of a Schumann checkerboard (Schumann, 1900) (see Figure 3.2).

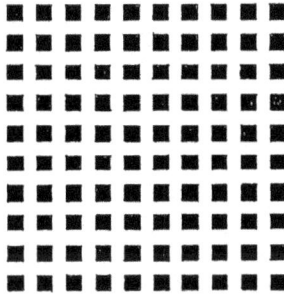

Figure 3.2 A Schumann checkerboard. With some practice, it is possible to impose various organizational principles upon the matrix of black squares, e.g. rows, columns, composite squares and rectangles, etc.

Normally, however, it is not the cognitive disposition that determines the content of perception. The content of perception is imposed upon the perceiver by the structure of perceptual information itself. Although this is particularly true for perceptual information gathered during movement through space, I can illustrate this point with a number of two-dimensional examples.

First, the figures which are determined by cognitive dispositions are characterized by a well-determined ambiguity, such as the Schumann checkerboard or the hexagon. It is very difficult, on the other hand, to see Figure 3.1(a) as a two- and Figure 3.1(b) as a three-dimensional configuration.

A second illustation is provided by visual illusions (see Figure 3.3). Visual illusions, such as the apparent curvature of the straight lines in the Hering-Wundt illusion do not cease to exist however sure the observer is about their illusory character.

A third example can be found in Johansson's moving-dot figures (see also section 6.2). A subject is provided with small lights on the joints and then filmed when moving in a completely dark room. Instead of seeing a number of unconnected dots describing particular curves in space, the observer has a very strong impression of a human body which executes a particular motion pattern.

The question as to what is specifically perceptual in perception may be answered if we can find a language or descriptive system that enables us to formulate statements about what we conceive of as typically perceptual. The phenomenologists have been at great efforts to find ways of describing our perceptual experiences in a way that would do full justice to their particular experiential qualities. The language of phenomenology, however, is no longer used to describe perceptual contents, though there are no motives of principle to reject it as unusable.

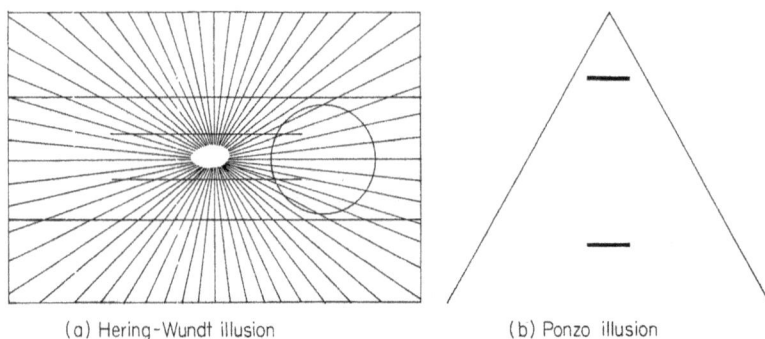

(a) Hering-Wundt illusion   (b) Ponzo illusion

Figure 3.3 Visual illusions. In the Hering-Wundt figure, straight lines look bent and the circle looks flattened at one side. In the Ponzo figure, the real and the perceived lengths of the horizontal lines do not correspond (the objective length of the lines is equal)

In the discussion of the main properties of perception, I shall follow the current trend of describing experiences as processes and operations. The perceptual process-language will have the following properties. First, it describes abstract processes, i.e. functional properties of perception which do not necessarily depict the real, internal spatiotemporal processes of the neurological perceptual apparatus. Second, the process language tries to meet the criterion of descriptive adequacy by describing the perceived world in terms which are acceptable by the metaphysics that underlies our thinking about the world. Thirdly, the process language imposes a particular conceptual limitation or perspective upon our field of inquiry and is not considered the only possible descriptive device.

The most obvious thing about perception is that our senses are responsible for it - they are 'the doors of perception' (Huxley). The senses are parts of our body and we can observe and describe them as we observe and describe other parts of the world. That is, we can describe our senses by means of the vocabulary that we employ to describe the basic properties of the perceptual world in general. In fact, this principle is the key to the understanding of the basic properties of the perceptual process and its development.

Let us now try to list a number of basic properties of the perceptual world and compare them with parallel properties of the sensory information. Our aim is not only to arrive at a description of perception but also at a specification of the conceptual point of view we shall adopt.

First, perception takes place through a number of senses which are qualitatively different. Nevertheless, the distinct modalities reveal one common perceived space. If a wet dog barks at me, I can see it where I can hear it and hear it where I can see it. An important consequence of this principle is that the space that I perceive may extend far beyond the part of space that I can see or hear. The difference between integrated space perception and knowledge of a connection between modality-specific information is illustrated by a desynchronized film. In such a film, I know or believe but do not immediately experience that the voice belongs to the speaker (or the sound to the event), whereas in a synchronized film, as well as in reality, the unity is immediately experienced. Summarizing, the first property of the perceptual process consists of integrating the qualitatively different streams of sensory information into one integrated perceptual space.

Second, the most salient property of normal sensory information is its continuous inconstancy. If I walk through a room, the projected image of the room will undergo complex changes in accordance with the changing angle of incidence from which I see the room. Some parts of the retinal image will move faster than others, dependent on the distance between my eyes and the objects that are projected. Moreover, the retinal image contains also the movement of the objects in the room themselves, such as a person who enters and takes a seat. In contrast with retinal information, however, the perceived content, the room, is stable, immobile and independent of the observer thanks to – and not in spite of – the fact that the retinal image undergoes particular changes during the observer's movements. Further, there is a clear perceptual difference between the perspective changes due to the observer's movements and the original movements of persons or objects in the room. Summarizing, the perceptual apparatus must be capable of analysing the total amount of stimulus variation and of discovering which variables are responsible.

Third, if one selected a particular descriptive system – let us take a Cartesian description of Euclidean space which is quite close to our commonsense image of space – the system might be used to describe and compare the spatial variability of the perceived world and the spatial variability allowed in the sense organs. One would discover that there is often a considerable difference between the spatial variability of the senses and the spatial variability of the perceived world. The classical example is provided by the eye. If I look at a room with one eye, I see the room as a three-dimensional spatial configuration, whereas the retina onto which the room is projected is a two-dimensional curved surface. The perceptual process is responsible for transforming the system of spatial variability of the various senses into perceived spatial variability, for instance two-dimensional retinal variability into three-dimensional variability of visual space.

A remark must be made, however, about the psychological reality of our description of perceived space in terms of three Cartesian dimensions (or of four, if time is added). The visual apparatus, for instance, transforms the retinal stimulus into a perceived world which, if a Cartesian descriptive system is applied to describe spatial properties, can be described as a three-dimensional extension, in contrast with the two-dimensional extension of the retina. If the transformation process is described in terms of a Cartesian language, it can be described as the transformation of a two- into a three-dimensional space. If, however, another system for describing spatial variability had been employed, another characterization of the perceptual process would have resulted which would not be logically incompatible with the Cartesian description, provided that the alternative system is also valid.

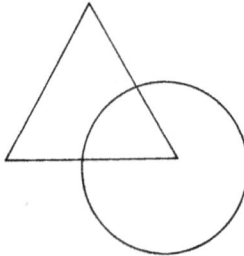

Figure 3.4 Superimposed figures: they are decomposed into a triangle and a circle

Fourth, if you listen to a record of an orchestra playing a piece of music, you will hear different instruments and, with some practice, you will also discern the different melodic lines which they follow. If you look at Figure 3.4, you will see two superimposed figures - a circle and a triangle. The examples show that our perceptual world does not consist of a totality of equally valid visual, auditory or olfactory variation, but that it is organized in terms of patterns, i.e. sets of places in space. If the system of Cartesian dimensions is applied, the only kind of coherence existing in the physical spaces is coherence specified in terms of sensory specific distance. In perceptual space, however, coherence is determined by pattern membership (see Figure 3.5 for an example in a simplified retinal space). Summarizing, the fourth aspect of the perceptual process can be seen as the organization of sensory variation in terms of perceptual patterns, i.e. of a variability of sensory places into coherent sets of perceived places that constitute forms or patterns.

From the combination of the previous perceptual processes, some very important features of perception follow. The percep-

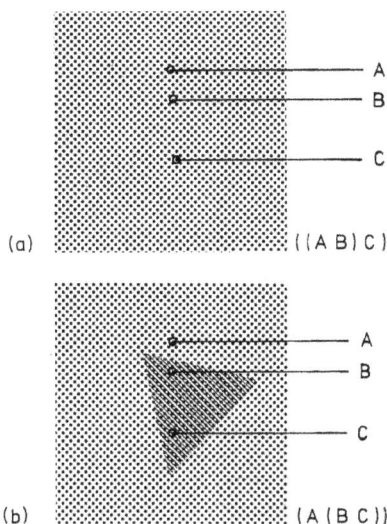

Figure 3.5 Two two-dimensional place systems with three specified places, A, B and C. In (a) proximity between places is
determined by mere distance; in (b) proximity depends on
the sub-spaces (forms, figures, etc.) to which the places
belong

tual apparatus can ascribe some types of variation, such as
perspective reduction of visual size or sound, to invariability
of an object (principle of constancy) in connection with variability in perceptual space, for instance movement along the
depth axis. There is also an important effect on how perceptual
occlusion is interpreted (which is particularly important in
visual perception). In terms of a Cartesian description, the
two-dimensional retinal stimulus has the form of a moszaic – it
consists of adjacent patterns of different size – whereas the
perceptual image consists of a three-dimensional space in which
patterns are situated before or behind others. Although the
nearest pattern is then seen as occluding the ones behind it,
the perceptual boundaries of the farther patterns are not
determined by their retinal boundaries with the adjacent ones.
We see them continue behind the nearer patterns (principle of
permanence). Husserl pointed out that if we look at a matchbox we not only see the three sides which are projected onto
the retina, we see the six sides, i.e. also the sides occluded
by the nearest ones. This seeing is an inferential or implicit
seeing but it is clearly different from making a cognitive
inference (e.g. inferring that the matchbox contains a beetle)
(see Figure 3.6).
    Fifth, a physical pattern can be distinguished from its
environment by sharp and clear boundaries, but it can also

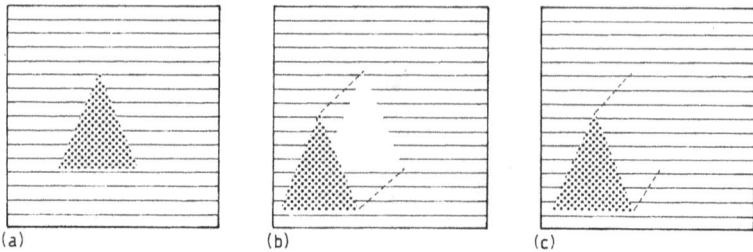

(a)   (b)   (c)

Figure 3.6 Although the proximal stimulus (a) can be described as a mosaic (b), the perceptual description consists of
partially occluding pattern elements, namely figure and
ground (c)

be weak and blurred. When I perceive patterns, however, their
perceptual quality does not differ so much in physical pattern-
definition (sharpness) as in perceptual centrality and peri-
pherality. Perception is determined by a mechanism we call
attention. We are not capable of processing the whole perceptual
field at one unique high level of detail but are forced to select
aspects and fragments of the field which are put into the focus
whereas the remaining aspects obtain a peripheral character
(Neisser, 1967). Another property of attention is that it
functions as a sieve. Attention prevents part of perceptual
information from becoming perceived. Van den Berg (1960)
gives a striking historical example of such a sieve function. A
demonstration of the fact that the valves of the veins open in
the direction of the heart led William Harvey to the assumption
that the heart is a kind of pump. Harvey gave further evidence
for this theory by stating that one could hear the pump work,
i.e. hear the heart beat. It is significant that Harvey's medical
opponents denied explicitly that the heart beats observably:
one of them sneeringly advanced the idea that in contrast with
the English doctors the Venetian ones were probably deaf. Van
den Berg mentions that nowhere in the medical literature before
Harvey is the observable heartbeat mentioned. The fact that
attention is cognitively determined does not alter the fact that
its effects are clearly perceptual: it is the perceptual image
which changes under the influence of cognition and belief, not
what we think or infer from an otherwise meaningless collection
of sense-data. That is to say, as far as the heartbeat was
concerned, the Venetian doctors were deaf.

According to our description of the minimal properties of the
perceived world, the perceptual process must fulfil five different tasks: first, sensory integration (integration of perceptual information across the various sensory systems); second,
analysis of the sensory variability in terms of variable and
invariable features; third, the construction of an adequate
frame of reference (e.g. spatial system reliably describable as

a three-dimensional space); fourth, the organization of the sensory stimulus in terms of patterns and pattern-relationships; and, finally, the selective focalization of the perceptual field. As we have seen, these five aspects of the perceptual process can be governed by perceptual stimulus-properties, by a conceptual disposition (knowledge, belief or goal) or by both, but, independent of its particular aetiology, the result of a perceptual process is a genuinely perceptual image which is perceptually meaningful in itself.

The idea underlying the foregoing analysis of perception was originally developed by Heider in 1926 and elaborated by Koffka in 1935 (Gibson, 1966). The idea concerns the basic difference between what is called the distal and the proximal stimulus. If I look at my cup of coffee or hear a car go by, the stimulus produced on my retina or my tympanic membrane has its causes in the actual cup or the car passing by. The car and the cup are the distal stimulus; the stimulation they produce on the retina or the tympanic membrane is the proximal stimulus. Our sensory apparatus has been constructed in such a way that we do not perceive the proximal but the distal stimulus. We do not see a changing two-dimensional configuration but a cup of coffee characterized by a particular three-dimensional, constant extension.

Films, pictures, mirror- and lens-images, stereophonic records or Ames rooms are examples of ambiguous distal stimuli. The actual distal cause of the perceptual image differs from the one that I perceive. Difficulties might arise, therefore, with the statement that I perceive the distal stimulus. In the case of a picture, for instance, the image is flat, whereas I see a three-dimensional scene. A frequently occurring but entirely wrong solution to this problem is that the distal stimulus is equated with the image in the perceiver's head. The solution that I would like to propose is that the distal stimulus should be regarded as the object of a particular perceptual activity. The question as to the properties of the distal stimulus cannot be answered as long as the psychological activity of which it is the object is not appropriately specified. Since a person can execute a number of different activities, a number of different distal stimuli may arise (the latter illustrates the thesis that there are as many worlds as there are ways of representing them). I can look to a picture as I look to a real scene. The object of my perceptual activity is the scene depicted by the picture. I can also look to the pictures as I look to a two-dimensional object. The object of my perceptual activity is a 'picture-qua-flat-object'.

The explanatory power of our perceptual theory depends on its ability to provide valid descriptions of the object of perceptual activities and their sensory causes, i.e. of the distal and proximal stimuli.

In principle, an adequate descriptive device might be found in the machine language of the system, i.e. the language that expresses the machine processes. The machine language, though perfectly sensible to the machine, does not represent the internal processes in terms of functional components that fit our theories of perception. The machine language of a pocket-calculator, for instance, does not represent what the machine actually does, i.e. calculating, unless the language is mapped on a mathematical theory (see Chapter 9).

An alternative to machine language is natural language. The perceptual theory would take the form of a transformational grammar which provides rules for transforming proximal-stimuli sentences into distal-stimuli sentences. It is very doubtful, however, whether such a perceptual grammar would be at all construable. In principle, a natural language description of a perceptual image can be infinitely variable. For most images, it is impossible to give a finite and exhaustive verbal description (in natural language terms) of what they represent.

In order to find a technically appropriate way of describing the perceptual material, we might return to our discussion of the five basic features of a minimal perceptual process. If we summarize these features, we come to the conclusion that the way in which we have described them requires a system of places. The proximal as well as the distal stimulus can be specified as a system of places in a space. Such a space is an abstract entity and consists of a formal system specifying the total possible variability of places. A simple and relatively commonsense form of such a system consists of a number of independent Cartesian dimensions which can be treated as co-ordinates. Take, for instance, the space required to specify the place-variability of the visual apparatus. In order to describe an instance of a visual proximal stimulus (e.g. the pattern of light which falls on an observer's retina for a given period of time) we need one dimension specifying light intensity, one for specifying frequency or wavelength, two dimensions for specifying the place on the retina and one dimension for specifying time of occurrence. A proximal stimulus, then, is specified as a (very large) six-dimensional set of places. The distal stimulus can be described as a specific derivation of the proximal place-set, consisting of one integrated instead of many sensory-specific place systems, characterized by the presence of place-clusters (patterns, forms and so forth). There exist various mathematical and logical ways for describing clusters or sets of places. Analytical geometry, for instance, is a well-known technique for describing clusters of places in terms of an equation which expresses the mathematical relation between their co-ordinates. In Chapter 6 I shall discuss a number of perceptual coding languages and show how they deal with form perception. It is important to note, however, that whatever descriptive system is employed, it should take into account that perception is a topological, i.e. place-set system, and not a propositional system, for instance. Moreover, each descriptive system represents a particular conceptual perspec-

tive of the contents that it describes. We would make a categorical mistake if we identified our description with a homeo-
morphic representation of the described content, implying that
only one descriptive system can be true.

I want to make a final remark on the status that can be
attached to the five subprocesses that mediate between the
proximal and the distal stimulus. I stated that these subprocesses have a purely formal meaning and that they do not describe
actual spatiotemporal operations or brain processes. They
specify the relationship that exists between a particular proximal and a particular distal stimulus description (e.g. in Cartesian terms). Moreover, the distal stimulus should not be viewed
as an image-in-the-head, but as something outside the subject,
as the object of a perceptual act. If we strive at an explication
of the formal subprocesses in terms of brain language or actual
internal processes, we have to make clear which kind of internal
states should be associated with acts that have a specific distal
stimulus as their object and a specific proximal stimulus as
their cause. In fact, it may be wondered whether translation
of the formal subprocesses into a 'brain' language' would actually increase our insight into the nature of perception and
its development.

In the next section I shall explore the consequences of this
view on perception for a theory of perceptual development.

3.2 THE CONCEPT OF PERCEPTUAL DEVELOPMENT

The study of perceptual development tries to provide an answer
to a number of basic questions. The first question concerns the
object of the perceptual activities during the initial state: what
are its properties, what is the nature of the perceptual operations that constitute this particular object and how do they
differ from the final state of perceptual development. The
second question concerns the transition from the initial to the
final state: how does the transition take place and what are
the properties of its dynamics.

In the previous section we have seen that the object of mature
perception is the distal stimulus. If we employ a particular
descriptive system, i.e. a Cartesian language of space, we are
able to describe the distal as well as the proximal stimulus and
define the act of perception in terms of five formal subprocesses.

The descriptive system that we employ should fulfil two basic
requirements. First, it should not be identified with the content of the perceptual processes, i.e. with the mind of the
perceiver. When I state, for instance, that the infant perceives
a three-dimensional instead of a two-dimensional world, I mean
that the child perceives a world to which the predicate 'three-
dimensional' can be attributed if a conceptual system is employed
in which this predicate is present and meaningful. I do not
intend to say that the infant himself describes the world he

perceives in terms of this conceptual system, for instance
that the infant employs an abstract system of underlying concepts one of which corresponds with our notion of three-
dimensionality.

Second, the descriptive system should be descriptively adequate, not only with regard to our basic scientific metaphysics
of the structure of the world, but also with regard to the way
in which the child perceives the world. The fact that I can
say that the infant perceives an object does not allow me to say
that the infant perceives a particular mass of molecules, just
because objects do consist of molecules. There is nothing in
the child's perceptual or motor activity that corresponds with
our notion of molecules, that is, there is no observable indication that the structure of the object (in the abstract sense of
the word) of the infant's perceptual actions can be described
meaningfully in terms borrowed from chemistry and physics,
such as 'molecule'. The structure of the object of the child's
perceptual activity is more compatible with a descriptive system
that consists of concepts such as 'object' (in the concrete sense
of the word), 'action', 'event' and so forth.

The model of perception put forward in the previous section
offers a description of the properties of the final state of
perceptual development, namely the state at which the formal
process of transforming the proximal into the distal stimulus
takes place:

$$FS: \quad PS \Rightarrow DS_F$$

(during the final state FS the proximal stimulus PS is transformed into the final distal stimulus DS_F).

Our next task is to define a theoretical initial state in the
light of the foregoing definition. Our definition will be theoretical, i.e. deductively and not empirically determined. As a
theoretical initial state we might postulate a state in which the
transformational process characterizing the final state cannot
yet be executed. The non-existence of the transformational
process implies that the subject at the theoretical initial state
perceives the world as it is proximally given (the distal stimulus equals the proximal stimulus):

$$IS: \quad PS = DS_I$$

The fact that the distinction between a final and an initial
proximal stimulus is not made implies that the model of development is limited to the period in which the physiological properties of the sensory system are fully developed.

It will be clear that the theoretical initial state is not necessarily the real, empirical initial state. It may be asked then,
which kind of other non-final states the model allows. Discuss-

ing these possible states will give us some ideas about the kinds
of empirical initial states which are theoretically possible. The
first possibility is that the empirical initial state equals in the
final state, such that within the framework of perception put
forward here there is no question of development. It is not
improbable that the newborn child is already capable of performing the five subprocesses, and that only the details, the process properties or power of the processes differ from the final
state (see further in this chapter). The second possibility is
that the actual, i.e. empirical, initial state of perceptual development is characterized by the ability to transform the proximal
stimulus into a distal stimulus which on the one hand differs
from the proximal stimulus, but on the other hand, also from
the final distal stimulus. Theoretically, such a provisional
distal stimulus can be constructed by employing some but not
all of the subprocesses, for instance only the rules of pattern
formation and analysis of variability. The resulting distal
stimulus would be characterized by the lack of sensory integration.

It is conceivable, however, that there are a number of theoretical limitations to the kind of initial states. We have taken
for granted that the perceptual subprocesses are totally independent, i.e. that none of the processes presuppose another
one. It is probable, however, that further investigation will
prove that some subprocesses actually depend on other ones
or on common underlying processes on a deeper level.

The main function of our theoretical speculation is to provide
programmes for empirical research, e.g. in the form of concrete
hypotheses. The theory tells us what kind of hypotheses are
possible and relevant if we accept the definition of perception
discussed in the first section of the present chapter. The
instrumental character of the underlying theoretical framework
makes it open to changes which improve its functionality,
e.g. its usefulness in formulating testable hypotheses.

Another function of the theoretical framework discussed thus
far is that it may help us understand the classical controversies
in the explanation of perceptual development, such as the
discussion between nativists and empiricists on the perception
of depth. How can we see depth, while our eyes are flat surfaces? Empiricists such as Berkeley explained depth perception
by postulating learned associations between tactile and motor
information about the third spatial dimension on the one hand
and the two-dimensional visual information about space on the
other hand. Later, Von Helmholtz also implicated the problem
of size and form-constancy in the discussion. He assumed that
the perception of size and form-constancy is merely due to
prolonged experience with reality which teaches the observer
that things only apparently change their form and size if he
moves. According to the nativists, the human species is provided with an innate knowledge of the basic structure of reality:
depth is seen and not inferred. In more recent times, the

controversy between nativism and empiricism took the form of
a discussion between learning theory and behaviourism on the
one hand and Gestalt psychology on the other hand.

In terms of our theoretical framework, the extreme empiricist's
position is characterized by the assumption that the theoretical
initial state of perceptual development provides a valid model
of the actual, i.e. empirical initial state:

$$IS: \quad PS = DS_I$$

The extreme nativist subscribes to the assumption that there is
no difference between the final and the initial distal stimulus,
i.e. that there is no perceptual development:

$$IS: \quad PS \Rightarrow (DS_I = DS)_F$$

Gestalt psychology offers an explanation for the above mentioned description of the initial state. According to Gestalt
psychology, the physiological properties of the perceptual
apparatus, in combination with the structural properties of the
perceptual stimulus, do simply not allow a transformation from
proximal to distal stimulus other than the above one, i.e. they
do not accept the kind of identity transformation that is required
by the empiricist's formula. It is clear that the application of
the theoretical framework entails a considerable theoretical
generalization for the nativistic and empiristic points of view.
The discussion is no longer focused upon the rather trivial
and unsolvable question as to whether either everything or
nothing has to be learned but rather upon the properties of the
initial state of development, i.e. the properties of the object of
perception during the initial state and the nature of the perceptual processes that constitute this object. Another advantage of
the theoretical framework is that it allows us to provide detailed
descriptions of theoretically and conceptually possible developmental states, which can be subjected to empirical investigation.

3.3 EMPIRICAL INVESTIGATION OF PERCEPTUAL DEVELOP-
MENT

In the field of perceptual development, important developmental
steps are taken during the first year of life. This fact implies
that we will have to draw a number of far-reaching conclusions
on the basis of research with very young children.

If we investigate the perceptual world of adults, we can rely
on our subjects' ability to use language for reporting the
properties of their perceived world. If we distrust the objectivity of introspective reports, we can rely on the adults'
capacity for handling non-verbal concepts, problem solving,

discrimination and so forth. The investigation of perception during the first year of life is hampered by the child's limited behavioural repertory, which makes it hard to find reliable empirical indicators for the properties of the infant's perceptually revealed world. Put theoretically, the basic problem in infant research concerns the lack of precision with which the empirical mapping rules have been elaborated in the field of perceptual development. In practice, the mapping rules are seldom made explicit. They consist of paradigmatic experimental examples and are mainly determined by our tacit, pre-scientific knowledge of the meaning of the theoretical terms. When the thinking of preverbal infants is concerned, however, our intuitions fail because they are primarily based on a conception of conscious, strongly linguistically biased forms of representation.

Infants differ from our model of the standard subject also with regard to the way in which they are involved in what happens around them. During the first weeks after birth, the child's behaviour is largely determined by his state of vigilance. Even when the child looks awake, there are considerable periodical and individual differences in his alertness and vigilance (Trehub, 1975; Ashton, 1976). Moreover, the state of vigilance is determined by the child's bodily position: according to Prechtl (1965) a two-weeks old child is never fully awake when lying on his back. Such a child will not or hardly react to stimulation to which it would react when sitting in a baby chair for instance (Bower, 1974). Neonates seem to be optimally sensible to stimulation when they are held across the shoulder of an adult, resting on the adult's breast, their back supported by the adult's hand (Frederickson and Brown, 1975). Another advantage of this method is that, with respect to visual stimuli in particular, the 'clever Hans effect' is avoided (the child might react not to the actual stimulus but to the unconscious discriminative bodily reactions of the adult who holds the infant and who can also watch the stimuli).

One of the conditions for the application of our model of perception to the entire process of development is that the proximal stimulus of the initial state is comparable with the proximal stimulus of the final state. This implies that the sensory organs must be sufficiently mature during the initial state. In reality, neonates are characterized by a relative immaturity of the sensory systems. The fovea, for instance, is less well developed than the peripheral zones of the retina. By means of peripheral discrimination, however, the visual system compensates its relative immaturity well enough to make the perceptual model applicable (see for instance Lewis et al., 1978; Maurer and Lewis, 1979; Kremenitzer et al., 1979).

Generally, the group of neonates and very young children who can be experimentally investigated is quite small: many children do not react to the stimuli, fall asleep or start crying (Poresky, 1976). It is highly probable that the group of

examinable children constitutes a rather unrepresentative
sample. Sensitivity to testing by means of the habituation technique, for instance, shows a high positive correlation with
cognitive and sensori-motor development at the age of fifteen
months (Miller et al., 1977a, 1977b; Johnson and Brody, 1977).

In the study of perceptual development, the magic word is
'discrimination'. The investigator relies upon his intuitive or
scientific information about qualitative properties of perception,
such as the integrative nature of the perceptual image. Then
he tries to find or create perceptual stimuli which he knows
will differ only in the qualitative property in which he is
interested. If the subject is aware of the differences, i.e. when
he can discriminate them, then it is clear that his perceptual
apparatus is sensitive to the investigated qualitative property.
The difficulty, however, is not only to design stimuli that fulfil the requirements, but also to find a reliable indication of
the subject's discriminative competence. The problem is that
children at the age at which we want to investigate the initial
state of perceptual development are still insensitive to most of
the common research methods. In order to overcome this difficulty, investigators have developed a number of specific baby-
research methods.

The best known technique is Fantz' fixation-time measurement
(Fantz, 1961; Friedman, 1972; Welch, 1974; Greenberg and
Blue, 1977). The experimenter measures the total amounts of
time the infant has spent looking at distinct stimuli. If the
amount of time of looking at one stimulus is significantly different from the time spent on the other one it is concluded that
the infant is capable of discriminating both stimuli. The technique does not only appeal to discrimination, but also to selective
attention: if the infant can discriminate both stimuli but finds
them equally interesting, there will be no significant difference
between the looking, i.e. fixation, times. Closely related to
the former technique is the eye-fixation method: by means of
an eye-fixation apparatus, the investigator registrates which
elements of the stimulus are most frequently fixated by the
infant (Salapatek and Kessen, 1973; Salapatek, 1975; Slater
and Findlay, 1975a). For this purpose, investigators often
employ the corneal reflection technique. It is based on the fact
that the cornea, i.e. the frontal surface of the eye-ball, behaves
like a convex mirror, i.e. the cornea reflects the presented
stimulus. In practice, the stimulus is provided with some
orientation light-bulbs. Then the subject's eye can be video-
taped in order to enable the observers to compute the centre
of the child's gaze.

The method that is most frequently used at present is based
on the habituation phenomenon. If an infant is repeatedly
confronted with the same stimulus, he will gradually lose his
interest, i.e. habituate to the stimulus. Habituation is indicated,
for instance, by a decrease in looking time at each repeated
presentation of the stimulus, a decrease in grasping and

touching the stimulus and so forth. After a number of repeated
presentations, the child is offered either a new stimulus or a
pair of stimuli, consisting of a new and a familiarized stimulus
(paired comparison technique). If the ability to distinguish the
new from the familiar stimulus is present, the child will show
a renewed interest, for instance, a longer gaze, or renewed
grasping (for a methodological discussion: Caron and Caron,
1969; McWorth and Otto, 1970; McCall and Kagan, 1970). Attention recovery after habituation is an inverted U-function of
the magnitude of discrepancy between the new and the familiarized stimulus (McCall et al., 1977b).

The advantage of the habituation method is that, contrary to
the fixation-time technique, selective attention cannot play a
disturbing role (few stimuli are so interesting that repeated
presentation does not affect their attractivity). The method's
main disadvantage is that it makes use of a rather complex
process, namely habituation, which involves, among others,
that the foregoing stimulus is remembered and compared with
the following one and that the effects of the comparison are
cumulative. For this reason, the habituation technique under-
estimates the discriminative abilities of children under four
months of age. Moreover, performance of these infants is limited
by three additional factors, namely position bias (which is quite
disadvantageous to the paired comparison technique), attention
tropisms which counteract habituation, and the length of
processing time (which is longer for the younger children)
(Caron et al., 1977).

Another technique employs behavioural frequencies as an
indicator of discrimination. The experimenter may measure
changes in heart-beat frequency at the appearance of a new
stimulus (auditive stimuli in particular) (Moffitt, 1973; Porges
et al., 1973; Sameroff et al., 1973; Gregg, Clifton and Marshall,
1976; Leavitt et al., 1976). A comparable indicator is sucking
frequency, measured by means of a pacifier connected with a
measuring apparatus (Franks and Berg, 1975; Mendelson and
Haith, 1975; Christensen et al., 1976; Crook and Lipsitt,
1976). Other investigators measure changes in pupil width
(Munsinger and Banks, 1974) and muscular tension (Boyle and
Hull, 1976) at the presentation of new stimuli.

In his experiments on size and form constancy, Bower (Bower,
1966) introduced the use of conditioned responses as an indicator of recognition (in fact, recognition is a kind of negative
discrimination). The infant learned to connect a response to a
particular stimulus. The elicitation of the response by another
stimulus, e.g. the same object now presented at another orientation, is taken as an indicator of recognition.

Besides these rather artificial techniques a number of more
natural indicators of discrimination are also frequently used.
Grasping and reaching for objects (Field, 1976a, 1976b), as
well as defensive responses (eye-blinks, withdrawal) are often
used as indicators of depth perception. Preferential grasping

can be used as a substitute for looking time in habituation
experiments. Smiling, crying and wariness of strangers can
give an indication of recognition of familiar persons (Sroufe,
1977; Watson et al., 1979). Tracking, i.e. following with the
eyes, is the classical indicator for the perception of movement
(Bower, 1974).

Like all experimental methods and techniques, the foregoing
ones also pose a number of particular problems concerning
reliability and validity. The problem of reliability is quite
particular. First, a large number of infants cannot be investigated: they simply do not fit the experimental techniques.
Consequently, it is impossible to compose a really representative sample. Second, there is the problem of the extreme
sensibility of the results to small changes in the experimental
method. A significant example of this problem is provided by
a series of investigations on the interference phenomenon (see
section 6.2.3.2). Although the results were contradictory
the experiments differed only in the kind of stimulus material
that was presented (Fagan, 1977; McCall et al., 1977a; Cohen
et al., 1977).

The next problem we have to deal with concerns the validity
of the experimental results. In the majority of experiments,
simple, largely artificial stimuli are employed which are presented
in an isolated way, i.e. in a non-distractive environment.
Second, most stimuli are static: the stimulus is immobile, the
observing infant is immobile, or the stimulus is not suitable
for being perceived from other points of view (e.g. pictures,
geometrical figures, etc.). Third, the stimulus does not form
part of an action other than the action experimentally required
from the child. Fourth, perception takes place in a socially
isolated situation: the child looks, hears and touches on his own.
It is very difficult to obtain optimally reliable results other than
by applying the above-mentioned conditions of stimulus presentation. But on the other hand it is equally clear that in
reality the child's mode of perception runs completely counter
to these experimental conditions. Normally, the child's environment is quite distractive, there is no such thing as a 'stimulus'
appearing in an isolated way. Moreover, the infant's perceptual
world is primarily dynamic: things change continuously, partly
due to place effects (such as perspective transformations),
partly due to real changes of the objects (such as the human
face). In most cases, the child's perceptual processes are an
aspect of a larger frame of action, e.g. exploratory or purposeful behaviour, in which it fulfils a particular function.
Finally, the child's perception frequently takes place in a social
connection: perceiving happens in a process of social interaction, in which the caretaker isolates objects or produces
events (in games, for instance) while the child follows the
caretaker's eye-movements, pointings and so forth.

It is necessary to improve the validity of our theories and
experimental findings as much as possible, for instance by

studying biologically and socially relevant patterns (Vurpillot, 1978; Harris and Van Geert, 1979) or by studying perception in a social context (Scaife and Bruner, 1975).

In addition to the unrepresentativity of the experimental methods with respect to real-life situations, a second problem concerning the validity of perceptual developmental research has to be posed. It concerns the question of the operationalization of the concepts the investigators want to examine. For instance, if an investigator decides to study the development of size constancy, he needs a set of decidable empirical criteria that can be used to determine the subject's state of size constancy development. The operationalization of the concept functions as a kind of measuring instrument. It is clear that for determining the different developmental states one measuring instrument should be used. In developmental research, however, it often occurs that measuring instruments, i.e. operationalizations of a concept, differ according to the state at which the measurement is carried out. With older children, size constancy is measured by means of verbal reports and experiments in which children have to adjust and compare the real sizes of experimental objects. In infancy, however, size constancy is measured by means of conditioned responses or habituation. Since the nature of the abilities involved in both methods is considerably different, it is quite probable that the methods measure different concepts. I assume that two concepts are involved: a sensori-motor and a conceptual-linguistic form of size constancy. Both forms follow their own line of development, but they also have a special connection: the sensori-motor is a necessary condition for the emergence of the conceptual-linguistic form.

In the following chapters I shall discuss the development of perception ordered according to the five subprocesses of perception: sensory integration, analysis of space and of variability, pattern and form construction and attention. It is very important to repeat, however, that these processes have a formal nature: they do not refer to concrete neurological processes. The processes make sense within the limits of our particular descriptive system - a Cartesian language of space - which we employed to describe the object of perception, i.e. distal space, objects and events, and its immediate physiological, sensory cause, i.e. the proximal stimulus. In the chapter on constancy phenomena, we shall see that a Cartesian language of space is not the only possible way of describing a space that is characterized by three-dimensionality, constancy and so forth. We shall see that the perceptual system employs its own particular way of representing such a space.

4 Sensory integration

4.1 THE NATURE OF THE PROCESS

In the first section we have seen that the proximal stimulus
consists of a number of separate sensory spaces, each characterized by their own physical and physiological peculiarities.
The distal stimulus on the other hand shows a definite unity:
we perceive one coherent perceptual space.

I shall try to explain the process leading to the perception of
an integrated space by means of an example, namely of how an
observer perceives the 'barking wet dog'. The dog simultaneously produces three kinds of penetrating sensory stimulation:
a loud, unceasing bark; a disgusting smell; and a frightening
sight. How is it that we see the dog where we smell him, and
that we smell him where we hear him?

In order to understand the integration process, we must first
take into consideration the physical properties of the different
kinds of stimuli. Information about smell is provided by the
dispersion of molecules emitted by an olfactory source. The
average density of the molecules depends on the distance from
that source. Sound is a phenomenon of airwaves propagated
with an average speed of 300 metres per second. The further
one is removed from the sound source, the later and fainter the
sound will be heard. Physically, vision is a matter of light
refracted by a lens and projected onto a concave screen, the
retina. Thus, the place of the projected image on the screen
will depend on the relative position of the lens and the screen
with respect to the projected object.

Figure 4.1 depicts a highly simplified case of sensory integrated perception of two places in space. The problem is to
explain how the perceiver determines that the dog is right in
the middle at position 1 and at the right at position 2. Both
positions correspond with three sets of sensory stimulation:
(v_1, v_2) (two places of retinal stimulation at both eyes);
(s_1, s_2) (intensity of smell in both nasal cavities); and (t_1, t_2)
(time of arrival of a sound at both ears).

With position 1, the subtraction of the members of each set
equals zero; with position 2, the subtraction results in three
integers, k, l and m, unlike zero. Although it would lead us
too far, it is possible to prove that, for any particular k, there
exists one particular l and m. The most important conclusion is
that a place in space does not correspond with a stimulus-value
but with a particular operation upon sensory stimulation.

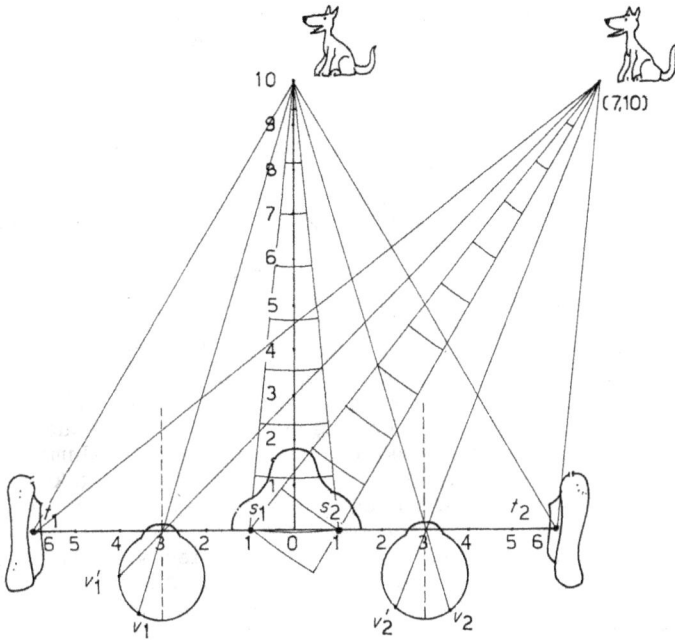

Figure 4.1 Sensory integrated perception of places. The barking wet dog produces visual, auditive and olfactory stimulation. The spatial position of the dog is represented in terms of a mathematical transformation of proximal stimulus values

In principle, there exists a one-to-one mapping relationship between a place in space and the resultant from an operation on sensory stimulus-values. The perception of places in space requires a system or a set of rules which are able to carry out this mapping relationship. It may be questioned whether these rules are innate or acquired. The complexity of the rules militates against a learning hypothesis, but at the same time the growth of the human body is a strong argument in favour of learning. The fixed mathematical relationship between values of v, s and t changes when the inter-ear, inter-nostril and inter-eye distances alter as a result of normal bodily growth (see Bower, 1974, for a more detailed discussion).

The fact that I demonstrated the sensory integration process by means of a simplified Cartesian model of space does not imply that the perceptual system operates with integers, Cartesian co-ordinates and the like. I merely set out to give a formal simulation of the integration process which the actual perceptual system executes in an entirely different way.

In addition to the integrated perception of space, there is a second form of sensory integration, namely integrated perception of pattern. Integrated pattern perception implies that our experience of pattern qualities does not depend on the sensory modality in which the pattern takes its form. A pattern can be seen, but can also be felt and heard (within particular limitations proper to the nature of the various sensory systems).

The intersensory perception of pattern should be distinguished from the perception of equivalences between sensory-specific patterns, such as the associative equivalences between sounds and colours. Intersensory equivalences were a familiar topic of research for scholars and artists at the end of the nineteenth and the beginning of the twentieth century (such as Zwaardemaker, Rimington, Scriabin, Huysmans and Kandinsky). Unfortunately, most of their work on the relationship between sounds, smells, taste, the musical scale, the timbre of instruments – to name only a few – has not been continued in recent research programmes. A favourite example of intersensory equivalences employed by the Gestalt psychologists concerned the visual form of the words 'maluma' and 'takete'. Most people see 'maluma' as the (nonsense) name of fluent, round forms, whereas 'takete' refers to sharp and angular ones (see Figure 4.2). Recently research has been done on the equivalence between musical and tonal patterns on the one hand and visual patterns on the other (Deutsch, 1975; Tolkmitt and Brindley, 1977). At present, most of the research is devoted to the integrated perception of sensory non-specific patterns, particularly in the field of visual-tactile integration.

Figure 4.2 'Maluma' and 'takete': an example of auditory-visual correspondences

In the standard experiment, the subject tangibly explores a visually masked object (normally by manipulating it). He is then visually presented with a number of objects among which he has to select the one formerly touched. Results currently obtained with this kind of research suggest that visual-tactile integration operates rather precisely, i.e. that tactile and visual information show a considerable degree of similarity. Nonetheless, the degree of accuracy and detail is much higher for visual than for tactile information.

For seeing subjects, the visual mode remains the dominant

one: in the case of experimentally induced deceptive contradiction between visual and sensory information, visual information dominates (Rock and Harris, 1967). The equivalence
between tactile and visual information does not only hold for
manually acquired information but also for information acquired
with any other part of the body. Forms 'drawn' onto the
subject's back can be easily recognized visually.

Research has also been carried out on the visual perception
of tactile qualities, particularly on graspability and tangibility,
which are non-tactile properties that provide information about
tactile explorability of objects (see Bower, 1974, for an overview). The perception of spatial boundaries is the major clue to
tangibility. Tangibility can be a property of objects represented
by images; graspability requires a spatial boundary extending
over three spatial dimensions.

I shall not go any deeper into the many different forms the
process of sensory integration may take but attempt to provide
a schematic theoretical explanation of the nature of sensory
integration.

In Chapter 3 we examined a method for describing formally
the content of perceptual proximal and distal stimuli, viz.
describing them as sets of places in a sensory place. The system
thus specifying perceptual contents was called a perceptual
coding language. In terms of the perceptual coding language,
the information, i.e. the images, conveyed by the various
senses are partly sensory-specific, partly sensory-uniform.
Sensory images have a number of sensory-specific qualities,
i.e. auditory, tactile, visual, gustatory or olfactory properties.
But on the other hand, sensory images may be characterized by
non-sensory-specific pattern properties. A tactile and a visual
exploration of an object may reveal the same pattern qualities
in spite of the different sensory modes. Translated into the
perceptual coding language, sensory integration is based on
the existence of a common sensory coding language in addition
to various specific sensory coding languages (the common coding
language might be either closely related to the system of motor
representation (Jones, 1975; Held and Hein, 1958), or 'abstract',
that is, based on a number of operations on sensory-specific
information (Van Geert, 1975; Leeuwenberg, 1971)).

The model of sensory integration discussed thus far provides
a theoretical base for speculations regarding the course of
sensory integration development. We may state that the sensory
integration model offers a description of what should be acquired
by the end of development, i.e. at the final state. Since the
final state is characterized by adequate sensory integrated
perception, expressed in terms of an intersensory perceptual
coding language, the theoretical initial state must be characterized by an inadequate sensory integrated perception. The
absence of sensory integration may be explained either by the
lack of an intersensory perceptual coding language or by a
perceptual coding language which is not yet at work. The

difference between the latter alternatives lies in the fact that
they have different developmental implications: either the
construction of a perceptual coding language or the learning
of how to employ it.

From our framework for thinking about development, it follows
that the theoretical description of the initial state of development - which will be termed the theoretical initial state - is
based on the conceptual properties of our final state description
and not on considerations of empirical plausibility. The description of the final and the initial state and the various possible
lines of development that connect them do not serve as empirical
statements but provide a theoretical and conceptual delimitation
of the kind of empirical statements that will be possible. They
point out within which conceptual boundaries statements about
empirical facts regarding sensory integration development will
be possible.

4.2 THE DEVELOPMENT OF SENSORY INTEGRATION

4.2.1 *The integrated perception of places in space*
When the adult perceives a place, he perceives it by means of
various sensory modalities: seeing, hearing and so forth. These
various sensory-specific modes of perception may be considered
intentional acts (a term introduced by Franz Brentano in 1874
and which is of great, if not always recognized, importance for
psychology). In our case, the object of the act is a specific
place in space, whereas the acts themselves are various sensory-
specific processes. When we state that the object of our various
sensory acts is one place in distal space, we mean that our
sensory acts are characterized by such experiential and behavioural properties that, given a descriptive system that specifies
distal space in terms of places, the various sensory acts can
be ascribed an object describable as 'a place in space'.

Why, one might question, is it so important to be so precise
about the fact that the object of our sensory acts is specified
in terms of a particular descriptive system. Isn't this trivial
and inevitable? It is inevitable, indeed, but it is not trivial.
What I finally mean to say is that a particular constitutive
relationship exists between our acts and their objects. The
objects are not just there in the 'real' world. The 'real' world
offers a number of conditions and possibilities and it needs a
particular act to make Objects of them. Since perception and its
sensory activities is simply another kind of act when compared
to the conceptual act that makes us speak about a distal space
characterized by places, the difference between both kinds of
acts should always be kept in mind. Nevertheless, in spite of
their differences, the acts - embedded in various representational systems such as perception or language - can be mapped
upon each other. The neonate's perceptual activities, for
instance, can be characterized by a number of properties that

enable us to state that he sees the same place as he hears. We never mean to state, however, that the neonate has some inbuilt spatial knowledge that is basically identical with the kind of knowledge the adult uses in order to describe and conceptualize space.

It may be questioned whether the neonate's perceptual activities are indeed characterized by properties that enable us to state that he sees, hears or feels distal places instead of as many places as there are place-sensitive sensory organs. What are these properties, however? One of the classical arguments for the existence of sensory integrated place-perception at birth arises from Wertheimer's demonstration of the neonate's ability to look in the direction of a sound source (Wertheimer, 1961).

Whereas Turkewitz et al., (1972) found supportive evidence for the existence of adequate looking by neonates towards an off-centre source, experiments by Butterworth and Castillo (1976) and McGurk et al., (1977) failed to confirm the previous results. According to Muir and Field (1979), this contradictory evidence is due to the fact that the experiments used different kinds and lengths of sounds and limited the neonate's response to eye-turning, whereas under natural conditions of visual-auditory co-ordination, the head as well as the eyes are turned. In Muir and Field's investigation, the experimenters held three-day old infants in an almost supine position, allowing the infants to move their heads freely. The experimenters themselves were wearing headphones such that they were unable to 'transmit' turning suggestions to the infants they were holding. The sounds were presented by means of two speakers located 20cm opposite each ear. The sounds consisted of a twenty-second long rattle sound averaging a sound pressure of 80db. The investigators concluded that there was a striking tendency for the infants to orient towards the sound. One would expect that the infant 'understands' that a place heard at the right can be seen by turning the head to the right. There is another plausible explanation, however, according to which the infant's orientation is a simple auditory tropistic reaction. The infant perceives a sound unevenly spread over both ears. The infant then seeks to find a position in which the auditory stimulation is maximal for both ears (just like a plant turns to the light). In Chapter 7 we shall discuss these explanations further.

Crassini and Broerse (1980) investigated four-day old babies' oculomotor responses towards sounds coming from different directions (with head movement restricted). The investigators found that the infants showed a significant tendency towards not responding to sound sources by means of eye turnings. When the infant responded, however, the majority of the eye turnings was towards the sound.

An experiment by Bower and Wishart (1973), carried out with much 'older' infants, namely five months old, showed that infants are capable of reaching towards a sound source in the dark. Thus, young children start from the implicit assumption that sound sources not only have a visual but also a tactile existence.

It may be questioned, however, whether these investigations definitely prove the existence of an innate intersensory perception of space. At first sight they merely prove the existence of sensori-motor integration, which might imply a common coding language for sensory and motor information. Our movements take place in the same experiential space as the space revealed by the various senses. It may be questioned, however, whether the child who looks at the direction of a sound source also sees the bell at the same place as where he hears it. Is there any connection, not to mention equivalence, between places heard and places seen?

Since we are not capable of experiencing what the child experiences, and since the child is not capable of telling it, we shall have to infer the child's experience of the integrative nature of place-perception on the basis of available empirical and theoretical evidence.

The observer has noticed that the child is capable of sensori-motor integration: the child has proved to be capable of directing his gaze towards a sound-source (auditory-motor integration) but also towards a source of visual information (visual-motor integration). If the sound and light sources are actually the same object, a bell for instance, the observer knows that both sources occupy the same physical place. It may be asked whether the subject also knows it. If sensori-motor integration is adequate, the grasping of the hand or the gaze of the eye must be directed towards the physical place, independent of whether the place has been heard or seen (see Figure 4.3(a)).

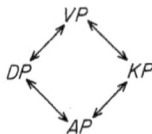

Figure 4.3(a)   The relations between distal (DP), visual (VP), auditory (AP) and kinesthetic (KP) places

It can be read as follows: distal place DP is equivalent to visual place VP and to auditory place AP. Visual and auditory places VP and AP are equivalent to kinesthetic place KP, i.e. the place indicated by the direction and/or place of the child's gaze or grasping. We shall examine whether or not the subject is capable of perceiving both the visual and auditory place of an object as one integrated distal place in space (see Figure 4.3(b)).

For the subject, P_1 is a place in a visual space, while P_2 is a place in an auditory space. Since both spaces are different, the

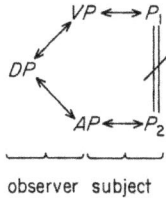

observer subject

Figure 4.3(b) The relations between a distal place (DP), visually and auditory presented places (VP and AP), and experienced spatial places (P_1 and P_2), for an observer and a subject

places are also different. The diagram represents a subject's knowledge of space at the theoretical initial state, that is, the state at which no intersensory perception of space is carried out. Now, it may be questioned whether or not the diagram is empirically tenable (see Figure 4.3(c)).

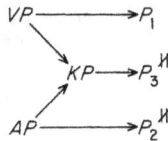

Figure 4.3(c) A diagram combining figures 4.3(a) and (b)

If the child were to believe that the visual, auditory and kinesthetic places are different since they belong to different spaces, then adequate grasping and looking would require that the child possesses a set of rules telling him how to connect a given visual or auditory place with a kinesthetic one. Since a rudimentary form of adequate sensori-motor co-ordination is present at birth, the system of rules would presumably need to be innate. It may be questioned, however, why a system of rules that runs counter to the real space in which the newborn child will have to live would be 'wired in'. Such a system of rules implies that the child would be equipped with a 'belief' in the difference between sensory-specific spaces. Would such a child be capable of discovering perceptually that there is in fact only one distal space which is the source of the various sensory spaces?

There are few arguments in favour of such a perceptual discovery. If the connections between the various sensory systems are relatively well established there will be hardly any behavioural failures that are due explicitly to the fact that the subject perceptually employs a 'theory' of separate sensory spaces. There is absolutely no reason to think that such a system, given the incredible connective capacities of our brains would lead to a highly inadequate sensori-motor co-ordination.

Is the theory of separate sensory spaces a 'wrong' theory?

It is, when compared with the theory of one sensory integrated distal space that we employ. As a way of describing or constituting space, however, it cannot be 'wrong' in the sense of 'false' or incompatible with the facts, since every fact that the child would experience is coherent with his constitutive theory of space. There are, however, a number of particular occasions that the child might use as evidence for the fact that the sensory spaces theory is wrong. Take for instance a visually and auditory perceived object, such as a rattle or a bell making noise. The visual place (the place seen) and the auditory place (the place heard) will be connected with the same kinesthetic place (the visual focusing or the grasping movement). It may be questioned, then, whether the fact that there is a common kinesthetic place connected with a visual and an auditory place would not force the perceptual system to accept that the visual and the auditory places are identical. I assume that this will not be the case. Firstly, the number of occasions in which visual, auditory and kinesthetic places are so closely coordinated is rather small. Normally, our visual space overlaps only slightly the auditory and kinesthetic space. What happens behind the back, for instance, cannot be seen though it can be felt or heard. It is quite doubtful, therefore, whether the whole system will be restructured because a quite limited number of occasions may be more easily processed if the perceptual system is changed entirely.

Second, the existence of visual and auditory places that are connected with the same kinesthetic place does not prove that the sensory spaces theory is wrong. Even if the subject had learned that for every place in the visual space there is a place in the auditory and a place in the kinesthetic space, the theory would not need to be cancelled. The fact that there exists a one-to-one correspondence between the spaces does not prove that they are actually only one space, just like one-to-one correspondence between members of logical sets does not imply that there is only one set instead of many. The subject would simply know something like 'If there is a sound "here" (in the auditory place), then there is a sight "there" (in the visual place), and a place at which I can grasp "there" (in kinesthetic space)'. The existence of intersensory correspondence between places is evidence that fits an intersensory space theory, but it fits a sensory-specific spaces theory as well. It will lead only to an intersensory space theory if the subject has an intersensory space hypothesis already at his disposal.

Summarizing, the sensory specific spaces 'theory' does not necessarily lead to inadequate sensori-motor behaviour, and it is also perfectly compatible with evidence such as the existence of intersensory connections. It is clear, therefore, that there are no reasons to change the theory and to adopt an intersensory spaces theory. The fact that (perceptually) adult people do employ an intersensory spaces theory is incompatible with the resistance to change that characterizes the sensory-specific spaces theory. Consequently, it is implausible that the human species is endowed with a sensory-specific spaces theory at birth.

This does not imply, however, that the neonate 'believes' that different sensory places refer to the same distal place. The infant does not believe that the places are different, yet the child does not necessarily believe that the places revealed by different kinds of sensory information are equal, i.e. that they constitute the same place. It is quite plausible, for instance, that young infants focus their attention uniquely on the sensory-specific aspects of the perceived world, i.e. the sounds, visual patterns, smells and so forth, and not on their non-sensory specific properties, such as their places in space. In this case, it would be incorrect to describe the object of the child's perceptual acts as an integrated, distal space or pattern. The objects of the child's acts would be sounds, visual stimulation and so forth. The development of a sensory-integrated perception, then, would imply a broad shift of attention from the sensory-specific to the non-specific properties of the world. Experiences with interesting bi-modally specified events or objects that can be grasped might stimulate this developmental process.

Is there any experimental evidence that might tell us whether or not the infant experiences different sensory places as one identical distal place? In an experiment on auditory-visual integration, Aronson and Rosenbloom (1971) started from the idea that if places are intersensorily perceived, any artificial segregation of sound and vision should produce distress or astonishment. The investigators place three-week old babies in a babychair behind a sound-proof glass wall from where they could see their mothers. By using loudspeakers, it was very easy to regulate the sound in such a way that it was heard coming from an entirely different place than the one at which the mother was seen. The investigators report that when the visual and the auditory place of the mother was disconnected the babies showed clear signs of surprise and puzzlement. It was conceived of as an unequivocal demonstration of the fact that the children do not perceive a visual or an auditory proximal place, but a distal place in physical space.

Aronson and Rosenbloom's results were not confirmed by a later experiment (McGurk and Lewis, 1974). Further, the experiments on intersensory pattern perception show four months as the age at which the earliest forms of intersensory patterns are observable (see section 4.2.2). We have also seen that the existence of adequate sensori-motor co-ordination in the human infant does not prove that space is perceived in an integrated way.

Are we allowed to conclude that very young children perceive space in an integrated way? This question cannot be answered without further preface. All the experiments start from the idea that the child does not only perceive an intersensory unity, but also recognizes any disturbance of an otherwise natural unity between sound and vision as explicitly abnormal, and therefore as threatening.

Now, it is quite plausible that the ability to perceive places intersensorily does not necessarily imply a kind of explicit expectation about the connection between vision and sound. That is, the young child will perceive places in an integrated way when the necessary physical stimulus conditions are fulfilled, without expecting such an integration however. If the integration between vision and sound is artificially removed, the child will accept it as well as he accepts the normal integrative nature of place perception. Put simply, the child perceives according to the rules, in the meantime accepting an unlimited number of (artificially produced) exceptions.

Summarizing, we may ascertain that there are no definite arguments deciding in favour of one of the proposed hypotheses regarding the nature of the real initial state of sensory integration development, except for the theoretical argument which proved that the neonate cannot be endowed with a sensory-specific spaces hypothesis. Presumably, the lack of empirical coherence is due to the large-scale character of the notion 'integrated perception of space'. It is conceivable that the real process of integrated space perception consists of a large number of small subprocesses and abilities which are connected in a very complex way. Some of these small-scale processes may be innate, others may have to be acquired or may follow from innate or formerly acquired ones. The only thing we may conclude is that future work in the domain of integrated space perception requires the construction of a much more refined and detailed definition of the process than the one we employ at present.

4.2.2   The integrated perception of pattern and form
In the foregoing sections, we assumed that a number of sensory modalities are sensitive to information about places in space.

Thus far, we have represented a place by a set of integers on two, three or four (the latter when we also take time into consideration) Cartesian co-ordinates that provide a kind of numerical representation of Euclidian space. We have seen that the way in which we have represented places in space does not imply a claim with regard to the way in which the perceptual apparatus itself represents and processes places.

Now, I shall try to show that the perception of pattern and form is based on the perceptual apparatus' ability to perceive and reliably registrate places in space.

Forms are determined by a specific organized boundary with surrounding space. The boundary and the part of space enclosed by it can be specified as a particular set of places, i.e. as the set of spatial places occupied by the boundary of the object. Different forms are characterized by different sets of places, identical forms by identical sets. Sets can be characterized in an extensional way, i.e. by enumerating all the members of the set, or in an intensional way, i.e. by specifying the properties that distinguish the members of the set from non-members. Probably, one will remember from school mathematics that a number of particular sets of places in a space determined by Cartesian co-ordinates are characterized by the fact that co-ordinates of their members answer to particular equations. For instance, all the members of a set of places in the form of an angle have co-ordinates that answer to a particular quadratic equation (see Chapter 6).

Complex forms or patterns can be characterized as particular arrangements of simpler sub-patterns. The arrangements can be specified as sets of places that are occupied by the constituent sub-patterns. The computation of formulas characterizing particular sets of places is formally analogous to the perceptual apparatus' perception of forms and patterns. Thus, the perceptual apparatus must contain a kind of physiological analogue to a system capable of specifying places in a space and of determining the spatial properties of sets of places.

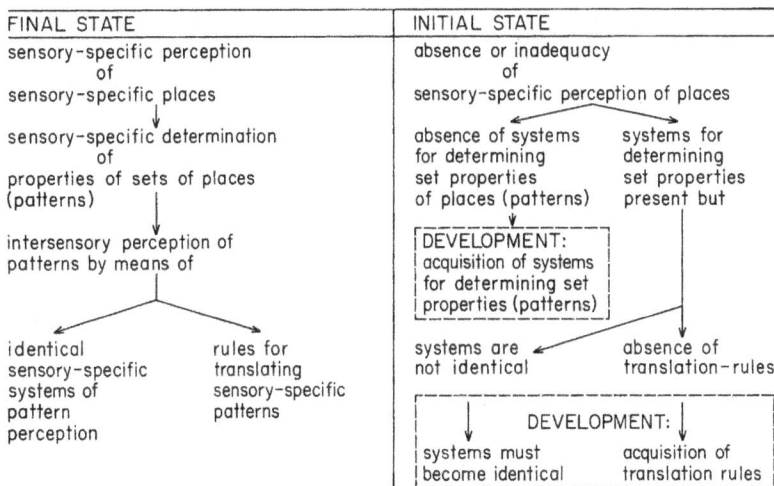

FINAL STATE	INITIAL STATE
sensory-specific perception of sensory-specific places ↓ sensory-specific determination of properties of sets of places (patterns) ↓ intersensory perception of patterns by means of ↙ ↘ identical sensory-specific systems of pattern perception / rules for translating sensory-specific patterns	absence or inadequacy of sensory-specific perception of places ↙ ↘ absence of systems for determining set properties of places (patterns) / systems for determining set properties present but ↓ DEVELOPMENT: acquisition of systems for determining set properties (patterns) ↘ systems are not identical ↙ / absence of translation-rules ↓ DEVELOPMENT: ↓ systems must become identical / acquisition of translation rules

Figure 4.4 Theoretically possible initial and final states based on the model of sensory-specific pattern responses

Now, we can determine the properties of a perceptual system capable of adequate intersensory perception of pattern. First, the various senses must be capable of adequate intersensory place-perception, since the perception of place is the primary requisite for pattern perception. Second, the various senses must employ an identical system for describing and specifying sets of places such that the various senses provide the same kind of pattern descriptions. Both properties characterize the final state of intersensory pattern development.

The theoretical initial state must be characterized by the absence of intersensory pattern perception (naturally, it remains to be determined empirically whether the theoretical initial state is also the empirical, real one). Unfortunately, the number of plausible models of the theoretical initial state that can be inferred from the models of the final state is quite extensive. I shall give an overview of these models in Figures 4.4 and 4.5.

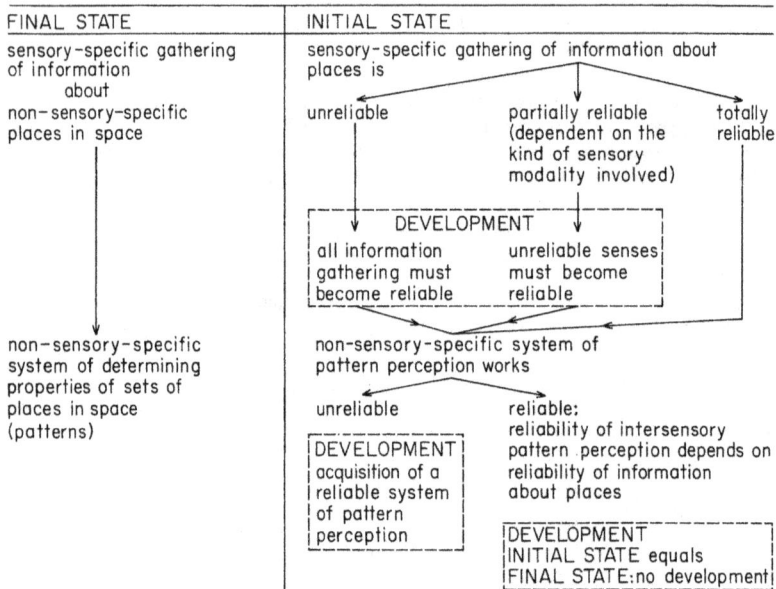

FINAL STATE	INITIAL STATE
sensory-specific gathering of information about	sensory-specific gathering of information about places is
non-sensory-specific places in space	unreliable partially reliable totally (dependent on the reliable kind of sensory modality involved)
	DEVELOPMENT all information unreliable senses gathering must must become become reliable reliable
non-sensory-specific system of determining properties of sets of places in space (patterns)	non-sensory-specific system of pattern perception works unreliable reliable: reliability of intersensory DEVELOPMENT pattern perception depends on acquisition of a reliability of information reliable system about places of pattern perception DEVELOPMENT INITIAL STATE equals FINAL STATE:no development

Figure 4.5 Theoretically possible initial and final states based on the model of non-sensory specific pattern perception

We shall now examine whether or not there is sufficient empirical evidence for deciding which theoretically possible initial state corresponds to the actual, empirical one.

In concordance with our discussion of pattern perception (Chapter 6) I shall start with experiments on the perception of spatiotemporal and temporal patterns. Spelke (1979) investigated whether infants are able to perceive bimodally (visual and auditory) specified events. Four-month old infants were presented with two motion patterns of two different objects and two sound sequences. The motion patterns consisted of bouncing against a surface, whereas the sound patterns consisted of the percussion sounds produced by the bouncing. When a

bouncing sequence is shown together with its concordant percussion sound, a bimodally specified event will be perceived
(provided that sounds and impacts are synchronized). It is
also possible to desynchronize sound and impact, such that the
auditory and the visual event show a common tempo but are
not simultaneous. The subject may perceive two different events
(a visual and an auditory one) that are characterized by a
higher order invariant property, namely tempo. The third possibility consists of a presentation of a visual sequence of
impacts and a different sequence of percussion sounds, such
that a common tempo as well as synchrony are absent. In this
case, the perception of a bimodally specified event is impossible.
Spelke carried out three experiments, employing visual preference and searching behaviour as the dependent measures.

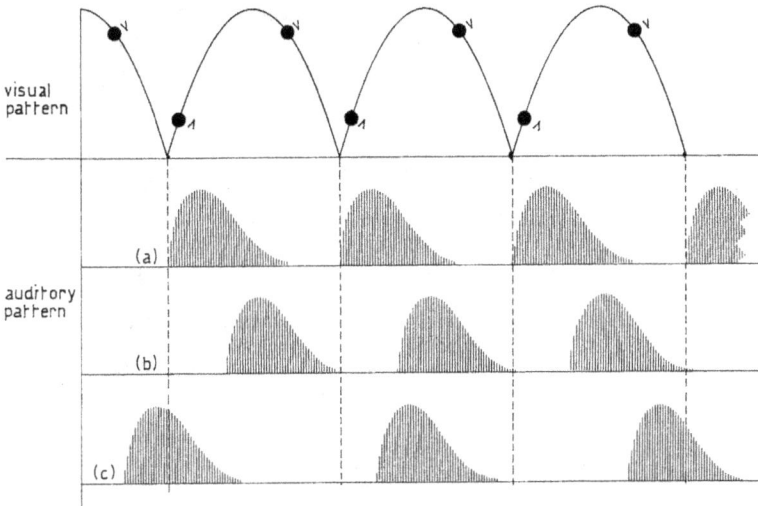

Figure 4.6 In Spelke's experiment, babies are presented with
a visual and an auditory pattern (a bouncing ball with corresponding sounds). In experiment (a), sound and sight are
synchronical; the infant perceives a sensory-integrated event.
In (b), sound and sight are asynchronical but characterized
by a common tempo; the infant perceives a visual and an auditory event characterized by a common higher-order property
(tempo). In (c) sight and sound are asynchronical and are
characterized by different tempo; two independent events are
perceived

The results of the experiment indicated that the infants were
able to detect invariant tempo and simultaneity in auditory and
visually presented events. In general, the results indicate that
temporal patterns are perceived in a sensory non-specific way

by infants as young as four months.

A comparable result was obtained by Allen et al. (1977). The investigators employed a habituation procedure. They familiarized seven-month old infants to a temporal sequence that consisted either of tone or light sequences. During the test trials, the infants were presented with different temporal sequences in a different sensory modality than the one to which they were habituated. Skin potential and heart rate measures of attention-recovery showed that the infants had discriminated identical from different temporal sequences, in spite of the different sensory modalities in which they were presented.

Lawson (1980) investigated the perception of bimodally specified objects in six-month old infants. The perceptual attribution of bimodal visual and auditory properties to an object required that the properties were spatially and temporally congruent. A sound synchronized with the movement of the object but coming from a different place, for instance, did not induce the perception of a bimodally specified object (as measured by means of habituation and attention-recovery). Lawson's results indicate that the perception of bimodally specified objects is not based on mere associative contiguity of sensory properties.

Bryant et al. (1972) performed an experiment that was one of the first to prove the existence of adequate visual and tactile integration of spatial form under the age of one year. The investigators worked with two different objects (see Figure 4.7), one of which could produce a buzz. The infants could touch the objects; they could not see them. Later, when visually confronted with both objects, the infants spontaneously reached for the object that had produced the buzz when it was touched. Thus, the infants were capable of transferring a tangibly explored form to the visual sensory mode.

Figure 4.7 Objects employed in the experiment by Bryant et al. (1972). Tactile information about the form of the objects must be transferred to the visual mode, and vice versa (after Bryant, 1974)

Gottfried et al. (1977) applied the habituation paradigm. The investigators not only confirmed the Bryant et al. findings but they also showed that intersensory perception of pattern could also be carried out by the mouth. In one of their experimental sessions, the objects, a little block and ball, were put into the babies' mouth (a small string attached to the objects prevented them from being swallowed by the children). During visual re-presentation of the objects, the children proved to be capable of visually recognizing the orally presented objects.

These experiments are typical both of the kind of research performed and the results obtained with intersensory perception of pattern. Do these experiments allow us to decide which of the theoretically inferred initial states of intersensory pattern development corresponds with the actual, empirical one? Unfortunately they do not. We may conclude that infants under the age of one year are capable of making adequate intersensory discriminations between a plain object and an object provided with a slot or between a ball and a block. We do not know, however, whether a child at that age is still at the initial state or whether he is already at a much higher state of development. Secondly, we are largely ignorant about the degree of accuracy and reliability of intersensory pattern perception.

Does the existence of a sensory integration ability in children younger than one year imply that intersensory comparison is the child's favourite and most effective way for exploring the properties of objects? The importance that is ascribed to action in development is easily understood as an argument in favour of such a hypothesis. Gottfried et al. (1978) investigated whether visual recognition is improved when the child is able to manipulate the object and to explore it by means of the haptic (tactile) mode. They found that with infants between six and twelve months visual recognition of familiarity or novelty of objects is hampered rather than facilitated when the object has been explored in a visual-manipulatory and visual-haptic way. The experiment does not prove that intersensory and manipulatory exploration is unimportant. It does prove, however, that intersensory exploration is not all-important and unique with regard to the acquisition of knowledge about the world.

Much research has been performed to investigate the development of visual-tactile pattern perception in children older than one year. The research is mostly carried out using nonsense-objects (see Figure 4.8) so that verbal recognition is difficult, if not impossible. Adequate pattern-perception is measured by the accuracy with which patterns are intersensorily discriminated and identified. The experiments are not only concerned with intersensory perception of pattern but also with intrasensory pattern perception, discrimination and comparison. This kind of research allows us to determine whether improvements in intersensory pattern perception are due to intersensory or to intrasensory developments (see Balter and Fogarty, 1971; Wohlwill, 1971; Rose et al., 1972; Jessen and Kaess, 1973; Jackson, 1973; Cronin, 1973; Bryant and Raz, 1975; Vaught et al., 1975; Northman and Norcross-Black, 1976).

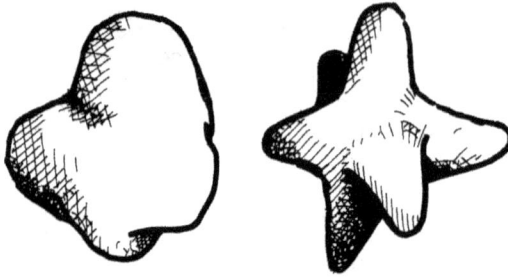

Figure 4.8 Nonsense objects employed in experiments on the development of visual-tactile pattern perception

The results obtained from the various experiments are quite unanimous. First, the adequacy of inter- as well as intra-modal perception of pattern and form gradually increases. The age at which it reaches its maximum level depends on a number of intervening variables, such as the complexity of the patterns, the possibility of using adequate strategies for comparing, the contribution of memory, etc. Vaught et al. (1975) find nine years to be the age at which optimal sensory integration is acquired.

Second, there are clear differences between the degree of difficulty of the various intra- and inter-sensory tasks. From easy to difficult we get: visual-visual comparison (intra-modal); visual-tactile and tactile-visual characterized by similar average difficulty (inter-modal); and tactile-tactile (intra-modal) as the most difficult. When the subjects are trained, most progression is obtained with the tactile-tactile comparison task. This fact might suggest that tactile perception is a rather neglected perceptual domain in seeing subjects. The difficulty of the task is probably due to the relative lack of adequate strategies of tactile information processing and not to a kind of inherent weakness of the tactile sense.

It may be asked whether the difference with regard to the difficulty of different intra- and intersensory pattern-discrimination tasks also holds for the youngest group of subjects in the experiments we shall now discuss, viz. three years old. According to research carried out by Rose et al. (1972) on visual-tactile integration and by Millar (1975) on visual-kinesthetic integration at the age of three years, there is no difference between the various senses with respect to the difficulty of discrimination tasks. Bryant and Raz (1975), however, did a critical replication of the experiment of Rose et al., and they were not able to confirm these authors' findings.

Kennedy and Sheridan (1972) 'wrote' simple lines and forms on the backs of their experimental subjects, children between two and ten years of age. The well-known difficulty of young children with the visual discrimination of forms which are mirror-images of each other also occurs with tangibly presented forms, viz. forms written at the back.

In general, the research on integrated visual-kinesthetic perception of distance confirms the results obtained with visual-tactile integration experiments (Millar, 1972, 1975). It does not, however, hold for visual-auditive integration, in which the difficulties are mainly due to the temporal nature of auditive patterns (Klapper and Birch, 1971; Kuhlman and Wolking, 1972).

The latter results pose the question of the extent of the influence of cognitive variables in sensory integration tasks. A number of investigations have demonstrated the influence of verbal mediation (Ford, 1973), memory (Davidson et al., 1974; Rose et al., 1972; Millar, 1972b), visual imagery (Ford, 1973; Cairns and Coll, 1977) and complexity of the stimuli (Northman and Norcross-Black, 1976). These experiments show that the integrated perception of pattern involves more than perceptual systems and strategies. The development of integrated pattern perception might be the mere reflection of a growing influence of cognition on perception, i.e. of what the subject can do with perceptual data.

Now, we may try to relate the empirical findings with the theoretical models of integrated pattern perception in order to decide which of these models coincides optimally with the real, empirical course of development. In the first model, pattern perception is entirely sensory-specific. Intersensory comparability of patterns is attained by means of identical pattern-perception systems or by means of translation rules that translate patterns from one sensory language into another one.

There is no empirical evidence in favour of the initial-state description provided by the first theoretical model. More precisely, the research only supports the hypothesis that, as far as the investigations have really captured the initial state of intersensory pattern development, there is no difference between the way in which the various sensory systems perceive patterns.

Is there empirical evidence in favour of the initial states predicted by the second model? We have seen that there is a gradual increase in the accuracy with which patterns may be intersensory discriminated. Three kinds of factors may be responsible for that increase, two of which are explicitly mentioned by the second model.

The first factor is concerned with the reliability of the place information provided by the various senses. Presumably, place information is initially only partly reliable. If information about places is relatively inaccurate, the perception of patterns which is based on place information will also be inaccurate.

The second factor explaining the gradually increasing accuracy of intersensory pattern-perception consists of the development of the intersensory pattern-perception system itself.

The third factor explaining the development of intersensory pattern-perception is not explicitly mentioned in the model. It

concerns the growing influence of cognitive strategies on
the tasks of intersensory pattern-comparison posed by the
experiments. A number of investigations have shown that
cognitive factors do play a considerable role. Consequently
the development of intersensory pattern-perception as indicated by the current experimental investigations is probably
highly cognitively determined. That is, the final state of mere
perceptual development may occur quite some time before
optimal integration is acquired as indicated by the experiments.

4.2.3. Intersensory anticipation
Assume that you hear a sound coming from a particular place
on your left. You turn your head and look at the place from
where the sound is coming. Instead of seeing the object which
might have been responsible for the sound, such as a loud-
speaker, an animal, an object, you see only an empty space.
It is quite probable that you will be startled by such an
absence of a sound source. In this case, you have relied on
intersensory anticipation. From auditive information, i.e. a
sound coming from a localizable place, you have anticipated
visual information, viz. the presence of a visible object acting
as a sound source.

Intersensory anticipation operates in a direction opposite
to those forms of intersensory integration discussed in the
previous sections. It is important to note that anticipation is
solely concerned with sensory-specific properties. When I
hear an object, for instance, I may also expect to see the
object at the appropriate place, i.e. visual information about
an object might be anticipated on the basis of auditive information. It is erroneous to say, however, that if I receive auditive information about an object, I may anticipate the presence
of an object (see Figure 4.9).

Adequate anticipation, which may be observed in adults and
older children, constitutes the final state of intersensory
anticipation-development. Theoretically, the initial state may
be characterized by the total absence of intersensory anticipation. Now it may be asked whether the empirical, real
initial state is adequately described by the theoretical initial
state.

One of the most serious difficulties with research on intersensory anticipation is to create a situation in which the subject's expectation can be – artificially – falsified; for example,
how to create an object that can be seen but not touched or
that can be heard but not seen. Bower et al. (1970a) solved
this problem in a very inventive way. By means of two
contrary-polarized light bulbs, they projected a double shadow
of an object on a semi-transparent screen. By employing
polarized glass, it is possible to construct spectacles which
transmit only a particular kind of polarized light. Bower
and his associates took babies between the ages of sixteen

non-sensory-specific properties

visual information   tactile information

(a)

non-sensory-specific properties

visual information   tactile information

(b)

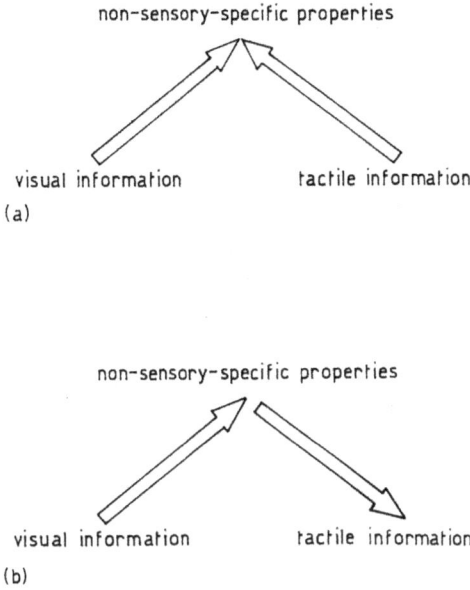

Figure 4.9 Sensory integration(a) and sensory anticipation(b).
In sensory integration, various sensory-specific systems contribute to the perception of non-sensory-specific properties (e.g.
form, place, etc.). In sensory anticipation absent sensory-
specific information is anticipated on the basis of non-sensory-
specific properties, which, in their turn, are based on sensory-
specific information

and twenty-four weeks and provided them with spectacles consisting of contrary polarized glasses. When shown the screen
with the double shadow, the information received by the child
is identical to the information provided by a real nearby object
under normal binocular vision. The infants saw an object at
a certain distance in front of them, even although the object
was not actually there (see Figure 4.10). Since infants between
sixteen and twenty-four weeks are capable of adapting their
reaching and grasping to perceived distance, it is possible to
use them as experimental subjects. Indeed, when the infants
discovered the deviant nature of the object, they showed clear
signs of surprise and distress: they started crying, pulling
faces, rubbed their hands together and so forth. Accordingly,
the investigators concluded that children between the ages of
sixteen and twenty-four weeks were indeed capable of adequate
intersensory anticipation. From such results it is not clear
whether children at that age are still in the initial state of
anticipation-development. If they are not, however, the development of intersensory anticipation has occurred with improbable

rapidity, which becomes an additional argument in favour of an innateness hypothesis.

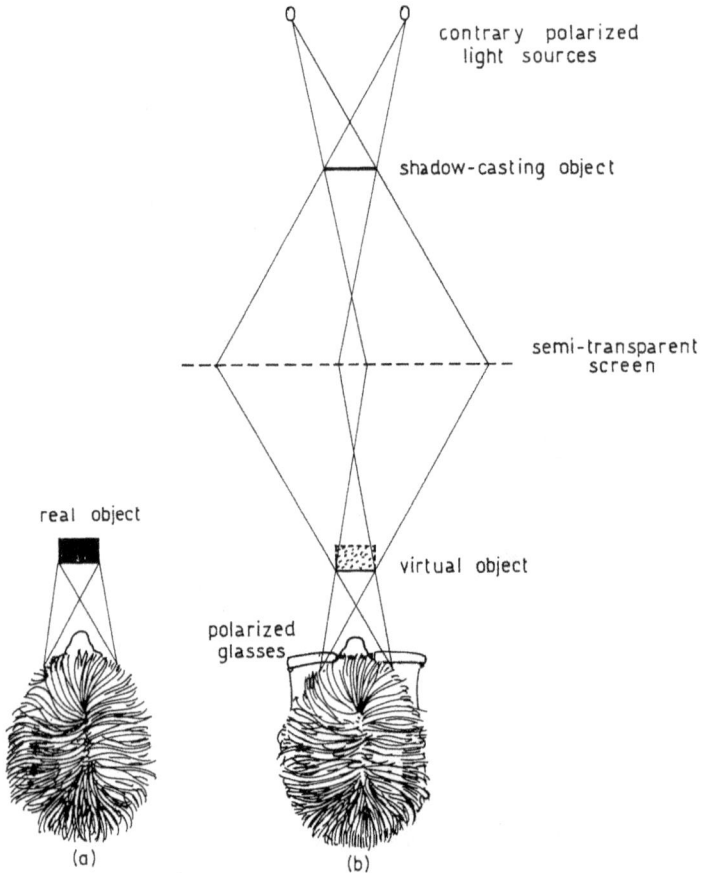

Figure 4.10 Bower's sensory anticipation experiment. (a) Optical diagram of the front of a real object. (b) Optical diagram of the front of a virtual object. The virtual object is based on a double shadow produced by means of contrary polarized light sources. The subject wears polarized glasses that transmit only the correspondingly polarized light. Consequently, the information received by the eyes approximates to the normal binocular disparity information produced by a real object under normal viewing circumstances

Unfortunately, the results of Bower et al., were not replicated by later experiments (Gordon and Yonas, 1976; Field, 1976a, 1977). Field used a Fresnell-lens which produces a virtual image of an object without the use of special spectacles. In Field's experiment, the signals of surprise and distress failed to appear. According to Field, the babies' reactions of distress and surprise were due to the unrealistic, somewhat threatening character of Bower's experiment. Although Gordon and Yonas' and Field's experiments failed to support Bower's conclusions about the existence of intersensory anticipation, it may be questioned whether they also proved that such anticipation is non-existent. We observed a comparable difficulty with Aronson and Rosenbloom's experiment of the integrated perception of place in young children.

Contrary to Aronson and Rosenbloom's topic of investigations, namely sensory integration, the concept of intersensory anticipation clearly implies the existence of an explicit expectation, namely the expectation that the information which has been anticipated will actually occur. It is possible that the experimental signals referring to an unconfirmed expectation have thus far been too crude.

A more reliable indicator of unconfirmed expectation has been used in an experiment carried out by Lyons-Ruth (1977). The investigator habituated four-month old infants to a particular sound-making object. In the novelty condition (which was one of the test conditions), the sound was produced by an object other than the familiarized one. If the infant has learned an association between a particular object and a particular sound during the habituation trials, the combination of a familiar sound with a novel object should produce signs of unconfirmed expectation. The results indicated that children presented with a familiar sound anticipated the presence of a familiar object, since they showed significantly different looking behaviour when their expectations were not confirmed.

In contrast with Bower and Field, Lyons-Ruth tried to find out whether a learned association between sight and sound results in mutual intersensory anticipation. It appeared that learned intersensory anticipation is operative by the age of four months.

4.2.4 *Summary*
We have started with a theoretical model dealing with intersensory perception in a purely formal way. The model allowed us to specify a number of theoretically possible lines of development.

On the basis of empirical and theoretical evidence we concluded that children at the initial state of perceptual development do not experience sensorily different information about one physical place as information about different places in different sensory spaces. The question related to the experience of an equivalence with regard to sensorily different information, however, could not be experimentally decided. The experimental evidence available showed that intersensory perception of pattern - if not present at the initial state of development - is certainly a very early acquisition. The experiments do not, however, provide evidence which enables us to decide which theoretically inferred line of development is the most adequate representation of the actual process.

The anticipation of tangible properties following visual presentation proved difficult to show. Anticipation of visual properties following sound representation after habituation to sight-sound pairs occurred at the age of four months.

The present lack of a sufficiently close connection between theory and empirical research can be solved not only by carrying out more investigations, but also by a further refinement of the conceptual framework within which the problem of intersensory development is posed. It is probable that we are dealing with concepts that are too broad with regard to the diversity of facts that they attempt to explain. The problem might be solved by dividing the original concepts, 'integrated space perception', for instance, into a number of concepts covering a much smaller but more firmly and certainly more consistently connected range of empirical phenomena.

Generally, it can be concluded that the basic properties of intersensory perception of space are innate. The way in which this statement is formulated, however, requires some caution. Properties such as the presence of one single distal space are attributed reliably to the world such as we perceive it, but they are attributed, nevertheless, on the grounds of particular commonsense, scientific or geometric ways of understanding and dealing with the world. When it is stated that four-day old infants perceive one single distal space, we mean simply that the object of their experimentally induced perceptual activities can be described in terms of an intersensory, integrated distal-space theory. The 'real' content of the infant's perception is represented in perceptual terms. Any attempt towards describing this content, i.e. the object of the infant's perceptual acts, requires the introduction of a particular descriptive device. We should not claim, however, that there is only one adequate way of describing the contents of perception or that our description is syntactically isomorphic with the object it describes.

5 The structure of space

5.1 DIMENSIONS OF SPACE

5.1.1 *The nature of the process*
In the previous chapter we discussed a rather abstract problem,
namely the way in which a single place in space is perceived
in an intersensory way. Places in space constitute a structure
which, within our Cartesian system, can be described as a
structure consisting of three independent dimensions (time not
included). Our Cartesian language, which describes a Euclidean
space, can be employed as long as we avoid a philosophical
error pointed out by Nelson Goodman (1960), namely to confuse
object (perceived space) and description (Cartesian description
of a Euclidean space). It is clear that a Euclidean description
of a child's perceived space - i.e. the space which is the object
of the child's perceptual act - does not imply that the child has
an implicit knowledge of Cartesian or Euclidean geometry.

The classical eighteenth-century authors such as Berkeley
started from the idea that vision is the primary sensory modality
for the perception of space. Since the eye is a curved, two-
dimensional surface, it cannot registrate variability along the
depth axis. Gibson (1950) showed that the Berkeleyean tradition advocated a very narrow view of the process of depth
perception (see Figure 5.1). Gibson's problem was to make clear
how the visual system makes a distinction between height and
depth, since both kinds of information are projected onto one
common axis of the retina. According to Gibson, depth and
height are separated because the perceptual system does not
operate with isolated but with clustered places. A place in
visual space occupies a specific position in a set of places that
form a gradient when they extend in depth (see further). The
perceptual differs from the Cartesian system, not because it
does not represent depth, but because it represents depth in
terms of a gradient membership instead of a depth co-ordinate.
Gibson's discovery of a complex relationship between the places
of the proximal visual stimulus - which he termed the optical
ecology - was directly inspired by the age-old knowledge of
figurative painters about how to represent a three-dimensional
scene on a flat canvas. Painters have developed a system of
two-dimensional cues of depth which can be construed geo-
metrically when a three-dimensional scene is projected onto a
surface by means of the central projection system (see also
Figure 5.1). A simple optical instrument, the lens, performs

such a central projection automatically. Since the retinal image
of the distal world is projected through the lens of our eye,
it corresponds to a central projection of the world to which
the painter's cues are applicable. In principle, however, it is
incorrect to speak about cues for depth: the perceptual system
does not infer depth on the basis of otherwise meaningless cues.
The cues are simply the way in which depth is represented by
the perceptual system. I shall demonstrate some of the cues and
explain why they occur.

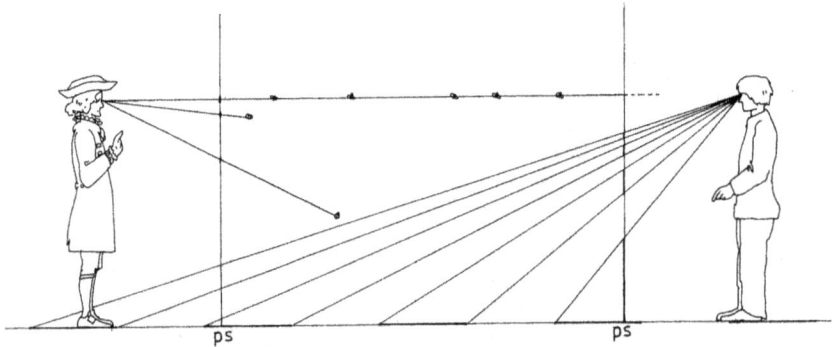

Figure 5.1 Berkeley's bees and Gibson's tiles. Berkeley watches
a number of bees flying around in front of him. The projection
places of the bees onto the projection screen give no information
about the distances between the bees and the observer. Gibson
turns his eye to the ground and discovers that the projection
places of the tiled floor convey sufficient information about
distance: the observer perceives depth and distance in the
form of decreasing projective size. For our purpose, the projection screens (ps) are sufficiently equivalent to the observers'
retinas

The average projected size of objects will be smaller the
farther the objects are removed from the observer. Texture
gradient is an application of this rule. In artificial and natural
surroundings, a succession of more or less identical objects
or forms, such as bricks, paving stones, grass, trees and so
forth, constitute a texture. The texture, if extended in depth,
constitutes a gradient, i.e. a regular one directional change of
projected Cartesian sizes.
   A second class of cues is based on the fact that a part of a
projected object is occupied by the projected image of an object
that stands in front of the first one. This cue is called
'overlap'.
   Since the painter's cues are based on the system of central projection, they imply an immobile, monocular observer (see Figure
5.2). Normally, observers are active: they move their eyes,
heads and body in space. Although the projected image will continue

to fulfil the properties of a central projection, it will now constitute a dynamic image, i.e. variable along the course of time.
Motion disparity is a typical dynamic cue. When the moving
observer fixates one spatial place, its retinal place will remain
the same whereas the retinal position of all the other places in
space will shift. The direction and speed of position-change in
relation to the fixated spot constitutes the way in which the
visual system represents depth (in terms of membership of a
class of spatiotemporal places). As we have two eyes which are
at a small distance from each other, there will be a small difference between the projection of one spatial place onto the
retinas (binocular disparity). Within certain limits, binocular
disparity can be transformed into genuine steroscopic sight (a
principle on which the stereoscopic viewer is based).

Figure 5.2　A pictorial representation of a natural situation, the
Garden of Eden, is based on a number of cues, such as texture
gradients, horizon, overlap, height in the picture plane, and
so forth. Depth is not inferred on the basis of these cues;
gradients, overlap, and height constitute the way in which
pictorial depth is seen

Besides painter's cues, that may also be termed 'pictorial',
and dynamic (and binocular) cues, a third kind of cue exists,
namely a kinesthetic one. When we fixate an object binocularly,
the lines of gaze of both eyes form an angle which becomes
smaller as the fixated object is moved farther away from the
observer. The angle is called the convergence angle. The observer receives information about the convergence angle because

he is sensitive to information about the tension of the muscles
that direct the movements of the eye-balls (see Figure 5.3).

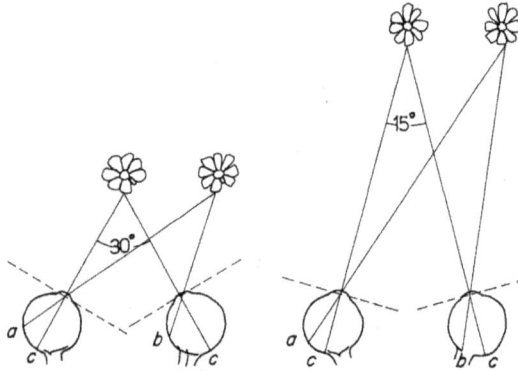

Figure 5.3 Binocular disparity and convergence angle. For any
pair of eyes, the projective places of the flower at the right are
different for the left and right eye (binocular disparity). The
left pair of eyes fixates a flower at a smaller distance from the
eyes than the flower fixated by the right pair of eyes. Consequently, the angle between the left pair of eyes is greater than
the angle between the right pair of eyes (convergence angle).
Binocular disparity and convergence angle are a mathematical
function of the distance of the perceived objects

In order to explain why a proximal stimulus containing these
cues is seen as a three-dimensional space, we need to extend
Gibson's theory by considering a further theory on the process
of perception put forward by the Swedish psychologist Gunnar
Johansson. Johansson views perception as a kind of computing
process. The perceptual computer analyses the mathematical
properties of the relations between proximal places. The mathematical properties are formally equivalent to the perceptual
image subjectively experienced by the perceiver. The three-
dimensional organization of visual space is in a way imposed
on the perceiver, given the nature of the perceptual apparatus
and the cues provided.

Since space is perceived in an intersensory way, visually
perceived space is but a fragment of our total perceived space.
This fact, which is obvious after all, is neglected in the experimental investigation of space-perception development. In order
to illustrate how senses other than the visual one contribute to
the perception of space, I shall discuss some aspects of auditory
space perception.

The auditory proximal space can be described by means of two
physical dimensions: amplitude and time. From these two physical
dimensions, the auditory system will perceive a space describ-

able as three-dimensional. Although the auditory perception of distance and spatial relationships is considerably less reliable than the visual one, a number of auditory cues may convey information about them which in turn may be important for the perception of parts of space inaccessible to the eye. Within specific stimulus conditions, a decreasing sound is not heard as a decreasing sound; the observer hears the constant sound of a receding object (this property is comparable with the function of decreasing proximal sizes in visual perception). Besides loudness, a number of additional acoustic properties will change as distance changes. Part of the sound reaches the ear after being reflected by objects, such as walls or the ground. Such reflection changes the acoustic properties of the sound: waves with the lowest frequencies will be more easily absorbed by the reflecting objects. The spatial position of sound-reflecting objects (slant, for instance) can be perceived on the basis of their reflection properties.

The acoustic properties of sounds produced on different spatial locations constitute a kind of auditive perspective whose principles are generally comparable with visual perspective (auditory texture gradient, for instance). There are also a number of differences between visual and auditory information. Overlap, for instance, does not hold for audition: we can hear around the corner or behind a screen. Since part of the structure of space (such as the place and distance of objects) is perceived on the basis of reflected sounds, the sounds emitted by the observer such as his voice and footsteps may play a role in the auditory exploration of the observer's immediate space. Part of the sound will be echoed and will reach the observer's ear at a time dependent on the distance of the reflecting object. Presumably, seeing adults only make very little use of the 'sonar' function of sounds, but it is probable that blind persons may use it adequately.

The foregoing discussion of how the structure of space is perceived offers a model of the final state of structure-of-space perception: the perceptual apparatus is able to organize the information provided by the various senses in such a way that a space is perceived which, in Euclidean terminology, can be described as three-dimensional. We may now think about the nature of the theoretically possible initial and transitory states. After deciding on a theoretical line of development, we examine a number of experimental investigations in order to determine which kind of theoretically predicted developmental line can be empirically established. If we want to understand the nature of the initial state of space perception, we must certainly take the intersensory aspect into account and not base our model on speculations that consider only isolated sensory modalities. Suppose, for instance, that the kinesthetic system of a newborn child is able to registrate kinesthetic places, such as the position of the hand, adequately in terms of three spatial dimensions, whereas the visual and the auditory system of three-dimensional registration fails. Does this fact imply either that perceived space is not three-dimensional or that the child perceives a three-dimensional kinesthetic and a two-dimensional visual and auditory space? Certainly not. The information provided by vision and audition should be technically represented by a set of three integers corresponding with the Cartesian dimensions of space, one of which is 'empty', i.e. can take any possible value. The idea behind this reasoning is that it makes an essential difference whether a sensory system specifies a place in terms of two dimensions or in terms of three dimensions in which one dimension will obtain an unspecified value. Both cases are different with regard to their developmental consequences. In the case of the two-dimensional representation, the sensory system will have to discover the existence of an additional, third, dimension. In the second case, the sensory system will not have to discover the third dimension but to learn how to specify information about the third dimension in a non-empty and unambiguous way.

It is probable that the accuracy with which the senses contribute to the structuring of space depends largely on the distance of the distal stimuli with respect to the observer.

In the next section, I shall examine the available empirical evidence and try to find out whether it allows me to make some suggestion with regard to the properties of the empirical line of development.

If we overview the available research, we may conclude that it is only loosely concerned with the kind of theoretical questions we are interested in. The research is concentrated mainly on visual perception, a fact which is partly due to the influence of the classical question of whether the two-dimensional retina can registrate depth. Second, it is hardly dealing with the question of how to find out the basic structural properties of the developing experience of space, or with the question as to whether the subjectively experienced space can be formally or technically described as three-dimensional (i.e. as far as a Euclidean language of space is employed). Third, the experiments are set up mainly to investigate whether young children understand the meaning of isolated spatial cues. Little attention is paid to the question as to how children employ and structure the 'perceptual ecology', i.e. the complex, intersensory structure of cues of the moving, acting perceiver.

5.1.2 Pictorial cues of natural space

Bower et al. (1970b) and Ball and Tronick (1971) investigated whether children between two and four weeks old are capable of interpreting variable perspective size as an indicator of depth. The children sat in a baby chair in front of a semi-transparent screen upon which a gradually expanding shadow of a block was projected. According to the investigators, the babies demonstrated that they understood the meaning of optical expansion - namely approach of an object - by showing defensive responses, such as withdrawal. Defensive responses occurred in the case of a 'collision path', i.e. when the projection centre of the block remained at the same projection plane, but not in the case of a 'miss path'. It was concluded that the infants also understood the meaning of different types of optical perspective expansion (miss- and collision-path expansion) (see Figure 5.4).

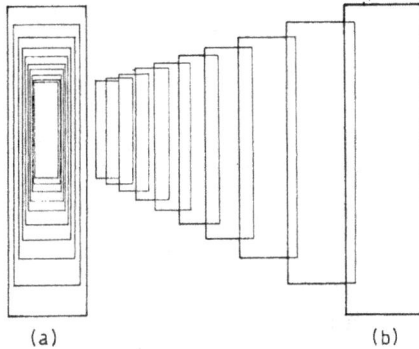

(a)   (b)

Figure 5.4 Successive projective images of a rectangular object approaching the observer along a collision path(a) and a miss path(b)

Yonas and co-workers (Yonas et al., 1977) replicated the optical expansion experiments and concluded that head withdrawal is not a defensive but an informational response: it has the function of keeping the expanding form in the child's visual field. Bower replied that in Yonas' experiments, the children were held by the mother instead of sitting in a baby chair, which might have reduced the threatening character of an optical impending collision (Bower, 1977a). It also reduces the sensitivity of the experimental criterion, namely head withdrawal. Bower also described an experiment carried out in co-operation with Dunkeld. Head withdrawal was recorded by a pressure transducer in the baby chair. In the experimental condition, one- to three-week old infants were presented with the optical image of a rectangle rotating towards their faces (a 'falling' rectangle). Pressure measures indicated that the infants responded with considerably more head withdrawal to the falling rectangle than to the control condition or to the 'rising' rectangle. If head withdrawal has a tracking function, as Yonas assumes, there wouldn't have been a difference between the falling and the rising rectangle conditions, which are both characterized by optical expansion. Dunkeld and Bower's experiment, therefore, makes plausible that adequate, i.e. defensive, responses are elicited by perspective expansions that refer to impending collision with infants as young as three weeks (see Bower, 1977a).

It is not necessary that the infant 'knows' or 'thinks' that the expanding image represents an object approaching along the depth axis. What is important, however, is that the infant's inbuilt or even reflexive responses are valid and make sense with regard to a space that we can describe as three-dimensional, i.e. not only extending in height and width but also in depth. This remark might suggest that it does not matter whether the infant responds to the proximal or the distal stimulus. I shall explain this point in the summary.

Yonas, Cleaves and Pettersen (1978) investigated static perspective cues. They found that twenty-six to thirty week old infants reached significantly more to the nearer (about 75%) than to the farther side of a rectangular window, rotated 45° about the vertical axis. The window was then photographed at the same position, enlarged and glued to a metal frame. The frame was shown to the infants along the fronto-parallel plane, which results in the same monocular retinal image as the real window presented in an angle of 45° (see Figure 5.5). When the infants viewed the trapezoidal window monocularly (by wearing an eye-patch), they reached significantly more to the pictorially nearer side (the trapezoidal form was presented in a fronto-parallel frame). When the infants were presented with a non-perspective form with a bigger and a smaller side, they did not reach significantly more to the larger side, which rules out the possibility that they were simply attracted by the size of the sides. Under binocular viewing, however, the infants were able to employ binocular and convergence information about the real, trapezoidal form of the window. In this case, the significant effect obtained under monocular conditions decreased considerably. These results show that infants between twenty-six and thirty weeks are able to employ pictorial cues of depth, provided that conflicting cues are avoided.

Texture and texture gradient are cues that are closely related with perspective size differences. From Bower's (1966) research on size constancy, it may be concluded that babies between six and eight weeks are not yet capable of employing texture gradient as a cue to depth. Further, Rosinsky and Levine (1976) have shown that the ability to use texture as a cue to depth significantly increases between primary-school age and adulthood.

Partial overlap of forms is an adequate cue for depth relations between objects if the perceiver is capable of perceiving the partially occluded form as a form which is only partially visible. That is, the observer must be capable of inferring that the occluded form continues behind the occluding one. Bower (1966) showed that infants between seven and nine weeks old are not yet capable of such perception of form, which implies that they cannot use the cue of overlap. Bower claimed that the infants saw the partially occluded form as continuing only if they had motional disparity information.

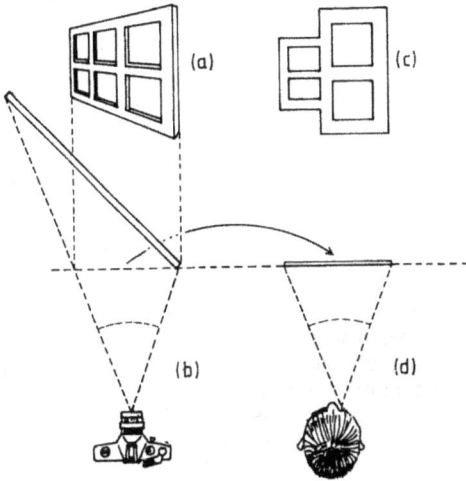

Figure 5.5 Experimental windows employed in the experiment
by Yonas et al. (1978). The window in (a) is a trapezoidal
photograph of a real rectangular window taken at an angle of
45° (b). The 'window' in (c) is used to investigate whether or
not infants reach to the larger side (instead of reaching to the
nearer side). Both experimental windows are presented in the
fronto-parallel plane (d). The optical angles in (b) and (d)
are equal.

5.1.3 Pictorial cues of depicted space

In principle, the study of the perception of depicted space, in
drawings and pictures, might offer an excellent opportunity
to study the development of the understanding of spatial pictorial cues. It may be questioned, however, whether the cues
used to refer to three-dimensional space in pictures are identical with the pictorial cues produced by natural three-dimensional
space. For most people living in western culture, it is a matter
of course to view the pictorial cues of pictures as being identical
with the natural spatial cues: drawings or pictures seem so
obvious as representations of three-dimensional space that it
would be hard to believe that cues for depicted space deviate
from the natural ones. According to Goodman (1968a), however,
the western pictorial perspective·representation of space is as
artificial as, for instance, that of the ancient Egyptians.
Goodman's point of view seems to be supported by a number of
findings concerning picture perception in non-western cultures

(see for instance Hudson, 1967; Mundy-Castle, 1966). Gibson,
however, has pointed out that pictures are made according to
the principles of central projection, according to which the eye
also works. To a certain degree, a picture is equivalent with
the retinal image of a monocularly looking ('Cyclopean'), immobile perceiver (see for instance, Hagen, 1974; and for a
thorough overview, Hagen, 1980). A picture is not a representation of space as we see it, but conveys the same information
as the projection of a real spatial scene on the retina of an
immobile observer. Our pictorial perspective system is 'natural'
under a number of conventional conditions, namely that the
observer closes one eye, remains immobile and integrates the
information provided by successive eye movements.

It is also possible, however, to integrate the effects of
various movements in space. The observer may go to each
object that is of interest to him and depict the fronto-parallel
image of each object onto the picture plane. This is what happens in Egyptian perspective. That is, given a moving observer
who integrates the visual information provided by the movement, the Egyptian perspective is as 'natural' as our perspective generated by central projection. Yet, one may state that
the central projection system is a better solution to the problem
of depicted space than the Egyptian (or Japanese or any other)
way. The picture plane invites the observer to stand still and
to suppress information provided by binocular looking and
eventual eye or head movements. That is because the picture
provides conflicting information (between depth of the depicted
space and flatness of the picture plane) when the observer
moves. Consequently, the observer is 'invited' to act in the
same way as the maker of the picture did, namely remain immobile and suppress kinetic, binocular and dynamic information.
It may be questioned, however, whether this 'inviting' property
of pictures should not be learned and whether each perspective
or picture system has its own correct 'inviting' properties for
the observer who has become accustomed to them.

  Investigations with rural African subjects have shown that
the inability to rightly interpret the Hudson-pictures does
not imply that the subjects are not capable of viewing pictures
as representations of spatial, i.e. three-dimensional, states of
affairs (Hagen, 1974; Deregowski, 1976). Jahoda and McGurk
(1974a, 1974b) asked African, Chinese and European children
between four and ten years old to make three-dimensional models
of depicted situations. The accuracy of the children's model-
building increases with age and shows only very small inter-
cultural differences. Even the four-year olds are capable of
a reasonable estimation of the real size and spatial relations of
depicted objects, though size estimation is better as more cues
are available, whereas spatial relations are better estimated on
the basis of a limited number of cues.

  The development of picture perception can be a source of
information with regard to the development of pictorial-cue

understanding if we reckon with a number of typical differences between natural and depicted space (see Kennedy, 1974). Depicted space normally contains less information than real space (line-drawings, for instance). A more serious difficulty concerns the informational contradiction present in pictures: though the pictorial cues refer to three-dimensional space, the binocular, kinesthetic and motion cues refer to a two-dimensional surface. Thirdly, every picture is made from a specific station point that only rarely coincides with the station point of the person who is watching it (Pirenne, 1970).

Pirenne (1970, 1975) and Eleanor Gibson (1969) have pointed out that the development of depicted-space perception is primarily concerned with the acquisition of the 'picture concept', i.e. the ability of the subject to suppress flatness if he has observed an informational contradiction between (pictorial) three-dimensionality and (kinetic and dynamic) two-dimensionality. It is probable that the African subject's inability to understand the pictures in the Hudson test is primarily due to his inability to solve the problem of pictorial conflict (which is merely a matter of familiarity with pictures).

The development of the picture-concept, i.e. the ability to cope with a conflict between pictorial and dynamic kinesthetic cues has been investigated by Yonas and Hagen (1973) and Hagen (1976). Yonas and Hagen asked their subjects (between the age of three years and adulthood) to estimate the size of depicted objects. They found that three-year-olds had great difficulties with this task. The estimations were improved considerably when dynamic kinesthetic information was artificially suppressed, for instance by making the three-year-olds look through a peep-hole. Hagen (1976) investigated the effect of a shifting station point. From the discussion on motion disparity we know that the perspective of a visual scene changes as the observer changes his position. Adults are capable of noticing the difference between the station point of the picture maker and their own station point (see Figure 5.6). When no other information is available, adults may use station-point difference to determine the pictorial character of a scene. Hagen (1976) discovered that three-year-olds are not capable of using the station-point cue, whereas seven-year-olds performed intermediately between three-year-olds and adults.

The presence of a picture concept is also expressed by the ability to use pictures as particular carriers of information about properties and positions of objects instead of true pictorial simulations of spatial scenes. Adults, for instance, will prefer a modified linear perspective that approaches parallel or axonometric perspective to rigid conic perspective following from applying the principles of central projection in a rigid way. The perspective image of a regular, cube-like object seen from a distance of approximately ten times the size of the object will be characterized by almost parallel, i.e. axonometric, perspective. This kind of perspective is least sensitive to changing

station point (i.e. the point at which the picture is viewed).
Three- to four-year-old children treat pictures as if they are
parts of the real world, i.e. as if looking at a picture is like
looking through a window. Therefore, they will prefer rigid
conic perspective produced by central projection since this
kind of perspective is most dependent on a particular station
point, which is also the case with perspective images of real
three-dimensional scenes (see Hagen and Jones, 1978).

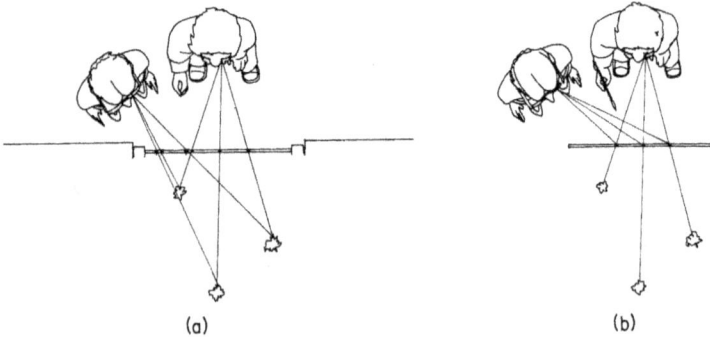

(a)   (b)

Figure 5.6 Station point and pictorial quality. In (a) two
observers watch a number of objects through a window-pane.
For each observer, the projective places of the objects on the
window-pane are different. They depend entirely on the observer's viewing position or station point. In (b) a painter and
a spectator watch a painted representation of the objects behind
the canvas. Since the projective places of the objects on the
canvas are determined by the station point of the painter, the
image of the spectator does not correspond with the station
point from where the image has been made. It is assumed that
observers are able to employ station-point deviations in order
to determine the pictorial quality of a scenery

Summarizing, the experiments suggest that the age at which
the picture concept is fully acquired falls between twelve and
fourteen years. Twelve years seems unrealistically late, however, when we think about the young child's manifest ability
to watch and understand pictures. Now, there exists a number
of differences between the experimental investigations and
natural circumstances. In natural circumstances, children are
primarily focused upon recognizing well-known, natural forms
(animals, houses, people) connected by rather global spatial
relationships. The ability to recognize depicted forms emerges
very early (it is probably innate) and is not limited to complete,
'naturalistic' pictures but also includes the recognition of
very impoverished and abstracted pictures (Hochberg and
Brooks, 1962; Van Geert, 1975). During experimental sessions,

however, the children have to watch geometrical forms lacking a 'canonical' size, such as triangles. Further, they are asked to make rather accurate estimations about distance or size. In natural circumstances, children have learned to recognize 'pictorial contexts', such as picture books, that disambiguate the perceptual information in favour of the purely pictorial aspects. In experiments, the contexts are mostly strange and unknown and the children have to rely solely upon their competence to understand the picture. If we want to understand the nature of picture perception and its development, we should start from the functionality of the picture, i.e. the picture as object in a structure of actions that expresses the purpose and meaning of picture making and use. If the functional value of the picture has been hidden (as in many experiments) or if its value is hardly known (as in the African experiments) the results of the experiments tell only very little, if anything, about perception.

Experiments on the young child's understanding of isolated pictorial cues are limited to rather global spatial relationships such as 'in front of' and 'behind'. The experiments have shown that 'overlap' can be used reliably at the age of three years (Olson, 1975; Hagen, 1976) and according to Olson and Boswell (1976) already at the age of twenty months. Olson (1975) and Olson and Boswell (1976) state that three-year-olds can use 'height in the picture plane' as a cue to depth, although Hagen (1976) and McGurk and Jahoda (1974) could not replicate this finding. Linear perspective and perspective size differences are not used before the age of five (Olson, 1975; Olson and Boswell, 1976; Olson et al., 1976).

Another way of studying the development of pictorial depth is to examine children's drawings of spatial situations. Drawing, however, is different from understanding. In section 5.3.2 we shall discuss an experiment carried out by Phillips et al. (1978) which shows that understanding of pictorial depth occurs even before the ability to copy depth cues. Nevertheless, the child's own effort towards the representation of pictorical depth is worth studying. Freeman et al. (1977) found that seven-year-olds represent the spatial relationships 'behind' and 'in front of' by drawing an object vertically above another, while Cox (1978) observed this phenomenon already with five-year-olds. The investigations indicate that height in the picture plane is the first cue for spatial depth that is used productively.

The main conclusion that may be drawn from our discussion on picture perception is that we must start from the thought that pictorial cues are connected within a rather peculiar optical ecology. Pictorial cues are part of a system of coherent though impoverished pictorial cues of space, that, in their turn belong to a contradictory system of cues (pictorial versus dynamic/kinesthetic). If we want to understand how the child learns to cope with this contradiction, we must not only take into account the child's growing mastery of the 'optical ecology' but also the pedagogical efforts of a culture in which 'looking at pictures' is a very important aspect of everyday life.

5.1.4 Binocular, motional and kinesthetic cues and natural cue-situations

Though binocular disparity is not a necessary cue to depth perception (Walk, 1968) it is a sufficient cue. Between four and six months, babies are capable of using it (Bower, 1966; Gordon and Yonas, 1976; Yonas, Oberg and Norcia, 1978). Further, the experiments on sensory anticipation show that babies can use binocular disparity, since they are able to reach for the virtual objects at the right (virtual) place.

As far as I know, there is no reliable experimental evidence on the understanding of binocular disparity in newborn children. The main difficulty is to find an adequate criterion. We know, however, that the basic condition for obtaining accurate information from binocular disparity, namely eye convergence, is present at birth (Slater and Findlay, 1975b). There is evidence, however, that convergence information alone, though reliably related to the absolute distance of observed objects, is a poor basis for distance perception (Gogel, 1961; Richards and Miller, 1969).

The development of depth perception by means of motion information is still badly understood, in spite of the fact that most of the spatial information pick up takes place during (loco-) motion. It may be concluded nevertheless, that motion disparity is operative by the age of three to five months (Walk, 1968; McKenzie and Day, 1972; see also section 5.3.2).

Degelman and Rosinsky (1979) investigated the development of absolute distance judgment on the basis of motion parallax. They examined subjects of eight, ten, twelve and twenty-two years of age. The investigators found an improvement in the ability to make distance judgments on the basis of monocular motion parallax. This improvement is due to the increasing accuracy with which the precise extent of bodily motion is registered, since the registration of retinal displacement during bodily motion does not change in the age range at issue. Carpenter (1979) investigated a more complex phenomenon, namely the perception of rotation in depth. When a row of dots rotates in depth, it produces a number of specific motion parallax cues, such as differential velocity of the dots dependent on their distance to the observer, movement direction, order of direction change and so forth. While six-year-olds were unable to infer rotation in depth from these cues, thirteen-year-olds were able to employ the cues in a reliable way. Between thirteen and nineteen years little developmental improvement was observed.

The development of auditory perception of the structure of space has been discussed in the chapter on intersensory perception (Chapter 4). Research on the olfactory perception of space has been executed by Rieser et al. (1976). The investigators concluded that children as young as sixteen hours are capable of discriminating the lateral position of an olfactory source, since the children turn their heads away from unpleasant smells.

One of the main difficulties in the investigation of spatial perception development is to find adequate empirical indications for the fact that the object of the child's perception of space can be described as a three-dimensional structure (provided that a Cartesian language of space is employed by the investigator). Normally, investigators reason as follows. An object is placed at a specific place in real space, conceivable as three-dimensional. If the experimental subject incorporates the object in his behaviour, for instance by taking it as a goal of an action, and the behaviour is such that it is directed towards the real physical place of the object, then the subject may be ascribed a perceived space that is describable as three-dimensional.

Now, it may be questioned what kind of behaviours are chosen as indicators of adequate space perception during the age of the initial state. Some of the investigators have employed defensive responses, such as eye-blinks, withdrawal, putting the hands before the face and so forth. The defensive-response indicator poses a serious interpretation problem: how defensive are the responses? Furthermore, it is probable that some clearly defensive responses are mere reflex reactions to proximal variables. Just as the eye closes reflexively when someone blows in it, a withdrawal may also be a reflexive defensive action to an optical expansion. In principle, it is possible to find out whether the child responds to the distal rather than to the proximal stimulus by confronting the child with a number of proximally different but distally equal stimuli. If the child shows a defensive reaction to optical expansion as a cue for an approaching object, he would also show the defensive reaction when another cue for an approaching object is given, for instance an artificially produced stereoscopic projection of an approaching object for which proximal size is kept constant.

Besides defensive responses, grasping and reaching for objects is also used as a cue to adequate depth perception. If the child were to see the world in a two-dimensional way, it would not be able to grasp an object at its actual physical place, but rather would show either an invariable or an accidental grasping distance. A difficulty with grasping is that it cannot be used as a criterion before the child is able to adapt muscular movements to perceived distance. In any case, with grasping, adequate sensory motor adaptation is possible at the age of three months.

One of the classical indicators of adequate visual depth perception is the child's behaviour at the visual cliff (Gibson and Walk, 1960). The visual cliff consists of a glass table-top, half of which is covered with a checkerboard pattern while the other half is transparent. Through this transparent half can be seen a similar checkerboard pattern drawn on the floor, thus providing a kind of cliff. The cliff is visual but not tactile, thanks to the strong glass table-top. The indicator of satis- factory depth perception is the child's refusal to crawl to his mother via the deep side of the cliff. Since the experiment demands that the subjects are able to crawl, the youngest age at which the experiments can be performed is six months. These children clearly refuse to crawl over the deep cliff, which demonstrates their spatial structuring ability. Unfortunately, in this form the visual cliff is a very poor indicator of spatial structure development, not only because the children are rather 'old' but mainly because the visual cliff actually creates a contradiction between visual information about depth and tactile information about flatness. Since space perception is an intersensory issue, the visual cliff is actually an experiment on the child's reaction towards sensory contradictions. It shows that vision is more trusted than the tactile sense, a result that is also obtained with adults (Rock and Harris, 1967). Walters and Walk (1974) avoided the above-mentioned methodological problem and employed the child's placing reactions as an indi- cator to depth. If a six month old child is put onto a surface, he will place his hands such as to reduce the shock when touching the surface. The investigators showed that defensive responses are elicited at the shallow and not at the deep side of the cliff.

5.1.5 Summary

If we summarize the experiments either directly or indirectly concerned with the perception of space, we may safely conclude that the object of the four month old child's perception of space is a space describable as a three-dimensional structure, pro- vided that we employ a Cartesian language of space. What about space perception in infants younger than four months? It is highly plausible that the object of their perception of space is also describable as a three-dimensional structure, although it is very difficult, if not impossible, to find reliable behavioural evidence for this statement.

It might be questioned which kinds of spaces infants might perceive if the space they perceived were not the three- dimensional one. The classical answer to this question is that infants would perceive a two-dimensional space. This hypo- thesis is based on the fact that the physical extension of retinal information is two-dimensional, provided that time is not taken into account. We have seen, however, that perception is an intersensory matter: perceived space could be two- dimensional only if the proximal structure of visual information were imposed on the other senses, but this is quite implausible. If space perception were based on the proximal aspects of sensory information, the child would not perceive one space, but a variety of sensory specific spaces. We have seen, how- ever, that this 'many-spaces hypothesis' does not mean that the child perceives a variety of spaces, in contrast with the

final state of perception in which there is only one, intersensory space. The child might simply limit his attention to
those aspects of sensory information that can be described
in purely proximal terms (i.e. in purely sensory specific terms).
The child would therefore only pay attention to the sensory-
specific, non-spatial aspects of space, i.e. he would not perceive space.

Is it possible that the initial state of space perception could
be characterized by a sensory integrated space characterized
by properties that are incompatible with three-dimensionality?
In order to investigate such a question, we must start from
the idea that basic experiential qualities of perception, such as
three-dimensionality of space or the structure of perceived
events, can be described in terms of formal specifications that
can be inferred from the structure of spatial information. If
we want to find out whether there exists a primitive perception
of space which is not three-dimensional, we should investigate
whether the proximal structure of space can be formalized in
terms which are less complex than three-dimensionality. If we
could find such a simple formalization, we could translate it
into experiential qualities of the perceiver and reliable behavioural indications. Needless to say, the simplicity of the spatial
formalization would have empirical consequences, instead of
being a mere matter of theoretical simplicity.

In summary, the investigation of early states of perceptual
development requires not only a thorough empirical investigation
of the perceiving subject but also a formal study of the objects
- space, objects, events - of the perceptual act.

An important question which has remained undiscussed up to
now concerns the perception of either a distal or a proximal
space by the infant during the initial state of the development
of space structuring. We have seen that the infant is able to
employ various sorts of information, such as motion parallax,
for instance. It may be questioned whether the infant's actions
are based on the depth-meaning of these cues or simply on the
cues themselves. That is, does the child react either to motion
parallax or to depth? This is a very difficult question, not
just because it is so difficult to examine empirically, but simply
because the question has a very complex meaning. One step
towards solving it can be taken by returning to our introduction
to the intersensory perception of a place in space. There, we
stated that perceiving either distal or proximal space means
that distal or proximal space is the object of our perceptual
acts, i.e. the object towards which our perceptual acts are
directed.

When we are dealing with the question of whether the infant
perceives either proximal or distal space, we are not concerned
with images and representations in the infant's head but only
with the object that can be attributed to his perceptual activities. We have seen that, given a particular system of description, the proximal space must differ in a number of basic

properties from the distal space. This difference should be
reflected in the different behaviours of neonates and perceptually mature subjects if it were true that neonates perceive
proximal whereas adults perceive distal space. When such a
difference is not found, however, isn't it possible that the
neonate responds to a very complex combination of proximal
variables, yet not to distal space? Presumably, this question
is very misleading. We have seen that the properties of distal
space are a very complex transformation of the properties of
proximal variables and vice versa. That is, we are free to
describe such a complex transformation in proximal terms, i.e.
as a complex function of proximal variables, or as distal space.
That depends on the point of view we want to adopt for descriptive purpose. The question of whether the infant responds
to either a particular complex function of proximal variables
or to distal space is psychologically meaningless, since it is
based on a confusion between our descriptive systems and the
object of our investigation, namely the child's perception.
Needless to say, the question of the object of the neonate's
perceptual acts is not solved by this theoretical exposé.

5.2 ORIENTATION AND DIRECTION IN SPACE

5.2.1 *The nature of the process*
Orientation and direction are structural properties concerned
with spatial relations between places or sets of places in space,
such as objects, forms and so forth. In order to understand the
nature of orientation and direction perception we shall have to
refer to Chapter 3 where we discussed the necessity of having
a perceptual coding language. A perceptual coding language
describes perceptual contents in terms of what is considered
to be a basic operational property of perception, namely the
processing of places and systems of places in a space. A simple
and rather well-known approximation of such a perceptual coding
language is the method of co-ordinates (see Chapters 3 and 6).
It is important to note that such a language has a merely
instrumental function. It is used to specify the object of perceptual acts and abstracts from a large number of empirical
peculiarities. It is also not meant to offer a model of what
really happens in the brain in the course of the perceptual
process.

In Figure 5.7 a number of right-angles have been drawn.
Angles 1 and 2 will be perceived as identical, though situated
at a different place with regard to the orienting co-ordinates
(x and y). Angle 3 will be seen as identical to 1 and 2 but with
a different orientation (it is tilted 30 degrees to the right).
Angle 4 is seen as a V-shaped angle, whereas 1, 2 and 3 are
L-shaped. Experiments by Beck (see Beck, 1967, 1972) have
shown that the foregoing differentiation with regard to V- and
L-types is a normally occurring property of the perceptual

process. Angle 5 is an exact copy of angle 1. Nevertheless, it will presumably be seen as identical to angle 4, since it is part of a rectangular figure.

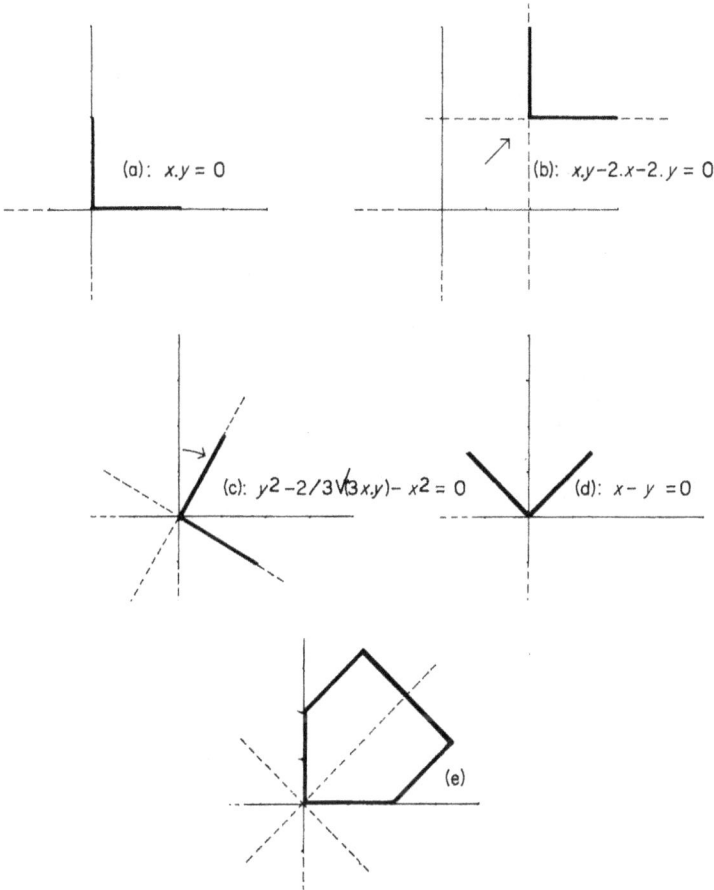

Figure 5.7 The effect of place and orientation on the perception of form. Although the angles 1 to 5 are identical, they are represented by different place formulas. They can be perceived as identical figures after translation and rotation of the co-ordinate system, i.e. after the 'proper space' of the angles has been determined. Angles (d) and (e) remain different from angles (a) (b) and (c) because their proper spaces are different. Angle (d) is characterized by symmetry axes, while angle (e) is characterized by the proper space of the figure to which it belongs

It may be questioned whether the method of co-ordinates is able to cope with these perceived differences. If we compute a formula expressing the relationship between the co-ordinates of the set of places occupied by angles 1 and 2, we will see that different formulas arise, due to the difference between the places of the angles. Since the perception of identity must be simulated by the identity between the formulas of both forms, an additional computing operation is required, namely the replacement of the co-ordinate system. Thus, formulas which were originally different can be transformed into identical forms that vary with regard to their respective places in space. The same kind of reasoning holds for the perception of form-identity between angles 1 and 3. If the co-ordinates are replaced and rotated, identical formulas will result. Angles 1 and 3 will be represented by identical formulas combined with a different rotation of the co-ordinates. Since angles 1 and 4 are perceived as different forms, their formulas must be different as well. It should be questioned, therefore, why the co-ordinates of angle 4 are not translated and rotated in such a way that its formula becomes identical with angle 1. In cases 1, 2 and 3, the overall co-ordinate system is closer to the orientation of the sides of the angles, whereas in 4 it is closer to the symmetry system. This will result in a different rotation of the co-ordinates and, consequently, in different formulas. Angle 5 may be explained on the basis of its belonging to a rectangular figure. The perceptual description of the rectangular figure requires a rotation of the co-ordinates. The rotated co-ordinates are parallel to angle 5's symmetry system, which explains why angle 5 is seen primarily as being identical to angle 4.

The foregoing formal example illustrates a number of principles that operate at the level of orientation perception. First, the perceptual apparatus makes a distinction between the overall co-ordinate system and the co-ordinate system adapted to a form's particular position in space. That is, there is a difference between overall space and the 'proper space' of a pattern or form. 'Proper space' means: the replaced and/or rotated co-ordinate system that has been used to compute the pattern or form's 'formula' (which is conceived of as the formal analogon of its perceptual image). The orientation attributable to a pattern or form consists of the relationship between the overall space and the 'proper space' of the pattern or form. Second, the 'proper space' of a form is chosen in such a way that it allows an optimally simple specification of the form and the smallest possible deviation from the orientation of overall space. Third, a form's proper space may sometimes depend on its being a constituent of another form, such as in Figure 5.7, angle 5. Thus, in addition to orientation with regard to overall space, there is also orientation with regard to the proper space of these patterns.

Everyday language has a number of terms for denoting a

number of 'canonical' orientations of patterns with regard to
other ones, such as 'under', 'above', 'at the left', 'at the
right' and so forth. It is very important to notice that these
'canonical' orientations are not only specified with regard to
the spatial relation between the patterns, but also with regard
to the orientation of overall space. Figure 5.8 illustrates this
principle.

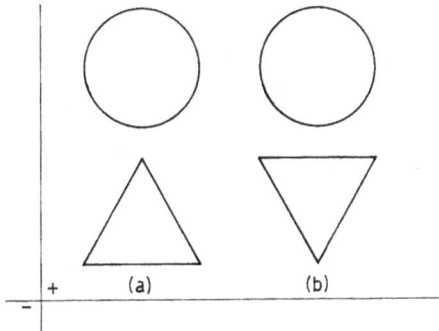

Figure 5.8 'Under' and 'above'. In the figure, the spatial
relation between the circle and triangle is not determined by
the proper space of the triangle but by the mutual relation
between triangle and circle in overall space. In both cases, the
circle is 'above' the triangle

It may be questioned how the overall orientation of perceived
space is ascertained by the perceiver. The simplest solution
to the problem consists of an egocentric, 'proximal' orientation.
The orientation of space will depend on the position of the
observer's body and, more precisely, of his space-sensitive
sensory organs. It is theoretically possible that this simple
solution to the problem is the one applied during the initial
state of spatial orientation development.

The second solution to the problem of how to determine the
overall orientation of space is to determine which kind of
orientation forms the most optimal 'proper space' for as many
forms as possible in a given perceptual situation. According
to Rock and Leafman (1963) the perceiver applies a kind of
'factor rotation': a system of spatial dimensions are rotated
until they optimally 'load' onto the various patterns discernible
in a space (a landscape, for instance) (see also Rock, 1974).
In natural space, the optimal loading will depend mainly on
the direction of gravity whereas the orientation ascribed to a
picture of a non-natural scene, geometrical forms for instance,
will presumably correspond with the frame or the edges of the
paper.

It is important to note that the problem of orientation is not
a matter of only one sensory system, namely vision, but of all

the spatially sensitive sensory systems. The difference between
the sensory systems is that their contributions to the intersensory perception of space and spatial structure may be different, for instance with respect to accuracy or level of detail.
Further, orientation is also concerned with dynamic patterns,
such as changes of place or more complex movements. In the
case of movement, we will presumably speak about 'direction'
but the basic problems remain the same.

Our discussion of the nature of orientation perception has
provided us with a model for the theoretical final state of orientation-perception development. At the final state, the perceiver
must be able to determine the overall orientation of distal space.
Second, he must be able to determine the proper space of a
form (of an object or event in distal space) and the relation
between the form's proper space and overall space (the orientation of the form). Third, he must be able to determine the
orientation of a form with respect to the proper space of another
form. Orientation is concerned with a relation between spaces.
However, since there exists no 'natural' rule or constraint with
regard to the kind of spaces that can be related, there may be
an infinite number of orientation specifications in space. Some
types of orientation depend on the orientation of the distal or
'real' space, for instance the spatial relations expressed by
the terms 'under' or 'above'. Other types of orientation are
determined by the place of the perceiver, for instance the
relations expressed by 'before' and 'behind' or 'left' and 'right'.
In still other cases, orientation depends on the properties of
objects, such as in 'in' or 'out'. With regard to their proper
frame of reference, orientations are absolute. For instance
'left' and 'right' are fixed with regard to the perceiver. The
absolute character of the left-right (under-above, etc.) is a
matter of (very practical) convention. It would have been
possible, for instance, to take left and right simply as opposites,
without fixing their absolute place with regard to the perceiver.

In order to constitute an optimal contrast with the final state,
the theoretical initial state - which provides a necessary conceptual delimitation to our empirical research and its interpretation - should be characterized by two essential properties.
Firstly, only the proximal space plays a role, and, secondly,
if orientation begins to play a role, it should be a relative form
of orientation.

The first property concerns the sole use of proximal space as
a system of spatial reference, i.e. the system of co-ordinates
necessary to specify formally the spatial and temporal extension of sensory stimulation. The assumption that the initial
state is characterized by the use of the proximal co-ordinate
system implies that no orientation perception will take place.
That is, no difference is made between orientation- and
form-specification. At the theoretical initial state, the perceiver
would see actually identical forms as different forms, if the

forms differed only with regard to their orientation (see Harris
and Schaller, 1971; Harris and Allen, 1974). Another consequence of the use of a proximal co-ordinate system is that forms
or patterns change as the angle of regard changes. If the head
bends to the right, for instance, a considerable change in the
orientation of the proximal co-ordinate system will result, which
in turn will lead to different form computations, which are
formally equivalent with experienced or perceived forms.

The second property concerns the relativity of initial
orientation and direction perception. Relativity requires that
the subject is able to perceive orientation, which implies that
it cannot occur during the theoretical initial state, when orientation is inexistent. Relativity is concerned with the absence
of a fixed direction in the place system. A movement from left
to right, for instance, will not be discriminated from a movement from right to left, unless they occur simultaneously.
Relativity can be represented in terms of a free numbering
direction in the space model (see Figure 5.9).

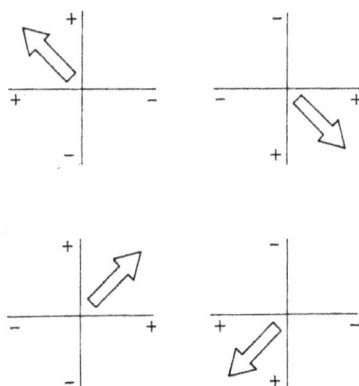

Figure 5.9 The four arrows represent the same direction (of
a movement, for instance). Although their direction with
regard to the paper differs, each arrow bears the same relationship with the numbering direction of the co-ordinate
system in which it is situated. It is plausible that a comparable
phenomenon is responsible for figural left-right reversals in
young children

5.2.2 Empirical investigations of orientation and direction development

Various fields of perception research have provided clues in
favour of an early emergence of 'proper space' perception,
i.e. the adaptation of a spatial co-ordinate system to the
specific properties of a form or pattern. Cornell (1975) showed
that the orientation of a figure is a determiner of the four- to
five-month-olds' attention towards figures. Fantz' classical

form perception research has shown that babies are sensitive to symmetry, which requires the adaptation of the co-ordinate system to the particular form or pattern (Fantz, 1961). Fagan showed that five to six month old babies have considerable difficulties in recognizing a face when it is presented upside down, which contrasts with the ease with which a normally oriented face is recognized (Fagan, 1972). This fact can be explained when one accepts that the up and down direction is already stabilized by that age.

The perception of orientation, however, requires more than sensitivity to orientation, symmetry or the direction of a face. Adequate perception of orientation means that the perceiver is able to distinguish a form's orientation from its form properties. That is, in spite of an observed orientation difference, the forms must be seen as identical. McGurk employed the habituation paradigm and offered six month old babies various sets of different and identical forms and orientations (see Figure 5.10).

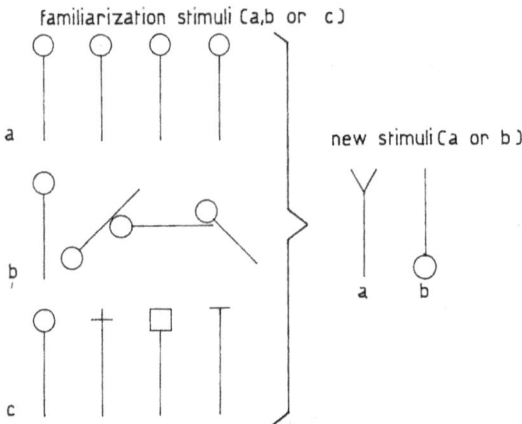

Figure 5.10 McGurk's experiment on form and orientation perception of infants consisted of six conditions, based on three sets of familiarization stimuli and two new stimuli. Form and orientation of the test figures were systematically varied over the six conditions (a-a: same orientation, same figure vs same orientation, different figure; a-b: same orientation, same figure vs different orientation, same figure; and so forth)

From the habituation diagrams it could be inferred that six-month-olds are indeed capable of distinguishing a form from its orientation. It is not clear whether children younger than six months are also able to distinguish form from orientation and, if so, to what extent they can do this. We do not know whether newborn babies employ a proximal rather than a distal system of co-ordinates. If it is assumed that newborn babies do employ a distal co-ordinate system, it may be questioned how general such a co-ordinate system will be. It is possible that the initial co-ordinate system holds for no more than one pattern at a time. In such a case the co-ordinate system will be adapted, e.g. rotated, to each new form that is focalized. Consequently, the child would be able to observe the identity between differently oriented forms but unable to see different orientations. If the distal system that the child imposes upon space is completely determined by the properties of one form or feature, there is no difference between distal and proper space, i.e. there will be no perception of orientation.

McGurk suggests that infants under six months of age might be able to detect either form identity or simple orientation differences, but not simultaneously form and orientation properties (McGurk, 1974).

As we have seen in Figure 5.7, orientation may also consist of a relationship between a form's proper space and the proper space of another form, which in its turn is seen in relation to the proper space of still another form or to overall space. For instance, one of the main technical problems that the beginner must cope with when painting portraits is the mutual placement of the facial features. In order to solve this problem, painters may use a system of lines connecting features such as the eyeball and the nostril, the eye and the corner of the mouth and so forth. All these lines form a complex system of interrelated orientations that in their turn must be connected with the contours of the face.

Children between three and five years of age cope with comparable problems. Olson (1970) asked children to construct a diagonal line in a kind of checkerboard, a simple task but one which highlighted a number of problems for the children. Other investigators have confirmed that the accuracy with which horizontal, vertical and diagonal lines were copied depends to a large extent on whether the copying sheet is rectangular, square or round (Berman et al., 1974; Berman and Colab, 1975; Berman, 1976; Berman and Cunningham, 1977). If squares, circles and triangles have to be drawn on normal, rectangular sheets of paper, circles are copied adequately by three-year-olds, squares by four-year-olds and triangles by five-year-olds (see for instance Piaget and Inhelder, 1956). If the paper is cut into the shape of the copied figure, no age differences are found (Brittain, 1976).

Presumably, the child experiences a kind of incompatibility between the spatial reference system, i.e. the co-ordinate system, imposed by the rectangular sheet and the orientation relationships of the line or figure. Consequently, he will have difficulties in expressing the line or figure in terms of the incompatible spatial framework.

Vogel (1977, 1979) investigated whether five and nine year old children and adults are able to remember the left-right

orientation of pictures. It was found that the five-year-olds
remember the picture, but do not remember its orientation.

Although we have stated that a purely egocentric, i.e proximal, space, is highly implausible even at the very beginning of
orientation and space perception, Piaget (1937) has claimed
that the child under the age of one year employs an egocentric
notion of space and imposes his own bodily orientation upon the
structure and direction of objective space. What he means,
however, is that the child has difficulties with mutual spatial
relationships, in particular when they have to be specified
in the course of locomotion or bodily orientation. This is
different, however, from the basic, perceptual form of orientation which is concerned with the relationship between the
proper space of a form and its simultaneous overall space.
A characteristic property of egocentric orientation is that
the egocentric spatial relationships (left-right, before-behind)
remain invariant during spatial replacement of the perceiver.
The existence of egocentric orientation can be made visible
when the perceiver has to rely on orientation information alone,
for instance, when he looks for a hidden object in a space
without objective points of reference. The effect of egocentric
orientation is counteracted, however, by the fact that early
orientation is also characterized by relativity of egocentric
orientation axes, left-right in particular. In practice, it will
be quite difficult to find reliable evidence for these contradictory operating orientation properties.

There is sufficient evidence, however, for a shift from an
ego- to an allocentric notion of space, which is determined
by mutual spatial relationships between objects (Acredolo,
1978; Bemner, 1978) (see Figure 5.11). Children with an allocentric model of space are not necessarily characterized by
the ability to distinguish an absolute left and right direction.
One of the classical illustrations of this phenomenon is the difficulty children have in discriminating mirror-images. Stein
and Mandler (1974) and Thompson (1975) have shown that the
difficulties will decrease considerably when the child is provided with some explicit orientation elements. The confusion
between opposite directions is particularly obvious in the
child's first attempts at writing. Four- to five-year-olds who
have just learned to write their names sometimes do so in the
wrong direction, that is, in mirror writing. Beginners often
confuse letters of the alphabet with their respective mirror-
images, which raises particular difficulties for letter-pairs such
as p-q and b-d (Firth, 1971). Explicit orientation training
helps children avoid such difficulties (Spectorman et al., 1977).
Other investigators have observed that training in reading and
writing coincides with considerable changes in the child's
strategies for orientation perception (Schaller and Dziadosz,
1976).

According to Bryant (1974) the child tries to find a fixed
reference orientation when he is asked to remember differently

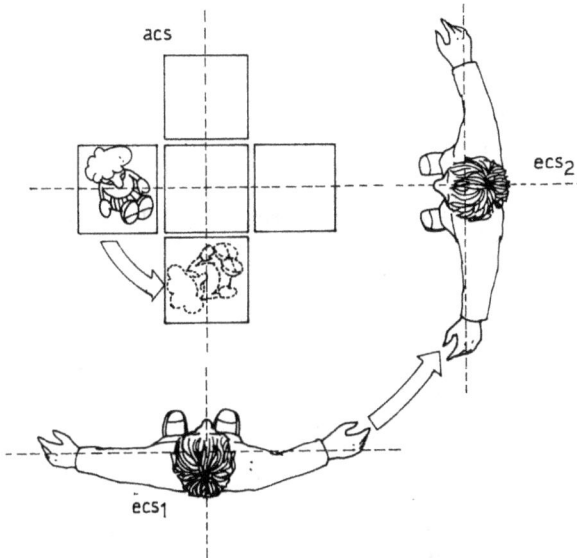

Figure 5.11 Although orientation in space is based on the co-ordination between an allocentric and an egocentric co-ordinate system (acs and ecs), Piaget believes that infants under the age of one year employ only the egocentric system. When a doll has been hidden in a box at the left, a ninety degree turn of the subject will change the egocentric but not the allocentric place of the doll. When the subject relies only upon the egocentric system, he will look for the doll in the wrong box

oriented lines. Since these lines are presented normally on rectangular cards, matching orientations can be found easily for horizontal and vertical but not for mirror-image oblique lines. Williamson and McKenzie (1979), however, have shown that five year old children do not employ reference orientations spontaneously. They presented the lines and reference figures in the form of luminous lines against a dark background. It is conceivable that these contradictory results can be explained by the degree of familiarity with reference systems. The child is accustomed to use rectangular sheets for drawing purposes and employs the lower edge of the paper as a reference orientation, e.g. as the ground of the depicted scene. Luminous lines against a dark background, however, are unfamiliar and it is conceivable that the child will not spontaneously employ them as reference systems. Hock and Hilton (1979) suggest that bodily orientation might provide a reference system for the discrimination of oblique lines. They have shown that children from five to eight years of age learned to discriminate between mirror-image oblique lines more readily when cards

bearing the obliques were shown vertically than when they were
presented horizontally. The superiority of the vertical presentation is explained by the fact that the objective (distal) and
retinal (proximal) axes are congruent for the vertical but not
the horizontal plane.

Many of the foregoing experiments may be criticized because
they do not measure purely perceptual but perceptual-motor
orientation. It is quite plausible that the child is able to perceive
the different orientations but has great difficulties with translating them into motor patterns. We shall see, for instance,
that most of the seven-year-olds are unable to copy a picture
of a cube simply because they see it as a cube and not as a
two-dimensional structure. Adults, for instance, are able to
distinguish the slightest differences between the faces of
people although they are completely unable to draw them.

It is conceivable that the perceptual specification of space
by a two year old child can be described in terms of a three-
dimensional Cartesian structure consisting of complex sub-
spaces, whereas the child's motor representation of space must
be described in terms of topological concepts such as proximity,
adjacency, closeness and so forth. It is also possible that the
complexity of motor space depends on its function. The visual
control of locomotion, for instance, is presumably much more
advanced than the visual control of manipulatory action, mainly
because locomotion is a much older system than manipulation.

5.2.3 Summary

The experiments that have been discussed thus far are characterized by a number of serious constraints. First, many experiments have operationalized the perception of orientation and
direction as the ability to copy or remember orientations and
directions of lines, figures or letters. Second, the experiments
are exclusively directed towards static place relations and not
to movement. Third, the experiments with children younger
than six months are not decisive with regard to their real
orientation-perception competence.

We may try to answer in a purely speculative manner whether
or not there is an empirical initial state of orientation development that possesses the properties attributed to the theoretical
initial state, namely the use of proximal space and the relativity
of the firstly emerging forms of orientation perception.

Our decision as to whether the neonate employs a proximal
system of spatial reference has to rely on indirect evidence,
particularly the research on feature detectors initiated by
Hubel and Wiesel (Hubel and Wiesel, 1962, 1965, 1968; Hubel,
1963; see also Carterette and Friedman, 1974 and Haber and
Hershenson, 1974). Very roughly stated, feature detectors are
sensitive to specific configurations of light on the retina, for
instance boundaries between light and dark with specific slopes.
If the neonate's perceptual apparatus equalled such a maximally
simple Hubel-and-Wiesel machine, orientation perception would

be based on a proximal system of spatial reference. The
detectors would detect horizontal or vertical lines as long as
they were horizontal or vertical with regard to the position of
the detectors on the retina. When the head and eye turned
ninety degrees, the horizontal line would be seen as vertical,
the vertical one as horizontal (see Figure 5.12).

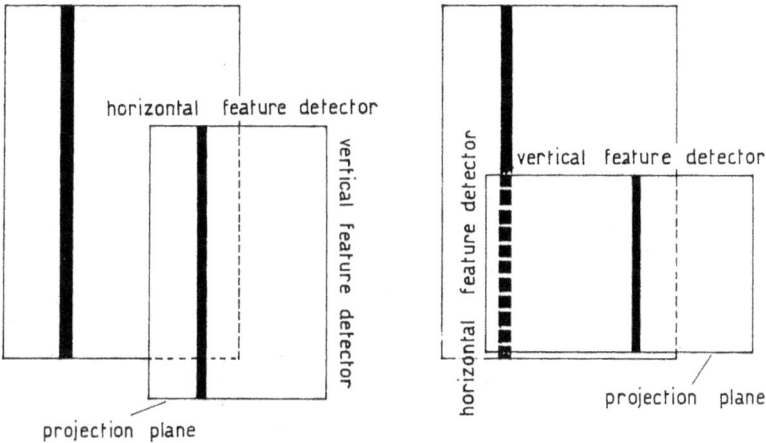

Figure 5.12 A feature detecting system is unable to account for
positional changes of the projection plane (the retina, for
instance). A ninety degree turn of the projection plane results
in the detection of different features

It is doubtful, however, whether the neonate's perceptual
apparatus indeed resembles such a simple Hubel-and-Wiesel
machine (see Neisser, 1967, p. 83 with regard to this question).
In principle, a Hubel-and-Wiesel machine contains not only the
lowest level feature detectors, but also higher order features,
such as texture sensitivity, and principles of feature organization, which constitute the neurological correlate of a perceived
three-dimensional distal space. Since even the earliest perceptual processes appear fairly complex, we may conclude that
the neonate's perceptual apparatus covers more than the basic
levels of feature detection. It may be questioned, however,
whether the neonate has organized the proximal visual information in a way that corresponds with distal space. The perception
of real orientation requires that the perceiver can determine
the average orientation of the objects and the surfaces on which
they stand. Thus, an extensive capacity for processing and
integrating information is necessary in order to detect what we
have called the 'real', distal orientation of the world. It is quite
conceivable that the neonate or even the six-month-old lack
such an information processing capacity. It is more probable
that the initial state of orientation perception is limited to

the perception of only one proper space – the proper space of
a simple object or arrangement of objects – i.e. the child probably adapts his spatial reference system to the extension of
only one focalized object. This, however, excludes the perception of orientation, since orientation is concerned with the
relationship between a space and a sub-space (a proper space,
for instance). Development may be characterized as a further
increase in the number and extension of spatial co-ordinate
systems that can be interrelated, until the general space contains a structure of interrelated objects and surfaces, including
the perceiver himself.

We have also questioned whether the firstly emerging forms
of perceived orientation are relative instead of absolute, i.e.
characterized by the absence of a fixed direction in the spatial
reference system. The experiments on the copying of diagonals,
letters or simple words (personal names) strongly suggest that
the early spatial co-ordinate system is indeed relative with
regard to orientation. Presumably, a distinction should be
made between top-bottom, before-after and left-right distinctions. The human body is relatively symmetrical only with
regard to the medial longitudinal plane through the body, mark-
ing the left-right distinction. Consequently, it is probable that
the top-bottom and before-after distinctions, if not innately
present, are acquired very early, whereas the discovery of
the absolute character of the left-right difference occurs
relatively late and is probably strongly determined by non-
perceptual factors, such as language.

5.3 CHANGE AND CONSTANCY IN SPACE

5.3.1 *The nature of the process*
From our analysis of the sensory organs (see part II, chapter
3) we know that the proximal stimuli change continuously, not
only because the objects or the surfaces are changing, but
mainly because perception almost always takes place during
bodily motion (a fact which is crucial for Gibson's account of
perception). Since the proximal stimulus is in principle entirely
determined by the relationship between the sensory state of
the perceiver (his own position in space and of the sensory
organs involved) on the one hand and the distal stimuli on the
other, movement will produce a regulated, law-governed change
of the proximal stimulus, the projection on the retina for
instance. In fact, the changing proximal stimulus forms only
the surface structure within which the perceptual system specifies a complex system of relationships – such as the relationships between a place and a place-gradient to which it belongs
– which, if the relationships are correctly established corresponds with a constant perceived world. When we walk around
the table, for instance, its proximal image undergoes a continuous perspective change, which corresponds, however, with

the objective properties of the spatial layout.

Before discussing the model of constancy perception, I should discuss a possible conceptual entanglement that might arise. Thus far, I have not particularly stressed the distinction between what the perceiver perceives and how he perceives it. When I say, for instance, that I perceive a space that I can describe as an infinite three-dimensional structure, I do not deny that I see a perspective world limited by the horizon. When I say that I see a rectangular wall, I do not mean that it has a rectangular proximal form. In fact, I see a three-dimensional infinite space because I see a perspective world limited by the horizon. There is no other way of seeing a three-dimensional world than as a world with perspective qualities.

In order to explain this, I refer to my theoretical definition of a form. I described a form as a set of places in a place-system or space. A form remains constant because the set properties, i.e. the particular relationships between the places and the place-system, remain constant. What matters is the relationship between the places and the place system and not the question of whether the place system has a Cartesian, a perspective or a variable structure. The concept of distance, length or size must be treated in the same way as the concept of form. Distance, for instance, is not a multitude or fraction of an absolute distance measure, such as the standard metre kept in Paris, but a numerical property of a particular set of places in a place system.

What is of primary concern in the present context is that the perception of form or pattern and distance, i.e. the computation of formulas and numbers of places, formally requires a system of places. The system of places is the framework within which sets of places are specified. Thus far we have employed a simple Cartesian co-ordinate system. Its main advantages are its simplicity and the fact that it answers our commonsense intuitions of space.

Since forms are described in terms of formulas that specify sets of places, it does not matter which kind of place system we employ, as long as the formulas can be applied to it. In Figure 5.13 two co-ordinate systems are represented. The first system (a) is a simple Cartesian one, the second system (b) is characterized by an angle of sixty degrees between the co-ordinates. It is clear that the graphic representation of a square will be different in both systems. Since the graphic representations answer exactly the same formula (see Figure 5.13) they represent exactly the same square. What matters is not the 'absolute' form of the squares, but the relationship between the form as a set of places and their place system. In fact, absolute form or size do not exist, since each form or size is a property of a particular distribution of places in a place system. It is only because we are used to imposing a Cartesian organization upon forms represented on a sheet of paper - except when they are clearly of a perspective nature - that we

see the square in Figure 5.13(b) as a parallelogram. Mapping
forms upon different co-ordinate systems is one of the 'jokes'
computer graphics has been used for (Reichardt, 1971). Csuri,
for instance, has mapped Leonardo da Vinci's famous Vitruvius
Man upon an L-shaped co-ordinate system. The result is almost
unrecognizable, although it is a perfectly adequate representation of Leonardo's drawing in an otherwise very uncommon
spatial system.

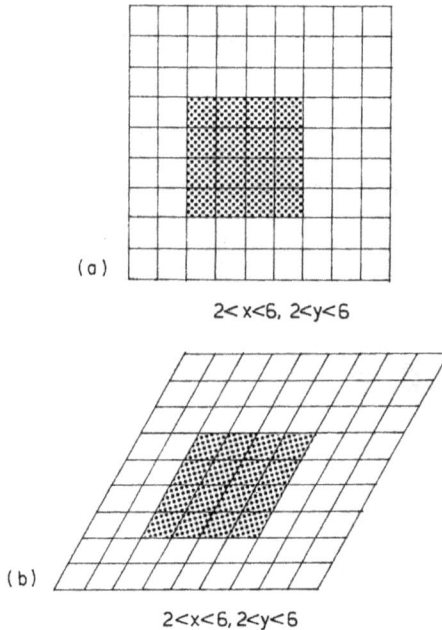

(a)

2< x<6, 2<y<6

(b)

2<x<6, 2<y<6

Figure 5.13 Two co-ordinate systems containing a square.
Although the 'absolute' form of the squares looks different
((b) looks like a parallelogram), they are identical. The
squares are characterized by an identical relationship with their
co-ordinate systems, expressed by the formula $2<x<6, 2<y<6$

   The fact that a form is not determined by a kind of absolute
template but by a relationship between a set of places and a
particular place system will be our key to the understanding
of constancy.
   Although visually perceived space can be described as a
three-dimensional Cartesian structure, the visual system itself
represents this space in a non-Cartesian, specifically visual
way which we might call the visual place system. Figure 5.14
represents a longitudinal section through a 'world' consisting
of an observer looking at a number of tiles lying at equal

distances in front of him. In order to see what is projected onto
the observer's retina, I have drawn a projection plane which
gives an enlarged image of the retinal projection (see for
instance Figure 5.1). We can use the projected image to make a
longitudinal section through the world that the observer perceives (Figure 5.14). We see that this world is not infinite, but
finite. It is limited by the horizon. More important is the observation that the 'absolute' size of the tiles or the distances between the tiles decrease as they are further from the observer.
The decrease is not arbitrary but can be represented by a
simple curve (Figure 5.14(b)).

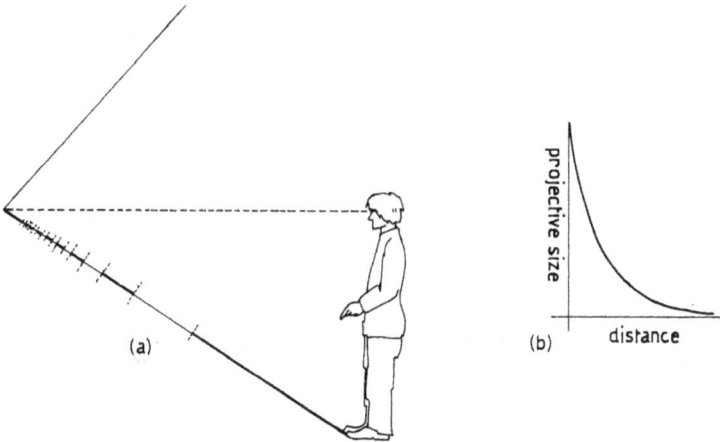

Figure 5.14 (a) An imagery longitudinal section through an
observer's visual world (based on the situation depicted in
Figure 5.1). In (b) the curve shows how the decrease of projective size is a function of real distance

It is also possible to make a representation of the visual place
system viewed from the top (Figure 5.15). The system takes
the form of a circle. The centre represents the position of the
observer, the circumference representing the horizon. The
circle can be drawn by plotting the projected distances from
Figure 5.14. In fact, the circular place system represents an
arbitrary section through the entire visual place system, which
would take the form of a globe. Besides, Figure 5.15 does not
offer a very precise representation of the actual visual place
system, since it has been tacitly assumed that the visual
system is completely identical with the projection through a
lens (see Figure 5.1). It can be very easily demonstrated,
however, that the perspective 'decrease' – which is only a
decrease with regard to Cartesian size - registrated by the eye
is less than the decrease registrated by a plain lens. The visual
system is characterized by an over-estimation of sizes that appear at a larger distance from the observer (see Figure 5.16).

It looks as though the visual system compensates for the fast perspective size-decrease provided by its natural, proximal lens system.

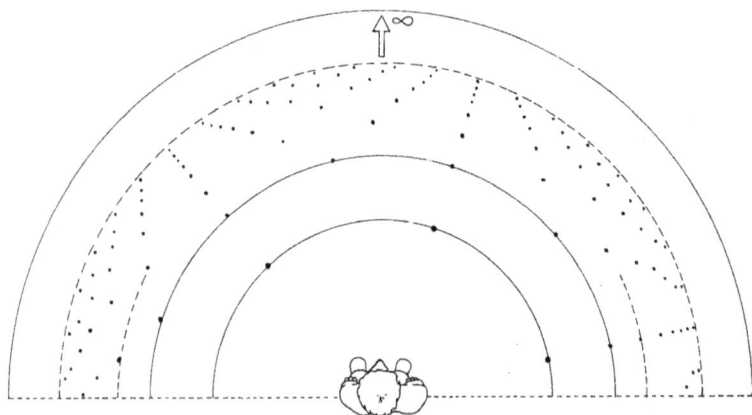

Figure 5.15 An imagery top view of a horizontal section through a visual place system. The circumference of the circle represents the horizon (the number of places is infinite). Since the number of places increases very quickly, no places have been drawn between the circular dotted line and the horizon

Perceiving a three-dimensional Cartesian, i.e. Euclidean, world does not imply that the perceptual image can only be represented by means of a Cartesian place system. The properties that characterize space-as-perceived, i.e. constancy of size and form, infinity and so forth, consist of particular relationships between the sets of places that constitute the sizes and forms and their place system. Consequently, a Euclidean space can be represented in terms of a non-Euclidean space, provided that the characteristic relationships between place sets and the place system remain constant. Constant size does not imply constancy in Cartesian terms and measured in centimetres or metres, but a constant relationship between a set of places and a place system, even if this relationship seems inconstant from a Cartesian point of view.

We could now arrive at the thesis that the classical question of size- and form-constancy development - how does the perceiver come to know that the trapezium he sees must be viewed as the perspective transformation of a square - is meaningless. According to the place system approach, we should not only specify the form - trapezium or square - but also the place system in which it is embedded - either visual or Cartesian. The perceiver would see a trapezium if he employs a Cartesian place system, but, since he employs a visual place system, he sees a square. That is, the perceptual apparatus has clustered a

Figure 5.16 Visual compensation of projective (proximal) size of objects at a distance. According to the rules of perspective, the boys A, B and C – who have a different projective size (length of the figure in the drawing) – possess the same real (distal) size. Although the projective sizes of C and D are equal, the projective size of C looks bigger

set of places that have the same distributional formula in a visual place system as the square set of places in a Cartesian place system.

The developmental question shifts from the development of constancy to the development of an appropriate visual place system. In order to understand this developmental process, we should take into account that place systems are not explicitly given, as in Figure 5.13, but implicit. The perceiver has information about place sets, their surrounding surfaces, properties of their place transformations and so forth. How should he discover the appropriate place system for a given set of places? There is one ideal case in which the place system can be made visible, namely when space is provided with a uniform texture of visible points in a transparent medium

(water, air, etc.). A uniform texture will correspond with a
three-dimensional lattice in Cartesian space and with a complex
perspective lattice, consisting of a set of gradients, in the
case of visual space (see Figure 5.17). Figure 5.17 shows that
the Cartesian and the visual place system are semantically
isomorphic (they are able to specify the same places or place
sets) but syntactically different (the form of the specifications
are entirely different).

Unfortunately, the ideal uniformly textured space would be
over-redundant and not informative. In practice, the perceiver
bases his place system (which always remains implicit) on partly
textured spaces, e.g. the natural, real space that surrounds
him. Generally, it may be stated that the place system is a function of higher-order properties of proximal spatial layouts,
particularly those properties that are affected by locomotion of
the perceiver.

At the theoretical initial state of constancy development,
the perceiver would not employ the visual place system determined by the properties of the projected image on the retina,
but the place system of the retinal surface itself. The distri-

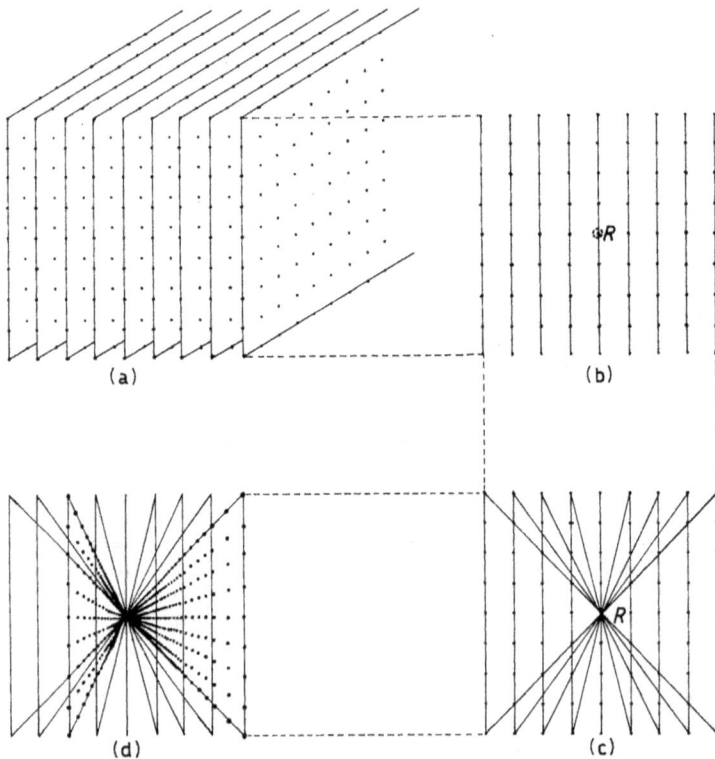

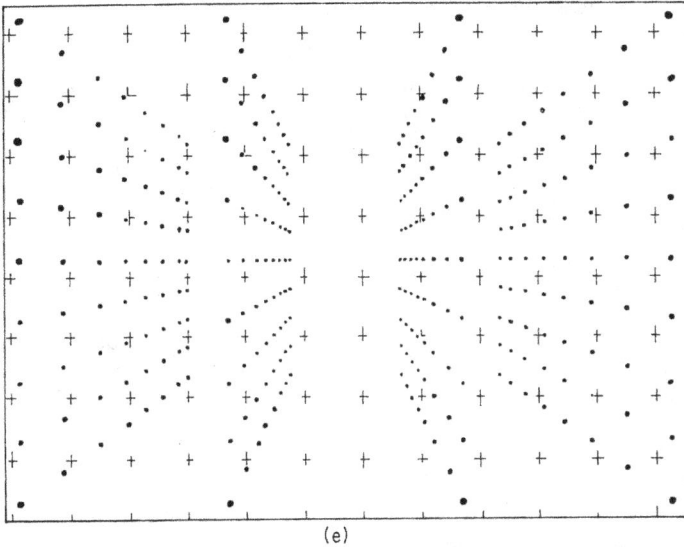

(e)

Figure 5.17 From a three-dimensional Cartesian to a two-dimensional visual place system. A uniformly textured three-dimensional Cartesian space is cut into parallel slices (a). A plane makes an orthogonal section through the Cartesian space; the plane corresponds with the proximal visual stimulus-space; a limit point R is chosen (b). The endpoints of the three-dimensional slices are projected onto the limit point R (c). Part of the uniform texture is projected onto the slices with a limit point in R, and a typical visual perspective texture arises (d). R corresponds with a point on the visual horizon, i.e. R defines the viewing point of the visual observer associated with the present image. (d) represents a (fragment of a) uniformly textured space in a visual place system. (e) represents a visual place system based on the projection of a rectangular grid of places extending one and a half metres in front of the observer. This place system is mapped upon a retinal place system (represented by crosses), which approximates a Cartesian distribution of places

bution of light sensitive cells on an idealized retina approximates a two-dimensional Cartesian place system. If this place system were imposed on the incoming retinal information, perceived size or form would depend on the distance between perceiver and perceived object. The theoretical process of constancy development would consist of the transformation of the initial Cartesian place system into the final visual place system. It may be questioned, however, whether this purely theoretical description provides a representation of what actually takes place during ontogenesis. Is the neonate's system of visually perceived spaces characterized by a two-dimensional Cartesian extension? If so, how would the infant discover which decreasing retinal size means constant real size? The classic answer to this question holds that the child learns the laws of visual constancy on the basis of tactile experience. When the child manipulates the same object at different distances from his eye, he may infer that the tactile size-experience remains constant, whereas visual size diminishes. This explanation is based on a number of dubitable assumptions. First, it implies a very close tactile-visual co-ordination: when the child manipulates objects, he must watch them closely. It may be questioned whether babies show this kind of co-ordination (see for instance Bower, 1974, pp. 151 ff.). Furthermore it is improbable that the child can make a sufficiently precise visual-size estimation of an object that is partly hidden by his hand. Second, the explanation presupposes a high level of tactile and visual preciseness. The difference between the smallest, visually possible, manipulating distance and the largest possible manipulating distance corresponds with an average decrease of 50 per cent of the retinal size of the manipulated object (an estimation based on the arm-length of the baby). It may be questioned whether the tactile system is precise enough to make an adequate correction of the apparent decrease of retinal size. Moreover, if the tendency to compensate decreasing retinal size is innate, it is even less probable that tactile information about size will be able to correct the corresponding visual information. Thirdly, the classic explanation of visual constancy development requires that the tactile dominates the visual system. When a child manipulates an object at different distances, he may experience a conflict between visual and tactile information. It is assumed, then, that the child suspects visual and trusts tactile information. With the visual-cliff experiment, however, we have seen that it is rather the other way round. If tactile-visual co-ordination was the explanatory factor, the child would not learn constancy but inconstancy.

Summarizing, it is rather implausible that the development of a visual place system necessary for a veridical perception of constancy takes place during ontogenesis. It is more plausible that the basic and formal properties of such a system have been acquired during phylogenesis and that the system is inherited. That is not to say that adequate, veridical constancy perception is an innate capacity, nor that the neonate employs an elaborate and overall visual place system. The fact that constancy perception is inherited means that the earliest forms of perception are not based on a retinal place system but on an - arbitrarily simple - place system based on relevant distributional properties of the visual stimulus, such as textural gradients and perspective size reduction.

It may be questioned whether the perception of depth, which we discussed in section 5.1, is a necessary prerequisite for the development of constancy. Although it is true that constancy phenomena are concerned with changing perceiver-object distances, I assume that depth and three-dimensionality are not formally necessary for the perception of constancy. A theoretical as well as an empirical argument supports this assumption. According to the theoretical argument, constancy is an inherent property of any place system, which may be two-, three- or simply n-dimensional. Although it is true that veridical constancy perception requires the exact estimation of perceiver-object distance, the principle of constancy in the perceived world depends on the relationship between a form (of an object, for instance) and its surrounding space. The empirical argument is based on a number of visual illusions.

In the Ponzo illusion, two lines of equal length are placed at different heights within an angular figure. The higher line is seen as longer than the lower one. Gregory (1966) has explained this illusion by referring to an inbuilt perspective tendency of the visual sense. The angular figure is seen as a perspective representation of two parallel lines. Consequently the highest horizontal line is seen as farther than the lower line and will be subjected to the kind of distance-compensation of length I illustrated in Figure 5.16. My explanation of this illusion is more general than Gregory's. I assume that the visual system considers the angular figure a place system comparable with the place system it imposes on the visual stimulus in general. The top of the angle is viewed as the limit point. The higher line occupies more places than the lower one and is also visually compensated, according to its position in the place system. The same explanation may be advanced for the Hering-Wundt illusion. The two parallel lines drawn in the ray figure look curved. The curvature may be explained by treating the ray figure as a place system comparable with the system imposed upon the Ponzo figure. The curvature is probably the result of size compensation for the line sections in the middle, which occupy a position nearer to the central limit-point where the density of the places is higher. The line-sections in the middle, therefore, occupy more places. Consequently, these lines are longer than the peripheral line-sections, which occupy less places, since the density of places is lower at the position where these line-sections occur. The curvature of the lines may be explained on the basis of visual length compensation of the middle sections.

The basic question that we shall have to answer on the grounds of empirical evidence concerns the emergence of a visual place system described in this theoretical introduction. To what extent is such a place system applied at birth and how does it develop further?

Besides, a number of additional questions may be raised. The first one concerns the relative inconsistency of the visual place system. The overall system has the form illustrated in Figures 5.15 and 5.17. In our western culture, focalized space often consists of a limited, two-dimensional surface, a sheet of

paper for instance, whose place system properties are basically
Cartesian. In such a case, children may be confronted with a
problem that is actually the reverse of the classical constancy
problem. The latter concerns the question of how the child
learns to understand that a perspective trapezium is in fact a
square or rectangle. I stated that this question starts from a
wrong assumption of how constancy perception works. The
problem is how the child comes to understand that the forms it
sees as squares or rectangles are in fact trapezia when they
are mapped upon a two-dimensional Cartesian place system of a
sheet of paper.

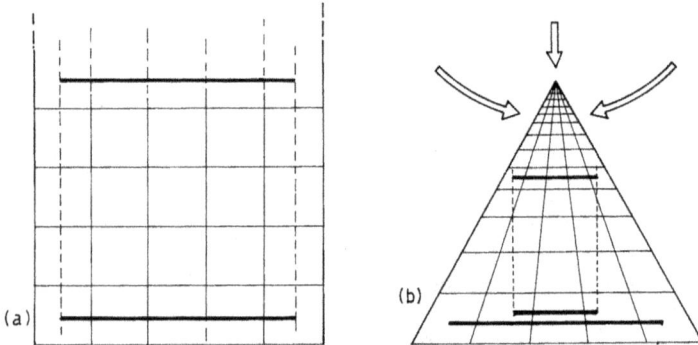

Figure 5.18 A place system explanation of the Ponzo illusion.
(a) represents a fragment of a Cartesian place system with
two horizontal lines of equal length. (b) represents a limit-
point transformation of this Cartesian place system. The limit
transformation consists of such a tilting and shortening of
parallel sets of places that they all meet at and are limited by
the limit point, which forms the top of the triangle of (a). The
length of parallel lines in such a place system is determined
by the properties of the system and not by a Cartesian measure
of length. It is assumed that the perceptual system adapts the
impression of length to the properties of the place system in
which this length is represented

The second problem, which is closely related with the first
one, concerns the ability to perceive proximal form properties.
This ability is an important aspect of drawing skills.
The third problem concerns visual illusions. Visual illusions
were mentioned because it was assumed that they might offer an
argument in favour of the visual place system approach. If the
tendency to apply the visual place system is innate, visual
illusions should occur very early in life and be universal.

5.3.2 The development of constancy
In their article on constancies in the perceptual world of the
infant, Day and McKenzie (1977) have made a distinction between

three different kinds of constancy. The first form, egocentric constancy, concerns the stability of the perceived world during locomotion of the perceiver. The second form, object constancy, refers to the constancy of form, size, colour and so forth during position changes of object or perceiver. The third form is identity or existence constancy and refers to the permanence of objects. According to Michotte (1962) permanence is a perceptual phenomenon, whereas Piaget has claimed that permanence is a concept that should be acquired in action. In Part III of this book I shall go deeper into this problem.

Thus far, I have limited the theoretical discussion to size and form, i.e. object, constancy. Egocentric constancy, however, may also be considered an inherent property of the visual place system. The visual place system is based on the projected properties of the distal world, that is, the distal world is taken as a frame of reference. Some parts of the body of the perceiver, such as the nose, legs or hands, are also projected onto the retinal image. During locomotion, these projected parts change their co-ordinates with regard to the visual place system. This enables the perceptual system to infer that the body moves with regard to surrounding space, how fast it moves and in which direction.

We have stated that the process of constancy development should be defined as a process of learning to apply the visual place system in an adequate, i.e. veridical way. That is, the child must learn to apply the visual place system in such a way that perceived form and size correspond as closely as possible with real form and size, within the limits of practical purposes and action.

Day and McKenzie have pointed out that the accuracy of size and distance perception in babies younger than four months is strongly dependent on two- or three-dimensionality of the perceived form and on objective perceiver-object distance. Size and distance are estimated accurately only when the infant looks to a relatively near, three-dimensional object. It may be concluded, therefore, that adequate constancy perception will not occur before reliable size and distance estimation has emerged, i.e. not before the age of four months.

It may be questioned, however, how accurate the child's perception of constancy must be in order to be acceptable as a definite proof for the existence of a (veridical) constancy principle in perception. It is possible, for instance, that the young child shows a tendency towards over-constancy or under-constancy. In both cases, constancy perception is largely inadequate and unreliable, though the principle of constancy is obviously present and active.

I shall first give an overview of the investigations that have tried to determine the properties of the empirical, initial state of constancy development.

Bower carried out two experiments, one about size, the other about form constancy, with babies between six and eight and seven and nine weeks of age respectively (Bower, 1966, 1974). The experimenter taught the babies a conditioned response to the stimulus, a cube with sides of 30 centimetres, placed at a distance of 1 metre in front of the child. In the testing stage, the children are divided into three groups. One group is shown a 30-centimetre cube at a distance of 3 metres (same distal size, different distance and different proximal size of the cube); another group is shown a 90-centimetre cube at a distance of 3 metres (different distal size, different distance, same proximal size of cube, since the real distance has increased the same number of times as the real size); whereas the third group has to look at a 90-centimetre cube at a distance of 1 metre (different distal size, same distance, different proximal size). The first and third group (same distal size and same distance group) showed twice as much conditioned responses to the test stimulus as the second group (same proximal size group). Bower concluded that size constancy is presumably an innate or very early emerging property of the perceptual apparatus. In general, it may be concluded that the child reacts to distal variables such as real size and distance and not to proximal variables such as retinal size.

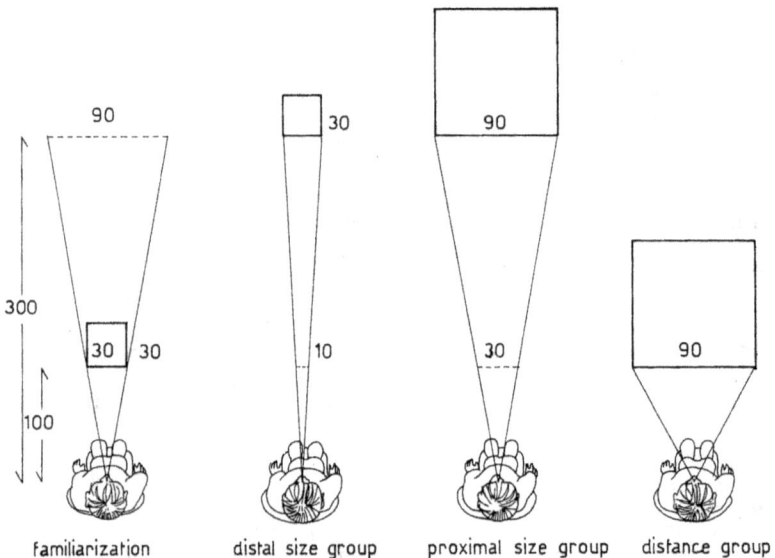

Figure 5.19 Bower's size constancy experiment. During the familiarization session, infants were taught a conditioned response to a 30-centimetre cube at a distance of 100 centimetres. If the infants had learned to respond to real size, they should show the conditioned response in the distal size but not in the proximal size or distance condition

Bower's form constancy experiment is similar in design to the size experiment. The conditional stimulus was a rectangle presented at an angle of 45 degrees. Test stimuli were: the rectangle presented in the fronto-parallel plane (same distal form, different proximal form, different angle); the trapezium presented in the fronto-parallel plane (different distal form, same proximal form, different angle); and, finally, the trapezium presented at an angle of 45 degrees (different distal form, different proximal form, same angle). The results showed that babies between seven and nine weeks reacted significantly more to the rectangle presented in the fronto-parallel plane. They did not react to the proximal form (the trapezoid retinal projection) but to the distal form (the rectangle having a trapezoid proximal form in the conditioning phase). Bower's results suggest clearly that form constancy is such an early emerging capacity that it cannot be but innate.

Day and McKenzie (1973) and Caron et al. (1978, 1979a, 1979b) confirmed the findings concerning the early presence of shape constancy. Day and McKenzie based their conclusions upon habituation curves obtained with eight and fourteen week old infants.

Caron et al. (1979a, 1979b) argued that the previous experiments on shape constancy were indecisive with regard to a proximal-stimulus- or a distal-stimulus-based explanation. It is possible for instance that the infants did not respond to real shape but to slant cues. This possibility, however, was ruled out on the basis of experimental findings (Caron et al., 1979a). In another experiment, the investigators desensitized infants to slant cues by habituating them to an object with a different slant during each habituation and test presentation. They found that the infants habituated to the object and showed considerable recovery to a test object with a different real shape.

Experiments carried out by Day and McKenzie (McKenzie and Day, 1972, 1976; Day and McKenzie, 1973, 1977; McKenzie et al., 1980) have confirmed Bower's results on form constancy but not those on size constancy. In the experiment carried out by McKenzie et al., four, six and eight month old infants were habituated to a three-dimensional model of a human head at distances of 30 and 60 centimetres. Response recovery in the testing conditions, which contained head models of different sizes and at different distances, showed that size constancy perception did not occur before the age of six months. Six-month-olds showed size constancy with the head model at a maximum distance of 70 centimetres. According to the investigators, the results also suggested that size constancy might occur at the age of four months, provided that the perceived objects are familiar and relatively near and that the subject shows a relatively low variance of responses.

At first sight, the fact that size constancy appears after form constancy is quite surprising, since the perception of

constant form requires the perception of constant size. If I
watch a rectangle turning around its right side, the rectangle
will keep its constant form only if I am able to see that the left
side keeps the same length as the right side. It may be questioned, therefore, how we can explain the experimental finding
that form constancy occurs earlier than size constancy.

A large number of experiments, including Bower's form and
size constancy studies have shown that babies base their perceptual depth and space judgments generally on dynamic cues,
motion disparity in particular. That is, the babies' visual
place system is based on a combination of the various kinds of
visual information, such as retinal size, retinal displacement,
convergence angle, motion disparity, texture gradients,
gradient changes and so forth. With regard to size and form
constancy experiments, we may suppose that the form experiments offer more perceptual starting points for an adequate
judgment of form than the size experiments do for an adequate
judgment of size. Suppose that the baby is taught a conditional
response to a stick with length l. In order to ascertain that
the stick presented during the experimental trials has the same
length, l, the visual place system used to represent the length
of the stick during the conditional trials must have the same
metrical properties as the visual place system employed during
the testing trials. The visual place system, however, must be
continuously adjusted to the properties of the visual image.
When visual attention shifts from a near to a remote object,
the properties of the local visual place system – which is
limited by the zone of focal attention – will change. The reason
for this is that the rate of perspective size decrease depends
on the distance between the perceiver and the object (see
Figure 5.14(b)). Adequate perception of size during perceptual
shifts to distant objects is possible when the perceiver is able
to keep the basic metric of the changing, local visual place
comparable. We shall see that this is a perceptual skill that
even adult perceivers hardly possess. It may be expected
that re-adjustments of the babies' visual place system during
object displacements of 100 centimetres – and probably less –
will give rise to mutually incomparable perceived sizes. We may
assume that babies do not yet perceive size constancy beyond
the limits of a local fragment of the visual place system
(Figure 5.20).

In the form constancy experiment, however, the requirement
that sizes must be represented in one visual place system in
order to make sizes comparable is fulfilled. Suppose that the
child has learned a conditional response to a rectangle, a
figure characterized by equal length of its opposite sides.
It is clear that the sides of the rectangle are visually present
at the same time, unless the rectangle is very large and exceeds
the extension of the visual field. The sides are represented
in one common fragment of the visual place system, based on
retinal size, gradients, motion disparity and so forth. Conse-

quently, it will be relatively easy to see the sides with an identical length. Even if the properties of the visual place system have been changed between the conditioning and the experimental sessions – for instance because the rectangle has not only been turned but also replaced – the form remains perceptually described as a form with equal opposite sides, i.e. as a rectangle (Figure 5.20).

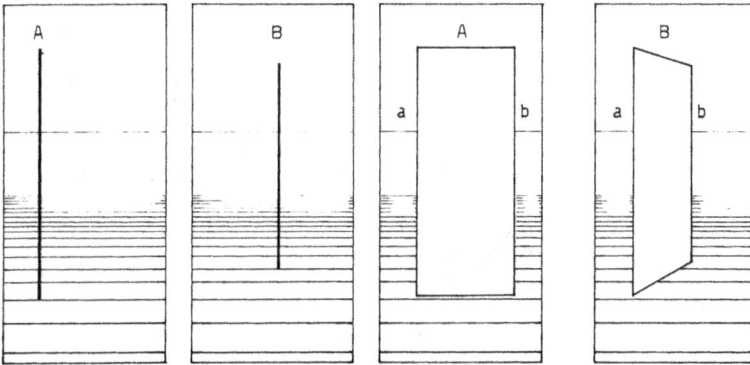

Figure 5.20 Although size constancy is a condition for form constancy, form constancy emerges earlier than pure size constancy. In the form constancy experiment, the infant has to compare length A and length B, without being able to compare them within one underlying place-system that would impose identical size and distance measures on A and B. In the form constancy experiment, the perception of a rectangular form is based on the size identity of the parallel sides. The perceptual judgment of size identity can be based on the fact that both sides are simultaneously present. It is quite doubtful, however, whether the infant would be able to perceive the size identity between rectangle A and rectangle B

It should be noted, however, that the previous explanation of the difference between size and form constancy experiments is limited and tentative. The results of size constancy experiments are contaminated by the infants' tendency to pay more attention to big than to small forms. Furthermore, infants might be particularly interested in events that occur with objects and not in the objects themselves. Examples of such events are the turning or enlargement of objects. Consequently, the constancy experiments may be much more decisive with regard to form than to size constancy during infancy.

The experiments on form and size constancy carried out after infancy are focused primarily on veridical estimation of size and form and not on the presence of constancy per se. It is clear that these experiments are directed towards another kind

of perceptual skill than the experiments on constancy carried
out during infancy.

The trends observed in the process of later constancy development differ according to the kind of constancy judgment that
is required. It is easier to make true estimations of the size
of an object when it is relatively close to the observer than
when it is far away. Although there is an average increase in
the adequacy of perceptual size judgments (Winters and Baldwin,
1971), there are different courses of development for the
estimation of near and of far objects (Vurpillot, 1976a, 1976b;
Kaess, 1974).

According to Vurpillot (1976b) the development of adequate
form constancy perception can be characterized in terms of an
inverted U-curve. She mentions that the age of optimal form
judgments differs according to the experimental method employed (the kind of forms used, the distance between the forms
and the observer, the instruction given, and so forth). Kaess,
however, found that form constancy judgments improve gradually (Kaess, 1971, 1974), although the results are also strongly
determined by the experimental method employed.

In the introduction, I stated that one of the problems related
to the constancy phenomenon is actually the reverse of the
classical constancy problem. The problem is not how the child
learns that the trapezia that he sees are in fact rectangles
or squares seen under perspective deformation: the child does
not see trapezia, i.e. proximal forms, but squares and
rectangles, i.e. distal forms. It may be questioned how the
child learns to understand that the rectangles that he sees are
transformed into trapezia when they are mapped upon a Cartesian co-ordinate system. If we look at the drawings of children,
we see that the understanding of this fact is a rather late
acquisition. It is often stated that children draw what they
know, not what they see. I think that this statement turns the
matter upside down. If we take the visual place theory seriously, we should say that the child draws what he sees, whereas
the adult (or at least some adults who have learned to draw)
draw when they know. (They know what has to be drawn, in
order to get a result that looks as if they have drawn what
they saw.) The child sees a rectangle, the wall of a house, for
instance, and he draws a rectangle on the fronto-parallel plane
of his drawing paper. Adults, on the other hand, have learned
the principles of perspective; they know that shapes seen as
rectangles or squares have a trapezoidal projection upon the
retina (at least when they are not lying in the fronto-parallel
plane). Adults draw rectangles in the form of trapezia, because
they know that the trapezium will be seen as rectangular shape.

Phillips et al. (1978) asked children between seven and ten
years to copy simple line drawings of perspective views of
cubes and also of similar designs that did not clearly represent
objects. The cubes were copied much less accurately than the
non-object drawings. The copies of the cubes contained elements

that were typical for the real object, such as square sides, for instance, and did not reflect the perspective properties of the model. This is quite surprising, because the task involved literal copying of two-dimensional configurations that only differ with regard to their representational value. The results support the formal approach to space perception I have been discussing. It is conceivable that the drawings of the cubes are perceptually specified by the children in a way that is compatible with a three-dimensional description, in spite of the fact that the actual appearance of the cubes is describable as two-dimensional. The non-representational designs, however, are specified more simply in a two-dimensional way (remark that the child is not attributed a Cartesian representational system but a representational system that, with regard to the present task, can be described reliably in Cartesian, two- and three-dimensional terms). The children see cubes, that is, they see a figure with square sides in an orthogonal mutual orientation. The child copies what he sees. The difficulty, however, is that the copying space is a two-, whereas the visual space is a three-dimensional system. The child is unable to transform a three-dimensional into a two-dimensional data structure, either because the transformation itself exceeds the child's processing abilities, or because the child does not possess graphic motor schemes that can be employed to carry out this task. The non-representative forms, however, are perceived and copied in a two-dimensional place system.

Some of the 'post-infancy' constancy experiments have also been focusing on the perception of proximal size and form, that is, the form or size which is drawn on the paper or projected onto the retina. Perceiving 'proximal' size means that the observer maps a two-dimensional Cartesian co-ordinate system upon the three-dimensional, specifically visual space he sees. In Figure 5.16 I gave an example, illustrating the difficulty of 'proximal' perception. It will not be surprising therefore, that the experiments demonstrated that the perception of the 'proximal' form – which requires the perception of 'inconstancy' – is much more difficult than perceiving the 'real' form and size (constancy) (Kaess, 1970; Vurpillot, 1976b).

The third problem that we should deal with is the development of visual illusions. In accordance with Gregory (1966) a great number of geometrical visual illusions have been explained in close relationship with constancy phenomena. Gregory explained visual illusions on the basis of perceptual perspective mechanisms. The ray figures, Muller-Lyer arrows or Ponzo lines are seen as perspective lines and the visual apparatus responds to them with an automatic compensation of apparent size, just like it does with real three-dimensional perspective phenomena. I have suggested that Gregory's explanation must be generalized: perspective must be seen as an application of the visual apparatus' tendency to impose a specific place system onto the retinal information. The form constancy experiments with babies have suggested that such a visual place system (or any functional equivalent of it) is presumably innate. If the system plays a role in the perception of visual illusions, we may expect that susceptibility to visual illusions must occur from birth on.

In Wohlwill's overview of research in perceptual development (Wohlwill, 1960) it is stated that the general trend consists of a gradual decrease of susceptibility to the illusory effects of the classical visual illusion displays. A reverse trend occurs with the Ponzo illusion (see Robinson, 1972, pp. 105 ff.) (see also Figure 3.3). It is quite plausible, however, that the Ponzo illusion is too 'impoverished' with regard to the number of cues pointing towards a place system interpretation of the figural display. The fact that illusions occur at rather early ages, and in general that illusions tend to decrease with age, supports the conclusion that illusion susceptibility is either an innate or a very early emerging property of the visual system. Visual illusions have also been studied with animals. Although the results of these experiments must be treated with great caution, they suggest that visual illusion susceptibility is a property of any organism that has a sufficiently complex visual system (see Gregory, 1966; Robinson, 1972). At first sight, cross-cultural research on visual illusions tends to contradict the conclusion drawn with the foregoing experiments. A number of investigators (see Robinson, 1972, for an overview) have tried to prove that the substantial inter-societal differences in illusion susceptibility are very probably due to cultural and natural differences in the environment. Traditional Zulu communities, for instance, live in villages that contain almost no rectangular forms. Their susceptibility to typical 'perspective' illusions, such as the Müller-Lyer arrows is quite low. Susceptibility to the horizontal-vertical illusion (horizonal lines are overestimated) is highest with people living on flat, open plains (higher than an average European sample), and lowest with people living in a jungle environment (Segall et al., 1963).

In an extensive review of visual illusion studies (Robinson, 1972) an investigation is mentioned which clearly contradicts the environmental hypothesis (Jahoda, 1966). A comparison between people living in open savannah in round huts and people living in dense forest in rectangular huts showed that neither of them was particularly more susceptible to the illusions that 'fitted' their natural environments (the same conclusion may be drawn from Gregor and McPherson (1965)). A study by Jahoda and Stacey (1970) shows that educational experience could not explain the differences between Scottish and Ghanaian subjects. Moreover, the fact that environmental properties might affect visual illusion susceptibility does not rule out the fact that visual illusions are based on mechanisms that are innate.

5.3.3 Summary
In the theoretical introduction to this section on constancy

phenomena, I have tried to make clear that the theoretical line of constancy development does not proceed from inconstancy to constancy perception in the strict sense of the word. Constancy is an inbuilt property of a place system. Constancy development may start theoretically with an initial state in which the place system is inadequate with regard to the constancy of the real world.

According to the classical approach, the initial system might be identified with the place system of the retina, a system we have thus far described as a two-dimensional Cartesian system. I have given a number of theoretical and empirical arguments for the thesis that the visual system is issued with a programme for construing place systems that deviate from the Cartesian retinal system on a number of essential points. That is not to say that the resulting visual place system has an inbuilt 'veridicality', i.e. that it automatically gives rise to size and form specifications that are true with regard to the 'real' world. We may state, however, that the principle of visual constancy corresponds with the principle of constancy in the real world, whereas the practical application of the principle must be improved during a developmental process.

It may be questioned in which way the visual system is provided with a visual place system of the kind required to make true estimations of the size and form of the objects. Empirical evidence suggests that babies define size and form on the basis of dynamic cues such as motion disparity, and kinesthetic cues such as binocular convergence. At a later stage the child will also be capable of employing pictorial cues such as texture gradients and perspective. These findings make plausible the conclusion that the visual place system is a function of the total amount of information provided by a changing visual stimulus. Perceived size, for instance, is a function of retinal size, retinal displacement, convergence angle, the place of the object in a texture gradient and so forth.

We have now come to the end of our discussion of space perception development. We questioned whether or not the infant perceives a space that can be attributed Euclidean properties, such as three-dimensionality and constancy, filled with objects whose forms do not depend on their orientations. We have seen that the empirical evidence shows a great number of missing links. Nevertheless, it has been shown to be plausible that the child's perception of space during the initial state of development is more closely related to a space with distal, Euclidean properties than a space with proximal, sensory-specific properties.

At different occasions, we have tried to clarify the meaning of our statements concerning the development of space perception. Our inquiry was concerned with the question of whether the child's perceptual acts are directed towards an object that can be described as a Cartesian space. We did not imply that the child should have a Cartesian representation of space.

Having a Cartesian representation of space is basically different from having a representation of Cartesian space. The latter refers to any kind of representation related to an object space that can be described in Cartesian terms. The acquisition of the ability to construct a Cartesian representation of space will take a long time. Although it is quite plausible that the construction of a Cartesian representation is supported by the fact that the child perceives a Cartesian space, the perception of Cartesian space itself does not automatically produce a Cartesian representation of space. The latter will be achieved only when the child is provided with concepts and formal and linguistic tools that make a Cartesian representation of space possible.

6 Perception of form and pattern

6.1 THE NATURE OF PROCESS

6.1.1 Properties of the pattern perception apparatus

In the previous chapters we have discussed the structural relationships between sets of places and space - such as three-dimensionality, depth and constancy - without taking into account why places are related and how sets of places are formed. In this section, I shall discuss this problem by outlining a theory of pattern perception and its development.

A system of places, a space, obtains its spatial character and structure through showing qualitative variability. This principle can best be illustrated with an example from visual perception. One of the many important conceptions Gestalt psychologists have put forward concerns the idea of a visual Ganzfeld. A Ganzfeld may be described as a textureless visual space, i.e. a space without variation in colour or brightness. In an experiment by Cohen (1957) (see Haber and Hershenson, 1974, for a discussion), the Ganzfeld was created by means of two connected, equally illuminated hollow spheres. The subjects initially experienced a foglike field, extending for an indefinite distance in front of them, but after 3 minutes some of the subjects reported complete cessation of all visual experience. Such an effect can be simulated by closing the eyelids, which are natural Ganzfelds. When a simple illumination-difference was created in Cohen's Ganzfeld, both the density of the perceived fog was reduced and its distance increased. It is possible that auditory Ganzfelds, consisting of a continuous noise, can be created in such a manner that will produce similar effects to those of visual Ganzfelds (the noise of the bloodstream in the environment of the ear is probably an example of such an auditory Ganzfeld). The Ganzfeld experiments show that stimulus variability is necessary in order to make normal space-perception possible.

In this section, I shall deal with a particular aspect of this variability, namely its organization into groups and structures of variability. This organization may be called form or pattern perception.

Without a particular perceptual apparatus that structures the perceived world into patterns and form, the world would always appear like a Ganzfeld, consisting of a coloured and differently illuminated indefinite fog. The perception of such a 'fog' seems impossible for an organism that is provided with a minimally complex perceptual apparatus: the existence of stimulus variability itself coerces the organism to organize the field in a complex and definite way.

I shall now try to define the nature and basic properties of the pattern perception process. Our aim is to find a purely formal theory of pattern perception, one that will provide the descriptive apparatus by means of which we can tackle the definition of hypotheses and empirical evidence. The formal theory describes the basic properties of any action to which the predicate 'pattern perception' can be assigned. It does not provide a model of how the process of pattern perception is actually carried out by the perceiver, the brain or a computer. In order to elucidate the function of a definitive theory of pattern perception I shall discuss two related examples, namely the formal theory of language provided by transformational linguistics and the theory of chess playing expressed in the rules of chess.

In transformational linguistics (I will take Chomskyan generative grammar as an example), an attempt is made to answer the question: what does it mean to produce language (form sentences, understand the meaning of sentences and so forth). The production of language is defined in terms of making and understanding grammatical sentences, or being able to judge whether they are grammatical or not (clearly, this is something of a caricature of what transformational linguists are doing). Transformational linguists define what producing grammatical sentences means. Producing or understanding grammatical sentences involves the construction of complex hierarchical relationships between grammatical building blocks (such as 'NPs', 'VPs', 'Dets', etc.). When the linguistic theory describes a sentence in this way, it is making a psychological statement, although not in a naive sense of the term 'psychological'. It does not assume that the construction of relationships between linguistic building blocks corresponds to the actual processing in the brain of sentences and linguistic material (it must be stated, however, that such a naive interpretation has been taken seriously in a number of experiments which have shown that the formal model did not coincide with the actual strategies of processing language: see for instance Mehler, 1963; Miller and McKean, 1964; and Savin and Perchonok, 1965). The formal theory is psychological in the sense that it states that the production of sentences by any system (a man, an angel or a machine) must be understood as a process that follows the rules and uses the building blocks described by the transformational, generative linguistic theory, independent of the way in which the system applies or follows such rules. Let us compare this process with playing chess. Playing chess implies that a number of rules related to specific chess-pieces are followed. Any process that follows these rules, irrespective of how the rules are actually employed is called 'chess'. Chess-masters employ the rules in a totally different way from novices, who may have to consult an instruction book before making any move. In spite of the tremendous differences between the actual cognitive processes of the chess-master and the novice, both are doing exactly the same thing, namely, they play chess. Without understanding the rules of chess, that is, without a formal theory that defines the meaning of the predicate 'playing chess', it will be impossible or at least very difficult to understand the nature of connection between the 'internal processes' of the master and the novice. Discovering the rules of chess is impossible when one has not even a minimal idea about what chess really is. How will the investigator know which kind of human activities are chess playing and which are not? The same conclusion holds for language: in order to study the concrete processes by means of which human beings produce and understand language, we must have a formal theory of language that enables us to determine whether or to which extent a given human activity is indeed language production or not.

Let us now deal with the question of how a formal theory of language or pattern perception may be constructed. Since the construction of such a theory is theoretically preliminary to the distinction between linguistic and non-linguistic or perceptual and non-perceptual acts, pure empirical induction, eventually in the form of experimental research and observation, will be an unusable method. The basic heuristic source for such a formal theory is the theorist himself, i.e. the theorist as a skilful subject, possessing the ability to employ language or perceive a pattern. Chomsky speaks about the linguistic 'intuition' or the tacit knowledge of the language user (or perceiver) (see also Polanyi, 1967). Intuition or tacit knowledge should not be identified with a mysterious private access to the basic internal 'machinery', but simply with the ability to use language or perceive, to judge linguistic or perceptual outcomes, such as sentences and perceived patterns or events. The technical description of linguistic or perceptual skill, however, requires a particular methodology that does not itself follow from the intuition or tacit knowledge of the theorist. A transformational grammar, for instance, may be based upon existing grammatical and syntactic theories and concepts or on logical and semantic models. A formal theory of pattern perception may be based upon existing mathematical methods, such as the methods of co-ordinates or of algebraic topology.

The method for describing perception that we have employed thus far started from a description of a proximal sensory stimulus, based on properties of the surrounding world and the position of the perceiver. In order to provide a coherent description, we should employ the same descriptive device for describing the relevant properties of the distal as well as the proximal stimulus. Perception should not be viewed as a translation of a meaningless stimulus into a meaningful perceptual image 'in the head', but as the assignment of a specific structure to the proximal stimulus, based on its proximal

properties. We have seen for instance, that the perception of
depth and object constancy is based on the visual place system
which is a particular organization of the set of proximal places.
The meaning of our statements about perception should always
be related to the properties of the descriptive system that we
employed to describe the nature of the perceived world and
of the stimulus. The method that we have followed thus far will
also be applied to the description of form and pattern perception
and its development.

There are specific basic requirements that any formal model
of form and pattern perception should fulfil. The first is that
the model should describe the resemblance between any system
that perceives, codes or recognizes patterns, independent of
the exact 'hardware' of the system or of the particularities of
the way in which the system carries out the perceptual act.
One consequence of this is that the model should not be sensory
specific, although it should be able to deal with any sensory
specific process of pattern perception. Second, the model of
pattern perception should operate in close connection with a
system of space perception, since the properties of patterns
are intimately related with the principles of the space in which
they appear. Third, the model should operate upon a complex
and spatiotemporal proximal stimulus and not be limited to
simplified, spatial stimuli.

I shall now give a short overview of models put forward by
Leeuwenberg (e.g. 1969, 1971, 1978), Koenderink and Van
Doorn (e.g. 1975, 1976a, 1976b, 1977, 1979a, 1979b, 1980) and
Pribram (e.g. 1977a, 1977b, 1979).

Leeuwenberg's model is primarily concerned with the coding
of perceived patterns. The pattern code should provide a formal
description of the perceptual properties of the patterns (and not
of the perceptual process that underlies them). The coding
starts with a description of the pattern (visual, musical, etc.)
in terms of angular deviations between elementary pattern constituents that are called 'grains'. This preliminary description
of the stimulus contains an extensional, summative description
of its properties, which is then further condensed by means of
a number of operators that detect regularities such as reversal
or alternation in the extensional description. The operators
function in a recursive way. They are applied to the pattern
description until a maximally simple coding of the pattern is
obtained. The number of coding elements (elementary angular
deviations between 'grains' and the structural formula provided
by the operators) necessary to specify a pattern constitutes
its information load. The coding theory predicts that patterns
will be perceived in the way described by the coding formula
that contains the smallest information load (see for instance
Leeuwenberg, 1971, 1978; and Restle, 1979, for successful
applications of coding theory).

Koenderink and Van Doorn have tried to provide a mathematical, topological explanation of the way in which ambulant

observers visually perceive solid objects in space. Besides the
fact that they deal with visual information and with ambulant
observers, the main difference with Leeuwenberg's model is
that they are interested in finding the general qualitative layout of the visual information field, whereas Leeuwenberg tries
to find exact quantitative descriptions (codings) of patterns.
Koenderink and Van Doorn deal with two qualitatively distinct
ways in which object properties are mapped upon retinal surfaces. The first way is concerned with the distribution of light
and shadow or the perspective transformations of textural
properties on the surface of an object, the second way with the
boundaries between visible and invisible parts of the objects
(contour lines). By means of differential topology, the authors
show that the qualitative structure of both forms of information
about objects is quite simple and rule-governed. Qualitatively,
solid objects consist of a limited number of structural elements,
such as 'humps', 'pits' and 'saddle planes'. The elements combine into objects according to rules that limit their structural
relationships. Under normal conditions of illumination and
station point, the object corresponds with retinal images that
contain all the structural information from the original, projected object. The information is contained in the flow of the
surface texture or in the field of isophotes. The structural
properties of objects are most clearly expressed in the 'optical
flow' that characterizes the visual information of an ambulant
observer. The way in which structural properties enter the
visual field, e.g. when the observer turns the object around,
specifies the spatial properties or 'form' of the object. Koenderink and Doorn's work on object perception is important
because it provides a starting point for a 'grammar of perception' that does not operate upon simplified visual displays
but upon the complex field of information picked up by ambulant
observers.

The third approach to pattern perception that I want to discuss is Pribram's holonymic theory. The theory states that
the brain operates according to the mathematical principles
upon which holography is based. Holography is a technique
used to project three-dimensional images of objects by employing the interference patterns of light waves. The complex wave
of the interference pattern can be decomposed into a number
of constituent harmonic waves by means of Fourier analysis.
The set of harmonic waves stores all the information contained
in the complex interference pattern, whereas the interference
pattern contains all the information of the solid object on which
it is based.

In spite of the increasing amount of neurophysiological evidence in support of the model, it may be questioned whether
the description of pattern perception in terms of wave decomposition techniques fits the large amount of empirical evidence
on the particularities of pattern perception. It is doubtful,
for instance, whether a Fourier decomposition of the line that

constitutes the profile of a face will correspond with the structure of local features that is typical for our perception of the profile.

The model that I want to present now tries to provide a formal description of the generative components of the psychological competence that we call 'pattern perception'. It should not be viewed as an alternative to the models of Leeuwenberg, Koenderink and Van Doorn and Pribram, but as an explicitation of aspects that I think have remained implicit in the previous models. The model defines perception as a process of assigning a 'deep structure description' - i.e. a particular structural organization - to the proximal stimulus, which can be either spatial or spatiotemporal. If perception is veridical, the surface/deep-structure pair should bear a one-to-one relationship with a characteristic description of the perceived object, event or space in terms of an object description language. The object description language we have employed throughout this book consists of a Cartesian system which describes objects or events as sets of places in a space (for an earlier version of the model, see Van Geert, 1975). One of the basic issues the model should deal with is the question of how relevant sets of places are formed and characterized. The sets are relevant if they correspond with properties of the environment that are important for the perceiver, such as objects, events, 'cliffs', obstacles and so forth.

The formal pattern perception model contains two sorts of operators, namely data and functional operators. The data operators form a strict hierarchy. The lowest level contains the spatiotemporal proximal stimulus. At this level, there is one data operator for every place in proximal space (I shall not deal with the question of how to find a physiological analog for 'place in proximal space'). Each of the lowest-level data operators contains one 'piece' of proximal information. In a two-dimensional visual display, for instance, consisting of black and white dots, data operators are characterized by a set of proximal co-ordinates and a specification of stimulus information, e.g. (1,1: black) or (1,2: white). The first-order data operators are followed by second-order data operators that contain information about stimulus resemblance or difference between pairs of adjacent first-order operators. This principle is recursive, such that second-order operators are followed by third-order operators, and so forth. The result is a hierarchy of levels of data operators that specify the proximal information and the resemblance or difference between sets of proximal data operators.

The data operators must be accompanied by a number of functional operators that have specialized tasks. Since most of the information contained in the data hierachy consists of information about resemblances or differences between underlying data operators, the first type of functional operator should be capable of comparing adjacent data operators at each

level of the hierachy and of telling whether they contain different or identical information. These operators might be called
comparing operators. One of the problems that a more elaborate
formal model of pattern perception should deal with concerns
the level of resemblance between adjacent data operators
necessary to establish a 'resemblance' - or 'difference' - specification.

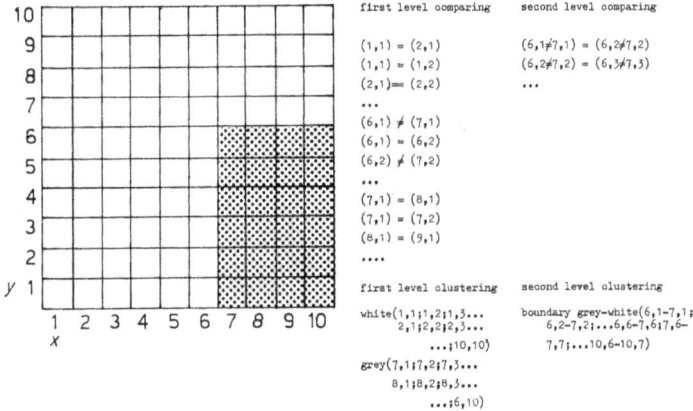

first level comparing

$(1,1) = (2,1)$
$(1,1) = (1,2)$
$(2,1) = (2,2)$
...

$(6,1) \neq (7,1)$
$(6,1) = (6,2)$
$(6,2) \neq (7,2)$
...

$(7,1) = (8,1)$
$(7,1) = (7,2)$
$(8,1) = (9,1)$
....

second level comparing

$(6,1 \neq 7,1) = (6,2 \neq 7,2)$
$(6,2 \neq 7,2) = (6,3 \neq 7,3)$
...

first level clustering

white(1,1;1,2;1,3...
2,1;2,2;2,3...
...;10,10)
grey(7,1;7,2;7,3...
8,1;8,2;8,3...
...;6,10)

second level clustering

boundary grey-white(6,1-7,1;
6,2-7,2;...6,6-7,6;7,6-
7,7;...10,6-10,7)

Figure 6.1 First- and second-order comparing and clustering.
The matrix consists of 100 data operators (small quadratic
segments). Comparing operators will compare each pair of
adjacent data operators. This will result in a list of first order
difference and identity specifications. Identical pairs will be
clustered, which will result in a cluster of 'white' and a cluster
of 'grey' data operators. Differences are compared at the second
level: the comparing operators will determine whether the first-
order differences are either different or identical. Identical
differences are clustered: they constitute the boundary between
the white and the grey region

Data operators form clusters. Clustering of data operators is
the task of clustering operators. All adjacent operators that
contain the same information should be taken together within
one cluster. Clustering appears at all the levels of the data
hierarchy. Figure 6.1 provides a very simplified example of
clustering: first-order clustering concerns the set of black and
white data operators, whereas second-order clustering concerns the boundary between black and white (second-order
clustering in the example is based on identical differences
between black and white, i.e. the boundary between black and
white). At higher levels of the hierarchy, comparing and
clustering is based on the general aspects of difference and
resemblance that characterize the entire visual display (see
for instance Figure 6.2). In normal circumstances, various

criteria of resemblance and difference interact, such as lumino-
sity, colour, texture, common rate of movement and so forth,
which implies that clustering is a very complex phenomenon.
The principle of clustering at various levels of the data hierarchy on the basis of the output of comparing operators is the
first principle upon which the model of pattern perception rests.

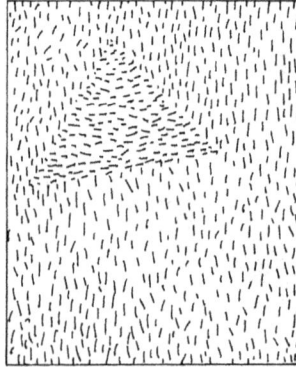

Figure 6.2 Forms are based on principles of clustering in place
systems. In this diagram a triangle will be seen because the
perceptual system clusters the places which are characterized
by the presence of averagely identical orientation

The second basic principle regulates the specification or
description of clusters. Like any other set of elements, clusters
of data operators can be specified in terms of either an extensional or an intensional definition. In an extensional definition,
a pattern is specified by listing all the elements of the set,
i.e. by listing the co-ordinates and stimulus values of the
clustered data operators. Such a definition is very extensive
and redundant. An intensional definition of a set specifies
a property that all the elements of the set have in common and
which distinguishes them from elements that do not belong to
the set. Since we have situated the data operators in a descriptive Cartesian space, we have at our disposal a classical method
for describing sets of places intensionally, namely analytical
geometry. In analytical geometry a set of places is defined
exactly by a formula that expresses a mathematical relationship
between the co-ordinates of the places (it is clear that simple
analytical geometry is not sufficient if we want to provide a
formal specification of more complex intensional specifications
of place sets; what matters now is that there are formal methods
for dealing with perceptually relevant properties of place sets).
In order to find intensional specifications of clustered data
operators, we need functional operators that are able to compute
intensional specifications. We may call them computing operators.

The computing operators come into action whenever a minimal cluster (i.e. a cluster consisting of two adjacent operators) has been formed. Consequently, the computing operators are organized according to the same hierarchical structure as the data operators. At the lowest possible level, they will compute the set property of two adjacent proximal data operators; at higher levels they deal with properties of lower-level sets (such as constituent features). The computing operators should be provided with a particular and limited computing capacity, which has to be specified in such a way that it simulates perception as closely as possible. Evidence of the limited computing power at low levels is provided by research on feature detectors (see for instance Hubel, 1963). Limited computing capacity at higher levels is demonstrated by a study on texture discrimination carried out by Julesz (1975). Julesz shows that we are able to discriminate textures of first and second order (created by throwing a unipole and a dipole a specific number of times on a surface), whereas we are unable to discriminate texture frequencies of the third order (created by throwing a tripole, such as a triangle, on a surface).

If we limit the computing capacity of the operators to hyperbolic and parabolic functions, the computing system would reach the ceiling of its computing abilities quite soon. Most of the place sets that are clustered – such as surfaces of objects – are much more complex than hyperbolic or parabolic place distributions. Since the system of operators is organized in a recursive and hierarchical way, it should be able to specify the properties of sets of infinite complexity simply by computing the properties of the relationships between sets situated at the top level of the operator's computing capacities. Koenderink and Van Doorn have shown that a limited computing capacity is able to specify the basic properties of visual information in a relevant and reliable way.

A system consisting of comparing, clustering and computing operators would be able to provide a rather complex description of a proximal data structure, but it would still differ considerably from adequate pattern perception. Imagine that we project a red ball provided with white circular patches on to the retina of a perceiver. The projective image of the ball will take the form of a circle, whereas the projections of the circular patches will depend on their respective places on the ball. The central patches will be circular, whereas the more peripheral ones will be elliptical, with a linear limit form. In principle, the computing operators will compute a different formula for each white patch on the ball. The differences between the white patches are such that they can be described in terms of a constant form, a circle, and a gradient, the surface of the ball.

A specification of the set of projected white patches in terms of a constant form plus a gradient would not only reduce the information load of the description considerably, but it would also correspond with the object description of the ball. The search for optimal simplicity in the formulas computed by the computing operators is the task of the fourth kind of functional operator, which we shall call the economizing operator. If the economizing operators are provided with the right kind of rules, their tendency towards economizing the computational output of the system should correspond with an increasing veridicality of the resulting perceptual image. In Chapter 3, on orientation perception, we have already discussed two simple techniques for economizing the computational output, namely translating and rotating of the proximal co-ordinate system. Of more interest for perception is the transformation of a set of congruent places (a texture for instance) into a gradient with a projective limit-point. In Chapter 5, on the structure of space, we have seen how gradients are the projective result of textured surfaces in three-dimensional space. Since a detailed discussion of this matter would exceed the scope of the present text, suffice it to state that the specification of a spatial place in terms of a position in a particular gradient is equivalent with the specification of that place in terms of three Cartesian co-ordinates. Also the specification of the form of objects is based on the principle of gradients. The projective image of the textured surface of the object depends on the orientation of the surfaces with regard to the station point of the perceiver. Instead of computing formulas for the different proximal projections of the textural elements, the economizing operators might try to find out whether they can content themselves with the specification of a constant textural form in addition to the necessary gradients. The relation between a set of gradients corresponds with the three-dimensional structure of the object, i.e. a description of the object in terms of an object-property language, such as Cartesian geometry. Music is a form of pattern perception where the economizing operators play a very important role by imposing a structure of categorical points (the musical scale) on the acoustic space in which the musical event takes place.

In principle, the information contained in the proximal data structure is sufficient in order to produce a veridical specification of its content. There are cases, however, where the information is not sufficient or ambiguous. Even if these cases are very rare, the formal theory of pattern perception would be inadequate if it could not deal with them. The operator that will make pattern perception possible under ambiguous and impoverished circumstances is called the testing operator. The function of the testing operators is quite trivial: their only function consists of inverting the order in which the various operations proceed. Instead of computing a formula for a given set of data operators, for example, the testing operators might test whether a set of data operators correspond with the description in terms of a given formula. The testing operators require a complex extra-perceptual component, which contains a set of testable, stored patterns, testing strategies and so forth.

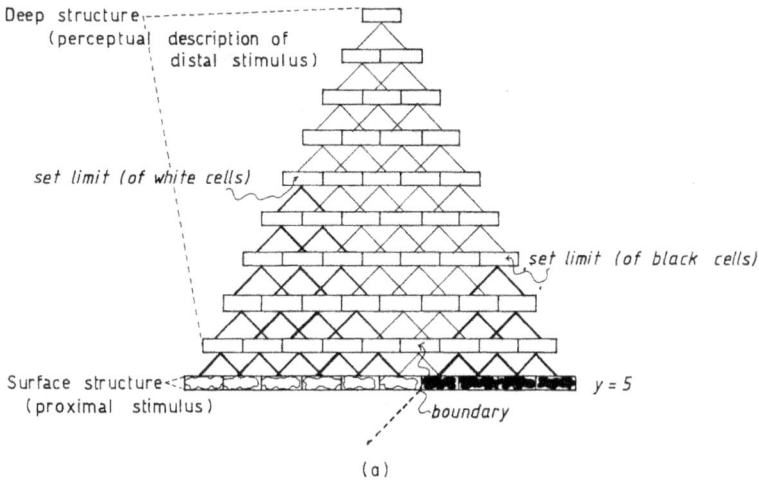

(a)

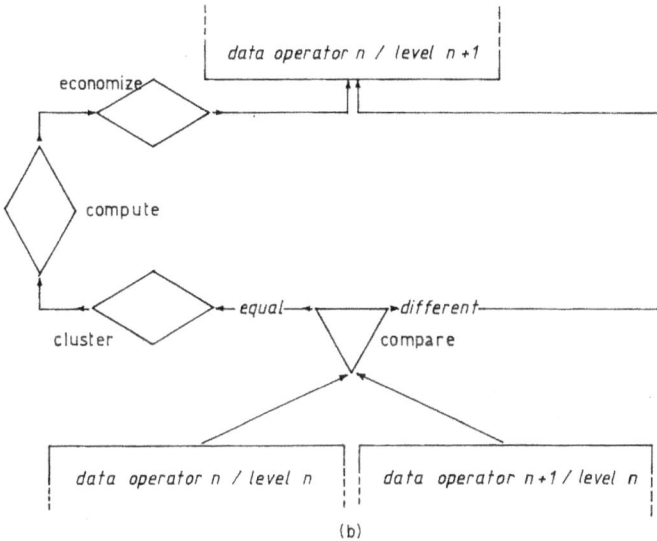

(b)

Figure 6.3 An overview of the formal pattern perception system.
(a) represents a cross-section through the pyramid of data
operators of Figure 6.1 at y=5. The lowest level contains the
proximal stimulus at y=5. The remaining levels contain the deep
structure, which consists of the appropriate clusters and place
formulas. (b) represents a unit consisting of two adjacent data
operators and one super-ordinate data operator. If the comparing
operators find that the content of the adjacent data operators
is equal, the data operators will be clustered by a clustering
operator. The computing operator computes the place formula
of the cluster, in collaboration with the economizing operators

who try to find a maximally simple place formula. The place
formula, together with a specification of the common content
of the subordinate data operators constitutes the input of
the super-ordinate data operator. If the comparing operator
finds that the content of the adjacent data operators is different,
the difference is directly fed into the super-ordinate data
operator. At higher levels of the data hierarchy, the comparing
operators might registrate identical differences. Then, the
clustering, computing and economizing operators will try to
find a place formula for these differences. The testing operator,
which is not explicitly represented in this figure, is able to
change the direction of the operator functions

Figure 6.3 summarizes the formal pattern perception model.
It is important to note that it describes perception as a process
of assigning a 'deep structure description' to the proximal
surface structure. The deep structure description specifies
relationships between proximal data elements. The way in which
it specifies these relationships in a given proximal data structure should show a one-to-one correspondence with a description of the distal stimulus in terms of an object-property language.
If the formal model of pattern perception is adequate, it
should also be able to deal with the basic properties of perception that have been discussed in the previous chapters.
The intersensory nature of the patterns may be explained
by the fact that the theory deals with sets of places in proximal
spaces, no matter what the actual properties of the proximal
spaces are. The model deals with visual as well as with auditive
spaces (see for instance Mak, 1981, for an application of the
model in the field of melody perception).
The principle of orientation results from giving a pattern its
proper space, which permits a maximally simple, i.e. economic,
specification of the pattern properties. Size and form constancy
is the result of applying the economizing operators to collections
of place sets (textures, for instance) characterized by gradients.
In the case of perceived three-dimensional objects, the application of computing and economizing operators leads to a specification of the perceived content in terms of a visual place
system which is formally analogous to a three-dimensional space.
Another important property of perceived patterns is that they
have a compound nature, i.e. that they consist of a structure
of pattern constituents or 'features'. The compound nature of
patterns plays an important role in most theories of pattern
perception. Selfridge's Pandemonium, for instance, defined
pattern perception as the recognition of the features of which a
pattern consists (Selfridge, 1959). Noton and Stark (1971)
explained the compound nature of patterns on the basis of an
eye movement theory (which leaves the compound nature of
non-visual patterns unexplained). In the formal model of
pattern perception that has been put forward here, the com-

pound nature of patterns results from the limited computing
capacities of the computing operators and from their hierarchical structure. If the computing powers were unlimited,
every form would have its own specific formula i.e. be perceived as a mono-featural whole of unlimited complexity.

As with most other properties of perceived patterns, the
principle of foreground and background stems from the pattern
system's striving towards optimal simplicity. If the system would
treat the perceptual display as a mosaic, it would have to
specify every pattern constituent in a positive (the constituent)
and a negative (the adjacent region) form. Instead, the system
imposes an arbitrary difference on the depth axis upon any
two overlapping place sets (overlap is indicated by T-junctions
between the boundary lines). The result is a considerable gain
in simplicity of the constituent structure (see for instance
Figure 3.6).

The Gestalt laws have long since been regarded as explanatory principles, i.e. laws that explain the formation and
perception of patterns (Wertheimer, 1923; Metzger, 1966; and
Murch, 1973). In fact, the Gestalt laws are largely descriptive.
The Law of Similarity, for instance, states that similar or
identical elements are grouped. Bartley (1969) and Kaufmann
(1974) have criticized this law because it is based on a property
(similarity) that is largely context- and experience-dependent.
Kaufmann cites an experiment by Henle (1942) that shows that
words in mirror writing are easily detected and grouped when
they occur in an environment of normally written words. The
difference between normal and mirror words is not primarily
perceptual but cognitive. The problem with this law is not that
it is untrue but rather that it is too general. Similarity explains
pattern perception only if it is submitted to a strict hierarchical
ordering, which is a basic property of the comparing operators.
Each new level in the hierarchy defines its proper kind of
similarity. Higher levels will be characterized by more 'abstract',
higher order forms of similarity (see for instance Figure 6.2).

The second Gestalt law, the Law of Proximity, states that
proximate elements are more easily clustered than less proximate
elements. Like the principle of similarity, the principle of
proximity is one of the principles upon which the operator-
model of pattern perception rests. Both principles, however,
are ordered in a hierarchical way, such that different levels
of similarity and proximity arise that are only apparently
incompatible. In Figure 6.4, for instance, most observers will
see three planes, AB, CD and EF, against a 'background' that
can be seen through the small inter-spaces between the planes.
At the lower levels of the clustering process, proximity will
hold between B and C, and D and E. At higher levels, the
BC and DE clustering is incompatible with the application of the
economy principle which demands a structuring in AB-, CD-
and DE-clusters (all line-segments are employed in the description of the pattern, all line segments have the same meaning).

Figure 6.4 The Law of Proximity leads to an incorrect prediction of the clustering of line segments in this figure. Although
the pattern perception system (see Figure 6.3) employs the
principle of proximity, it does so in a hierarchically ordered
way. Low-level proximity will lead to a clustering of B with
C and D with E. Under the influence of the economizing operators, the actual clustering will occur with A and B, C and D,
and D and F

Another Gestalt law, the Law of Good Continuation, tries to
explain why and how overlapping or adjacent forms will be
separated into isolated patterns. The Law says that this separation is not arbitrary but should obey the rule that a form should
be maximally simple and continuous. In Figure 6.5, for instance,
there will be no doubt about the way in which the figure should
be separated into two-line segments (although the separation
can be easily directed by the testing operators, which is also
shown in Figure 6.5). The Law of Good Continuation follows
from the application of computing and economizing operators.
If good continuation at a lower, i.e. more local, level is incompatible with good continuation - or any other principle - at a
higher, less local level, the organization of the pattern will be
determined by the higher-level properties.

6.1.2 Theoretical implications for development
The pattern-operator model offers a starting point for a strictly
theoretical description of the development of pattern and form
perception. Since we are primarily concerned with psychological
development and not with biological maturation, we shall start
with a model of the theoretical initial state in which the basic
neurological apparatus, simulated by the structure of the data
operators, is present. The main problem, then, concerns the
development of the functional operators.
   According to the most extreme definition, the initial state of
pattern perception must be characterized by the absence of
pattern perception. Complete absence of pattern perception
implies that data operators are not compared and clustered,
that no distributional formulas are computed and so forth.
   Assuming that there exist organisms that are characterized
by this theoretical initial state of pattern perception, how
would such organisms perceptually experience the world? The
answer to this question can be found in the experiment with
which we started this chapter, namely the Ganzfeld experiment.
A Ganzfeld is a perceptual experience characterized by the
complete lack of place-clustering and place-set specification.
Since patterns are primarily characterized by contrasts with

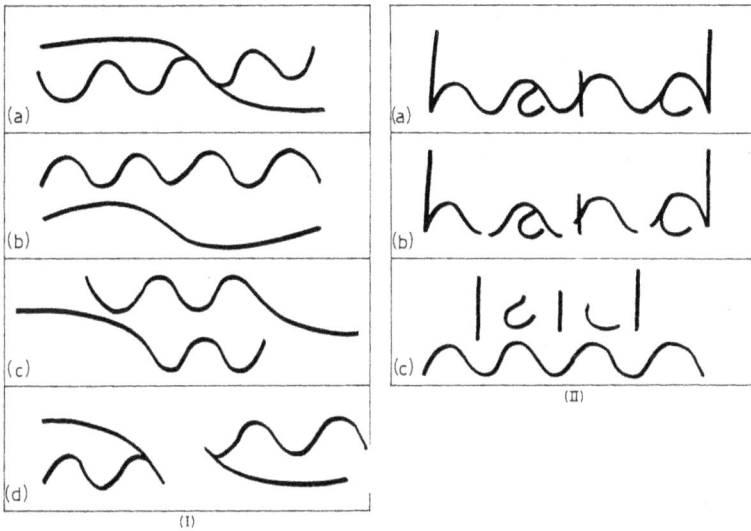

Figure 6.5 Although (Ia) can be decomposed in various ways, some are more plausible than others (the order of plausibility is (b)-(c)-(d)). When the complex figure consists of known, pre-structured elements, the testing operators, provided with the distributional formulas of the elements, will force the perceptual system to a perceptually less plausible decomposition (see (II))

other patterns or with the space that surrounds them, we may conclude that the Ganzfeld impression simulates the experience of a patternless world. An organism characterized by the absence of functional operators would see nothing or hear nothing, though it would not be blind or deaf. It is very doubtful whether such an organism could exist. Even the simplest unicellular organisms must be capable of perceiving changes (of light, temperature, acidity, etc.) in order to survive. It is clear, therefore, that our theoretical initial state of pattern perception should be defined in a less extreme way if we want our theoretical speculation to be more realistic.

Less extreme forms of theoretical initial states of pattern perception can be constructed either by allowing a limited number of functional operators or by limiting their capacities. The functional operators are ordered in a functional hierarchy, such that each successive operator needs the operator of the preceding level. The order of the functional operators is as follows: comparing operators, clustering operators, computing operators, economizing operators and testing operators. We shall examine the properties of an increasingly complex series of pattern-perception systems.

The simplest system is one which is simply provided with
comparing operators. The only thing such a system could
perceive are differences or equivalences between places in
the sensory proximal spaces. If such a system were to be
provided with normally sensitive sensory systems, it would
'perceive' an infinite amount of differences and equivalences
that would carry no informational value. If such a simple
system could be less sensitive to sensory stimulation, that is,
if it had only a small number of data operators, it might have
some functional value. The less proximally sensitive the
system, the more general, overall differences or equivalences
it would identify. The system would perceive gross differences
between brightness levels (light and dark, for instance),
temperature and so forth. The organic representative of such
a system might be found at the level of unicellular organisms.

A less simple perceptual system would contain comparing and
clustering operators. The system is capable of clustering
identical data operators at various integrative levels. Such a
system is capable, for instance, of making the distinction
between a boundary and the sensory content that it encompas-
ses. It is also capable of making a distinction between the
building blocks of a pattern (for instance the dots of a dot
pattern) and the pattern itself. Since it is not provided with
computing operators, however, it cannot specify the various
clusters it perceives. Consequently, every set of data operators (the basis of a pattern) it has clustered is identical with
any other set of data operators at the same hierarchical level.
That is, the system can discriminate between a plane and its
boundary (sets at two different hierarchical levels) but not
between various planes or various boundaries. For such a
system there would be no difference between a square and a
circle, for instance.

A system provided with comparing and clustering operators
would be able to perceive a qualitatively important property
of the environment, namely changes in the general constellation
of place clusters. The perception of a change requires the
same functional operators as the perception of a spatial boundary, since a change can be characterized as a boundary between
two spatiotemporal - instead of merely spatial - sets of places.
Since the system would not be equipped with computing operators, it would perceive all changes as equal.

It may be questioned whether there exist organisms that are
characterized by the presence of only the comparing and
clustering operators. The perception of place-sets without
discrimination is very inefficient, although it requires a rather
complex perceptual apparatus. But on the other hand, the
apparatus can be extended quite easily, for instance with computing operators. This relatively small extension would produce
a considerable increase in the system's efficiency. It may be
concluded therefore that, if such a system exists in the organic
world, it must be a system at an initial, or at least low, state

of perceptual development.

The introduction of computing operators into a perceptual system creates the first actual pattern perceiving system. The role of the computing operators in the formal pattern perception model consists of specifying the properties of all the places that belong to one set (a pattern) in such a way that they are distinguished from any other place that does not belong to the set. Since we employed a Cartesian language for describing the stimulus space, the properties of the places belonging to one set are specified in terms of formulas that describe the mathematical relation between their co-ordinates. The power of a pattern perception system, therefore, depends on the power of the computing operators, that is, on the maximal level of mathematical complexity they can achieve.

It may be questioned what kind of limitations have to be imposed upon this perceptual system in order to characterize it as being in its initial state of development. The most rigorous limitation that might be imposed consists of an absolutely minimal computing capacity. The operators are only capable of specifying a set of places in the most general way possible, for instance by means of the predicate 'SET'. With such a limitation, the initial state would have the same pattern perception properties as a system without computing operators, the only difference being that it need not discover that computing operators belong to its necessary outfit.

The basic disadvantage of a system that is provided with comparing, clustering and computing operators characterized by a relatively high mathematical power is that its discriminative capacities are too strong, i.e. they would largely overestimate the relevant variability in the object world. It would compute different formulas for different perspective images of the same object. In order to overcome this difficulty, we might provide the system of pattern operators with rudimentary economizing operators. The economizing operators are responsible for translation and rotation of the proximal co-ordinate system, in order to find the least complicated formula for a set of places. They also compare families of place sets - elements of a texture, for instance - and try to find out whether they can be simplified by introducing a gradient. The economizing operators try to assign fixed co-ordinates to places whose proximal co-ordinates vary by specifying those places in terms of fixed positions in gradients. A system also provided with economizing operators can still be very rudimentary, for instance when the extension of the proximal domain upon which it can operate is limited or when its computing or economizing powers are limited. Structurally, however, it does not differ considerably from a complete pattern-perception system, except for the presence of the testing operators.

It may be questioned whether an initial pattern-perception system equipped with comparing, clustering, computing and economizing operators can do without some rudimentary functioning testing operators. The testing operators are able to invert the functional operations. They make pattern perception possible when the proximal conditions are ambiguous. The question of whether testing operators should be present during the initial state depends on the amount of information contained in the normal proximal stimulus. According to the Gibsonian theory of perception, all the biologically relevant information is present in the normal proximal stimulus. In the previous chapters, we have seen that Gibson's point of view is more valid than the view that proximal information is basically ambiguous, incomplete and without functional meaning. On the other hand, it is quite plausible that not every relevant perceptual strategy - for instance the various ways in which the economizing operators work - is directly based on the structure of proximal information. The testing operators might play an important role in the acquisition of new perceptual strategies. Learning to see interrupted figures, for instance, might be impossible without the help of testing operators (see Figure 6.6). The testing operators might impose various place formulas upon the set of unconnected dots and examine whether one of them describes the spatial distribution of the dots. If such testing operations are successful they might result in computational strategies for finding place formulas for arbitrary sets of elements that are characterized by particular proximal properties (i.e. proximal properties that are characteristic for elements that constitute interrupted figures).

Figure 6.6 A triangle consisting of dots. The places of the dots are specified by the distributional formula of a triangle. In order to compute a distributional formula, it is not necessary that all the places specified by the formula are actually present in the visual image. In principle, one dot placed at each angle is sufficient to determine a triangular distribution. In practice, however, a distribution of places should be much more redundant in order to make an adequate computation of formulas possible

For any model of the theoretical initial state of pattern perception that we might choose we are obliged to specify the nature of the factors that explain the transition of the initial state to more advanced states. In the chapter on the concept of development, we have seen that the transitional dynamics

of a developmental process can be characterized in terms of
internal stability versus instability of the states and open
versus closed states. A maturational explanation of development
is based on internally unstable, closed states. The state
transitions take place on the basis of internal dynamics and
are not determined by external factors. In this case, the pattern perception programme would be 'wired in' to the structure
of the sensory system. Experience would play only a very
general, conditional role (in the sense that experience might be
necessary to 'trigger' the internal programme).

The development of the pattern perception apparatus might
be based on learning principles, which are incompatible with a
maturational explanation. A learning model requires internally
stable, open states: transitions take place on the basis of
external influences and, if they are absent or insufficient,
the system will remain in its current state. There is a third
possibility for explaining the development of pattern perception,
which is based on relatively open and relatively instable developmental states. Change is based on internal dynamics, although
the direction or speed of the state transitions depend on external factors, i.e. experience, exercise and so forth. Various
explanatory principles have been put forward to deal with this
interactionist view of development. Piaget has advanced the
concept of equilibrium. The system is in a state of disequilibrium
at the beginning of development but actively strives after final
equilibrium. A Piagetian explanation of pattern perception development would require a close connection between action and
perception. A second interactionist explanation of development
defines the instability of non-final states in terms of 'hypotheses' about the possible next developmental steps. One of
the main disadvantages of a hypothesis-testing explanation of
development is that any less complex developmental state should
contain the ability to represent the characteristic properties of
a set of more complex states. In Chapter 7 I shall sketch an
interactionist explanation of perceptual development based on
the concept of attention. We shall see that the process of
attention exceeds a limiting and constitutive influence upon
the experiences that can be acquired. The nature of the possible experiences is not only determined by the properties of
the actual developmental state but also on the properties of
the environment.

We shall now examine which model of the theoretical initial
state of pattern development provides the most plausible description of the actual, empirical initial state.

It may be questioned whether a perceptual system provided
with a limited set of functional operators (e.g. comparing,
clustering and computing operators) is able to introduce new
operatory functions (e.g. economizing operators) on the basis
of ontogenetic adaptation (learning, experience, exercise,
etc.). Although the emergence of qualitatively different properties is a basic characteristic of any ontogenetic process,

the process of development itself must be based on a limited set of functional invariants. These functional invariants have emerged during a process of biological evolution whose principles - mutation and selection - are basically different from the principles that govern ontogeny. It may be questioned, therefore, whether the functional operators must be conceived of as structures that can be acquired during ontogeny or whether they constitute the functional invariants that underlie the actual development of pattern perception. Upon closer examination, the various functional operators appear to be based on two elementary functions, namely comparing and clustering. The comparing operators cluster adjacent data operators and compare them with regard to difference or identity; the clustering operators compare pairs of data operators and cluster them; the computing operators compare place properties of clustered data operators and cluster the places in terms of place formulas; and, finally, the economizing operators compare place formulas and cluster them according to higher-order resemblances. The elementary clustering and comparing functions (which should not be identified with the functional operators of the same name) constitute the functional invariants of the development of pattern perception.

From this it follows that the attribution of functional pattern operators to a perceptual system is concerned only with the quantitative complexity of the operations that the system is carrying out. From a qualitative point of view the various sorts of functional operators are implicitly present, or at least not alien to the system as soon as such a system contains at least one functional operator (i.e. if it minimally contains the comparing operator).

The initial state of pattern development can be characterized as the state in which the pattern operations are maximally simple. At this level, the various operatory functions are present, but their activities are so structurally simple that they cannot be distinguished from the activity of the lowest operator, namely the comparing operator. In addition to minimal operative capacity, the initial state of pattern development is characterized by a minimal degree of recursivity of the functional operators. If the operators were not qualitatively limited, but yet functioned at the lowest levels of the data operator structure (i.e. with a minimal level of recursivity), pattern perception would be limited to small local details of perceived space.

In the next section I shall discuss the empirical evidence on the development of pattern perception. I shall start with the most basic form, namely the perception of spatiotemporal patterns. Traditional accounts of pattern perception development begin with a discussion of static, geometric stimuli, followed by the perception of objects, and, finally, the perception of interactions between objects. The logic of this order, however, is not psychologically valid. Under normal circumstances, perception takes place during locomotion and action. Consequently, the most obvious sort of perceptual image is the event (e.g. perspective deformation, gradual occlusion and so forth).

6.2 THE DEVELOPMENT OF PATTERN AND FORM PERCEPTION

6.2.1 *Spatiotemporal patterns*
A spatiotemporal pattern can be defined as a structure of changing places in space. The co-ordinates that determine the distribution of these places are spatial and temporal. In general, two types of spatiotemporal patterns can be distinguished. The first type consists of the effect of ego movement on the properties of the perceptual image and is represented by the various sorts of motion-disparity effects which have been extensively studied by James J. Gibson. According to Gibson, the main cause of our perception of static and constant objects is not a static stimulus display but a specific pattern of stimulus changes connected with a specific pattern of ego movement, such as walking, head-turning and so forth. The second type of spatiotemporal patterns consists of 'object'-event patterns, i.e. events situated in the object-world and carried out by the objects themselves. The most obvious examples of spatiotemporal patterns are auditory events such as speech and music.

In visual perception, too, spatiotemporal patterns are numerous and of central importance. Rolling movements, the movement of a pendulum, the various movement types of the human body, such as running, walking or dancing, are only a few examples. Johansson in particular, has studied the perception of motion patterns in a long series of investigations that started in 1950 (Johansson, 1950, 1964, 1973, 1974, 1976, 1977). Johansson's experiments, besides many others, have shown that the perception of spatiotemporal patterns proceeds according to the same type of structuring rules that are known with spatial patterns. The perceptual apparatus tries to find the basic, invariant components of the temporal place changes and determines which of them will function as a reference component for the others. Johansson has called it the process of perceptual vector analysis (see also Kalveram and Ritter, 1979). The most striking illustration of the power of vector analysis processes in perception are the experiments on the perception of biological motion.

Much research has also been carried out with simple mechanical motion-patterns, for instance two dots moving along a perpendicular path (see Figure 6.7). Restle (1979) has shown that Leeuwenberg's coding theory is able to explain the process of vector analysis necessary for motion perception. Earlier, I have tried to show that the principles of movement perception can also be dealt with by the 'geometrical' theory of pattern perception that has been applied throughout our discussion of perceptual development (see Van Geert, 1975).

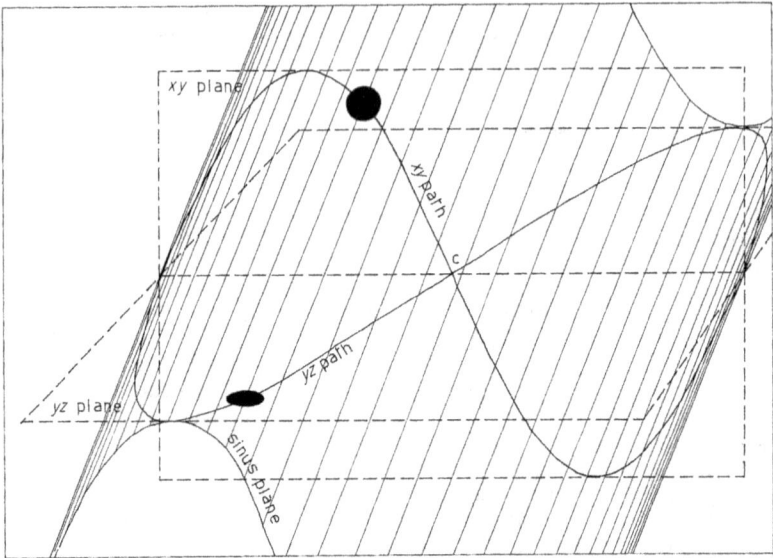

Figure 6.7 A spatiotemporal representation of two dots moving along a perpendicular path. Physically, the *xy* path occurs on the *xy* plane, while the *yz* path occurs on the *yz* plane. In the perceptual presentation, however, both paths occur on one common sinus-plane. The subject sees two dots that move towards and away from each other. The sinus-plane represents the common movement of the pair of dots, namely an oblique movement towards and away from the central point (c)

There is a class of interaction patterns that may be considered of great importance for the cognitive domain, namely the causal interactions and the interactions between objects that result in partial or complete visual occlusion of one of the interacting objects. This kind of interaction has been studied by Michotte and his collaborators (see for instance Michotte, 1946, 1962). According to Michotte, causality is a perceptual phenomenon. When a pattern of movements responds to a number of very precise stimulus requirements, it is seen inevitably as a causal interaction.

Another type of cognitively important pattern of movement is concerned with the principle of object permanence. The progressive occlusion of an object that is moving behind another object that acts as a screen can be studied as a particular movement pattern that is completely different from the spatiotemporal pattern that accompanies the real vanishing of an object. The principle of permanent existence of objects disappearing behind a screen, therefore, is rooted in the perceptual properties of occlusion patterns and may not be considered a genuinely cognitive discovery (a point of discussion between Michotte and Piaget).

The classical topics of auditory pattern studies are speech and music (see for instance Roederer, 1975). Besides, simple tone patterns are used to study fundamental mechanisms of auditory pattern perception, such as temporal grouping.

In this section I shall discuss only the perception of object motion. The perception of ego-movement effects has been dealt with in the section on constancy (Chapter 3, section 3.3). Before dealing with the various sorts of spatiotemporal patterns, we shall examine whether and how the effects of object movement play a role in the early perceptual activity of the infant.

It is a well-known fact that movement quickly elicits the interest of an infant. More recently, a number of studies have shown that movement can exercise a facilitating influence upon the perception of spatial patterns in infants. Goren et al. (1975) showed that newborn babies can discriminate between a normal and a scrambled face-pattern only when the patterns are moving. Girton (1979) investigated the externality effect with patterns in which internal elements were moving. The externality effect implies that five week old infants are able to scan the external boundaries of a compound form and are unable to scan internal elements (they scan the contour of a face but are unable to scan the eyes, for instance). Girton found that this particular limitation of the infants' perceptual abilities did not occur with moving internal elements. A comparable result has been obtained by Bushnell (1979).

An experiment by Rose et al. (1977) has provided evidence for the fact that neonates are able to observe internal figural detail when the figure, a model of a face for instance, moves and when visual following is employed as a discrimination criterion.

One of the main developmental questions concerns the amount of spatial and temporal variability the neonate can process. The perception of spatiotemporal patterns requires a process of abstracting information from temporal changes within space. It is plausible that such a process is limited by a specific level of complexity. Bower (1974) assumed that the infant is not capable of perceiving spatial (i.e. form) equivalences between a moving and a stationary object: when an object sets into motion, it turns into a completely new one. This assumption implies a rather severe restriction on the infant's perceptual abstracting capacities (see for instance Bower, 1971).

Experiments carried out by Hartlep and Forsyth (1977) and Burnham and Day (1979), however, indicate that ten-week-old infants are able to abstract spatial pattern information from moving objects. Hartlep and Forsyth used an operant technique to train a preference response to either the sphere or the cube in a simultaneously presented stationary cube-and-sphere pair. During the test trials, the effects of this preference training technique were tested with a stationary and a moving cube-and-sphere pair. The results showed that preference obtained with stationary objects generalized to moving objects (the cube and sphere described separate circular paths). Preference generalization is possible only when the child is able to identify the moving objects either as a sphere or a cube. Although it is possible that comparable operant training effects are obtained in natural situations (think about the mother's face, for instance, or noise-making toys suspended in the infant's cradle), it is rather implausible to assume that the training takes place with stationary objects and is generalized to moving ones. It seems rather the other way round: the mother's face is more interesting and more easily discriminated when it moves, the toys in the cradle make a noise when they are shaken or swung.

We might question, however, whether the perception of identity between stationary and moving objects either occurs as a result of learning or is an 'inbuilt' property of perception. Burnham and Day (1979) carried out an experiment based on the habituation technique. They tried to establish whether infants in the age-range eight to fourteen and fourteen to twenty weeks can detect the colour of stationary and moving objects and maintain this discrimination over changes in velocity. Since their generalization measure, colour, is quite simple, their experiment, unlike Hartlep and Forsyth's, cannot give information about the ratio between the spatiotemporal variability of the stimulus situation and the complexity of the spatial pattern that may be abstracted from it. Burnham and Day are only concerned with the question of whether the child abstracts anything other than velocity features from a moving-object stimulus. The infants were familiarized with either a green or a red cross. One group of infants was familiarized with the stationary, the other with the rotating figure. The attention-recovery measures obtained during the test trials showed that even the youngest subjects were able to detect colour change and colour equivalence during changes from a stationary into moving stimulus and velocity changes. These results indicate that even with spontaneous attention, the infant between eight and twenty weeks is able to differentiate motion from object properties when both are simultaneously present in a spatio-temporal stimulus. We may conclude that motion, which is predominant in infant perception, plays a facilitating role in isolating objects and object properties from their background.

We shall now examine whether infants are capable of discriminating motion patterns of objects, and, if so, whether these discriminative abilities provide information about the nature of the early motion-pattern mechanism.

Two experiments carried out by Gyr and collaborators (Gyr et al., 1973, 1974) show that children of between one and three years are able to discriminate various transformation patterns of a geometrical form, such as contraction, expansion, rotation and so forth. Unfortunately, the subjects are too old for the experiment to be decisive with regard to the initial properties of the motion perception mechanism. Two more recent experiments

have shed light on earlier motion-pattern perception abilities.
Gibson et al. (1978) habituated five month old children to
three types of visually presented rigid motion. By varying the
rigid motions, such as rotation around the vertical or the horizontal axis, during one habituation series, the infants were
habituated to the rigidity of the motion and not to a particular
type of rigid motion. During the test sessions, the infants were
either presented with a fourth rigid motion or with a deformation (a squeezing of the object). The stimulus difference between rigid motion and deformation is that with rigid motion the
spatial interrelationships between the surface features of the
objects (black dots) do not change whereas they do change
during the deformation. It was found that recovery of attention
during the test trials was significantly greater for the infants
viewing a deformation than for the additional rigid-motion
group. Unfortunately, it is not clear from the description
whether the object in the deformation trial also underwent a
change of size. The latter is quite plausible, since the investigators carried out a 'squeezing' deformation. The attention
recovery of the deformation group, therefore, might be explained
by the fact that the deformation, in contrast to the additional rigid motion, was accompanied by a specific size-reduction.

It is clear that the current state of the experimental data
does not allow us to clarify the properties of motion-pattern
perception at the actual initial state of development. It is quite
probable that further investigations will strengthen the assumption that neonates or at least very young children are capable
of perceiving spatiotemporal organization in the form of motion
patterns. Some of the theoretically relevant questions that
deserve further study are the following. What is the earliest
age, for instance, at which discrimination of minimally complex
motion-patterns, such as left to right or upward-downward
movements, is possible? A second question concerns the infant's
ability to perceive biological motion, such as walking, running
or climbing patterns, in a relatively abstracted form (for instance as dot patterns). It may be investigated, for instance,
whether the infant is able to discern biological dot patterns,
such as in Johansson's experiments, from randomly moving
dot patterns of the same complexity and spatiotemporal extension.

A particular class of motion pattern that is of great cognitive
importance consists of interaction patterns between objects.
An interaction pattern may be defined as a set of motion patterns that are co-ordinated in a particular way. When I open
the cover of a box, for instance, the motion pattern of my
hand and arm are specifically related to the motion pattern of
the cover. I mentioned before that the basic research in the
field of interaction perception has been carried out by Michotte
and his collaborators. Michotte's basic interests lay in showing
that a number of cognitive categories, such as 'causality',
'permanence', 'tool' or 'goal', were determined by specific

perceptual-pattern properties. A causal interaction, for instance, must not be inferred but is seen immediately. It is very
important, however, to make a distinction between a causality
percept and a causality concept, i.e. between a perceptual and
a conceptual definition of causality. The perceptual definition
concerns the ability to perceive causal situations in a way
described by Michotte. The conceptual definition can be exemplified by means of a description of the situation, for instance
in terms of a simple theory of mechanics. It is clear that the
conceptual form does not emerge together with the perceptual
form (see also Part III for further discussion).

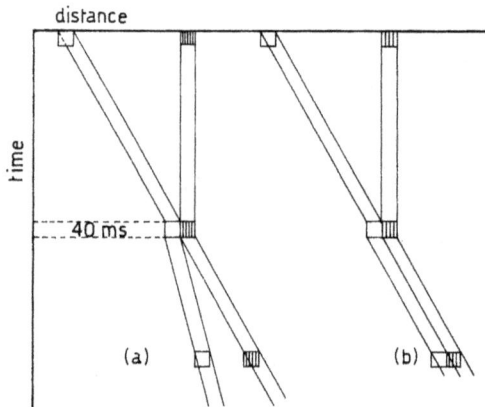

Figure 6.8 A spatiotemporal diagram of two Michottean causal
situations. In (a) the white block launches the striped block:
in (b) the white block pushes the striped block. In order to
achieve an optimal impression of causality, the blocks should
remain immobile for a period of about 40 milliseconds after
touching

The classical investigations by Piaget (1927, 1937) and more
recently by Olum (1956, 1958) and Lesser (1974, 1977) have
shown that children's reactions to Michotte's situations deviate
considerably from adult reactions. Young children do not seem
to see them in a causal way. It is a question of perceptual
development, however, whether children perceive the situations
in the same pattern-like way as do adults. That is, if adults
specify the Michottean situations perceptually by means of a
spatiotemporal place formula 'C", do children, then, apply the
same formula? This question is completely independent of the
question of whether they both conceptualize the situation in
causal terms.
    Leslie (1982) investigated whether infants are able to dis-
criminate causal from non-causal interaction situations. The
infants involved in the experiment were four, five and eight

months respectively. The subjects were habituated to either
a causal Michottean film of a launching situation or a Michottean
non-causal situation. Leslie's dishabituation situations were
non-causal (see Figure 6.9).

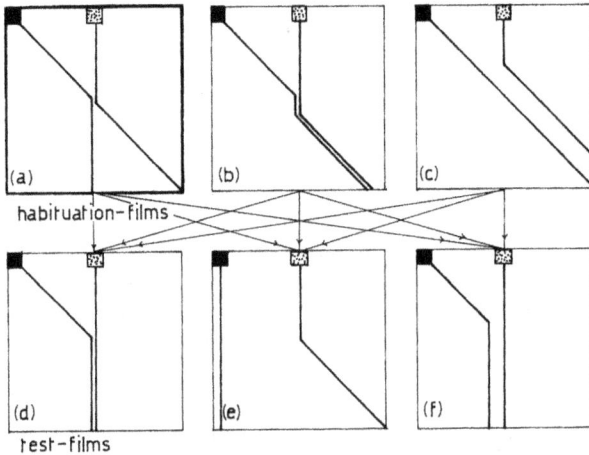

Figure 6.9 Leslie's experiment on the perception of causality in
infancy. Infants are familiarized with one of the three habituation films ((a), (b) or (c)). Then, they are presented with one
of the test films ((d), (e) or (f)). Only film (a) shows a causal
interaction. It is expected that, if the infants are able to perceive the causal character of the interaction in (a), only the
group of infants habituated to the (a) film should show considerable recovery of attention during the testing stage. The (b)
and (c) groups of infants are presented with non-causal situations. The (b) and (c) group should not show recovery of
attention during one of the test films, since the test films show
non-causal interactions

    The attention recovery during the test trials can be explained
by two experimental parameters. Firstly, dishabituation can
be explained on the grounds of order reversal. The infant has
registrated that, in the given pair of objects, always the left
object starts. In order to see that the reverse is the case in
the test film, the infant must notice the spatial reversal of the
familiarized temporal order of movement. Secondly, attention
recovery is significantly greater for the group that was habituated to the causal situation and received a non-causal situation in the test trial. It may be concluded that the difference
between perceived causal and non-causal situations is a second
parameter that determines experimental dishabituation with
four-and-a-half-month-olds.
    The central question is how to explain this discriminative

ability: do the infants perceive causality and therefore distinguish perceptually the causal from the non-causal situation,
or do the infants simply distinguish both situations perceptually
without attributing a predicate 'causality'? In his article, Leslie
discusses the adequacy of a pictorial explanation of the test
results, i.e. an explanation based on perceptual differences
alone. He shows that a spatiotemporal, pictorial representation
of these situations cannot account for the experimental outcome.
If a pictorial representation of causal situations is employed,
however, it must structurally resemble the kind of perceptual
representation the perceiver himself applies.

In accordance with Michotte's and Johansson's investigations,
it may be stated that causal situations are represented in terms
of a motion vector (or vector system) that is inferred from the
actual properties of the movements of the blocks that are involved. In a typical causal situation, the 'dependent' block is
taking over the motion pattern (speed and direction) of the
active, causing block. Michotte has called this particular property 'ampliation' (see Figure 6.8 for an illustration). It is
plausible that causal and non-causal situations are distinguished
on the basis of the same perceptual vector-analysis processes
as those that explain the perception of motion patterns, either
mechanical or biological, which were studied by Johansson. If
this 'higher-order' explanation of causality perception is
accepted, it explains as much of the experimental results as
does a non-perceptual, propositional explanation such as Alan
Leslie employs. The definite choice between a perceptual or
propositional explanation of the infant's experimental behaviour
cannot be decided on the grounds of the empirical evidence
alone, but must be evaluated in a larger framework of arguments. Such a discussion will be presented in Part III of the
book.

The Michottean causal situation may be conceived of as the
prototype of an action. An agent (the causing block) is exer-
cising an action (pushing, launching) upon a recipient that
causes a change in the recipient's present state (the recipient
is pushed or launched). Many theories of early language acquisition have stated that the learning of language, notably its
grammatical or syntactic aspects, is based on prelinguistic
knowledge of concepts such as 'agent', 'action' and 'recipient'.
I shall deal with these theories in Part III of the book. In this
chapter we have seen that the perceptual basis for distinguishing the concepts of action, agent and recipient is present in
infancy. Besides the distinction between causal and non-causal
situations, infants must also be able to make a distinction between the constituents of causal situations, for instance, the
different roles played by the objects involved.

In Leslie's experiment the effect of order-reversal is already
an indicator of the fact that infants can make a distinction
between the normal initiator and the normal 'follower' of the
action. More detailed evidence has been sought by Golinkoff

in two experiments on the semantic development of infants
(Golinkoff, 1975; Golinkoff and Kerr, 1978). In the first experiment, subjects of fourteen and eighteen months of age had to
watch short films showing an action sequence. The results of
the experiment suggested that the subjects might have been
able to distinguish action initiation from recipience. In a second
experiment (Golinkoff and Kerr, 1978) a more sensitive method
was used, namely habituation, with heart rate deceleration and
visual fixation time as indicators. Moreover, the hypothesis
contained two distinct predictions: first, that infants can perceive action-role reversals regardless of the direction of the
action (pushing from left to right instead of the other way
round, for instance); second, that anomalous reversals (chair
pushes man after habituation to man pushes chair) would
receive more attention recovery than normal reversals (man y
pushes man x instead of x pushes y). The subjects were infants
between the ages of fifteen and eighteen months. The results
supported the first but not the second hypothesis: either
anomalous reversals do not puzzle the infants any more than do
normal reversals or the indicators, fixation time and heart rate
deceleration, are not sufficiently sensitive.

Unfortunately, the experiment did not make a distinction between causal and non-causal situations. In a non-causal situation where the recipient sets into motion before being touched,
for instance, we cannot speak about action-role reversal but
simply about movement-initiator reversal, since the reversal
concerns only which object starts moving first. Nothing can be
concluded, therefore, with regard to the perceptual differentiation between agent and recipient.

A second cognitively important type of interaction pattern is
that concerned with permanence. We have seen that Michotte
has shown that the conditions of permanence are perceptually
determined and unambiguous. Starting with Piaget's classical
work on the development of the object concept (Piaget, 1937)
a great number of investigations have been carried out to
determine how the child reaches the understanding of the object
concept. In these experiments, a similar difficulty to that found
with the causality experiments may arise, namely a rather
confused theoretical mixture of a perceptual and conceptual
approach. This research on permanence and the discovery of
the object concept will be discussed in Part III of the book.

A particular type of spatiotemporal pattern consists of auditory patterns. The nature of the auditory stimulus itself,
namely the fact that it is constituted by complex wave patterns,
makes the use of the temporal axis inevitable. Auditory space
may be conceived of as the overall stimulus domain within which
perceivable auditory changes are possible (except for place
changes of the sound source in distal space). This space consists of co-ordinate axes such as pitch and loudness. Sound
patterns of speech constitute an important class of auditory
pattern. It is a well-known fact that children and adults have

a tremendous capacity for distinguishing and remembering complex speech sounds. Another typical example of complex auditory patterns is music.

Several investigations have shown that newborn children orient to sounds (Wertheimer, 1961; Muir and Field, 1979; Field et al., 1979, 1980). Neonates are also able to discriminate between auditive patterns (Miller, 1975; Lester, 1975; Wormith et al., 1975).

Infants between one and two months can discriminate speech sounds such as (a) and (e) (see for instance Trehub, 1973; Williams and Golenski, 1978). Infants between two and three months not only discriminate vowels but also consonants. They are able to perceive the difference between syllables that differ in only one of the consonants (Eimas, 1975; Fodor et al., 1975; Juszyk, 1977).

Phonemes constitute the intra-linguistic variability of a language, whereas the pattern of phonemes constitutes its inter-linguistic variability (the phoneme pattern of English is different from Dutch, for instance). Spoken language is also characterized by inter-individual variability. Due to the particular structure and use of the articulatory apparatus, every man is characterized by a specific voice, i.e. a specific quality of the produced speech sounds.

Like the human face, the voice is a socially and biologically important kind of pattern. The ability to recognize voices and faces of people may be responsible for the earliest social and cognitive structuring of the environment of the infant. Voices and faces are otherwise characterized by extreme complexity and variability. Probably, the typical character of a voice is not explained by a number of 'stationary' parameters, such as a fixed intensity for instance, but rather by temporally variable parameters, such as a particular pattern of intensity changes. Likewise, the face is characterized by a typical changeability, due to the complex mobility of the facial muscles.

Research by Friedlander (1970) has shown that nine months old infants can distinguish their mother's from an unfamiliar voice. Bartholomeus (1973) showed that some nursery-school children were almost as good as their teachers in identifying the voices of their class-mates. These results suggest that the development of voice perception reaches the final state at a rather early age (it is clear that the adequate perception of voices is conditional for adequate recognition). According to Mann et al. (1979), however, a significant difference exists between recognition of familiar and unfamiliar voices. The investigators worked with subjects between six and sixteen years old and with adults. The subjects were offered series of spoken sentences consisting of one or two inspection sentences and two or four recognition sentences respectively. The subjects had to tell which of the recognition sentences was uttered by the person(s) who had produced the inspection sentence(s). Mann et al. found that recognition ability increases

considerably until the age of ten, when recognition ability closely approaches the adult level. Between ages ten to thirteen,
however, performance declines markedly. From thirteen years
on, performance levels increase towards adult level. Almost
identical results were obtained with face-recognition experiments. The authors conclude that such a common developmental
course might point towards identical mechanisms underlying
both voice and face recognition development.

It may be questioned how far Mann and his co-workers'
recognition experiments are relevant with regard to the perceptual abilities of their subjects. Is the increasing recognition
level attributable to increasing perceptual abilities or to increasing storage abilities? It is probable that the youngest group is
unable to store all the information they might have distinguished
with the voice being present.

Formally, a resemblance exists between musical and speech
perception with respect to the role played by a framework of
tones and speech sounds. In music, tonal structures are perceived against the background of a musical scale. In speech
perception this background is provided by the phonemes of the
perceiver's particular language. In principle, the acoustical
boundaries between different speech sounds are inexistent. A
language, however, operates with a number of speech-sound
prototypes, which constitute the phonemes, i.e. the acoustic
building blocks of the language. It is quite probable that
adults and older children, who have acquired the particular
phonemic system of their language, will perceive speech sounds
in a different, more prototypical way than infants who have got
less experience with language. According to Trehub (1976)
prelinguistic infants, lacking the acoustic category system of
a particular language, will more easily discriminate the typical
sound contrasts of various languages, because their perception
is still 'acoustical' and not 'phonemical'. In fact, it is found that
some sound contrasts are, whereas others are not, discriminated
in the 'phonemic' way by prelinguistic infants (Swoboda et al.,
1976; Juszyck et al., 1977; Eilers et al., 1979). Actually, pre-
linguistic infants might lack production experience with a
language but they certainly do not lack receptive experience
(unless they have extremely taciturn parents). It is quite
improbable, therefore, that prelinguistic infants are still in a
'natural state' as far as their speech perception is concerned.

In contrast with speech perception, the development of musical pattern perception is relatively unknown. According to
Dowling (1978) adult perception of melodies is the product of
two kinds of underlying schemata: first, musical contour, which
is the pattern of ups and downs; and second, musical scale,
which is a framework of tone intervals (the C-scale or F-scale,
for instance). The perception of musical patterns in a framework
of tones may be compared with the perception of speech sounds
in the phonemic framework of language. It may be expected
that the development of musical perception will tend towards

increasing categorization (i.e. reduction to patterns fitting the framework) as the child becomes better acquainted with the system of musical scale and the musical habits and preferences of his environment.

The basic ability underlying musical perception, namely the discrimination of tone sequences, is present at an early stage of life. Kinney and Kagan (1976), for instance, have shown that infants of seven-and-a-half months are able to discriminate between auditory patterns comprising different tones. Chang and Trehub (1977a) habituated five month old infants to short melodies. The attention recovery measures showed that these infants were able to recognize transpositions of these melodies.

The construction of prototypes is a typical property of pattern recognition in general. Williams and Aiken (1975), for instance, showed that prototype construction also appears in tone pattern perception and that it is relatively age-independent.

The categorical perception of musical patterns depends on the acquisition of the musical-scale patterns. Since experience with music is a necessary condition, this categorical perception of music will not appear early in life. Dowling (1978) cites a number of experimental investigations which show that at the age of eight years musical scales are employed in the same way as the phonemic system is employed in speech-sound perception. It is probable that at the age of five musical scales do not yet play a role in perception (see for instance Imberty, 1969; Zenatti, 1969).

From the experiments, it may be concluded that the perception of spatiotemporal patterns is either an inbuilt or at least a very early emerging property of perception. In order to arrive at more specific conclusions, however, the investigators should solve a number of very difficult methodological problems, particularly those that are concerned with the investigation of very young subjects. One of the most striking gaps in our knowledge concerns the patterns that are socially or biologically relevant, for instance the visual form of human motion and the pattern of the expressive face.

6.2.2 Temporal patterns
Temporal patterns may be characterized without reference to spatial or other qualitative dimensions. A typical example of a temporal pattern is rhythm in music. This example makes clear that a temporal pattern may be characterized by the same kind of hierarchical structuring as spatial and spatiotemporal patterns. A simple 1/1 march rhythm, for instance, may be recognized as the underlying structure in a $\frac{1}{2}.\frac{1}{2}/\frac{1}{2}.\frac{1}{2}$ or $\frac{1}{2}.\frac{1}{2}/1$ pattern. Despite its importance in adult perception, little is known about the development of temporal pattern perception.

Chang and Trehub (1977b) investigated the perception of temporal grouping in auditory patterns with infants of four-and-a-half and five-and-a-half months. Their subjects were habituated to a six-tone stimulus with a 2/4 grouping. Attention recovery was measured by heart rate deceleration. Significant attention-recovery during the testing stage showed that the infants were able to discriminate a 4-2 from a 2-4 grouping of elements along the temporal axis.

Allen et al. (1977) showed that infants of seven months are capable of intersensory perception of temporal sequences. Two groups of infants were habituated to a standard auditory or visual sequence, consisting of pure tones or flashes of light of equal duration, separated by pauses of different length. During the test trials infants were presented with a new temporal sequence in the same or in a different modality. The results showed that infants discriminated between temporal sequences, independent of the sensory modality in which the different sequences were presented.

6.2.3 Spatial patterns
Spatial patterns can be described entirely by using only spatial co-ordinates, in addition to a number of qualitative co-ordinates which belong to a specific sensory mode, such as brightness and colour for the visual mode and pressure intensity for the tactile mode. Most of the research on spatial pattern perception is based on patterns with the following properties: they are visual; they have a geometrical and two-dimensional form; they are presented in the fronto-parallel plane to an immobile observer. The experiments on pattern perception and its development reflect our historically achieved preoccupation with reduced two-dimensional forms. A considerable part of the visual information in which we are interested has been abstracted and projected onto the page of a book, a sheet of paper or a screen. From this point of view the use of impoverished flat stimuli in most of our experiments is something more than a reflection of the experimental reduction of irrelevant situational aspects and variables. It also reflects a particular 'Gutenbergean' academic bias towards perception.

The experimental investigation of pattern perception development has focused primarily on a number of classical themes, such as the discrimination of simple geometric stimuli by very young infants, the perception of the facial scheme (without either depth or movement) and the discrimination of letter forms. Recently, more emphases have become placed on the higher-order or structural aspects of spatial patterns. Higher-order aspects concern properties of spatial forms that can be situated at the 'higher' levels of the pattern perception process, for instance where the form-properties are 'abstracted' from the colour- and size-properties of the observer's object.

Our discussion of the current research will be organized around three main themes. The first is concerned with the properties of the initial state, i.e. the neonate's perception of spatial patterns. The second theme centres on the increasing complexity of the pattern-processing abilities during perceptual development. We shall discuss the child's growing ability to

detect higher-order variables of patterns and the construction
of perceptual schemes and prototypes. The third theme will be
an illustration of the abstracting and constructing properties
of the developing pattern-perception process applied to a
socially and biologically relevant pattern, namely the human
face.

6.2.3.1 Properties of the initial state   In section 6.1.2 I
discussed a number of possible properties of the initial state
of pattern perception. The question that I want to explore now
is which of these theoretical properties are also characteristic
for the empirical initial state, which I shall - artificially - limit
to the first month of life.

Before discussing a sample of the many experimental investigations that have been carried out with neonates and children
in the first month of life, I wish to mention some methodological
problems which are closely related to the question we are trying
to solve. The first problem concerns the lag between 'competence' and 'performance'. It is possible that the perceptual
system of the neonate is provided with the various pattern
processes (competence), whereas the expression of this competence is limited either by considerable quantitative limits
(the amount of information that can be dealt with in the various
processes) or by limitations imposed by supportive functions,
such as memory. A further possibility is that some of the processes (for instance the processes carried out by the economizing and the testing operators) might require a minimum level of
pattern complexity in order to be applicable. It is probable that
this minimum level cannot be achieved by the more basic processes, and therefore the question of whether or not the more
complex processes are potentially present at birth cannot be
answered.

The second problem is concerned with the difficulty of finding a reliable observable criterion for the presence of the pattern processes. Since both the behaviour and the ability of
neonates to respond are minimal, the main behavioural index
of discrimination which has been employed is selective attention
expressed by different fixation times between two or more
simultaneously presented stimuli, recovery of fixation times
after habituation, heart rate decrement, selective fixation or
scanning of particular parts of the total stimulus, bodily
orienting reactions, reaching for objects and so forth.

The neonate, provided that he is born at full term, shows
a distinctive pattern of selective attention. Attentiveness is
determined mainly by quantitative pattern-properties, such as
size (the bigger the pattern, the more it is preferred) (Fantz
and Fagan, 1976). With patterns of equal size, presented
simultaneously, the child prefers the pattern with the highest
number of elements (Miranda and Fantz, 1971). Brennan et al.
(1966) showed that the preferred number of pattern elements
is an optimum, not a maximum. They investigated the preference

of three, eight and fourteen week old babies to checkerboards of variable consistency (2 x 2, 8 x 8, 24 x 24). The results indicated that the youngest infants preferred the smallest number of elements, whereas the older infants preferred the intermediate number. Number of patterns, however, is not the only determiner of the neonate's selective attention. When presented with patterns of horizontal and vertical stripes, babies show preference for a particular, optimal number of constituent stripes and not necessarily for the pattern with the highest number of stripes (Slater and Sykes, 1977). Other non-quantitative determiners are: curved rather than straight lines (Fantz and Miranda, 1975) and orientation with horizontal patterns being preferred to vertical lines (Slater and Sykes, 1977). This latter finding corresponds with data obtained by Kessen et al. (1972) about the neonate's preference for horizontal over vertical boundaries in pattern-scanning. Neonates prefer high figure-ground contrasts (Rose et al., 1977) and sharp figural boundaries (Fantz et al., 1975). The latter authors have given the name 'pattern definition' to properties such as contrast and sharpness. In general, it may be stated that the amount of pattern definition is directly related to attention. Pattern definition is also related to another strictly quantitative property of patterns, namely the total amount of light falling on a pattern display. McGarvil and Karmel (1976) have shown that neonates prefer well-lit patterns (see Figure 6.10).

When scanning geometrical figures, neonates, as well as one month old infants, tend to focus upon only one feature of the pattern, such as an angle (Salapatek and Kessen, 1973; Salapatek, 1975). Until the age of one month, infant's scanning is characterized by the externality effect, i.e. they scan the external boundary of a composite pattern (Salapatek, 1975; Milewski, 1976). We have seen, however (section 6.2.1), that such an externality effect can only occur with static patterns.

In general, habituation is not appropriate for investigating the perceptual capacities of neonates. This fact is largely due to the limits of the neonate's visual memory (Salapatek, 1975; Fantz et al., 1975). When the differences between the habituated and the new pattern are sufficiently large, however (a 2 x 2 and a 12 x 12 checkerboard, for instance), some newborn babies do show habituation and attention recovery during the test trials (Friedman et al., 1974).

Various investigations of newborn and slightly older infants' perception of colour have shown that its fundamental properties remain unchanged during development (Bornstein, 1975; Bornstein et al., 1976; Bornstein, 1976a and 1976b; Gaines, 1972; Gaines and Little, 1975; Glass et al., 1974; Bornstein, 1978; Jones-Molfese, 1977). These properties include the subjects' preference for highly saturated colours and categorical colour perception (perceiving the colour-circle in terms of a limited number of prototypical hues, such as red, yellow, blue instead of intermediary hues such as yellow-orange, green-blue, etc.).

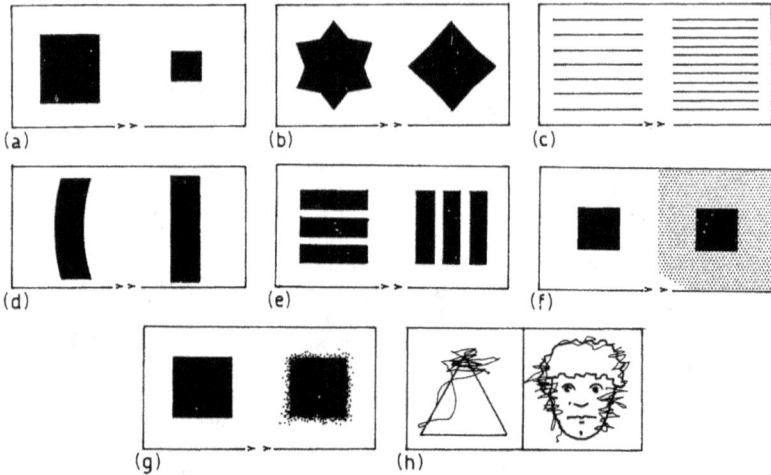

Figure 6.10 An illustration of preference principles in geo-metrical patterns. Determiners of preference are: size(a); total amount of contour(b); optimal textural gradient(c); curved versus straight(d); horizontal versus vertical(e); optimal figure ground contrast(f); sharpness of contour(g). During the initial stage of pattern development, children prefer to scan salient figural features and external boundary(h)

Our main concern is to explain the current data on neonate pattern-perception. According to Karmel (1974; Karmel and Maisel, 1975) the neonate and young infant's preferential atten-tion can be explained on the basis of the total amount of con-tour within a pattern (the sum of the contour-lengths of the various pattern constituents or elements). Total amount of contour summarizes lower-order quantitative properties such as size and number of pattern elements. Some of the previously cited experiments, however (Slater and Sykes, 1977, for instance), have shown that contour can be defined subjectively. Neonates prefer horizontal to vertical striped patterns, for instance. Since the magnitude of the neonate's eye movements proceeds along the horizontal axis, horizontal boundaries are more easily captured. Consequently, the horizontally striped patterns contain more perceivable contour for the infant than the other patterns, and this could explain their preferential status.

How far Karmel's contour-explanation can be related to the kind of question we are interested in, namely whether the various pattern-processes - clustering, comparing, computing,

and so forth - are present and operative at birth, is questionable. If contour is sufficient to capture an infant's attention,
then the perceptual system could operate with comparing and
clustering operators only (that is, provided that the actual
number of clustering operators involved plays a role in determining selective attention). The finding that curves are preferred to straight lines (Fantz and Miranda, 1975) shows, however, that neonates are sensitive to a minimal difference between
boundary distributions (i.e. form). However simple such a
discrimination may be, it does require computing operators
which are capable of 'computing' the difference between the
curved and the straight boundary. A straight and a curved
line can be discriminated by the fact that a straight line shows
a boundary with a constant direction, whereas a curved line
shows a constant direction-change. Properties such as direction
constancy and direction change are closely related to the simple
quantitative measures that the neonate child employs to distinguish between patterns.
    The existence of clear limits in the neonate's ability to dis-
criminate between patterns, i.e. in the activity of the computing
operators, may be inferred from the relative immaturity of his
fovea. Although peripheral discrimination of form is certainly
possible, even at the age of three months (Maurer and Lewis,
1979), the fovea plays a crucial role in pattern perception.
We might state that the fovea is the place where the pattern
perception operators are the most dense. According to Mann
(1964), the fovea or central retina (in contrast to the peripheral retina) is very immature at birth. This immaturity
explains part of the functioning of the neonate's visual apparatus (Kremenitzer et al. 1979). Since the fovea is supposed
to contain the most sophisticated pattern-perception abilities,
the infant's immature fovea might be responsible for the almost
complete lack of pattern discrimination on other than simply
quantitative grounds. Lewis et al. (1978), however, found that
newborns can detect simple lines by means of the central
retina. It can be concluded, therefore, that although the
immaturity of the central retina or fovea may exert a purely
physiological or maturational constraint upon the neonate's
pattern perception, it does not completely prevent the child
from detecting patterns. Moreover, since the peripheral retina
is structurally mature at birth and contains at least a minimal
number of pattern-processing abilities, the minimal sensory
conditions for pattern perception are fulfilled.
    The most important finding, however, is implied in the method
that is used to study the neonate's perceptual abilities, namely
the existence of selective attentivity. It is an extremely important fact that the neonate's gaze is not determined by completely
occasional factors, such as the eventual place and position of
the eyes and head. The infant is active in exploring the visual
field - as far as his postural and motor limitations allow him to -
and is provided with a number of 'criteria' that determine the

goal of his explorative and seeking behaviour.

According to Bornstein (1978) these criteria have a specific physiological form, namely the amount of neural excitation produced by a pattern or pattern property, such as colour. It is quite probable that selective attention plays an important role in perceptual development (see Chapter 7).

6.2.3.2 Developmental after the initial state: the perception of higher-order properties   The concept of higher-order properties is basic to our model of pattern perception, and in fact to any account of pattern perception that attributes a central role to the perceptual coding process. Patterns consisting of a texture (a triangle consisting of dots, for instance) are coded at higher levels of the process than the texture elements of which they consist. Before discussing any research, a number of underlying factors have to be clarified.

First, order and hierarchical relationship are properties of a processed pattern and cannot be used as a classification of the pattern itself, i.e. the distribution of places in space.

Second, a distinction must be made between processing patterns in terms of a hierarchy of levels on the one hand and isolating higher-order levels on the other. When the perceiver processes a triangle in terms of a triangular relationship between three connected constituent angles, it is not necessarily implied that triangularity will be isolated from the total pattern description. The investigator, however, can only decide about the existence of higher-order processes if the subject is able to generalize a response such as fixation time to a class of patterns that differ with regard to lower-order variables, but have a higher-order property in common.

Third, higher-order levels of pattern processing depend on the various types of functional operators. Clustering and computing operators are responsible for the processing of properties such as boundary, repetition and internal pattern structure, economy operators are responsible for properties such as orientation or continuation of partly-occluded forms, whereas testing operators investigate whether patterns fulfil particular internally-stored pattern formulas. It is clear that higher-order properties determined by the testing operators will occur later than higher-order properties inferred from the lower-order, proximal properties by the clustering and computing operators. It is impossible, therefore, to study the development of higher-order properties 'per se'.

Our discussion of the research will be divided into a number of current topics: isolation of higher-order variables (perceptual class or concept formation); isolating a form from its actual two- versus three-dimensional appearance; pattern structure determined by the testing operators; prototype formation; and regular differences between patterns.

At the beginning of the second month, the child's ability to process qualitative pattern properties gradually becomes manifest. One month old babies discriminate between triangular and cross-figures (Milewski and Siqueland, 1975). At the age of three months, qualitative differences come to dominate quantitative differences between patterns.

The results of preference research may be summarized as follows. Three month old babies prefer curved to straight lines, concentric to parallel lines, horizontal and vertical lines to diagonals, irregular and checkerboard distributions of squares to row- and column-distribution, texture gradient to uniformity, and angles to straight lines (Fantz et al., 1975; Ruff and Birch, 1974; Ruff, 1976; Ruff and Turkewitz, 1975; Bornstein, 1978).

An experiment by Cook et al. (1978) shows that the perception of higher-order variables must be distinguished from a form of quasi-abstraction which results from the immaturity of the perceptual system. With three month old infants the investigators found no evidence of discrimination between a cube and a wedge or truncated pyramid. On the other hand, the infants discriminated composite (an L-shape) from non-composite forms (a wedge, for instance). It is clear that their perceptual distinction between composite and non-composite forms is not based on higher-order abstraction but on the inability to provide adequate and complete perceptual formulas for different kinds of spatial forms.

Milewski (1979), however, showed that three month old infants are able to detect configurational invariance despite variation in size of the constituent dots. We know from selective attention research that three-month-olds are able to discriminate size, which allows us to conclude that Milewski's experimental subjects abstracted a higher-order property (the dot pattern) from a lower-order property (various sizes). We know also that size is a very attractive variable for three month old children. Therefore, the experimental results - abstraction of dot-pattern - could only be achieved because the experimenter cancelled the attractivity of size in an artificial way. We may conclude that higher-order abstraction does not lie beyond the perceptual competence of three-month-olds, although it will not or only very rarely occur in natural situations. At the age of one year, form has become the dominant perceptual dimension for the child. The children find a form discrimination task much easier to learn than a colour discrimination task, although colour might seem a more salient and simple feature than form (Casey, 1979).

One of the questions that have been investigated in the domain of higher-order perception of forms is whether children are able to perceive form-identities across dimensional changes (an object and its two-dimensional representation, for instance). At the age of one month, the infant is capable of discriminating two- from three-dimensional forms in general (Pipp and Haith, 1977). Rose (1977) has shown that at least at the age of six months, children are able to see the form resemblance between a three-dimensional object and its two-dimensional representation. This ability to abstract a form from its actual dimensional appearance is presumably common to all complex perceptual systems. Cabe (1976), for instance, has shown that pigeons are able to recognize the identity between two- and three-dimensional identical forms.

One of the main problems with higher-order variables is that they may be made arbitrarily complex and difficult. There is no such thing as a single 'higher-order level' connected with a specific level of perceptual complexity. This difficulty was demonstrated in an experiment carried out by Ruff (1978). Ruff investigated whether six-to-nine month old infants are able to extract invariable form from a number of objects varying in size, colour and orientation. The results suggest that form detection depends largely upon the particular form that has to be extracted (see Figure 6.11).

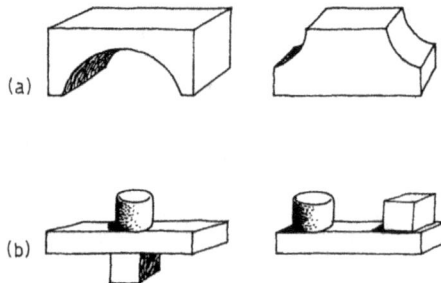

Figure 6.11 Objects employed in the experiment on discrimination of higher order features by Ruff (1978). Objects of type (a) are more difficult to discriminate than type (b) objects. The experiment shows that the complexity of higher order variables depends on the figural characteristics of the objects that are employed

Hopkins et al. (1976) demonstrated another form of categorical or 'classificatory' form perception, based on the detection of higher-order properties of patterns. They habituated ten month old infants either to a series of different straight lines or to a series of different curved lines. Attention recovery in the first group was tested with a curved line, in the second group with a straight line. The results showed that attention recovery was higher in the first than in the second group. That is, a curved line differs more from a set of straight lines than does a straight line from a set of curved lines. With curved lines as a reference set, a straight line may be described as a zero-curved line (measuring 0 degrees of arc). With straight lines as a reference set, however, a curved line is simply another type of line.

Cohen and Strauss (1979) have studied higher-order perception at the age between four-and-a-half and seven-and-a-half months, using pictures of faces. The oldest group showed a high level of perceptual categorization. This experiment will be discussed in more detail when we deal with the perception of the human face.

The investigation of Hopkins et al. (1976) is closely related to the experiments concerned with the perception of forms by means of prototypes. When we observe objects or events, we do not only registrate their individual properties but also their family resemblances with other objects and events. The traditional view on this form of perceptual classification is that it is based upon the detection of a number of common, relatively independent features. According to the competing point of view, a class - the class of birds, for instance - is represented by a prototype - a relatively unspecific singing bird, for instance, such as a blackbird. The extension of the class is determined by a rule of permitted maximal deviation from the prototype. Prototypical representatives play a considerable role in the use of names of objects, actions, properties and so forth (Rosch, 1973; Smith et al., 1974).

A number of experiments have shown that perceptual classification also employs prototypical representatives. The experiments carried out by Hopkins et al. (1976) and Cohen and Strauss (1979) suggest that prototype formation may be operative before the end of the first year of life. The evidence does not, however, discriminate between a feature and a prototype explanation. Williams et al. (1977) employed geometrical non-sense stimuli in a study with three-, four- and five-year-olds. The results suggest that the ability to use single features develops prior to the ability to use a feature list or prototype and that both distinctive features and prototypes are important. In another study, Williams and Aiken (1977) investigated whether prototypes could be used across sensory modalities (auditory and visual). They showed that eight and twelve year old as well as adult subjects mainly employed a-specific (modality independent) prototypes in the same way. Most of the experiments on perceptual prototype-construction have shown that there is little development after the age of five to six years (Lasky, 1974; Aiken and Williams, 1973; Posnansky and Neumann, 1976).

A particular type of higher-order variable consists of the aspect 'regular difference'. Gaines has studied the ability of young children to detect regular changes in matrices of elements. In such a matrix, two dimensions may vary simultaneously, for instance 'growing smaller' along the horizontal dimension and 'growing bigger' along the vertical dimension. Gaines (1973, 1977) showed that children as young as four years old are able to detect where the order of the matrix has been (artificially) changed, which indicates that the children have discovered the simultaneous principles of variation (see Figure 6.12).

The perception of higher-order variables may be formally attributed to the computing and economizing operators. The way in which the computing operators specify the spatial distri-

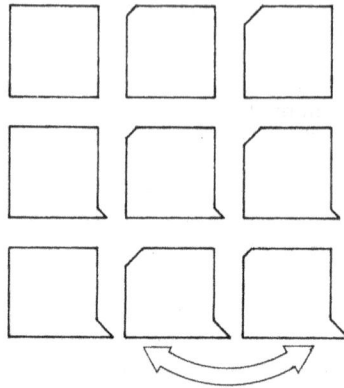

Figure 6.12 An example of Gaines's matrix problems (Gaines, 1973, 1977). Children from four years on are able to discover which polygons have changed places

bution of places that constitutes a pattern is directed by the economizing operators. The latter are responsible for 'cutting of' pattern properties that are determined by accidental factors or properties that make the pattern too complex and specific. In the experiment by Gibson et al. (1978), where children were shown rigid and deforming action patterns, the perceptual specification of the exact inter-dot distances or the precise number of the dots would make the pattern too specific. The economy operators compare the pattern with patterns that were presented previously during the habituation session, and decide how much of the low-level information must be cut off in order to make the series of patterns processable. It is important to note that the operator description is not meant as a description of the course of the perceptual process but as a specification of the functional aspects of such a process.

It might be questioned whether there is evidence for the development of the testing operators. In general, the testing operators are responsible for testing whether a specific proximal stimulus corresponds with an internally stored structural formula of a pattern. In section 6.1.1 we have seen that this activity requires a certain amount of ambiguity in the proximal stimulus. Ambiguity implies that the proximal stimulus can be assigned more than one 'deep structure' specification, i.e. that it forms the basis for more than one distal stimulus. The majority of spatiotemporal proximal stimuli in the normal environment, contain information that is so specific that it is compatible with one pattern-specification or 'deep structure' only. The testing operators, however, might play a role in masking and selecting a large part of the incoming information. Generally, the proximal stimulus is overburdened with information. An active, selective attitude, expressed by the testing operators, is required in order to reduce the perceptual environment to relevant foci. Selective attention, for instance, might be a very early expression of testing operativity. Selective attention means that the perceiver seeks patterns with particular quantitative and qualitative properties. During the initial state of pattern development, these properties are very simple and rudimentary.

A plausible indicator of more complex testing operations is the habituation phenomenon. The fact that looking time decreases after repeated exposure might be due to the fact that the testing operators test whether the new pattern equals the familiarized pattern that has been stored in perceptual memory. It is also plausible, however, that habituation is based on the fact that repetition of a particular pattern-perception process increases its speed and efficiency. In order to decide on these conflicting explanations of the habituation phenomenon we might investigate the nature of the scanning processes during repeated exposure to a pattern. Qualitative instead of merely quantitative changes in the scanning programme during repeated exposure might indicate that the process changes from a scanning to a testing programme.

A still more complex form of testing operativity is investigated in the so-called interference experiments. In these experiments, the infant is first habituated to a test stimulus. Then a second process of habituation follows, this time with a new stimulus which is employed as distractor. Finally, the infant is again habituated to the original test stimulus. When the distractor has exercised no interfering effect, the second habituation session with the test stimulus should be a mere continuation of the first session, just as if the distractor had never appeared. With interference, however, a relationship should exist between the properties of the distractor and the course of the second test stimulus habituation session. That is, the distractor co-determines the perceptual processes that take place during this session.

The results of interference experiments are quite contradictory. Fagan (1977) employed faces as stimuli and found an interference effect, with the level of interference being determined by the resemblance between the test stimulus and the distractor. Interference was also found by DeLoache (1976). McCall et al. (1977a) also found interference, using pictures of faces, buildings and checkerboards, though their explanations were not based on test-stimulus/distractor resemblance, but rather on whether the distractor had been decoded by the infants or not. Cohen et al. (1977) used geometrical and nonsense figures and found no interference effect. The same result has been obtained by Bornstein (1976b) using colour stimuli. The main conclusion that may be drawn from these experiments is that the appearance of interference is largely determined by the nature of the stimuli that are employed. This may be attributed to the fact that the various stimuli, faces and geometric forms, for instance, appeal to different perceptual strategies or processes. The theoretical problem with these experiments, however, is that testing operators might explain the presence as well as the absence of interference effects, and, more importantly, that any experimental effect may be explained either by testing operativity or by increasing processing efficiency.

A more reliable indicator of the testing operators consists of the perception of ambiguous and incomplete figures. Most of the research has been done after infancy. In principle, however, it must be possible to study whether infants employ an internally stored pattern in order to solve perceptual ambiguities. Take the rabbit-duck ambiguous figure, for instance (see Figure 6.13). One group of infants might be habituated to a group of duck heads, whereas another group might be habituated to a group of rabbit heads. During the test trial, one half of the duck and one half of the rabbit group might be shown the ambiguous figure. The other half of the duck group is shown one of the habituation trial rabbit heads, whereas the other half of the rabbit group is shown one of the habituation trial duck heads. Although much depends on the exact nature of the stimuli, the results might show whether the infant has imposed the habituated pattern upon the ambiguous form. As far as I know, no such experiment has so far been carried out.

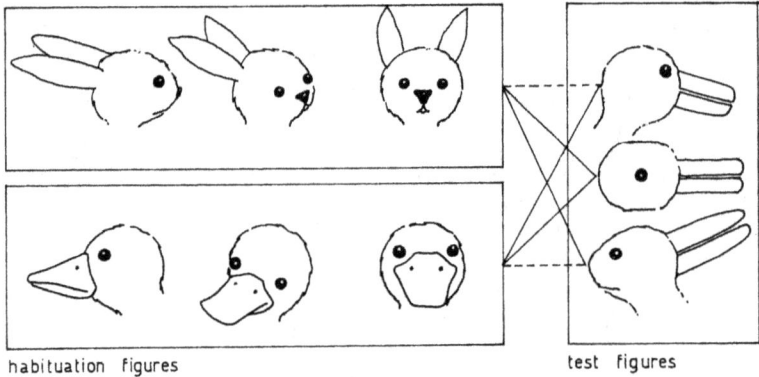

habituation figures   test figures

Figure 6.13 A possible experiment on the perception of ambiguous forms in infancy. One group of infants is familiarized with pictures of rabbit heads; another group is familiarized with pictures of duck heads. One of the test figures is ambiguous (the figure in the middle). If the infants are able to impose a familiarized form onto the ambiguous figure, they should show recovery of attention to the non-familiarized test figure but not to the ambiguous and the familiarized figure. It is doubtful, however, whether an experiment like this one can be carried out with the appropriate age group

Figure 6.14 A figure consisting of nine dots. Children under
the age of four years are unable to abstract its visual structure
(a cross)

An example of an incomplete pattern is provided by the nine-
dot figure in Figure 6.14. Such a figure is not perceived as a
cross by children under four years. Chipman and Mendelsohn
(1975) have shown that the ability to detect the visual structure
of dot patterns increases during the child's primary-school
years. Visual forms can also be reduced by omitting parts of
their contour lines (see Figure 6.15), such that a lack of closure
results. Vurpillot (1976b) discusses a great number of investigations on the effect of closure upon pattern detection and con-
cludes that detection of figures lacking normal closure gradually
develops until the age of twelve years. The present writer (Van
Geert, 1975) has studied the ability to recognize incomplete
figures with a twenty-two month old child, employing verbal
labelling as a criterion for recognition (see Figure 6.16).

Figure 6.15 The ability to detect the form of figures with
incomplete contour gradually develops until the age of twelve
years

The child recognized highly reduced figures with great consistency (only spontaneous labelling was accepted). The drawing of these incomplete figures was guided by the investigator's
intuitive assumptions about salient parts or general form-
properties. The child was also shown a simplified face in front
view (Figure 6.16). It was not recognized as a face, however;
the child isolated the external circular boundary and the mouth
and called them 'moon' and 'banana' respectively. Even at
repeated exposure there was no attempt to label the composite
form (with 'doll', 'man', 'daddy' or any other word referring
to a person). This lack of recognition may seem strange when

Figure 6.16 A twenty-two month old child was able to find appropriate names for highly abstracted and simplified figures; a frontal face was not recognized (banana)

compared with experiments that have shown that the ability to recognize the facial character of a face-like stimulus emerges at the age of fifteen weeks (see further). The contradiction is less alarming, however, if we accept that recognition of patterns is not an autonomous activity but depends upon its relationship with other activities or goals of the subject. Recognition of forms during the period of active word-meaning acquisition may differ considerably from recognition at the pre-verbal age of fifteen weeks or from recognition at later stages, when other and less perceptually dependent aspects of meaning are explored by the child. At a later date, the same child no longer recognized many of the simplified forms he had directly and consistently recognized at the age of twenty-two months.

Dworetzki (1939) and Elkind et al. (1964) employed figures made of deviant constituents, such as a face whose eyes consisted of light-bulbs. The aim of these investigations was to find out whether children are capable of detecting a pattern that is made of constituents which are incompatible with it. Three-year-olds see only the elements. Seven and eight year old children can see either the overall pattern or the constituents, but they are not yet capable of seeing the constituents in terms of their place in the overall pattern. Twelve-year-olds are able to integrate the various constituents in the overall pattern - they know, for instance, that the light bulbs represent eyes (see Figure 6.17).

Whereas the form-abstraction experiments rely more upon the activity of the clustering, computing and eventually also the economizing operators, the incomplete figure experiments tend to rely exclusively upon the testing operators. It is plausible, though certainly not investigated by the present experiments, that the perception of incomplete figures is based upon the subject's increasing stock of patterns and his knowledge about the occasions in which they may occur. The same kind of processes that directed the child's perception of incomplete figures may occur at much later stages of perceptual learning, where the subject is acquiring skills such as musical structure perception or the perception of composition and structure in paintings or in the layout of printed matter. Although these skills require more than perception alone, it is clear that perception plays an important role in them.

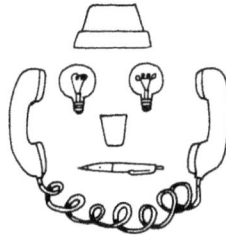

Figure 6.17 Elkind's Turk. Children under the age of seven years are unable to see the figure as a face composed of non-facial elements (after Elkind et al., 1964)

6.2.3.3 The human face: an example of higher-order property perception Because of its social and biological importance, the human face constitutes one of the favourite patterns in perceptual developmental research. Although the normal environment confronts the child almost exclusively with a moving face, undergoing not only perspective but also expressive changes, most of the research is concentrated on the immobile and inanimate face. Field (1979) measured visual and cardiac responses to animate and inanimate faces by three month old infants. She found that the infants looked longer at the inanimate stimulus and that the heart rate level was lower than during looking at the animate face. According to Field, this combination of looking time and heart rate indicates that the inanimate face provided much less information to the child than the animate face. The children's looking away from the animate faces is not an expression of passive disinterest, but rather of active concentration upon a stimulus with a high information level. In addition to the fact that the (inanimate) facial scheme starts to emerge at the age of three months (see further), and that pattern perception may be facilitated by movement (see section 6.2.1), Field's results suggest that the animate facial scheme has emerged earlier than the inanimate one, in spite of the fact that animate faces look more complex than inanimate ones. Probably, the correct explanation for this fact is not that the child has built up different schemes for animate and inanimate faces but simply that the animate face provides more information about the spatial and spatiotemporal properties of the face than does the inanimate face.

The main problem with most of the experiments is whether and when the infant employs a facial scheme, i.e. a higher-

order property common to all representations of the human
face, either inanimate, simplified and two-dimensional, or
animate, complex and three-dimensional. Gibson (1969) has
given an overview of the literature up to 1969 and finds con-
firming as well as disconfirming evidence for the statement that
the young infant employs a facial scheme. Wilcox (1969), Haaf
(1974) and Jones-Molfese (1975) concluded that before the age
of three months, selective attention is only determined by
pattern-complexity and not by facial resemblance.

Haaf and Bell (1967), Haaf and Brown (1976) and Haaf (1977)
constructed patterns on the basis of two independent pattern-
dimensions, namely complexity and facial resemblance. The
general finding is that at an age between three and four months,
preferential attention is clearly determined by the facial resemblance dimension. It may be questioned, however, whether the
infants see the face either as a configuration or as a set of
separate facial features, such as the eyes for instance. By
employing these features in a non-facial configuration, the
experiments were able to rule out the latter explanation. An
indication for the fact that slightly older infants (five- to six-
month olds) employ a facial scheme is provided by Fagan (1972).
Fagan found that the infants had considerable difficulties with
recognizing and discriminating facial patterns when they were
presented upside-down. Although the physical complexity and
constituent features remain the same in an upside-down presentation, recognition of such a face is more difficult since (as
a consequence of its deviant orientation) it does not fit the
facial scheme. The same difficulty with recognizing turned-down
faces is observed with older children and adults (Ellis, 1975).

The importance and function of the facial features is changing
along the course of development. With inanimate faces, one-
month-olds mainly scan the external boundary of the facial
pattern, whereas two-month-olds prefer to scan the internal
features, the eyes in particular (Maurer and Salapatek, 1976;
Bergman et al., 1971; Haber and Hershenson, 1974). Caron
et al. (1973) investigated the saliency of the facial features. At
the age of four months the eyes are the most salient, whereas
at the age of five months the mouth has become just as salient
and differentiated as the eyes. It is plausible that the very
frequent eye-to-eye contact with the mother at the age of four
to five months is related to this development and plays a role
in the construction of the facial scheme (eyes-nose-mouth-
relationship) of a particular person (Friedman et al., 1974).

Besides the development of the frontal facial scheme, investigators are also interested in the emergence of facial constancy
(orientation invariance) and the ability to perceive faces in a
categorical or classificatory way. The frontal view and the
profile of a face differ considerably with regard to proximal,
lower-order variables, although they are both the representation of one facial pattern. A number of investigations (Fagan,
1972, 1976; Cornell, 1974) have suggested that from the age of

five months the child has learned to identify different orientations of a face as representations of the same facial pattern. It is quite plausible, however, that the perception of normal facial constancy is much easier and occurs much earlier than with inanimate, photographed faces. Not only are the animate faces more interesting, they also contain more complete information, for instance information based upon binocular and motion disparity. It is plausible, therefore, that the experiments underestimate the infant's face-perception abilities. The same remark also holds for an investigation by Cohen and Strauss (1979) on the ability of four-and-a-half to seven-and-a-half months old infants to perceive faces in a categorical way. The investigators employed a habituation method and found that the oldest group was capable of categorical perception. Attention-recovery measures indicated that they were able to perceive a specific female facial pattern, regardless of its orientation and of object differences between the faces.

Experiments by Fagan (1972) and Dirks and Gibson (1977) have shown that five and seven month old infants were able to detect the invariant facial pattern in a two- and three-dimensional presentation of a face.

The question about the development of face perception and recognition, in particular at later stages, is at present only partially answered (see Ellis, 1975, for an overview). Hess and Pick (1974) examined the contribution of the various facial features to children's discrimination of schematic faces and found that with pre-school children, the eyes are most discriminative. Goldstein (1975) investigated the recognition of turned-down faces and found that recognition appeared to increase between three and fourteen years. Cross et al. (1971) and Ellis et al. (1973) found that there is no considerable development of recognition when the subjects had to discriminate between faces which were new and which had previously been viewed during a familiarization stage.

According to Diamond and Carey (1977) and Carey and Diamond (1977) the representations and recognition of familiar and unknown faces develops along different lines. Children under ten years of age are comparable with adults as far as recognition of familiar faces is concerned. The encoding of unfamiliar faces by subjects under ten years of age, however, is considerably less than is adult recognition. Between six and ten, there is a marked improvement, followed by stagnation or even decrease between ten and fourteen, and finally between fourteen and sixteen a gradual increase toward the adult level can be observed (Carey and Diamond, 1977). Mann et al. (1979) showed a clear parallel development between face- and voice-recognition (see also section 6.2.1 for further discussion). The authors suggest that face- and voice-recognition are based upon the same perceptual mechanism, which is of considerable social importance and probably very typical for the human species.

One of the most interesting properties of the face as a higher-order pattern is that it is characterized by a large range of typical configurational changes, namely the various facial expressions. Facial expression does not change the facial scheme in itself (the eyes are not turned upside-down, for instance) but changes a number of relationships within the scheme, such as the places of the corners of the mouth. Furthermore, the various expressions (anger, fear, pleasure and so forth) have their own typical higher-order form. Although individuals may vary in the precise way in which their faces express pleasure, the various expressions are characterized by a higher-order resemblance. Young-Browne et al. (1977) employed a habituation procedure in order to find out whether three month old infants were able to see the difference between a sad, happy and surprised face. The results showed that the infants discriminated the surprised face from the happy and sometimes from the sad face. There was no evidence, however, that the infants discriminated the happy from the sad face. It is quite plausible that the infants based their differential response upon feature differences, such as the eyes. Moreover, the generalization from this experiment to the normal situation requires greater caution. In the normal situation, facial expression by the mother is accompanied by vocal expression and actions such as touching. The range of diversity within one facial expression is also very extensive (the many changes of the talking, pleasure-expressing face of the mother for instance). It might be more relevant, therefore, to habituate the child in a normal, active situation to a specific emotional attitude of the mother, such as pleasure or happiness and then examine whether the child dishabituates more to an inanimate test stimulus consisting of a sad or surprised face than to a happy face. Discrimination of facial expression by four-to-six month old babies is also shown in an experiment by La Barbara et al. (1976) in which the infants preferred a happy face to an angry or a neutral face.

The discrimination between sad and happy faces is only a very rudimentary ability when compared to the many refined distinctions older children are able to make between facial expressions. Abramovitch (1977), for instance, showed that four-to-five year old children were able to tell whether their mothers were interacting with a friend or a stranger. Their judgments were based on video-tapes without sound, which showed the mother's face and upper torso. A group of adult subjects was similarly successful when an unknown person was concerned. A particular expressive feature of the human face which is quite relevant for social contact is gaze direction. Gaze can be detected by observing the relationship and place of the pupils of the eye. Lord (1974) and Thayer (1977) investigated children's and adult's ability to detect on- and off-face gazes. Thayer in particular found that six-year-olds detect on-face gazes rather well, although they are far less accurate than adults.

6.2.4 Summary

We based our discussion of development on a formal model that
defines pattern perception in terms of various functional operators. The operators work with complex spatiotemporal proximal
stimuli provided by the various senses. In one of the previous
chapters we stated that perception of a distal property implies
that this property may be conceived of as the object of the
perceptual act. In the current chapter, we stated that a distal
object of a perceptual act formally corresponds with a specific
deep structure or organization imposed on a proximal stimulus.
The function of the operators is to assign a specific deep structure or principle of organization to a proximal stimulus. The
normal proximal stimulus is so specific that it can be assigned
one and only one deep structure by the functional operators,
i.e. that it corresponds with one and only one distal stimulus
which is complex, detailed and veridical.

We tried to infer a set of theoretical initial-state models starting from the structure of the functional operators. We concluded that the most plausible initial-state model is the one in
which all the functional operators are present, at least in a
rudimentary state. We have seen that the empirical initial state
of pattern perception - which we shall limit to the first month
of life - is characterized by pattern preference based on quantitative properties, such as size or pattern definition. In principle, quantitative properties can be dealt with by comparing
and clustering operators and do not require operators of a
higher level. We have also seen, however, that, quantitative
properties being equal, pattern preference can also be determined by simple qualitative properties - such as curvature -
which require rudimentary computing operators.

The question as to the presence of economizing operators
during the empirical initial state cannot be answered on the
basis of the available evidence on early pattern perception.
Economizing operators are operative in the perception of higher-
order properties of patterns. These higher-order properties,
however, require a level of lower-order property-computing
which exceeds the computing power of the operators at the
initial state. Since the economizing operators are also responsible for the perception of three-dimensional spatial structure
and constancy, we could go back to the relevant chapters in
order to answer the question of whether economizing operators
are manifestly present during the empirical initial state. We
have seen that there is no evidence for constancy or spatial
three-dimensionality in infants younger than six weeks. There
is also no evidence, however, for the fact that one month old
infants are not able to perceive constancy or a three-dimensional
spatial structure, which implies that the question as to the
presence of economizing operators during the empirical state
must remain open.

The evidence is inconclusive also with regard to the initial
activities of the testing operators. It is conceivable that

selective attention, habituation and interference phenomena can be explained on the basis of the testing function, but at present it is not clear whether this explanation is the only or most plausible one. We have seen that the perception of incomplete and ambiguous figures – which we considered an illustrative example of the activity of the testing operators – develops during the whole period of childhood. Such a long development is compatible with the particular nature of the testing operators which, of all functions, are the most sensitive to learning.

Besides the question of which pattern operators are present and active during the empirical initial state of pattern perception, we must also deal with the problem concerning the nature of pattern development. What happens with the functional operators once they have made an appearance: does development consist of a gain in the operative powers (computing power or economizing power, for instance) or of a gain in the level of recursivity at which the operators can be applied (the higher the level of operative recursivity, the greater the extension of the perceived patterns and the level of pattern abstraction). Although it is highly probable that both aspects are involved in pattern perception development, it is unclear which one provides the principal contribution. It is plausible, for instance, that a relatively small increase of the level of operative recursivity has a more considerable effect on pattern perception than a relatively strong increase of the computing or economizing powers.

One of the most striking findings of the research carried out during the first stages of perceptual development is the existence of perceptual preference. Preference is closely related to attention, in as far as every form of attention implies selectivity and differences in the importance attributed to various parts of the total stimulus-field. We have seen that, during the first months of life, preference undergoes a number of clearly discernible changes. During the first month, preference is based on quantitative properties, such as the amount of contours or saturation of colour. During the following months, qualitative properties, i.e. pattern and form, become dominant. During the third stage, beginning by the age of six months, typical preferential attention disappears and is replaced by forms of attention that are part of action schemes involving goals, motives and interests (see also Fantz et al., 1975, for a comparable division into three periods).

The first and second form of preference may be explained on either a physiological or a functional basis. The physiological explanation is based on the physiological mechanism that is responsible for these forms of attention. According to Bornstein (1978), the infants prefer the forms that are particularly appropriate for stimulating the geniculostriate or primary visual system. The author states that 'the level of bioelectrical activity which is evoked by selected stimulation may serve as a neuronal substrate for the level of gross attention displayed by infants'

(p. 186). In addition to this physiological explanation of the attention mechanism, Bornstein also stresses its ethological significance which may be inferred from a functional explanation, i.e. an explanation based upon the function which the mechanism fulfils with regard to development. Attentional preference is important because it constitutes a stimulus-behaviour interaction that may serve important organizing functions early in life (p. 187). It is suggested that attention, a perceptual function which we have so far not discussed in any depth, plays a crucial role in perceptual development. It may indeed be the mechanism which determines the transitions between the various developmental states. The next two chapters will be devoted to the role of attention and to an explanation of the dynamics of perceptual development.

7 Attention and the dynamics of perceptual development

7.1 THE PROCESS OF ATTENTION

7.1.1 Components of attention

The concept of attention implies that behaviour, and perceptual behaviour in particular, always contains an aspect of selectivity and an aspect of intensification (Berlyne, 1960). In this chapter we shall focus on the aspect of selectivity.

Selectivity is never a matter of all or nothing. Besides the focus - the aspect which is particularly selected - attention contains a peripheral zone, that is, the zone that surrounds the focus and that is processed with decreasing intensity as the distance to the focus increases (see Neisser, 1967). If we look at an object, for instance, we focus on one feature, while the rest of the object, together with the surrounding space, constitutes the periphery of the looking action. The looking action consists of a series of successive foci and a series of corresponding focal shifts. The periphery associated with one single focus constitutes the domain in which possible focal shifts will take place.

Besides the focus-periphery distinction, there is a second distinction which is of particular importance, namely the subjective versus the objective component of the attentional process. Perception is primarily directed to an objective world outside the subject; the objects of perceptual acts constitute an exterior world. This principle holds for all perceptual acts (with the exception of proprioceptive perception), even those of neonates and very young children. Any perceptual act is directed to a specific spatiotemporal, physical extension. The external domain will be called the external or stimulus domain of perception. It can be divided into an objective or stimulus focus and periphery.

Perceptual acts not only involve a specific objective domain, they are also composed of specific perceptual functions. By perceptual function we mean the particular sorts of processes that take place: sensory-specific versus integrated perception; perception of places, sets of places, constancy, the structure of space, etc. Perceptual acts always contain a variety of perceptual functions (in fact, it is impossible to separate the various functions). The difference between perceptual acts consists of the different hierarchical relationships between the functions. Attention might be focused either on the sensory specific or the sensory integrated aspects. The non-focal function will be peripherally present. The structure of functions involved in a perceptual act is called the subjective or function domain of attention. It is divided into a subjective or function focus and a corresponding periphery (see Figure 7.1).

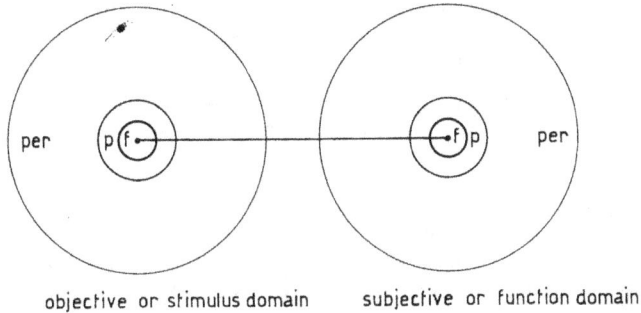

objective or stimulus domain   subjective or function domain

Figure 7.1 Attention is a bipolar process, consisting of an objective or stimulus domain and a subjective or psychological functions domain. Each domain can be divided into three zones: a focal zone, f; the zone of proximal attention, p; and the periphery, per

The model of attention has a purely technical function. It does not describe a set of processes that could be observed during attentional activity. The model specifies the formal components of attention. In the following sections we shall see why the distinction between the subjective and the objective domain is necessary.

It is important to note that the subjective domain, i.e. the structure of perceptual functions, is state-specific (a develop-mental state corresponds with a specific structure of perceptual functions). The development of perception, therefore, can be described as the development of the underlying structures of perceptual functions. The problem, then, is to explain how the structure of functions may change on the basis of perceptual acts that are based on these functions. That is to say, the structure of functions determines the properties of the external world. For instance, if the child is inclined to look at the external boundaries of objects, his phenomenal world will consist of external boundaries. How can we explain that the child gradually changes his focus of attention, for instance towards internal features of objects? In fact, the connection between the dependent variable - perceptual development - and the independent variable - the perceived world, perceptual activities - is a typical problem of developmental psychology in general.

7.1.2 The zone of proximal attention
The focus of attention is spatiotemporally limited. We have seen

that a perceptual act consists of a series of foci, i.e. a series
of focal shifts. The peripheral domain, associated with a specific focus, is the set of all possible successors of the actual
focus. It may be questioned whether it is possible to predict
the new focus, f_2, given a present focus f_1 and a corresponding periphery p_1. Do all the objects or properties within p_1
have the same probability of becoming the next focus?

In order to answer the previous questions we shall introduce
an imaginary observer, O. O perceives an imaginary ideal
object space that is characterized by a uniform distribution of
objects and properties. The objects of the imaginary space consist of coloured circles with various degrees of colour saturation. Let us assume that one out of every eight spots is optimally saturated, three are medium and four are minimally
saturated. Since the object space is uniformly distributed, it
can be divided into a number of subspaces containing spots that
average the same distance from the present focus f_1 (see
Figure 7.2).

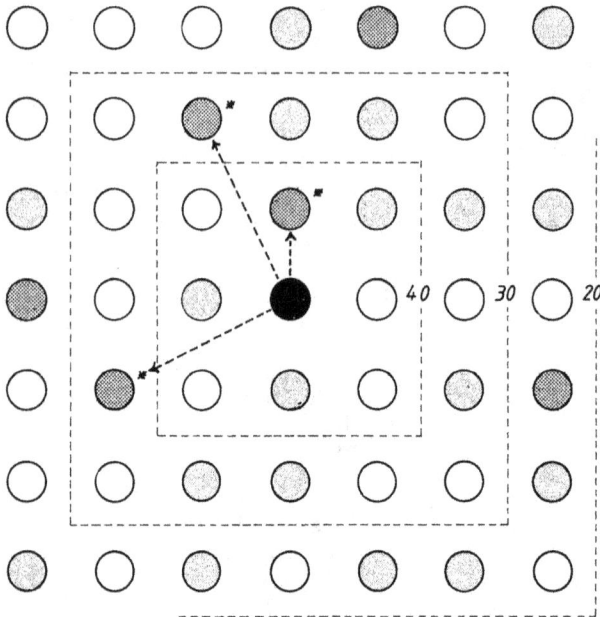

Figure 7.2 A fragment of an ideally-distributed object space
filled with coloured circles. Dark grey circles are optimally,
light grey circles are medium and white circles are minimally
colour saturated. The black circle in the middle represents the
present focus. The circles with an asterisk form the present
zone of proximal attention. The arrows correspond with the
most probable focal shifts

It may be assumed that the observer, O, will show definite perceptual preferences. Provided that O resembles a neonate observer, we may also assume that he will prefer saturated colours on the one hand and that he will select his focal shifts as close to the actual focus as possible. Suppose that the focal shift probabilities are as follows. First, highly saturated circles will be selected in 50 per cent, medium saturated spots are selected in 30 per cent and minimally saturated spots in 20 per cent of all focal shifts. Second, the probability that a focal shift will occur in a subspace is inversely proportional to the distance between the subspace and the present focus, according to the ratio 40 per-cent-distance 1, 30 per-cent-distance 2, 20 per-cent-distance 3, 10 per-cent-distance 4, 0 per cent for all further distances.

If both forms of selection probability (preference) are combined, the following list of values will result:

1 element belonging to the first distance zone has a probability of 40% x 50% = 20% of becoming the next focus (f_2)
3 elements of distance zone 1 have a probability of 40% x 30% : 3 = 4%
4 elements of distance zone 1 have a probability of 40% x 20% : 4 = 2%
2 elements of distance zone 2 have a probability of 30% x 50% : 2 = 7.5%
6 elements of distance zone 2 have a probability of 30% x 30% : 6 = 1.5%
8 elements of distance zone 2 have a probability of 30% x 20% : 8 = 0.75%
3 elements of distance zone 3 have a probability of 20% x 50% : 3 = 3.33%
. . .

In Figure 7.3 the relation between probability and number of circles is represented by means of a curve. We see that there is a difference between a set containing a relatively small number of circles with high shift probability and a set with a large number of circles with an increasingly small shift probability. The former set is called the zone of promixal attention, the second set is called the periphery. The line between the proximal and the peripheral zone will be arbitrarily drawn at a shift probability of 7.5 per cent. In consequence, the zone of proximal attention in our imaginary ideal object space will contain three elements.

After all, we are not primarily interested in predicting the focal shifts, i.e. the actual objects that will constitute the content of f_2, f_3, etc. Since we are dealing with development, we want to be able to predict which selection criteria - brightness, global size, global amount of contour, etc. - will succeed the present selection criterion, namely saturation. As we know, the succession of selection criteria and functional modes -

preference, exploration, generalization, etc. – constitutes an essential observable expression of perceptual development.

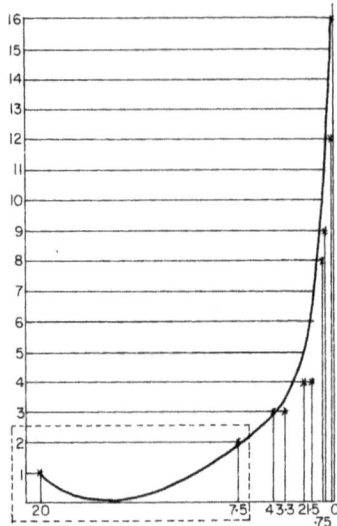

Figure 7.3 The relation between probability of becoming the next focus and number of points characterized by this probability. The area within the dotted line is the zone of proximal attention

To begin with, we might apply the principles of focal, proximal and peripheral attention to the set of selection criteria (i.e. the set of preferred object properties). If the child is presently interested in highly saturated colour, we might simply state that saturation constitutes the focal selection criterion during this particular state of perceptual development. Consequently, the course of development can be described as a set of focal shifts that take place over weeks, months or years, according to the actual speed of development.

Focal selection criteria – let us simply call them focal (object) properties – belong to the objective or stimulus zone of attention. These properties correspond with specific functional properties of the perceiving subject, namely the structure of perceptual processes and strategies. That is, if the child is able to select highly saturated spots and if saturation is a preferred property, he should possess a specific perceptual programme (process, strategy, etc.) that enables him to carry out this particular selective activity. Changes in the focal object properties should correspond with changes in the function domain, i.e. the domain of perceptual processes and strategies.

If one particular property occupies a focal position during one particular developmental state, every other perceptual property of objects belongs to the peripheral zone. In order to apply the concept of proximal attention, the peripheral zone should possess the properties of the 'ideal' object space. The ideal object space – which we have discussed previously – is a metric space, filled with uniformly distributed metric objects that do not mutually interfere (circular objects, for instance). The peripheral zone is metric if, for any pair of peripheral object properties, there is one definite distance (in practice, the number of different distances should exceed one).

A set of properties can be expressed in terms of a metric space if it is possible to make a similarity judgment for any possible pair of properties in the set. The degree of similarity is synonymous with distance. The metric space implies that the set of compared properties is based on a limited number of underlying variables (see for instance Miller, 1967, for an application in the field of verbal concepts).

It is quite plausible that similarity measures also occur with perceptual properties: 'saturation', for instance, seems more closely related to 'global size' than to 'triangularity'. The degrees of similarity are not based on intuitive judgments; they emanate from the fact that perceptual properties correspond with perceptual functions, i.e. perceptual programmes, processes or strategies. First, it will be quite obvious that distinct perceptual processes are not equally different: some processes are clearly more directly related than others (see, for instance, processes that regulate the perception of quantitative object properties versus processes that regulate the perception of distributional characteristics of place sets, i.e. form properties). Second, we may assume that the differences between perceptual processes are not one-dimensional. In the previous chapters we have seen that perceptual processes may be directed towards the perception of change versus constancy, dimensionality, orientation and direction, distributional properties of place sets, and so on. In summary, the set of perceptual properties can be represented by means of a formal, metric space consisting of n variables (dimensions) with k values (the number of values refers to the number of validly distinguishable differences within one variable; at least, the number of values should be two, namely '0' and '+').

The concept of proximal attention is applicable to the space of object properties if any increase in the distance from a given standard property corresponds with an increase in the number of possible properties (i.e. if there are x properties at distance d_1 and y properties at distance d_2, y should be greater than x if d_2 is greater than d_1). Let a be the number of variables in which a subset of properties differs from a standard property (a clearly represents a distance). The number of properties in the distant subset is given by the formula:

$$N_p = (k-1)^a \cdot \frac{n!}{a! \cdot (n-a)!}$$

The formula shows that any increase of 'a' corresponds with an increase of N_p (except if k is quite small); consequently, the concept of proximal attention is applicable to the space of object properties.

It is quite conceivable that not all the processes of selective attention that take place during one developmental state will be directed towards the focal selection criterion. Saturation, for instance, is a state specific selection criterion because the majority of selective perceptual processes is directed towards it. Since the set of perceivable object properties is character- ized by a focus-proximity-periphery-structure, we may assume that 'non-focal' perceptual processes will take place within the zone of proximal attention associated with the current focal selection criterion. Any focus on the current selection criterion - saturation, for instance - will have a consolidating, but probably also a habituating effect. Any focus on a proximal selection criterion - global size for instance - might have a potentially developmental effect.

Needless to say, attention shifts can take place only if the observable world contains more than one object and more than one object property. It may be questioned how a development- ally ideal world should be like. Suppose that a selection cri- terion SC_1 characterizes the initial state, while SC_n character- izes the final state of perceptual development. How should observable properties be distributed among the set of observ- able objects in order to provoke the required developmental process (i.e. $SC_1 - SC_2 - SC_3 - ... - SC_n$)?

Any SC corresponds with a specific object property, i.e. $p_1.p_2.p_3,....$ Before determining the properties of a develop- mentally ideal object space, we must accept the following assumptions. First, we assume that preference is subject to habituation (it does not matter whether the cause of habituation is either external or internal). We must also assume that habit- uation increases the probability that the current selection criterion will be replaced by a new one. Second, the origina- tion of new selection criteria (i.e. of developmental state transi- tions) will be determined by the distribution of observable properties among the set of present, observable objects.

We shall now try to formulate a set of minimal requirements that an object space should fulfil in order to make the required developmental process possible. Let p_m/p_n be the probability that an object with property m also possesses property n; p_a, p_b and p_c are the proximal properties associated with p_1; p_d, p_e and p_f are the proximal properties of p_2; etc. The developmental process consisting of the chain $SC_1(p_1)-SC_2(p_2)- ...SC_n(p_n)$ will occur if, first, p_1/p_a is significantly greater than p_1/p_b and p_1/p_c and if $p_a = p_2$; second, p_2/p_d is signi- ficantly greater than p_2/p_e and p_2/p_f and if $p_d = p_3$; third, p_2/p_3 is significantly greater than p_2/p_1 (it will be clear that p_1/p_2 and p_2/p_1 are entirely different values).

The previous conditional probabilities are related to the

objective properties of the observable world. The fact that p_2 belongs to the proximal zone of p_1 is based on the properties of the perceptual processes. It is possible, however, that the child's environment contains no objects with property p_1 and property p_2. Consequently, the probability that attention could shift from p_1 to p_2, provided that p_1 is the currently preferred property, would be zero. Then, the subject would not be able to explore the proximal properties of p_2, and so on.

Let us now try to recapitulate the entire model of attention shifts. First, we have seen that focal shifts take place at the behavioural level, i.e. the level of actual perception. During the course of a short-term perceptual process, attention shifts from one focus to another. The shifts are determined by the zones of proximal attention (ZPA) associated with each focus (see Figure 7.4).

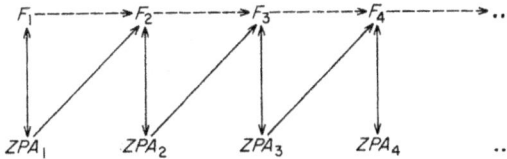

Figure 7.4 Temporal structure generated by foci (F) and associated zones of proximal attention (ZPA)

Second, we have seen that a state-specific set of focal shifts is characterized by an underlying state-specific selection criterion. The focal preference – i.e. the preference that occurs most frequently – is directed towards one particular observable property (e.g. saturation). The selection criterion has its proper zone of proximal attention that consists of a relatively small number of related perceptual properties. Shifts at the level of selection criteria constitute the developmental process. We have seen that these shifts are based, first, on a set of shifts at the behavioural level, and, second, on the specific distribution of perceptual properties among the set of observable objects. Moreover, shifts at the level of selection criteria (SC) are also determined by the proximal zones associated with the current selection criterion. The combination of the behavioural with the developmental level results in a nested structure (see Figure 7.5(a)).

Third, it is plausible that the hierarchic structure of the process is recursive. As sets of focal shifts at the behavioural level are characterized by an underlying selection criterion, so sets of shifts at the level of selection criteria might be characterized by an underlying meta-selection criterion (MSC). Empirically, this assumption seems reasonably tenable. The first stages of perceptual development, for instance, are clearly based on quantitative properties of patterns. At later stages, preference is based on qualitative properties. It may

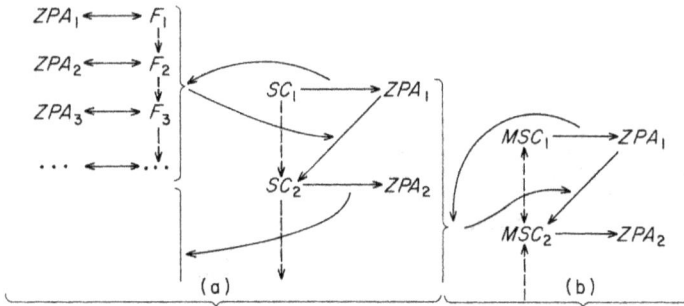

Figure 7.5 Nested structure of focal (F), selection criterion (SC), and meta-selection criterion (MSC) shifts

be assumed that shifts at the meta-level are based on shifts at the selection criterion level (see Figure 7.5(b)).

Before discussing the empirical meaning of the attention model, I want to elucidate the scope of the employed concepts. It should be clear that the model has an explicitly formal meaning. The concept of preference or selection, for instance, implies that the subject prefers or selects certain kinds of perceptual properties. It has no implications at all with regard to the specific motives behind this preference or selection, e.g. either physiologically or functionally determined. The concept of the proximal zone has no implications with regard to the actual origin of this zone. It does not matter, for instance, whether the object space is either natural and arbitrary or artificial and purposeful. In practice, however, the object spaces will be explicitly created, e.g. by parents or teachers. The basic property of an educational process is that the 'object' space (objects, questions, information, problems, etc.) is explicitly structured and adapted to the current developmental state of the educated subject. The adult might limit the proximal zone to one item only and decrease the distance between the current and the successive focus. Such is the case in particular forms of programmed instruction, for instance. The adult might assist the child in making a focal shift, e.g. by helping the child in solving a problem. The adult might also reinforce one focal shift and obstruct another, e.g. in operant conditioning. Finally, the model should not only be valid in the field of perceptual but also in the field of cognitive development in general.

7.1.3 Attention shifts and programmes
The zone of proximal attention is expressed by the structure of the actual attention shifts. A limited - though probably fairly extensive - set of attention shifts should enable us to discover the probabilities with which the various shifts take place. Although a succession of attention shifts can be dealt with from a

purely statistical point of view (e.g. as a Markov chain) I shall
concentrate upon the functional meaning of successive shifts.
A structure of shifts fulfils a function and may be compared
with an action programme which is employed in order to achieve
a specific goal. In this section I shall discuss the notion of
'programme' starting from an example concerning Muir and
Field's investigation of the neonate's tendency to orient to
sounds (Muir and Field, 1979; see also section 4.2.1). At the
beginning of the experiment, the child's head is centred. Since
the infant is in an alert state, it is highly probable that he is
focusing attention on something (Muir and Field, 1979, p. 432).
Let us assume that the child visually focuses on a place in
space (the stimulus focus). This place is visually inspected,
since its interest is probably determined by its visual properties
(visual inspection is the functional focus).. At left and right of
the infant, two stationary loudspeakers are placed. One of
them will produce a rattle sound, lasting for a maximum of 20
seconds. When the right speaker produces the rattle sound,
the infant will shift his attention. The shift takes place both in
the stimulus domain (change of place and change of stimulus
quality, i.e. sound instead of a visual pattern) and the function
domain (auditive instead of visual inspection). The fact that
such a shift arises may be safely assumed on the basis of auditory discrimination research, which has shown that the emergence of a new sound produces attention arousal.

It is unclear whether the child's attention to the sound produced by one of the speakers is directed towards the properties
of the sound itself or towards the sound's place. We may assume
that the first shift is concerned with the pattern properties of
the sound (the functional focus consists of auditory pattern
specification). After that, a functional shift towards the place
of the auditory pattern may arise (the order of the shifts has
been determined in a speculative way, though in principle it
must be possible to investigate the order empirically).

The third functional shift can now take place: the child shifts
from auditory to visual inspection of the place on his right from
where the sound is coming. A direct shift is impossible, however, since the auditory specified, lateral place at the child's
right does not belong to the set of central places which the
child's visual field is covering during the onset of the sound.
In order to achieve this functional shift to visual inspection,
the child has to take a number of intermediate steps, namely
head and eye turning. These intermediate steps may be processed in two different ways. The first possibility is that the
orienting response, head and eye turning, is a tropistic,
centring response. The child will turn his head until the auditory stimulus and its visual correspondent have occupied a
central place. The second possibility is that the child employs
a sensory-uniform spatial 'map', i.e. that there exists a one-to-
one correspondence between the set of auditory and visually
specifiable places. The child 'knows' that the lateral place

occupied by the sound source does not belong to his present, centrally oriented visual field and that he has to turn his head and eyes to the right in order to find it. Muir and Field state that their experiment cannot determine which of these possibilities actually holds for the child's orienting response, the tropistic or the spatial method of orientation. If the child's orienting response is of a tropistic nature, it is not attracted by places in space but by laterally occurring auditory and visual stimuli. In this case, the child might not be interested in a visual inspection of the auditory specified lateral place but only in getting the auditory pattern at a central position.

Whether the turning response is either tropistic or not, it will result in a new auditory and visual orientation towards the observable world. That is, the spatial origin of the sound will arrive at the centre of the auditory and visual fields. It is quite plausible, then, that an attentional shift will occur, particularly when the spatial origin of the sound is occupied by a visually attractive sound-making object. The child may now visually explore the properties of the object, i.e. he may perform a number of stimulus shifts based on one particular function, namely the registration of distributional properties of visual place sets. After a while, when the child habituates to the visual and auditory properties of the stimulus, the probability of a new functional or stimulus shift will increase. When no particular additional stimulation occurs, the child will probably return to his central head position, simply because the lateral direction of the head takes too much effort. In this case, the functional shift is determined by the child's motor functions and not by stimulus properties and perceptual functions.

Let us assume that the earliest orientation reactions of the child are based on a tropistic reflex and not on sensory integrated place perception. The set of attention shifts can be represented by a focus diagram. The columns represent the stimulus and the function component. A double arrow indicates a shift (see Figure 7.6).

Focus diagrams represent perceptual actions. The programme from Figure 7.6 might be called a 'visual inspection of an auditory revealed place' programme. Other kinds of programmes include 'cross-modal exploration of pattern', 'separation of pattern and orientation' and so on. These programmes have a number of particular properties.

First, they do not consist of a uniform, pre-programmed series of steps; they are based on shift probabilities. Second, the programmes do not consist of completely separate steps. The diagram in Figure 7.6 represents only the focal units. With each focal unit corresponds a proximal and a peripheral zone. The latter contain the succeeding foci. In fact, a programme resembles a chain of partially overlapping circles that represent attention domains. Third, the structure of the programmes is more complex than the actual linear succession of attention shifts. It may be stated that the attention shifts

F_1 visual specification of place ⟷ central place (occupied by an arbitrary object)

F_2 auditory specification of pattern ⟷ sound pattern at right

F_3 auditory specification of place ⟷ place of sound source

F_4 tropistic reaction: head turning
in order to level the stimulus—
differences between both ears ⟷ changing stimulus-difference between ears

F_5 auditory specification of place ⟷ central place, occupied by sound-making
object

F_6 visual specification of place ⟷ central place, occupied by sound-making
object

F_7 visual specification of pattern ⟷ visual pattern property of sound-making object

$F_{8,9,10...}$ visual specification of pattern ⟷ successive visual pattern properties of
sound-making object

increasing muscular effort
and habituation to pattern

head is turned back

F_n ... ...

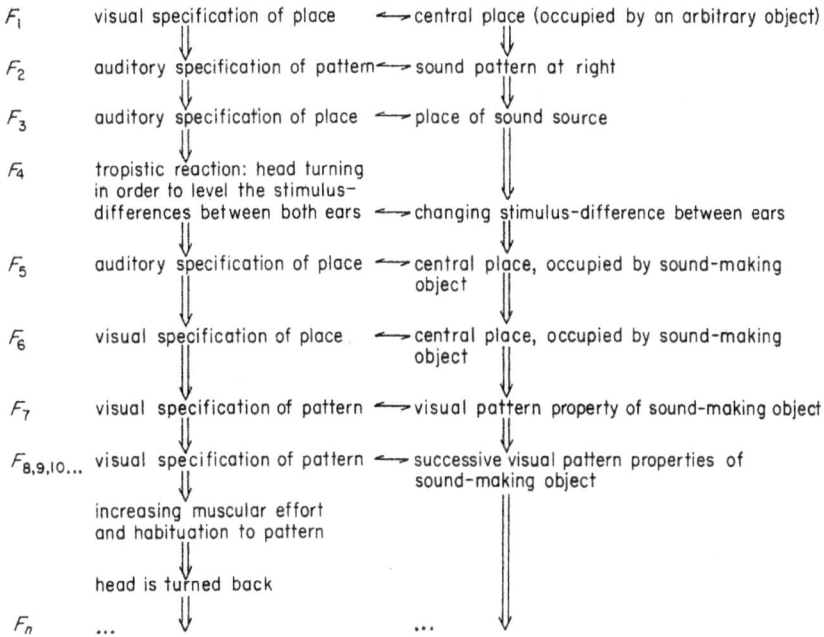

Figure 7.6 The structure of stimulus and functional shifts
during a tropistic action pattern

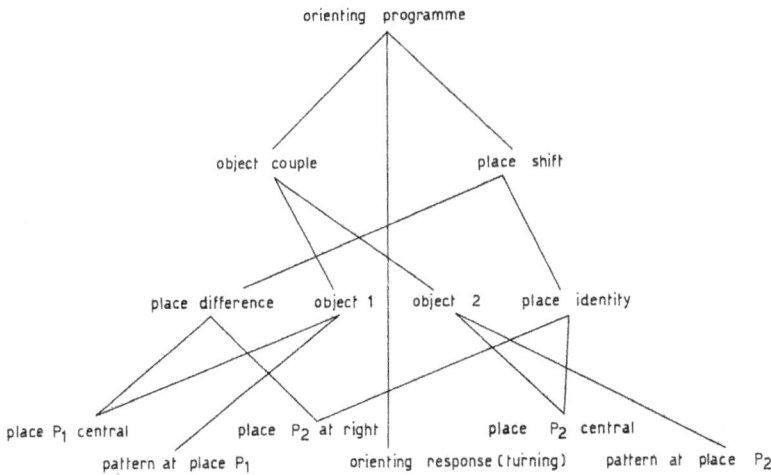

orienting programme

object couple   place shift

place difference   object 1 | object 2   place identity

place P_1 central   place P_2 at right   place P_2 central

pattern at place P_1 orienting response (turning)   pattern at place P_2

Figure 7.7   The 'deep structure' of an orienting programme

constitute the 'surface structure' of the programme. The 'deep
structure' consists of the relationships between the shifts. In
Figure 7.7 I have tried to represent the deep structure of the
visual inspection programme by means of a tentative tree
structure.

Although the temporal structure of the shifts is linear and
successive, we see that their functional structure is complex
and hierarchical. The importance of the various shifts, therefore, is not equal. The shift between 'place P_2 at the right' and
'orienting response: turning' is represented at a high level of
the functional hierarchy and is more important than the shift
between the last and the last focus but one. When the child
starts a new programme (from visual inspection to·reaching, for
instance), the corresponding attention shift should be represented at the highest level of the functional hierarchy, namely
the 'programme' node. These examples illustrate that shifts,
which equal others from the viewpoint of duration or difficulty,
may differ considerably in their functional importance.

7.2 DYNAMICS OF PERCEPTUAL DEVELOPMENT

7.2.1 *The orienting response and the development of a pro-gramme of object perception*
Perceptual development is concerned with changes in the struc-
ture of the perceptual functions, such as auditory place perception, pattern perception and orientation, and, consequently,
with changes in the nature of the perceptually revealed world.
During our discussion of the development of various perceptual
functions, we have never attempted to answer why these functions changed, improved and became more complex. We concentrated upon a conceptual explanation – the structure and
logic of developmental states – and were not concerned with
the causal explanation of the process. I shall now try to show
that the structure of attention shifts within the domain we
have called the zone of proximal attention provides a basis on
which a causal explanation of development may be found.

For the sake of simplicity, I must introduce a number of
limitations to the scope of the discussion. The first limitation
is that development is concerned only with changes in the
function domain. That is, we shall assume that the environment
remains fairly stable and that the child lives in a reasonably
rich environment that is adapted optimally to any possible
developmental state of the perceptual functions. In reality,
however, close relationships exist between a child's state of
development and the kind of environment in which he lives.
Although the general environment may not change, the 'proximal' environment, i.e. the part of the environment with which
the child is most intensively confronted, is constantly adapted
in close connection with his abilities. Development is not an
individual but a social matter. The child does not develop alone,

but in a constant interplay with other people. Parents, for instance, are very attentive to the child's developmental needs. This attention is expressed in many ways, e.g. in the changing formats with which they talk and interact with the child and the toys they offer. The discussion of how perceptual functions develop, however, will not explicitly take account of the fact that the environment is actively adapted to the child's developmental process. I shall take for granted that the environment is always optimally adapted to what the child needs from a developmental point of view.

The second limitation is that the normal stimulus domain is taken to resemble the properties of the ideal stimulus domain which has been employed to determine the properties of the zone of proximal attention. In practice, the whole domain, i.e. everything that may provide a stimulus to the perceptual functions of the child, will never show such a close correspondence with the ideal domain. I assume, however, that the stimulus domain that is of maximum importance, the young infant's cradle or his social interaction with the mother, for instance, resembles the ideal domain fairly well.

The first example I shall discuss concerns the development of a programme of visual inspection of an auditory localized place, based on the investigation of Muir and Field which I have discussed in the previous section. I shall start from the assumption that the child's initial orienting responses are merely auditory tropistic reactions. In this case, there is a high transition probability between the auditory localization of an off-centre source and the auditory inspection of an on-centre source. That is, when the child localizes an off-centre source he will try to get this sound source at an on-centre place by turning his head. On-centre inspection constitutes the proximal function zone of a functional focus consisting of off-centre localization. In the normal environment there is a very large number of off-centre sound sources, but only a few of them meet the criteria for producing the attention shift we are discussing (see Muir and Field, 1979, for a discussion of the sounds that will evoke an orienting response). This limited number of specific sounds constitutes the proximal stimulus zone that is connected with the auditory localization function. Whereas the proximal, stimulus zone depends on the properties of the environment, the proximal function zone at this initial state of development depends on innate relationships between functions ('reflexes'). The problem is to explain why an innate tropistic auditory reaction leads to the emergence of visual auditory programmes for the inspection of places or patterns in space.

In the case of the orienting response, this explanation is not very difficult. The child lives in a world where most places that 'contain' an interesting sound also contain an interesting visual form. That is, sounds are produced by objects, and most sounds are produced by visible and discernible objects.

The child's tropistic reaction to the sound source also produces
a change in the visual stimulus domain: the object that has
produced the sound becomes visible. When this object has an
interesting form, it will probably belong to the visual proximal
stimulus zone, i.e. it will be one of the few objects that have
a considerable chance of being focused visually given that the
actual focus of attention consists of an auditory inspection of
the sound localized at the same place as this form.

This set of attention shifts, originally based on a tropistic
reaction, constitutes an interesting 'programme' since it not
only led to getting the sound at an on-centre place but also to
an interesting sight. It is quite probable that successful programmes will become 'institutionalized' very easily, because
the young baby is a fast learner (see for instance Papousek
(1969) and Siqueland and Lipsitt (1966) discussed in Bower,
1974). The new programme - 'visual inspection of an auditory
localized place' - has been built upon the old programme -
'tropistic reaction to off-centre sound'. This change is based
upon two aspects; first, the structure of the proximal function
zone and, second, the structure of the proximal stimulus zone.
A particular property of the latter, for instance, is that interesting sounds are mostly connected with interesting visual
forms.

We have explicitly stated that our first example is highly
speculative, since it has not been proved that the child's
orienting response is tropistic. For, if we look at the general
style of the orienting response we might become convinced
that it is not tropistic at all. At the onset of the sound the
eyes open wide and then close somewhat while the head is
turning. When the turn is completed the eyes open again and
the child appears to inspect the sound source. The wide opening of the eyes at the onset of the sound might be interpreted
as a kind of audio-visual alertness response: a sound is
registered and the eyes open widely, optimizing the chance
for detecting a visual pattern associated with the registered
auditory one. The closing of the eyes during head turning
optimizes the processing capacity of the auditive channel by
reducing the flow of visual information. Meanwhile, the visual
apparatus cannot be attracted by a more interesting form that
is not exactly located at the place where the sound has been
localized.

Although the connection between auditory and visual functions might suggest that the orienting response of the neonate
is based on an innate 'visual inspection of an auditory localized
place' programme, one property of the orienting response
argues against this interpretation. Muir and Field report that
the eyes are rarely seen to move towards the sound source
before the onset of the head turning. In fact the eyes and head
move as one, i.e. there is no independent eye movement anticipating the place of the sound source. It might be assumed
that a genuine visual inspection programme would show this

relative independence of head and eye movements clearly enough.
Crassini and Broerse (1980) investigated whether infants would
turn their eyes to a lateral sound source if they were prevented
from turning their heads. They found that the infants will not
display eye turns in the majority of cases, but when they do,
most of the eye turns will be directed towards the sound
source.

Orienting programmes not only illustrate the effect of the
proximal zones of attention, they also allow us to make a further
distinction in the structure of the programmes, namely the
distinction between 'carrier' and 'subordinate' programmes.
The tropistic orientation programme we have discussed previously (see Figure 7.5) provides an example of a carrier
programme. The carrier programme consists of the main transitional steps, i.e. the steps that are the necessary and typical
constituents of a tropistic orientation programme. The successive functional steps of the carrier programme constitute possible initial steps of the subordinate programmes. The opening
of the eyes at the onset of the sound or the closing of the eyes
during head turning are typical examples of subordinate programmes. These programmes may play an important role in the
development of the visual inspection function on the basis of
a tropistic orientation. The eye-opening and -closing subordinate programmes, for instance, optimize the visual information
flow in a very effective way. They increase visual attention at
the onset of the sound and decrease visual attention during
head turning.

The development of a 'visual inspection of an auditory localized place' programme is only one small step in the development
of the structure of perceptual functions. In the following example, I shall employ the visual inspection programme and discuss
how it may lead to a 'permanent object' programme.

With the tropistic programme, it does not matter whether the
sound-making object is visible or not, for instance hidden
behind another object or under a blanket. The only thing that
matters to the child is getting the sound source in an on-centre
position. With the visual inspection programme, however, it does
indeed matter whether the sound-making object is occupied by
a visible object. The visual inspection programme expresses a
learned expectation that an auditive place corresponds with a
visual place, or, put differently, that a topological break in
auditive space (a set of distinct places in auditive space) corresponds with a topological break in visual place. Assume,
for instance, that a sound-making object - a music box - got
under the child's blanket. When the child visually inspects the
place where the sound comes from, he does not see any particular object except for the blanket, which is an object that
extends far beyond the locus of the sound. Since there is no
visual topological break that corresponds with the auditive
topological break, the perceptual system might create the topological break itself. This can be done by attaching a foreground-

background programme to the visual inspection programme: the visible object - the blanket - which does not correspond with the auditive topological break, might be put at the foreground, whereas the expected topological break might be put at the - hidden - background. The effect of this programme is that the child has created a screen-function and has shown a rudimentary form of object permanence.

Although I cannot go into the details of this new perceptual programme, two important conclusions may be drawn. First, a developmentally important fact belongs to the zone of proximal attention connected with one but not with another programme. That is, the hidden sound-making object belongs to the zone of proximal attention of the visual inspection but not of the tropistic orientation programme. If the infant has learned that auditory revealed patterns correspond with patterns that can be inspected visually, he will be struck by the absence of a corresponding visual pattern. The second conclusion concerns the effect of proximal attention at the 'internal', i.e. function, side of the process. We have seen that a foreground-background programme will be attached to the visual inspection programme when the visually expected object is hidden by another object. Put differently, the foreground-background programme belongs to the zone of proximal attention of the visual inspection but not of the tropistic orientation programme.

A new programme - visual inspection of an invisible, auditory localized place - has emerged, based on the zones of proximal attention of the simple visual inspection programme. It is clear that this new programme constitutes an important step towards the permanent object programme, which is basically a programme of search and action connected with invisible objects. In order to find out how such a final permanence programme develops, we have to investigate its functional antecedents and examine how they relate in terms of the model of the zone of proximal attention.

Before I continue with a tentative explanation of the development of spatial pattern perception, I want to elucidate a number of differences and similarities between the notions 'programme' and 'zone of proximal attention' and Piagetian notions such as 'scheme', 'assimilation' and 'accommodation' ('adaptation'). The 'scheme' concept is closely related to concepts such as 'programme', 'frame', 'skill' or 'algorithm'. They imply that behaviour and the environment in which it is executed can be explained in terms of possibilities of action that form complex, interrelated conditional structures (instead of linear S-R connections, for instance). These concepts refer to a basic notion in the psychology of higher behavioural structures and are not unique to the Piagetian approach. They express the same basic idea but differ with regard to the theoretical background from which they have been derived.

The 'zone of proximal attention' plays a role that is functionally equivalent with the Piagetian notions 'assimilation' and 'accommodation' ('adaptation'). Assimilation implies that the subject is not sensitive to any kind of environmental information with which it is presented but only to that kind of information that fits his processing abilities, 'schemes', 'knowledge' and so forth. The concept of accommodation is concerned with the changes that the internal apparatus undergoes under the influence of external stimuli, i.e. experience. The function of assimilation can 'reduce' the environment, but it cannot reduce the environment to a mere reproduction of the internal apparatus. In that case any development other than mere maturation would be impossible. The proximal zone concept plays roughly the role attributed to assimilation and accommodation although it is not implied that it has the same far reaching theoretical and philosophical importance as in Piaget's theory. The 'proximal zone' concept is based on the assimilation idea, according to which the stimulus world is necessarily determined by the scope of our stimulus defining abilities, i.e. the structure of sensory functions. An important consequence of this starting point is that the number and nature of the targets of a possible attention shift are severely limited. Nevertheless, this limited set of possible foci (the zone of proximal attention) contains exactly the kind of information upon which developmentally relevant changes in the logic of the focal shifts will be based (the idea of accommodation).

A question that is closely related to the foregoing point is whether perceptual development is a process of integration or of differentiation. In the Piagetian tradition development proceeds by the integration of schemes, for instance the schemes of hearing and seeing. According to Gibson (1969) perceptual development is a process of differentiation. The child starts with the perception of undifferentiated wholes and gradually acquires the ability to differentiate them into their constituents. I think that it will fully depend on the nature of the stimulus as well as on the nature of the function whether a developmental process will have an integrative or a differentiation character. When a tropistic orientation programme evolves into a visual inspection programme, a process of integration as well as differentiation occurs. The process of differentiation is concerned with the separation between the auditory localization function and the tropistic reaction. The process of integration takes place between auditory localization, visual localization (by means of intermediate head turning) and visual inspection.

The following example deals with the influences of place perception on the development of pattern perception and illustrates that processes of differentiation and integration are mutually conditional.

It is conceivable that the initial state of pattern perception is characterized by a 'mono-featural' tendency, that is, every pattern is perceptually specified in terms of only one feature, such as 'curved' or 'closed', 'angular', 'multi-angular', 'regular' and so forth, dependent on its most salient properties (the term

Premisses. At the stimulus side: a triangilar figure specified in terms of four place sets S_1, S_2, S_3 and S_4. At the function side: a function 'mono-featural specification of pattern' that specifies S_1 as 'ma' (multi-angular), and S_1, S_2 and S_3 as 'a' (angular); a function 'place specification', specifying S_1 as p_1, S_2 as p_2, and S_3 as p_3 (see (a)).

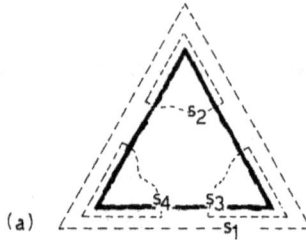

(a)

Question. How does the child acquire a multi-featural pattern specification function that specifies a triangle not as a single feature 'ma' but as a structure of spatial relations between angles?

Demonstration. The child's visual inspection of the triangle is determined by a stimulus parameter, containing four possible place sets (S_1, S_2, S_3 and S_4), and a function parameter containing two functions, namely place specification (PIS) and pattern specification (PaS). This implies that any inspection programme can be described in terms of a finite state automaton that contains eight possible states (see (b)). The states can be specified as the products of the interaction between function and stimulus parameter (see Premisses). The network describes the total set of possible attention focuses in a visual-inspection-of-the-triangle programme. The attention shifts (jumps between focuses) must be governed by transition rules. The simplest rule is to allow any possible shift. In this case we shall postulate a stricter transition rule. The rule states that within one functional domain, a shift to any possible place set is allowed, while shifts from one functional domain to another require that the stimulus focus remains the same.

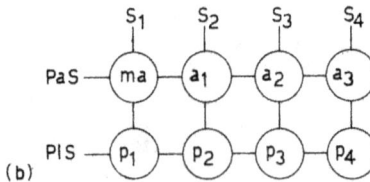

(b)

Diagram (c) summarizes the possible shifts, starting from focus $a_1(S_2 \times \text{PaS})$. A formal description of the transition rules might look as follows:

If $(\text{PaS}-S_i)$ then $\left[(\text{PaS}-S_i \Rightarrow \text{PaS}-S_j) \text{ and } (\text{PaS}-S_i \Rightarrow \text{PIS}-S_i)\right]$

If $(\text{PIS}-S_i)$ then $\left[(\text{PIS}-S_i \Rightarrow \text{PIS}-S_j) \text{ and } (\text{PIS}-S_i \Rightarrow \text{PaS}-S_i)\right]$

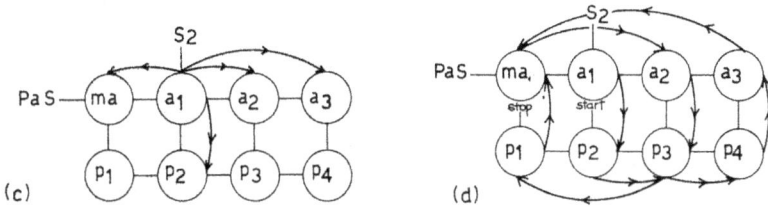

(d) represents a programme constructed according to the transition rules. In linear form:

$$a_1\text{-}p_2\text{-}p_3\text{-}p_4\text{-ma-}a_2\text{-}p_3\text{-}p\text{-ma}$$

In order to explain the effects of such programmes, we should start from the principle that the functional structure of the pattern perception system (see Figure 6.5) applies also to the components of these programmes, i.e. that comparing, clustering computing and economizing operations are carried out with the successive components. It is also assumed that the length of a processable programme should be limited (e.g. it should not succeed ten successive steps).

We may expect that three kinds of clusters will be made: one consisting of place specifications; another of pattern specifications, and a final one consisting of place- and pattern-specification pairs characterized by the same place set. The computing operations can be described in terms of general categories, such as adjacency (adjac) and subordinateness (subord), identity (=) and difference (≠). The result of the computing operations is that sub-clustering will occur in the three general clusters. The clusters can be represented as follows.

$$\left[(a_1, a_2, a_3)^=, \text{ma}\right]^{\neq} ; \left[(p_2, p_3, p_4)^{\text{adjac}}, p_1\right]^{\text{subord}};$$

$$\left[(a_1, p_2)^{S_2}, (a_3, p_4)^{S_4}, (a_2, p_3)^{S_3}, (\text{ma}, p_1)^{S_1}\right]$$

In terms of one place formula:

$$\left\{\left[(a_1, a_2, a_3)^=, \text{ma}\right]^{\neq}, \left[(p_2, p_3, p_4)^{\text{adjac}}, p_1\right]^{\text{subord}}\right\}^{1:1}$$

One of the most important implications of this formula is that the spatial relationship between the ma feature and the cluster of a features is described by the adjacency-subordinateness formula. That is, the ma feature is equalled to a particular spatial relationship between a features

Figure 7.8 A formal representation of the development of some pattern perception rules

'mono-featural' is closely related to 'undifferentiated Gestalt').
Mono-featural perception applies to complete figures as well as
to their constituents. The child may perceive a star as a 'multi-
angular' figure and each of its constituent angles as an 'angular
figure'. First, because of their spatial and functional proximity,
the complete figure - the star - and each of its constituent
angles will belong to each other's zones of proximal stimulation.
That is, when the infant fixates one angle of the star and sub-
mits it to the function 'pattern-specification', it is highly
probable that the focus of attention will shift either to another
constituent angle or to the complete figure (see Figure 7.8).
Second, the zone of proximal function connected with the focal
function 'pattern specification' will presumably contain the
function 'place specification'. It is conceivable that programmes
consisting of pattern- and place-specification-shifts on the one
hand and stimulus-shifts between angles and the multi-angular
pattern on the other hand will lead to a programme that is able
to specify the perceived star as a collection of constituent
angles with a particular spatial relationship (see Figure 7.8 for
more details). If we overview the developmental process, we
shall see that it consists of differentiation as well as integration.
The originally mono-featural multi-angular pattern has been
differentiated into a structure of constituent angles, which in
its turn consists of an integration of the original 'angular'
constituents.

7.2.2 Changing preferences and the development of spatial pattern perception

We have seen that the initial state of spatial pattern perception
is characterized by pattern preferences based on quantitative
properties. Further, the neonate's perception of spatial patterns
is characterized by the tendency to scan one salient element of
a pattern, e.g. one angle of a triangle. It may be questioned
what kind of events are responsible for the development of
preferences for qualitative properties of patterns, complex
scanning programmes and the ability to detect higher-order
properties of patterns.

Fantz et al. (1975) discuss the effects of institutionalization,
length of gestation and the effect of Down's syndrome (Mongo-
lism) on the development of pattern perception. The comparison
between babies living in a low perceptually stimulating environment (a home for unmarried mothers) and a highly stimulating
environment (babies living at home) showed no differences with
respect to the form but did differ with respect to the duration
of the developmental curve. Experimental enrichment of the
'poor' environment did not produce significant results. It is
quite conceivable, however, that perceptual enrichment means
more than the simple suspending of a number of toys in the
infants' cradles (which actually happened in the enrichment
experiment) and that enrichment should be achieved by increasing the social interaction with the infants, such as taking them

out of their cradles, pointing out things and talking to them.
It is highly probable that early perceptual development is
stimulated and directed by the contingent social and interactive
behaviour of caretakers and infants. This fact does not contradict our formal model of perceptual development via the zone
of proximal attention, but specifies the practical conditions on
which the formal model actually operates.

Fantz et al. (1975) also discuss the difference between premature infants and infants with normal gestation age (40 weeks).
Post-conceptual age (age in weeks after conception) showed to
be a much better predictor of pattern development than post-
natal age (weeks after birth). It might be concluded, therefore,
that early pattern development is a matter of mere maturation
(see also Miranda, 1970; Sigman and Parmelee, 1974; Fantz and
Fagan, 1976). A comparison between normal and Down's syndrome infants shows that the differences occur only in the field
of qualitative pattern properties. The preference for quantitative patterns shows no differences between normal and Down's
syndrome children, due to the fact that this form of preference
is regulated by more basic processes and neural components of
the pattern perception apparatus.

A number of investigators have shown that there are differences between neonate boys and girls with respect to the
level of discrimination-ability or preference-patterns. Girls
appear to be more advanced than boys, although it is possible
that the difference is not due to the perceptual but rather to
the response component (see Sigman and Parmelee, 1974; Weizmann et al., 1971; Cornell and Strauss, 1973; Friedman et al.,
1974; Fagan, 1972; Rose et al., 1976; Greenberg and Weizmann,
1971; Cohen et al., 1975).

Summarizing, all these investigations point in the direction
of a maturational explanation of the first developmental state
transitions in pattern perception. It would be wrong to conclude, however, that learning and experience do not play a
role in this developmental process. In our discussion of the
development of perceptual programmes we have seen that
programmes, such as the visual inspection programme, are
based on a number of innate programmes, such as the auditory
tropistic reaction and auditory-oculomotor programmes. The
visual inspection programme cannot originate from the tropistic
reaction when there is no visual preference programme that
moves into operation when an interesting visual property is
detected. If the presence of such a preference programme
depends on the infant's maturational level, the visual inspection
programme cannot emerge before that level is achieved, in
spite of numerous experiences with the auditory tropistic programme and its structuring effects on the perceived environment. However, since the neonate's and young infant's learning
rate is quite high, the emergence of new programmes based on
perceptual experiences will follow the emergence of their
maturational conditions quite closely. Once all the conditions

are present, it will not take long before the new programme
becomes established, provided that the child is allowed normal,
that is to say quite active, perceptual exploration. As I stated
earlier, the neonate's and young infant's opportunities to
explore a sufficiently rich perceptual environment will depend
largely on other people's willingness to compensate for their
immobility by carrying them around and extending and structuring their perceptual field. From this point of view, the
development of perception depends not only on biological and
experiential factors, but also on social conditions.

One of the most striking results of the study of pattern
perception development is that it starts with highly structured
visual behaviour. The initial state is not characterized by
arbitrary and unstructured scannings and shifts, but rather
by a quite rigid and predictable set of visual-motor programmes.
The structure of visual behaviour is based on both a motor and
a sensory component. The motor component consists of complex
natural looking patterns, which are present at any early stage.
Tronick and Clanton (1971) have studied such looking patterns
with infants between three and fifteen weeks of age. These
patterns are functional, in the sense that they can serve as
'search' or 'fixation' patterns and they consist of complex co-
ordinations between eye and head movements. On the sensory
side, the structure of looking behaviour is determined by the
presence and distribution of preferred pattern properties in
the explorable environment.

Before discussing the effects of scanning strategies and preferences upon pattern perception development, I must compare
the notions of 'scanning' and '(shifting) focus of attention' more
closely. At first sight, both terms seem to have the same meaning. The focus of attention, however, covers a domain that
is usually more extended than the visual fixation point. Since
the focus of attention is not only determined by the stimulus
domain but also by the perceptual function involved, it is possible that attention is focused on properties of forms that do
not strictly belong to the fixation point and that are not explicitly scanned. When adults focus upon a triangle, for instance,
they will presumably fixate the top angle and its relation to the
base, although they are able to shift the point of fixation to
other parts of the triangle quite easily (see for instance Yarbus,
1967). When a one month old infant scans a triangle, it is probable that a conservative scanning of one interesting feature of
a pattern is the only way in which the infant can maintain the
whole pattern as the focus of attention. The extension of the
focus of attention, however, remains a matter of theoretical
decision. The focus of attention can be defined at various levels:
first, it can be defined as a point of fixation during one single
fixation point of the eye or during one elementary temporal
quantum; second, it can be defined as a point of fixation during
a set of elementary shifts; finally, it can be defined as the
maximally preferred property during one specific developmental

state. The choice of the descriptive level depends on our
explanatory purposes. I would suggest not to go below the
level of a set of coherent scanning activities or eye movements
that are directed towards one pattern or pattern property.
Lower levels of focalization, e.g. the focus that corresponds
with the static phase between two eye movements, might be
relevant for detailed analyses of the processing aspects of
visual perception, but I assume that they are at a level below
that which we conceive of as functionally valid.

Figure 7.9 Total amount of contour, which is not linearly
related to size, is a simple and relatively adequate criterion
for figural complexity

The visual inspection of the one month old infant is determined by his preference for quantitative properties of patterns.
At the initial state of pattern development, these inbuilt preferences might play the same role as 'motives' or 'goals' at a
later age. In general, there are three kinds of quantitative
preferences at the initial state of pattern development: pattern
definition, total amount of contour, and constancy of contour

direction. The order in which these quantitative criteria have
been mentioned corresponds with their increasing connection
with qualitative pattern properties (i.e. form and pattern).

In the normal visual environment, patterns that have a high
degree of pattern definition, high total contour length and a
high level of directional change of contour are normally patterns
that have also a high probability of having interesting and
easily discernible qualitative properties. When two arbitrary
patterns have different amounts of total contour, the highest
contour pattern probably has the highest number of qualitative
features, since most features consist of typical breaks and
changes in the contour direction (see Figure 7.9). Put differently, the properties of natural objects are such that the set
of quantitatively optimal patterns has a zone of proximal attention which is characterized by interesting qualitative properties.
Remark that the level of attention to which I refer is the second
level in the theoretical model of attention shifts (see section
7.1.2), i.e. that of the selection criteria. The change in the
selection criteria is based on a variety of shifts at the lower
level, i.e. the micro-level of attention activities.

I shall now try to illustrate the development of pattern preference in more detail. The pattern space that I shall employ
is purely artificial but it is designed to make the demonstration
as clear as possible.

The basic principles that we must start with are, first, that
the perceptual system avoids increasing entropy and, second,
that it tries to find optimal topological breaks. A topological
break is defined as a change in sensory quality (brightness,
colour, pitch, loudness, etc.) over at least two places or sets
of places in space. Entropy is defined as the probability with
which a place in space (i.e. equivalent regions in space) carries
a topological break. We say that entropy is maximal when every
place in space has the same probability of carrying a topological
break (a very rough definition, but it will do for the moment –
see figures 7.10(a) and 7.10(b) for illustrations). Textures,
for instance, are characterized by a relatively high level of
entropy (although the local entropy can be quite low, e.g. when
the texture consists of clear-cut, specific textural form-ele-
ments). Textures are nevertheless important because of their
relationship with the surrounding texturally different space:
textures circumscribe objects, constitute supporting surfaces
and so forth.

The development of pattern preference is concerned with the
precise meaning of 'optimal' in 'optimal topological break'. I shall
try to show that any particular definition of 'optimal' – which
specifies a state of pattern perception development – will lead
to a set of preferred patterns that define zones of proximal
attention that contain the developmentally subsequent definition of 'optimal topological break'.

The most obvious initial pattern preference rule based on the
principles of minimal entropy and maximal topological break is:

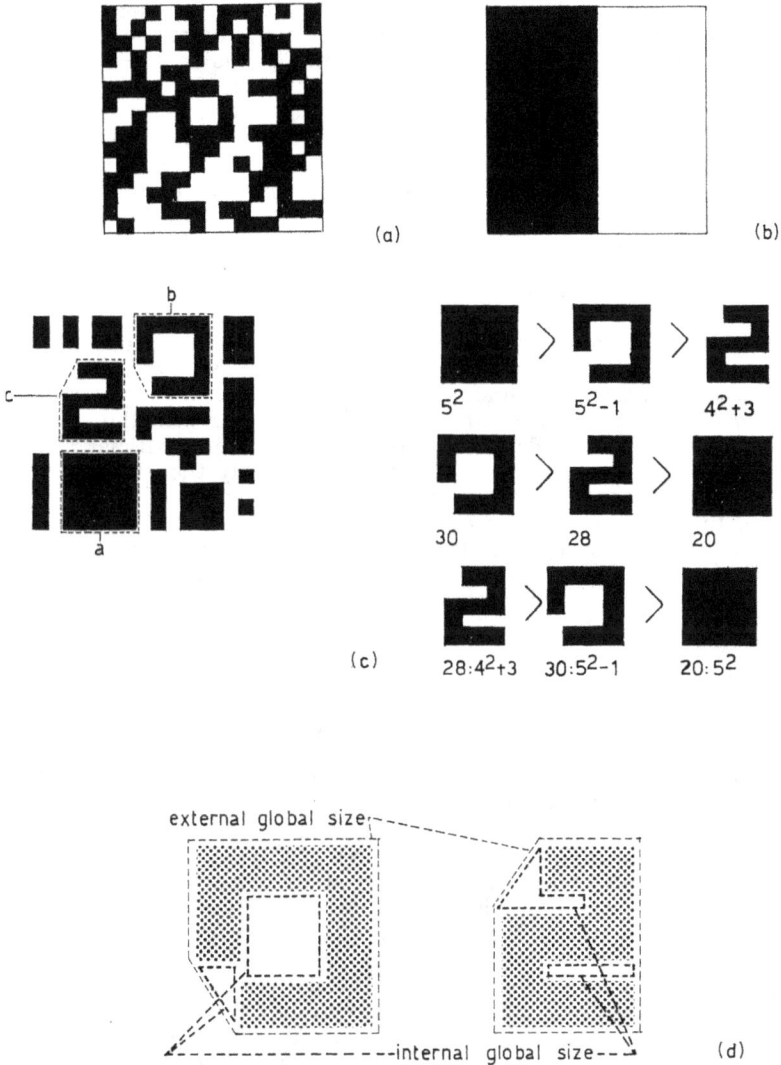

(a)

(b)

(c)

5^2 5^2-1 4^2+3

30   28   20

$28:4^2+3$ $30:5^2-1$ $20:5^2$

external global size

internal global size

(d)

Figure 7.10 (a) A 15 x 15 places space with a black saturation of 50 per cent (50 per cent of the places are occupied by black spots). The space shows maximal entropy: each place has a probability of 50 per cent of containing a black spot. (b) The same space as in (a). Entropy is minimal: the places at the left have a probability of 100 per cent of containing a black spot, the places at the right have a probability of 100 per cent of containing a white spot. (c) The same space as in (a). The black

spots have been distributed in the form of fifteen place sets.
If global size is the main parameter of attention, the order of
visual preference for the three most salient figures is a-b-c; if
absolute amount of contour determines preference, the order
will become b-c-a; with relative contour, the order of preference
will become c-b-a. (d) In principle, global size specifies the
external contour of an object. If also the internal contours are
submitted to the global size function, the resulting size specification equals the total amount of absolute contour. Relative
contour is the result of dividing absolute contour by global
external size, i.e. relative contour represents the relationship
between global size and the amount of internal detail

attend to global size of topological break. Global size represents
the general quantitative relationship between a cluster of places
and the perceivable surrounding space. It determines the
global amount of space taken by a cluster, together with the
density of the cluster. Figure 7.10(c) represents an artificial
space filled with a number of patterns. If we apply the global-
size rule to the set of patterns, the order of preference
(limited to the three most important patterns) is a-b-c. The
order results from computing the global size of the patterns
(the field within the dotted line) and the density (in Figure
7.10(c) I made an abstraction from the latter). When the
observer prefers global size, the zone of proximal attention will
consist of the criterion 'absolute contour'. Within each global
field that circumscribes the patterns of the ordered set a-b-c,
the application of the global-size rule leads to a new criterion,
namely absolute contour (see Figure 7.10(c)). Absolute contour
is simply the result of applying the global size measure to each
constituent of the pattern on which it is applicable, i.e. external as well as internal boundaries of the pattern. The reason
why the global size criterion is applied to the internal boundaries of the figure is that, although external boundary is the
most salient aspect of the figure at this stage of pattern development, internal boundary lies within its zone of proximal
attention (viewed from the micro-level of attention processes).
The result of applying this new criterion, i.e. absolute contour, to the set of patterns in our artificial space is that the
order of preference will change into b-c-a. In a normal pattern
space, the application of the absolute contour criterion will
lead to the selection of patterns that have a high amount of
absolute contour but a relatively small global size. Since the
criterion of global size preceded the absolute contour criterion,
it still belongs to the zone of proximal attention of the latter
(the reason for this will become clear when we look at Figure
7.2). If global size belongs to the zone of proximal attention of
the absolute-contour criterion, a second, more important,
property will also belong to this zone, namely relative contour.
Relative contour is the relation between absolute contour and
global size. By paying attention to relative contour, the conflict

between absolute contour and global size (which is characteristic for many natural patterns – see Figure 7.9) can be solved, and thereby also the danger of a circular process of development, which would be characterized by an increase in the speed with which the cycle would take place, i.e. from global size to absolute contour and vice versa. If the criterion of relative contour were applied to the artificial-pattern space, the order of preference would become c–b–a.

When relative contour determines pattern preference, the zone of proximal attention will contain an important property of patterns, namely the distributional characteristics of the contours, i.e. form properties. Relative contour excludes global size and absolute contour as preference criteria. The only quantitative differences that may exist between patterns characterized by equal relative contour are concerned with the way in which the contour is distributed in space, i.e. with the degree of complexity of the distribution principle. Infants will prefer a scrambled to a regular checkerboard, provided that both have approximately identical relative contours. The difference between the scrambled and the regular checkerboard lies in the complexity of the rules according to which the constituent squares are ordered. The same holds for a straight and a curved line: the distributional formula of a curved line is more complex than that of a straight line (although the complexity depends on the kind of space we employ or have to ascribe to the visual system). Distributional properties of the contours constitute the form characteristics, i.e. the qualitative appearance of the form or pattern. In summary, qualitative properties have been inferred from very general quantitative properties on the basis of a process of attention shifts in the proximal zones.

The 'topological break-minimal entropy' rule served as a meta-rule which determined the nature of the shifts between preference rules. Once the qualitative-preference rule has been acquired, it is highly plausible that the meta-rule will be replaced, i.e. the nature of the subsequent developmental state transitions will change. The reason for this change is that, once qualitative rules have come to determine pattern preference, the object (in the logical sense) of the perceptual act takes the form of an object (in the material sense, i.e. things, persons, etc.). When preference will be directed to properties that constitute forms-qua-things, the zone of proximal attention will be determined by thing-properties, i.e. properties that permit comparison, interactive use of objects (e.g. putting something in something else), and so on. The object (i.e. thing) quality of perceived patterns and forms will become the new meta-criterion of pattern perception development.

Finally, I must state that the previous analysis of the development of pattern perception mainly serves a theoretical function. The concepts and parameters of the model are highly simplified and abstract. Nevertheless, I assume that it should be possible to find adequate empirical mapping rules that enable us to test the model experimentally.

8 Description and explanation of development

8.1 DESCRIPTION AND EMPIRICAL INVESTIGATION

The basic aim of developmental psychology is to discover adequate descriptions of development and to determine the explanatory principles lying behind them. Unfortunately, there is no general consensus about what we mean by 'adequate' description or explanation.

The naive empiristic, inductive approach to this question is clearly untenable. It is not possible to find an observer who is able to 'empty his mind' and carry out an uninfluenced observation of what 'really' happens. Observation without specific selection, abstraction and strategies for observing is impossible. Besides, the idea of a theoretically not-contaminated observation language appears as untenable as the idea of undisturbed observation. An observation language is 'pure' only with respect to a number of basic theoretical decisions made in the general language in which it is embedded (see for instance Hanson, 1958).

Naive falsificationism, which is often but partly unjustly identified with Popper (see for instance Lakatos, 1970) constitutes another extreme: it is possible to prove that a theory is false but impossible to prove that it is true. Falsification occurs when an observation has been made that does not tally with the basic statements and beliefs of the theory. The main critique against naive falsificationism is that nothing exists that is so easily replaced as a theory or hypothesis that has been falsified. A simple, conservative revision of the theory may intercept the criticism and in turn be accepted as a new theory.

In the first part of this book, I sketched an approach which viewed theories as descriptive and interpretive frameworks. The conceptual kernel of a theory consists of a framework for describing the nature of psychological phenomena, i.e. for defining the nature of the events and properties with which the theory deals. It may be questioned from where a theory, viewed as an apparatus for description and interpretation, comes and according to which principles it develops.

In the first part of this book, I have tried to give a speculative answer to this question. I stated that a theory of development is inferred from an existing 'theory' of any psychological, cognitive, social or other state or skill that can be conceived of as the final point of a process. The content of such a theory and the reason why we have chosen it reflects our basic

assumptions about man and his place in nature and culture. Our
theory of the development of perception started from a definition of the mature perceptual process. The definition involved
a number of assumptions that are basic to our view of the
structure of perceivable reality; for instance, that there is one
world instead of as many worlds as there are senses; that this
world exists independently of our presence; that space can be
described reliably in terms of three dimensions, and so forth.
These assumptions are broad enough to allow considerable freedom with regard to the kind of aspects we wish to accentuate.
We might have chosen another definition of perception than the
one we actually did, without going beyond the boundaries of
what is found to be a philosophically, socially or empirically
acceptable account of perception. Instead of the individual we
might have accentuated the social aspects of perception; instead
of the stimulus-side we might have accentuated the internal,
cognitive constraints upon the process of perception, and so
forth.

Starting from a definition of perception that is rooted in the
conceptual and practical worlds of the sciences, of philosophy
and of commonsense, we have tried to make a theoretical inference with regard to the kind of initial state that underlies it.
We have seen that the choice for such an initial state is not
always obvious and unambiguous, but we have also seen that it
is not totally arbitrary. The choice of an initial state definition
depends on the way in which we have defined the final state,
i.e. it must be conceptually coherent with it. Within these close
conceptual relationships between our final and initial state
definitions, clear limitations exist with regard to the nature of
the steps that may lead from one to the other.

We may state that our theory of development constitutes a
particular way of constructing a 'world of mental development
of the child' (e.g. the contemporary western child). The constructive activity takes two forms, namely a conceptual and
a practical form. The conceptual form is based on a descriptive
and interpretive framework necessary to build a conceptual
representation of developmental phenomena, whereas the praxis
consists of a specific 'style' of experimentation and observation,
a number of favourite topics of investigation and discussion,
specific educational or practical applications (or the lack of
such applications) and so forth.

However, if the world of mental development is the object –
more precisely the result – of our constructive activities, it
may be questioned whether any limitations can be imposed on
these activities. In order to understand that these limitations
are indeed present, we must take into account that the world of
mental development is not only the result, but also the domain
of our scientific constructive activities. This domain – which is
itself the produce of former biological, cultural and scientific
processes of construction – offers a number of well-defined
possibilities and limitations. However much an experiment may

be a theory-dependent construct, for instance, the range of
possible meaningful experiments is anything but occasionally
determined, whereas the actual empirical outcome of the experiment may answer our questions in an unexpected way. In fact,
there is no structural difference between the constitutive effect
of the infant's perceptual functions on his perceptual world
and the effect of our theoretical instruments on the world of
mental development that they construct. In both cases, the
domain in which the activities take place limits their possible
outcomes and creates a small but therefore also significant zone
of new possibilities or insights.

The classical methods for evaluating developmental statements
empirically are observation and experiment. These methods serve
different functions. In principle, the formulation of a descriptive and interpretive theoretical framework can be done behind
the desk, independent of any contact with the empirical world.
As I stated before, this is a mere theoretical possibility. In
practice the development of such a descriptive frame will arise
in close connection with empirical investigation. Observation is
the method that is most appropriately applied during the stage
of theory and concept formation. Observation is a method of
confronting ourselves with the conceptual, descriptive and
methodological possibilities that are implied by our theoretical
starting point but which we are unable to make explicit without
the inspiring influence of observation. Many developmental
theories are the result of an interaction between a broad conceptual framework and careful observation. Piaget's theory is
probably the best known example. Another example is provided
by the history of theories of language development (see for
instance Tiedemann (1782), Preyer (1881), Stern and Stern
(1907) and Brown (1973)).

The experimental method is particularly suited when decisions
must be made between alternative statements generated by a
sufficiently elaborated conceptual framework or theory. Experimentation alone can never be the key to a deeper understanding
of reality: if we didn't have a conceptual and descriptive framework, where would our experiments come from? How would we
formulate the hypotheses we want to test and determine their
relevance? Experiments are relevant when they give an answer
to a precise and relevant question. The relevance and preciseness of a question, however, depends on the theory in which
it is embedded.

When I state that an experiment is 'embedded' in a theory, I
mean that it is designed in order to answer a question that is
posed by this theory and it does not matter whether the experiment is carried out with the intention of answering this question
negatively or positively. Negative intentions are often inspired
by theoretical backgrounds that are different from the theory
that has generated the experiment (the mother theory). By
proving that the mother theory is wrong, the concurrent theory
tries to improve its own position. Piaget's theory of cognitive

development offers an interesting example of a 'mother' theory
which has been attacked experimentally from various sides.
Trabasso's investigation of children's transitive reasoning, for
instance, is an example of a specific Piagetian theme - transitive
inference making - that is used to support an alternative
approach to cognition, namely information processing theory
(Trabasso, 1975). Other examples are provided by experiments
on conservation by Bruner (e.g. Bruner et al. 1966), Brainerd
(e.g. 1978) and Bryant (e.g. 1974). It is often quite difficult, however, to determine in which theory an experiment is
actually embedded. When Trabasso, for instance, proves that
children can solve transitive inference tasks without making
use of transitive inferences but by linear ordering and mental
comparison, his experiment is not a transitive inference experiment but an experiment on ordering and comparing. The same
might be said about Bruner's and Brainerd's conservation
experiments, which extended the kind of acceptable criteria
for conservation. Piaget's answer to this kind of experiments
(see Piaget, 1968) is that these experiments do not measure
conservation-as-defined-by-Piaget and that they are not suitable for deciding whether and where Piaget's theory is wrong.
Put differently, a controversy exists about what happens in
these experiments. A nice example of such disagreement is
provided by Watson's (1968) interpretation of a conservation
experiment in behaviouristic terms.

In Fregean terms, various theories - behaviourism, Piaget,
information processing theory - discuss the same experiment
insofar as its actual referent - the experiment as a spatiotemporal event - is concerned, but a different experiment when
its sense is taken into account. The 'sense' of the experiment -
or, more precisely, its Saussurean 'value' - depends on its place
in the structure of events and concepts, which is clearly
theory-dependent. It may even be questioned whether the
referent can remain unaffected when such basically different
views on the nature of psychological reality are concerned.
In accordance with the viewpoint that I have discussed in this
book, the referent should also be defined as the object of a
particular (scientific) act of observation and interpretation,
and, as such, the nature and extension of the referent depends
on the properties of the observation - and interpretation -
practices, which are often specific to the distinct theories.

This leads us to still another point concerning the relation
between experiments and a theory or descriptive framework.
When we refrain from the conceptual plurality of an experiment,
the experiment as such is characterized by a particular degree
of relevance with regard to a particular theory. Kendler's
reversal shift experiment is highly relevant with regard to his
theory about response mediation in cognitive development
(Kendler and Kendler, 1970; Kendler, 1964). It is certainly
possible to give a Piagetian interpretation of this experiment,
but this does not make the reversal shift experiment relevant

for Piagetian theory. That is, experiments differ with regard to the importance they have for a theory, i.e. they occupy different hierarchical levels in the conceptual structure of a theory. A nice example of this principle is provided by the experiments that have shown that problem solving skills are highly dependent on the kind of content to which they are applied. This phenomenon is especially typical with formal operational thinking. Most subjects pass only a limited number of formal operational tests, mainly the ones for which they have had explicit training or schooling.

At first sight, this finding contains a serious attack on Piagetian theory, which claims that cognitive structures are independent of concrete contents and are united into coherent, closely connected structures. Piaget, however, has never denied this experimental finding but he has attributed it with a relatively low status in the hierarchy of theoretically relevant facts. The concept of vertical 'décalage', for instance, is one way of solving this difficulty. It implies that a developmental stage does not consist exclusively of cognitive contents and structures that are typical for this stage, but will in practice also contain remnants of previous stages. Although the concept of 'décalage' often causes resentment amongst students of Piaget's theory, it is perfectly compatible with one of Piaget's basic principles, namely that his theory is a 'competence' and not a performance theory of cognitive development (see Brainerd, 1978). The reason why these décalages occur might be explained on the basis of differential resistance of cognitive contents to their assimilation by particular, e.g. formal, operational structures (see Smedslund, 1977). This explanation is again perfectly compatible with the basic notions of Piagetian theory.

Whereas the finding that cognitive ability is closely related to cognitive content occupies a rather low position in the Piagetian hierarchy of theoretically relevant facts, it is of central importance in a skill theory of cognitive development (Smedslund, 1977). This is not difficult to understand when we consider skill to be a specific ability with regard to a specific content or domain of application. The fact that skills are not completely unconnected and form clusters characterized by relatively content-independent properties is not incompatible with the theoretical concept of 'skill'. It is a secondary finding, however, in comparison with the finding that skills are primarily content-bound. Summarizing, a fact that is typically 'illustrative' with regard to one theory may be merely 'compatible' for another theory and vice versa. That is, facts are related to theories at various levels of relevance.

It might look as if this view of the constitutive relationship between a descriptive framework and facts paves the way for complete arbitrariness, theoretical anarchy and relativism. In fact, this criticism bypasses what actually happens when a new theory or new concepts of development are created by an individual, a group or a 'school'. Suggesting a new theory, concept or point of view is a human activity that contains productive as well as creative aspects. On the productive side, a new theory, such as the one introduced by Piaget in the early 1920s, is always rooted in a variety of existing theories, concepts or problems that may stem from various fields. The nature of human cognitive production is such that no conceptual construction can be made that is entirely arbitrary and without meaningful relationship with the existing conceptual constructions. On the creative side, the making of a new theory or point of view cannot simply be predicted from an existing set of theories or points of view. When a theory is new, it is usually relatively immature and contains a large number of weak or unelaborated aspects. It must be able, however, to defend itself against the attacks raised by adherents of existing theories. The theory has to take part in a scientific discussion that is determined by generally accepted rules (with a few exceptions that prove how much is actually generally accepted). The theory will have to defend itself against attempts to disprove the consistency or necessity of its concepts, against experiments carried out to falsify the theory's empirical statements, and so forth. The new theory, therefore, should always be meaningful with regard to the existing theories and, in a broader sense, also to accepted philosophical and epistemological points of view and questions.

The constitutive relationship between a descriptive framework or theory on the one hand and facts on the other hand holds at the conceptual but not at the phenomenal or existential level. In fact, a descriptive framework or theory describes a universe of conceptually possible facts. Only a limited part of them will actually occur. The explanation of these empirical limitations will give the theory its empirical value, i.e. its relationship not with a possible but with the actual world. It should be taken into account, however, that the facts have only a severely limited freedom to resist the attempts towards verification, realization and construction that originate from the various theories. Nevertheless, the structured uncertainty of an experiment or observation is characterized by a zone of proximal (scientific) attention which contains the conditions for later, eventually drastic, changes of the descriptive and interpretive framework.

The prediction criterion, stating that the theory which predicts best is the best theory, is often used uncritically as an ultimate criterion for evaluating competitive theories. One must question, however, whether different theories also agree about what must be predicted, i.e. about the content and form of the facts that are worth predicting. The theory of perceptual development that has been sketched in this book has led to a particular hierarchy of the available empirical evidence and to suggestions with regard to the kind of new experiments that have theoretical priority. That is, we have pointed out which kind of facts are worth predicting and which ones are simply irrelevant.

Primarily, theories must be evaluated on instrumental or functional grounds. In order to make the instrumental criterion clearer, I shall have to rely on a metaphor, namely a comparison between a theory and a tool. A tool, such as a hammer, is made to serve a particular function, namely driving nails into wood. Certainly it may serve other functions, such as knocking boards into two pieces (although a saw is much better suited to this purpose). The value of a hammer, therefore, depends on the kind of activity one wants to fulfil. On the other hand, an available instrument creates its own function and its own expedients. When one has a hammer, for instance, one also needs nails and pliers otherwise the hammer will be useless.

In fact, a tool-kit is a better metaphor for a theory or descriptive framework. The concepts and methods contained in the theory might be compared with the individual tools that serve mutually adapted functions. One kit might contain a small and a large hammer, nails of various sizes, pliers and a driving-punch while another kit contains screwdrivers, screws and a drill. Tool-kits that are designed to serve largely identical functions, such as the screwdriver and the hammer kit, are metaphors for theories that cover largely identical phenomena, such as theories of perceptual development or memory processes. When such theories must be compared and evaluated, one has to employ roughly the same criteria as with the tool-kits. The choice depends not only on the particular function they have to fulfil, the particular affinities and abilities of the user, but also on considerations of quality (which might suggest that it is more practical to use a good screw set than a bad hammer set, even when the job might be done better with a good hammer set). The tool-kit metaphor also illustrates why eclecticism is a bad habit, insofar as eclecticism is understood to be simply mixing the tools of various sets, i.e., the concepts and methods of different theories. Such a mixture would imply that the user of the 'eclectic' kit might try to screw a nail into the wood. That is to say, that, as long as theories are kept separately and carefully distinguished, the user is free to choose a theory that serves his actual goals and affinities best.

The goals we want to achieve will be determined, at least partly, by the possibilities of the kits themselves. Applied to theories, it means that our goals, such as improving perceptual development for instance, will be circumscribed by the conceptual potentialities of the theory that we employ. This fact sets a plain limit to a purely functionalistic approach of scientific theories. As far as the functions that will be fulfilled by the theory are co-determined by the theory itself, a functionalistic evaluation of the theory is partly self-fulfilling.

Finally, I want to remark that the tool-kit metaphor, however illustrative, underexposes a number of important aspects. In practice, the metaphor will lead too easily to a simple and untenable form of pragmatism, which views theories as ways for solving problems. The fact that the problems themselves are co-determined by the theories that are employed to solve them makes a naive pragmatic interpretation less obvious.

Theories are very complex instruments, which mediate between the exploring subject and the explorable world. In fact, the world acquires its specific explorable form by virtue of these instruments. The world of mental development, for instance, is the object of a particular instrumental act, namely the use of a developmental theory (in experimentation, observation, educational application, explanation, and so forth). We have seen, however, that the world is not only the object but also the domain of our acts, i.e. an objective field within which our acts are carried out. In this sense the domain offers a number of functional possibilities and limitations to the acts, which will result in products that will indirectly reflect the functional slots of the domain.

The question of whether a theory is either a constructive tool-kit or an image of reality can be answered at two levels: the level of actual use and the meta-theoretical level. At the level of actual use, theories are tool-kits if and when they are used as tool-kits; they are images of reality if and when they are used as images of reality. The making of reliable distinctions between various types of scientific acting requires a morphological theory which would constitute an important contribution to the philosophy of science (see for instance Gobar, 1968, for a morphology of psychological theorizing). At the meta-theoretical level, it should be questioned which properties are common to the various morphological types of scientific (psychological) acting. The meta-theoretical answer that I have tried to illustrate in this chapter holds that the common property of all scientific acting consists of the constructive relationship between the investigator and the investigated universe, taking into account that the constructive relationship takes the form of a theory, experiments, practical application, and so forth. The successses and failures of our theories and experiments are the expression of the power of our constructive abilities with regard to the reality in which we carry out our constructive acts. This implies that we adhere to a form of ontological pluralism as far as reality as object of our constructive acts is concerned, whereas we start from reality as an objective datum if it is viewed as the scene on which the constructive acts are carried out. It should be noted, however, that even in this sense objectivity is not a simple concept and that reality as the product and as the scene of our scientific activities pass into each other.

8.2 DESCRIPTION AND EXPLANATION

Explanation occurs at two distinct levels. First, at the conceptual level the explanation of developmental transitions is finally a matter of definition. We 'explain' the occurrence of a concrete operational state after a pre-operational state by elucidating the definitions of these states. In practice, however, we are more interested in a second form of explanation, based on the causal and conditional factors that determine whether and when a developmental transition will take place with a specific subject.

Both kinds of explanation are closely related to description, as I shall try to illustrate by means of a few alternative descriptions of an (artificial) developmental sequence, generated by different theories. We shall assume that the theories employ an identical data base (e.g. a set of daily video-recordings of a child during the first three years) and that the various theories agree that one whole year corresponds with one developmental state (a very artificial but practical assumption).

For each theory, we can draw a scheme consisting of four levels. At level 1 we find the ages of the subject (1, 2 and 3 years), at level 2 the corresponding data base (B_1, B_2 and B_3), at level 3 the theoretically determined data descriptions, based on a specific way of data-weighting, selecting, conceptualization and so forth (D_1, D_2 and D_3) and at the fourth level we find the state labels that correspond with the descriptions of properties at the previous level. Explanation at the fourth level is purely conceptual, i.e. it consists of a theoretical justification of the necessity of this particular order of states. At the third level, the explanation is causal or conditional: how can behaviours described by D_2, for instance, emerge on the basis of D_1? If this succession were merely a matter of contingency, the description and explanation would be both useless and uninteresting. It may be assumed, however, that the succession of described behaviours is not accidental, i.e. that causal and conditional relationships between D_1 and D_2 properties do exist (see Figure 8.1).

Theories differ in the way in which they employ the data base. A typical developmental theory will employ the data base in a cumulative way. At the age of three, for instance, it will describe the behaviour of the subject on the basis of the sum of data collected over the first, second and third year. But on the other hand, the behaviour characteristic for the first year will be described in connection with the behaviour that is characteristic for the second and third (and following) years. Data are meaningful with regard to the chain of data in which they occur.

A non-developmental behavioural theory may also try to explain the succession of behaviours provided by this data base. Such a theory, however, will not employ the data base in the cumulative or retrograde way that is typical for developmental theories. That is, the contextual meaning of the behaviours is limited to a relatively small section of the data base (D_1, for instance).

We can now show what a developmental and a non-develop-

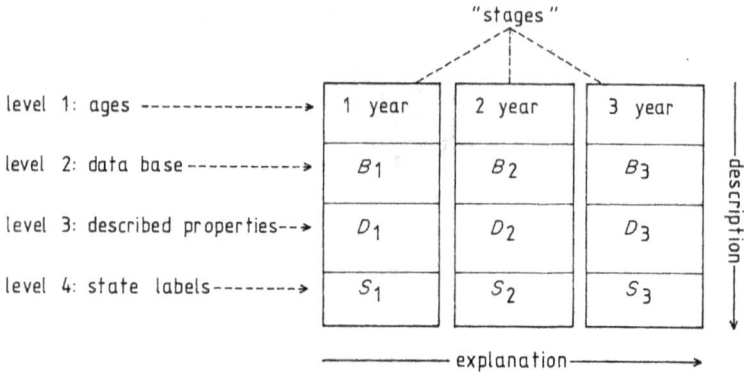

Figure 8.1 Levels of description (vertical) and levels of explanation (horizontal) in models of development

mental theory of behavioural change will do when, for one or another reason, the data base at age three is roughly identical with the data base at age one. The non-developmental theory will apply a state description to the limited data base and assign the same state-label to the ages of one and three. The succession of stages is $S_1-S_2-S_1$. We see that this theory accepts reversible development: behaviour can be learned as well as unlearned. Such an approach is typical of a rather naive kind of theoretical learning approach. In a developmental theory, the data base upon which the description and labelling of age three rests consists of the entire series of observations carried out during the whole three years. That is why age three behaviour will be described and labelled in a different way than age one behaviour even if the degree of phenomenal resemblance is very high. It is not the behaviour alone, but also its particular place in a succession of behaviours that determine its meaning. The developmental theory may describe the age three behaviour as an instance of regression (which is entirely different from mere developmental reversibility) or it may state that the resemblance with age one behaviour is superficial and not structural. There are perfectly good reasons for such a cumulative mode of data description. 'Behaviour' is a theoretical category that does not only contain spatiotemporal aspects such as amount and form of bodily motion, nervous processes and so forth, but also, and most importantly, functional aspects that explain why the motions or processes took place, what they were intended for and which previous events have caused them. Gregory (1966) and Von Senden (1932) have provided case studies of previously blind patients who recovered sight after an operation. Although their reactions to visual information might show a number of resemblances with infants, the lines of development are not identical, simply because the adult's visual development has totally different antecedents and functions than that of the infant. The same kind of problem can be met in Papalia's studies of cognitive regression by the end of life. Although the conservation responses of a senile eighty year old subject may show striking resemblances with four-year-olds' reactions to the test, their reactions are based on totally different antecedents, serving totally differing functions and leading to different endpoints. The danger with cumulative data bases is that they might give occasion to theories where statements are no longer connected with particular and specific data bases but simply with mere behavioural succession. That is, any behaviour occurring after state 2 behaviour, for instance, will be employed as a criterion for a 'state 3' ascription, simply because the behaviour occurs after state 2 and not because the behaviour has particular state-specific properties other than its place in the succession. Such a theory is not sufficiently connected with the reality upon which it is mapped.

Explanation is concerned with the relationship between the stage columns or 'stages' distinguished in Figure 8.1. We have seen that different opinions exist with regard to the way in which a data base must be used. One of the most obvious properties of explanation concerns the distinction between the explaining and the explained variable. If the explained variable is the occurrence of state 3, for instance, then the explaining variable is the sum of the properties, experiences and events that are the necessary and sufficient antecedents of state 3.

In order to explain a variable, we should not only specify its temporal, behavioural and theoretical extent, but also the properties and extent of the explaining variable. It makes an enormous difference whether we are interested either in a non-cumulatively defined set of behaviours that we want to explain on the basis of non-cumulatively defined behavioural variables or in a cumulatively defined set of behaviours, i.e. a behavioural state, that we want to explain on the basis of cumulatively defined antecedents, i.e. the entire developmental history of the subject. I assume that it is impossible or at least very difficult to tell which kind of explanation provides the best and most reliable predictions of developmental phenomena. I think that the answer depends on the kind of explaining and explained variables, i.e. either cumulatively or non-cumulatively defined, that one wants to employ. Traditional Piagetian stage theory, for instance, is a typical example of the latter, whereas learning theoretical approaches to development provide a typical example of the former kind. It is also conceivable that a broad, cumulatively defined variable explains non-cumulatively defined, specific behaviour. This might be the case with relatively unique, stage-specific expressions of stage-specific abilities. An adult's ability to solve a complex, unknown mathematical problem, for instance, can be described in a non-

cumulative way, since it is an ability that has no relevant
resemblance with a kind of ability that occurred before adulthood. The explanation of this ability, however, requires an
explaining variable that has a very broad, cumulative scope.
It would be different, however, if the adult had just learned
how to solve such a problem. In this case the explaining variable would be relatively specific and non-cumulative. The
adult's ability to learn how to solve such a problem in such a
short time, however, might again ask for a broadly defined
explaining variable, and so forth.

8.3 FROM EXPLAINING TO DETERMINING THE COURSE OF DEVELOPMENT

One of the classical issues of developmental psychology concerns the question of whether skills and abilities that are
acquired on the basis of strictly guided training and teaching
have the same meaning and developmental effects as skills
and abilities that are acquired spontaneously. Stated in this
form, the question is highly misleading, however, since it suggests a fundamental difference between learned and spontaneously acquired forms of behaviour. In fact, the gist of the
question concerns the 'degrees of freedom' in the order and
speed of developmental phenomena: how much depends on the
autonomous decisions with regard to training practices or
'laisser-faire' attitudes of the parent, caretaker or teacher?

Let us examine which kind of theoretical considerations may
contribute to solving the question concerning the developmental
effects of training and explicit teaching. The presence of a skill
or ability (knowledge, forms of thinking) is indicated by a
specific kind of behaviour. This behaviour is employed as a
decisive criterion for the presence of this skill or ability. The
critical behaviour is generated by 'programmes', i.e. structures
of functions applied in particular contexts. Programmes are the
expression of the global structure of functions that characterize
the perceptual (and cognitive) abilities of a subject at a given
time. This global structure constitutes a 'grammar', a complex
set of transition probabilities between functions and function
groups. It may be stated, therefore, that the acquisition of a
new skill or ability implies a new programme, and consequently
it also implies a change within the global structure of functions
(I exclude 'new' skills or abilities that structurally conform
with the existing ones). The extent to which the structure has
changed depends on the structural distance between the newly
acquired skill or ability and the 'old' ones.

Piaget's viewpoint on the effect of training is that if training
has resulted in the emergence of an ability before the 'allowed'
time, the effects of such training are superficial, easily revoked
and without effects on further development. Brainerd's extensive review of Piaget replication studies has shown that at least

some of the training experiments have had reliable and more
than superficial effects at times that were not theoretically
permissible (Brainerd, 1978). In early perceptual development,
training experiments have remained unsuccessful (see section
7.2.2). Since these experiments are so few in number, however, it is impossible to give a definite answer to the question
of whether trained and spontaneously acquired perceptual skills
have the same developmental meanings and implications. I shall
try to show that the answer to this question will depend on
the nature of the function programmes that underlie the behaviour at issue.

Assume, for instance, that we succeeded through training
to evoke interest in qualitative form discrimination several
months prior to the time the child would spontaneously express
such interest. The child will possess a form discrimination
programme embedded in a structure of perceptual functions
that are still limited to 'selection of saturated colour' programmes
or programmes for selecting optimal amounts of pattern
contour. At first sight the form discrimination programme is
incompatible with the structure of functions in which it is
embedded. This incompatibility can be explained in two different
ways which have one basic feature in common, namely that they
do not accept that a specific programme and the structure of
functions in which it is embedded are really incompatible. The
justification for this assumption is that the 'structure of functions' represents a theoretical concept that is inferred from
the properties of programmes, i.e. that it is a structural
'translation' of a set of observed programmes in one subject.

The presence of a seemingly incompatible discrimination programme that has been learned long before the time that it is
spontaneously acquired can be explained either by assuming
that the entire structure of functions has been drastically
changed or by assuming that the behaviour at issue is generated by a programme that differs entirely from the programme
that will generate it at a later point in development, i.e. at its
normal time of occurrence. The first explanation can be tested
by examining whether or not the trained child is able to carry
out untrained behaviours that are typical for the changed
structure of functions (transfer criterion). The difficulty,
however, lies in determining the kind of structural changes
that have taken place as a consequence of the training. It is
clear that these changes are not identical to the changes that
take place when the trained ability occurs normally, simply
because 'normal' development involves more than the single
discrimination ability that has been acquired artificially. The
second explanation of the trainability of discrimination long
before its normal time can be tested by examining whether the
discrimination behaviour at issue can be explained on the basis
of stimulus and function variables other than the ones involved
in the genuine discrimination programme. We have seen, for
instance, that a number of experiments on the perception of

higher-order variables can be explained on the basis of lower-order variables, simply because both types of variables co-vary in most of the patterns in which they occur. Accordingly, neonates might be taught to discriminate forms on the basis of simple quantitative feature discrimination.

How pessimistic or optimistic are we with regard to trainability of perceptual and cognitive abilities, functions and structures in general? Certainly, one of our basic points is that no ability can be acquired before a number of necessary and sufficient conditions are fulfilled. These conditions are quite specific and do not allow much freedom with regard to the order in which abilities can be acquired. This point of view, however, is not necessarily pessimistic with regard to educational and training possibilities. The fact that things cannot be acquired before a number of necessary conditions are fulfilled is quite trivial. Our main educational interest, however, lies in the difference between time and order of trained or taught abilities on the one hand and the 'spontaneous' emergence of the abilities on the other hand. It is quite plausible that a wide gap exists between the time at which the necessary functional conditions are fulfilled and the time at which abilities based on these functional conditions are acquired when one lets matters take their own course. In the previous chapter we have taken for granted that the external or stimulus side of attention is always optimally adapted to the child's developmental needs, such that the 'zone of proximal attention' is always sufficiently rich. I have stated, however, that the adaptation of the environment to the child's developmental needs rarely occurs spontaneously. Without the active educational interest of parents, teachers and peers, the environment would be more frequently developmentally inert than operative.

The most realistic solution to the problem of development, education and 'readiness' is to make distinctions between abilities and behaviours on a scale determined by two extremes, one of which consists of maximally internally, the other of maximally externally, determined abilities. Although nothing can develop when its internal and external conditions are absent, we should make a distinction between two kinds of abilities: first, abilities that can be easily acquired in almost any sort of environment, provided that the necessary conditions are present: and, second, abilities that are based on relatively simple internal conditions in addition to very complex external conditions of acquisition (i.e. carefully planned interaction between a competent subject (the tutor), a non-competent subject (the pupil) and the subject matter of teaching). It is wrong to think that the difference between these abilities coincides with the difference between basic, structural aspects of development and aspects that are more concerned with specific contents and which are identified with more superficial aspects of competences. It is quite plausible, for instance, that formal thinking has little opportunity to emerge spontaneously when explicit teaching is lacking. The mere presence of the necessary prerequisites for this form of thinking is presumably insufficient to make it arise spontaneously, for instance on the basis of active self-discovery without guidance.

The question as to which kind of ability emerges 'spontaneously' and which emerges only on the basis of explicit educational interaction cannot be answered without specifying the additional main parameters that are involved in the process. How rich is the environment of a particular child and how active is the child with regard to exploring it? How far is the environment of the child educationally involved and what is the quality of its educationally relevant interactions with the child? Finally, I think that the difference between 'spontaneous' and 'directed' emergence of abilities reflects a matter of gradual differences within one particular context of development instead of a structural distinction.

Piaget's theory is one which is not obviously associated with a strongly educationally inspired approach. The meaning and extension of the environment with regard to the subject is determined by his actual developmental state ('assimilation'), while the subject changes on the grounds of possibilities and properties enclosed in this subjectively limited environment ('accommodation'). Both aspects of the developmental process result in a progressive adaptation between the subject and the world. In Piaget's theory, adaptation has reached the level of final equilibrium when the subject has acquired a formal operational cognitive system. Piaget's approach to the final state of cognitive development suggests a 'one-dimensional' relationship between the subject and his world. In contradistinction to this, I am in favour of a more pluralistic worldview in which the 'making' of worlds (Goodman, 1978) is given a central place. Concepts such as 'causality', 'weight' and so forth are not acquired because they are sufficient and necessary tools for understanding the world as it really is, but because they constitute useful ways of creating a particular kind of 'world' that forms the universe within which our practical and cognitive activities can take place. 'Logical', formal operatory structures, however, are only one route to 'worldmaking' that is characteristic for the final state of development. Other routes to worldmaking are the arts, imagination, perception, politics, religion and so forth, which may go far beyond the specific formal operatory principles (without necessarily becoming incompatible with them).

The 'zone of proximal attention' shows a close terminological relationship with one of the basic concepts in Vygotsky's theory of development. Vygotsky attributes central importance to the 'zone of proximal development', by which he understands 'the distance between the actual developmental level as determined by independent problem solving and the level of potential development as determined through problem solving under adult guidance or in collaboration with more capable peers' (Vygotsky,

1978, p. 86; the selection of the quotation is by Wertsch, 1979). This quotation shows that Vygotsky's proximal zone concept has an entirely different meaning from mine, although both concepts are compatible within one theory. What the child can do under adult guidance certainly depends on the way in which he can employ the information that the adult is providing in the form of directed questions, limitation of the total amount of information and so forth. That is, it depends on the way in which the adult is able to contribute to a zone of proximal attention that has high developmental relevance. The problem with Vygotsky's concept is that the notion of guidance is difficult to define. Teaching, assistance during problem solving, the way in which the adult converses with the child, the kind of toys and books which are bought, the kind of things that are forbidden and allowed, all express particular ways of guidance. Just like the concepts of training or teaching, the concept of guidance is only useful as a gradual distinction within one particular developmental environment.

Bruner's conception of development as the resultant of an internal push and an external pull is also clearly compatible with the zone of proximal attention concept. His detailed studies of the behavioural ecology between parents or teachers and children offer excellent examples of the way in which the adults are directing and employing the child's attention in close correspondence with the child's actual developmental level.

I think that the primary function of the proximal attention concept is to offer a specific point of departure for the explanation of development. It tries to make clear the nature of the relationship between the subject and the environment during a process which is conceptualized as a process of development. Further, it tries to make clear that the concepts of 'teaching' or 'guidance' on the one hand and 'laisser-faire' or 'spontaneous acquisitions' on the other hand can be viewed at various levels of generality. Finally, it can be employed to explain the relationship between short 'low-level' processes of attention and learning and the 'high-level' processes of cognitive development.

Part III

The development of language and cognition

9 Cognitive development and the attribution of knowledge

9.1 THE PROBLEM OF THE POCKET CALCULATOR

When somebody says that a pocket calculator calculates or that it solves calculation problems, we would not accuse him of speaking nonsense. Isn't calculating what pocket calculators are made for? Is it true, however, that pocket calculators calculate? Certainly, this is not the kind of problem the user of calculators will be interested in. If the calculator does not calculate, it is not useful. For the cognitive psychologist, however, the question of whether or not the machine calculates is interesting enough, not because the psychologist is interested in pocket calculators but in the statement 'This man or machine calculates'. Moreover, calculating is only an example of an extensive range of activities that were originally concerned only with the human mind.

Traditionally, mental acts, such as calculating, are concerned with what happens inside the mind. Does this also hold for the calculating of the calculator? Suppose, for instance, that I change the key-symbols and the numbers on the screen to names and descriptions of extinct animals and events and that I change the mathematical operation symbols to transitive verbs. Needless to say, such a machine is a completely useless toy and nobody would be inclined to say that this machine calculates What this modified calculator actually does is to 'answer' questions such as 'What happens when a dinosaur loves a mosasaur' with statements such as 'They go to the market'. Even if the machine combines the statements in a fixed and reliable way, it would be very difficult, if not impossible, for the uninformed observer to discover that this fancy machine is identical with a pocket calculator as far as its internal processes are concerned. Suppose that a particular form of dysphasia exists which is characterized by the use of sentences comparable with the ones produced by the modified pocket calculator. The language of the dysphasic patient is limited to sentences such as 'When a pterodactyl touches a tyrannosaurus, his hair will fall out'. A closer examination of this form of dysphasia might reveal that these sentences follow a particular kind of logic, i.e. that they obey a number of rules. For the sake of the argument, let us assume that the sentences produced by the modified calculator are constructed according to the same rules. That is, the limited set of sentences produced by the modified calculator and the sentences uttered by the dysphasic patient form two, probably intersecting, subsets of the total set of possible sentences based on these rules. The modified calculator has now been transformed into a particular 'dysphasia machine'.

The highly speculative example makes clear that the normal, unmodified calculator calculates because the results of its operations upon number symbols obey the rules of the theory of calculations. The set of formal rules is also necessary in order to determine which part of the internal processes is meaningfully related to calculating and which is merely epiphenomenal (e.g. processes concerned with the presentation of the results or with retrieval from memory).

The fact that the processes themselves do not contain the essence of the behaviours that they underlie has been discussed also by Wright (1978) and Dennett (1979). Dennett, for instance, discusses the way in which a Martian believes something, for instance 'Bill has been murdered'. The Martian's internal processes might differ completely from the terrestrian's, yet they both believe that Bill has been murdered.

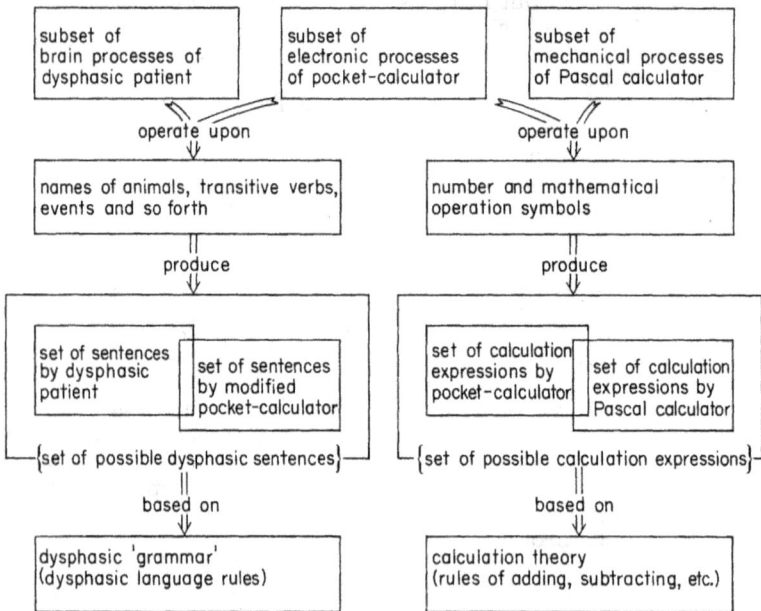

Figure 9.1 Relations between processes, symbols, behaviour and underlying rule systems

There is a second argument, however, to lend force to the assumption that the calculating is not in the internal operations themselves. Calculation can be carried out by small electronic devices but also by more solid mechanical machines, such as Pascal's calculators or the calculators that were widely used until the 1960s. Pascal's calculator and a modern electronic chip calculator both calculate. Nevertheless, an incredible difference exists between the operations performed by them. The human brain is also able to make calculations, but the way in which it executes them is totally different from an electronic as well as a Pascal calculator. In principle, it is possible to provide a computer with a very extensive memory that stores an enormous amount of calculation-sentences, such as '29 + 34 = 63', for instance. Such a computer will calculate also, be it in a very circuitous way (see Figure 9.1). In the diagram, the set of sentences produced by the dysphasic patient and the modified pocket calculator intersect. The same holds for the expressions produced by the electronic and the Pascal calculator.

The intersection between the subsets as well as their extension within the set of possible sentences or expressions is determined by a number of accidental and a number of structural factors. The accidental factors concern the particular use made of the devices. It is possible, for instance, that a very complicated calculator will be used only for a small number of very simple additions. The structural factors concern the possibilities and limitations of the processes. A Pascal calculator, for instance, may be limited to the four basic calculation operations, whereas an electronic calculator is able to carry out very complicated operations. In spite of its structural limits, however, the Pascal as well as the electronic calculator are executing basically the same kind of task.

It may be questioned how extensive a set of sentences or mathematical expressions must be and how much they might extend beyond the limits set forth by a calculation theory in order to account for the underlying processes as calculating processes. In principle, a process that produced one expression that obeys the rules of calculation theory and no expressions that do not obey them can be attributed the status of a calculating process. For practical purpose, however, this evidence is too poor as well as too strict. On the one hand, it is possible that a two-year-old child, for instance, can give a correct answer to the question 'How much is two plus seven' without understanding the nature of the answer he is giving. That is, a certain degree of productivity is a necessary prerequisite for the ascription of a competence to a subject or a machine. On the other hand, the rule that not a single error may be made is clearly too strict. Human calculators, for instance, are fallible, yet the ability to calculate may be ascribed to them reliably, unless the errors that are made reflect a systematic deviation from the theory of calculation.

Let us now try to summarize the answer we have found to the question of whether and why the pocket calculator calculates.

First, the calculator should be able to carry out a number of operations upon a number of mathematical symbols (i.e. upon inputs that are a linear function of these symbols). These operations are based on spatiotemporal processes expressed in terms of a machine language. In principle, the operations may be realized by means of various machine languages (it is only a matter of technological competence whether or not machine-alternatives to operations can be construed).

Second, the products of the machine processes form a set of calculation expressions (e.g. '2 + 2 = 4'), i.e. a subset of the set of possible calculation expressions.

Third, the set-qualification of the machine products is based on a formal theory of calculation (the 'competence' theory). An expression belongs to the set of calculation expressions if and only if it obeys the rules of the formal theory. Because the theory of calculation is a strictly formal construction it should not be sought in one material form or another, although there is a variety of material exemplifications of the theory, such as pocket and Pascal calculators, a set of correct calculation expressions, correct judgments about the truth or falsity of calculations, and so forth.

9.2 THE RELATIVISTIC NATURE OF PSYCHOLOGICAL STATEMENTS

Our most important conclusion concerns the complicated nature of a statement about a property such as calculating. The reason why I have devoted so much attention to the problem of the pocket calculator is that I want to employ it as a model of the problems that arise with statements about mental states, actions and properties in general. Cognitive psychologists are concerned with the question of whether and when a subject 'knows something', 'believes something', 'is able to do something', and so forth. Predicates such as 'knowing' and 'believing' are basically identical with a predicate such as 'calculating' and I think that the question of whether a subject 'knows' something must be solved in the same way as our question of whether the pocket calculator was able to calculate. The human subject 'believes Q' or 'knows P' if he executes operations - or is able to execute operations - that respond to the rules determined by a theory of believing Qs and knowing Ps. The internal operations and their corresponding mental states and processes are components or expressions of the act of knowing and believing; they are not the knowing and believing itself. An act is an act of knowing or an act of believing in that it obeys the rules of a competence theory of knowing and believing. The theory of knowing, believing and so forth, is an abstract struc-ture of rules. It does not reside within the brain or the head of the knower or believer or within textbooks of psychology or the philosophy of mind. We could state, however, that the set of possible - or actual - acts of knowing and believing is an exemplification of the theory of knowing or believing. Other exemplifications can be found in statements about knowing and believing or in attributions of knowledge and beliefs.

The fact that a mental act is theory-dependent instead of internally self-defining does not imply that it is entirely arbitrary, i.e. that the defining competence theory can be constructed in an entirely arbitrary way. A competence theory is based on arguments of descriptive adequacy. It should take into account that concepts of mental acts and states have a proper history and sociocultural meaning. This does not necessarily imply, however, that the science of mental acts and states should consist of analyses of mental state-terms from natural language.

Before giving a few more examples of analyses of mental states, activities or structures, I shall try to clarify some of the reasons that underlie my preference for this particular approach to the nature of statements about the mind and mental contents.

The first reason is that a considerable diversity exists in the actual processes that underlie the way in which a man or a machine carry out activities that belong to the mental state, such as knowing, information processing, deciding, believing and so forth. Empirical examples of this diversity are provided by artificial intelligence investigations (see for instance Schank, 1982), which have shown that very complex 'human' processes can be carried out by electronic devices such as computers. Independent of the existence of empirical illustrations, we should question whether words such as 'knowing' and 'believing' are applicable to systems that differ to a greater or lesser extent from the human systems to which these words are applied normally (such as Martians or computers). Although such questions seem irrelevant, especially for empirical psychologists, they highlight the meaning of the concepts that are employed in psychological investigations.

Second, empirical investigations of a psychological concept imply that the concept has been applied to a set of variables that determine the actual empirical extension of this concept. The criteria employed in applying the concept to the empirical universe, however, escape from empirical research. These criteria have been discussed in the first part of the book. They consisted of the mapping rules associated with the theoretical concepts. In the second part of the book, we have seen that an analysis of the concept of perception is a necessary pre-requisite to any understanding of empirical data on perception and perceptual development. That is, a mental (or behavioural) act is a perceptual act relative to a descriptive framework that functions as a competence theory of perception. In this sense, psychological phenomena are relativistic phenomena. An ordinary psychological statement should be considered an elliptical form of a statement that renders explicit not only the mental phenomena, processes and properties, but also the formal, descriptive

and definitive framework within which the statement has been
formulated and justified.

Theoretical arguments in favour of a relativistic view of the
nature of psychological phenomena have been put forward by
philosophers like Goodman, Dennett, Davidson, Sellars and
Ryle (see, for instance, Goodman, 1960; Dennett, 1978, 1979;
Davidson, 1963; Sellars, 1968; Ryle, 1949). Goodman has
explained the importance and function of interpretive and
representational systems for understanding the world. Understanding, however, is primarily a process of making a world.
Dennett (1979) analysed explanations of 'belief' and 'desire'
within three kinds of 'intentional psychology', which consist of
conceptual frameworks characterized by particular ways of
dealing with psychological concepts. These frameworks are:
folk or naive psychology, which is embedded in our colloquial
psychological terms vocabulary; intentional systems theory,
which Dennett describes as a kind of logical behaviourism that
describes and defines the observable properties of intentional
and meaningful behaviours; and, finally, subpersonal cognitive
psychology, which seeks for an explanation of intentional
behaviour in terms of underlying structural processes. While
folk psychology might be reduced to intentional systems theory,
the latter cannot be reduced to subpersonal cognitive psychology,
since the processes and procedures described by the latter
achieve their meaning by virtue of the concepts provided by
intentional systems theory. The analyses of developmental
processes that I have sketched in this book are closely related
to Dennett's approach. Two basic differences, however, are
that I accepted a greater variety of theories and, second, that
I would attach greater importance to the problem of how these
theories originate and which functions they play.

The relativistic theory of mental phenomena is disputed by
philosophers such as Kripke, Putnam and Donellan (see
Schwartz, 1977, for an overview). According to the traditional
theory of meaning, the extension of a term is based on its
intension, i.e. the set of properties common to all its exemplifications. Kripke and others state that reference – the relationship
between a term and its actual extension – is not based on a preliminary intensional definition. Reference consists of a direct
relationship between a term and its referents. The extensional
meaning of 'water', for instance, consists of a direct relationship
between 'water' and all instances of real water (H_2O) in any
possible world.

If the previous theory is applied to mental property terms,
the idea of relativism should be abandoned. The meaning of
'belief', 'knowledge' and so on consists of the direct relationships
between these terms and all their true exemplifications, i.e. all
true instances of 'belief', 'knowledge', etc. Finding the properties of 'belief' or 'knowledge' is a matter of empirical investigation, not of conceptual analysis.

Schwartz thinks that the previous claim is too strong. He

makes a distinction between 'natural kind terms' ('gold', 'water', etc.) and 'nominal kind terms'. The latter refer to whatever satisfies a certain definition (e.g. 'bachelor' refers to whatever is male, unmarried and of marriageable age). Probably a considerable number of mental property terms are of the nominal kind, that is, their meaning is relative to a definitive framework.

In contradiction with Schwartz's suggestion, I think that the nominal aspect should be viewed as an aspect of any kind of term, that is, of natural as well as nominal terms. The nominal dimension could be combined with a referential dimension in order to constitute a space in which the problem of rigid reference and nominal flexibility could be solved. Medieval scholars, for instance, would speak about aqua (H_2O), about aqua fortis (nitric acid) and aqua vitae (alcohol, distillates). In accordance with Putnam, we might say that the medieval scholars were misled by the apparent similarity between water, nitric acid and alcohol, such that they presumed that nitric acid and alcohol were particular forms of water (H_2O). We might also claim, however, that the medieval 'aqua' referred to a set of liquids containing H_2O, nitric acid and alcohol. That is, the medieval 'theory' of water - the rules that describe how and when 'water' can be used - simply differs from the modern theory. Chemical analyses have shown that the medieval 'aqua' covered a set of chemically distinct liquids, which has led to a considerable change in the meaning of 'water' (this change needn't have been necessary, i.e. even the modern meaning of 'water' could have corresponded with a set of liquids containing H_2O, HN_3 and C_2H_5OH). Put differently, the medieval aqua and the modern water occupy distinct positions on the nominal dimension; these positions co-determine the referential extension of the terms. Further, the nominal positions are clearly historically related.

In practice, the nominal position of the speaker is left implicit and is usually shared with the addressee (e.g. a scientific discussion, in which 'water' necessarily means 'H_2O' and not 'a transparent, colourless liquid'). In psychology, however, the possible nominal positions are less rigid (compare, for instance, the folk psychological with the cognitive, behaviouristic and psychoanalytic view of mental properties). The nominal diversity of psychology is frequently interpreted as one of the growing pains of a young science. I believe, however, that nominal diversity is simply an essential property of psychology, although I presume that it will finally lead to a disintegration into distinct scientific disciplines.

The principle of relativity is valid not only with regard to static propositional attitudes such as knowing and believing, but also with regard to active processes such as thinking and the use of meaning in understanding and producing language. Usually, thinking is identified with a covert, genuinely mental process, i.e. thinking is the stream of internal images, frag-

mentary sentences and schemes that occur when people think.
In contrast with the previous, current view on thinking, I
claim that any activity - in principle it does not matter which
one - can be called thinking in that it obeys the rules of our
definitive theory of 'thinking'. Thinking is not an internal
feeling, such as 'pain' for instance; it is an intensional act,
i.e. it is intensionally related to a definite content. The competence theory of thinking should specify how various kinds
of acts can be related to contents. The naive theory of thinking,
for instance, is quite tolerant in attributing thinking, for
example, to preverbal infants or to animals. Rationalist and
idealist traditions, however, seem to have created a more
sophisticated theory of thinking, which attributes thinking
only to processes that involve internal representations of the
thought content. Piaget's theory, on the other hand, views
thinking as intelligent acting. When babies manipulate and
explore objects, they are thinking externally.

If we accept that thinking is a relationship between certain
internal and external activities and dispositions, and a theory
of thinking, we are able to describe the rules according to
which the thinking proceeds without implying that these rules
must be present in the head or brain of the thinker. What must
be present are the conditions that enable the subject to act in
a way that forms the expression of these rules of thinking.
The rules themselves, however, should not be identified with
these conditions. Just as there were different sorts of calculators that operated according to the rules of a theory of
calculation although the basis upon which these operations were
grounded differed considerably, there might exist subjects or
machines that think according to the same rules but on the basis
of totally different mechanisms and conditions.

Also the production and understanding of linguistic meaning
by speakers and hearers can be understood by means of the
relativistic theory of mental phenomena. If asked where the
meaning of what they say or hear can be found, most people
will say 'in my mind' or 'in my head'. Is meaning in the head of
the speaker or hearer? It is certainly not in the words themselves. The meaning of a word can be stored in many different
ways, for instance in the neurological component that forms
our memory, in the memory of a computer, in a dictionary
description, on magnetic tape and so forth. Consequently, the
meaning itself cannot be identical with either of the ways in
which it is stored. According to our relativistic view upon
mental contents and processes, meaning must be defined as a
relationship between particular activities (inner speech,
imagery, overt actions, etc.), and a theory of meaning
(exemplified by the various ways in which we employ meaning,
react to nonsense and so forth). The way in which meaning is
given to words and sentences - i.e. the way in which they are
understood - does not matter as long as we deal with these
words and sentences in a way that answers the rules set forth

by the theory of meaning. The question of whether the meaning of a word is stored in the head of a language-user - a two year old child, for instance - should not be understood literally. What it means is: does the child possess the operative conditions necessary for acting in such a way that the understanding of the word can be safely attributed to him. As we have seen in the chapter on attention (Chapter 7), these conditions have a subjective - internal - and an objective - external - aspect. The subjective aspect might consist of a functional organization of the brain, whereas the objective aspect depends on the possibilities of the environment. In an environment without alternatives for acting, there is nothing to know or to believe, since the conditions for expressing the knowledge or the belief, namely the presence of crucial alternatives, are absent. Theories of meaning can be exemplified by naive as well as very sophisticated systems. The naive - but highly functional - theory exemplifies meaning in terms of verbal paraphrasing, pointing or showing, answering questions, carrying out instructions, and so forth. These exemplifications underlie the idea that meaning is a structure of mental words or an internal image of the referent, and that understanding a word means that it is connected with its internal 'dictionary' description or with an internal image.

The 'translation hypothesis' of understanding is a nice example of how a social, communicative process - communicating meanings of new words by paraphrasing them or by pointing at their referents - is transformed into an image of how the brain works. Computer simulations of such a model should be successful, simply because they simulate a successful social practice. There is absolutely no reason to believe, however, that the 'translation hypothesis' has any validity with regard to the actual working and structure of the brain.

The thesis that mental states and events and behaviour are dependent on a theoretical descriptive framework has been discussed in the second and first part of this book, with regard to theories of development in general and the development of perception in particular. In this part of the book we shall be concerned with the development of knowledge and representation in the first three years of life.

10 General aspects of representational development

10.1 IMITATION AND PRE-LINGUISTIC REPRESENTATION

Recently, a number of papers have been written, dealing with the transition from the pre-linguistic to the linguistic stage, particularly with respect to the kinds of knowledge that are assumed to support this important developmental step (see for instance: Sinclair-De Zwart, 1973, Moerk, 1975; Morehead and Morehead, 1974; Bowerman, 1974; Schlesinger, 1974; Bruner 1975; Moore and Meltzoff, 1978; Lock, 1982; Campbell, 1979).

I shall begin by attempting a conceptual analysis of a number of statements put forward in a representative article by M.K. Moore and A.N. Meltzoff, 'Object-permanence, imitation and language development: toward a neo-Piagetian perspective on communicative and cognitive development' (1978). The article deals with the nowadays much discussed problem of the relation between pre-linguistic cognition and the emergence of language, in terms of a general Piagetian framework which the authors have adapted to incorporate a number of recent findings in the field of infant development.

Moore and Meltzoff begin by discussing the development of imitation in relation to the development of the representational system. According to these authors, the 'major prerequisite determining the onset of meaningful speech is the development of the infant's rules for maintaining the identity of objects through spatial and featural transformations of them' (p. 152). In other words, the infant has to develop a system of internal representation in which objects are represented in terms of object identity and permanence.

As a basic premise for the internal development of a sensori-motor representational ability in the infant, Moore and Meltzoff accept Piaget's claim regarding the importance of imitation and the crucial stages of imitative development. During the first stage of imitation development, imitation of gestures is possible only under full visual control: the infant must command a visual field which comprehends the gesture which it wants to imitate, e.g. the movement of an adult's fingers, as well as its own imitation of that gesture. In the second stage the infant proceeds to master his imitation without being dependent on visual control of his effort to imitate (that is to say, he can copy the gesture before him without watching himself do so). Finally, the infant is able to imitate something from memory without visual control of either the object being imitated or his own imitation. It is only at this final stage that the question of internal representation is raised (by Piaget, among others). Imitating something which is not actually present requires the existence of an image or model of the imitated 'in the head of the child', because otherwise imitation would not be possible.

Nonetheless, contrary to Piaget's predictions, some of Moore and Meltzoff's experiments showed that two to three week old infants performing under optimal testing conditions could imitate such facial gestures as the opening of the mouth and protrusion of the tongue – in spite of the fact that the infants could not see their own faces. It is therefore clear that any explanations for such imitative gestures fall completely outside any hypothesis suggesting the necessity of visual control by the infant (Moore and Meltzoff, 1978).

Before I continue with examining Moore and Meltzoff's explanation of early imitation, I shall discuss an experiment by Jacobson (1979) which contested the authors' claims on empirical grounds. According to Jacobson (1979), the child's tongue protrusion does not represent imitative behaviour, but a released response elicited by a broad but delimited class of incentive stimuli. Six week old infants replied with tongue protrusion after tongue protrusion of the experimenter as well as when they were presented with a small object moving toward and away from the infant's mouth. The movement and shape of these objects operate as releasers of a tongue-protrusion response which has no imitative meaning. At present, however, I shall not deal with the question of who is right in the imitative-versus-released response debate. We shall discuss the explanations of early imitative development, regardless of the actual existence of the phenomenon in question.

Moore and Meltzoff explain the early imitative competence of the child by postulating a supra-modal format, similar to Fodor's basic computational language (Fodor, 1975), which is used to represent information from the various senses in one common format or 'underlying language'. According to Moore and Meltzoff, the significant implication of their experiment is that the capacity to act on the basis of some internal representation of the external world 'may not be the culmination of psychological development in infancy as Piaget conceived, but merely its starting point' (p. 157).

The problem, then, is why – in spite of the infant's actual competence – spontaneous imitations of facial gestures never emerge before the time predicted by Piaget. Moore and Meltzoff explain this by observing that Piagetian stages in the development of imitation mark changes in the function that the imitation serves; the facial imitations of a one year old child, for example, show that the child realizes that when he imitates another person, 'he looks like the other and the other looks like him'. The infant is thus capable of understanding in visual terms the correspondence between his imitation and the person imitated. That is, whereas Moore and Meltzoff are concerned with unconscious representation, Piaget is mainly interested in conscious representations. Moore and Meltzoff claim, however, that unconscious representation is a necessary prerequisite for the emergence of Piagetian conscious representation. On the other hand, Moore and Meltzoff, as well as Piaget, consider conscious representation the precursor of linguistic reference. Conscious imitations are the first signs of the child's growing consciousness that he is representing something, that his actions are referring to the objects or events he imitates.

One of the main problems with the previous - unfortunately rudimentarily sketched - theory of representation by imitation is that the crucial notion, 'representation', is left undefined, which is perhaps understandable if we bear in mind that representation is a troublesome and hard to define concept (see, for instance, Black, 1972, and Goodman, 1968a). What is clear from conceptual analyses of 'representation' is that it is not an objective link between a representing and a represented object (a picture of a scene and the depicted scene, for instance). Representation is a relationship between an observation function (a real observer; a theory of observable objects and possible forms of appearance, etc.), a represented 'object', and, finally, a representing 'object' (anything that has a sign function). An object is a representation of X if there exists an observation function that is able to view the object as a representation of X. In the section on picture perception, for instance (section 5.1.3) we have seen that a picture becomes a 'picture' when the child is able, firstly, to recognize the contradiction between three-dimensional information (perspective, texture gradients, etc.) and flatness (based on motion disparity, stereopsis, etc.); and, second, when he is able to suppress the information for flatness. As long as the child is unable to take this internal contradiction into account, he may see the picture as a particular presentation of an object, just like the appearance of the object itself constitutes a particular form of presentation.

Our definition of representation implies that an 'object', such as a neurological structure or a retinal image can be considered a representation by a particular observer - a psychologist, for instance - whereas it is not a representation for the subject who employs it. For the subject himself, such underlying 'representations' are functional and instrumental conditions in order to arrive at or generate presentations, representations, and examples of objects, events, properties and so forth. The underlying computational language which Fodor has postulated can be considered a representational system by somebody who employs a theory of underlying representations. For the subject himself, the underlying system has a functional, i.e. procedural, and not a representational meaning.

The fact that the representational function of behaviour is based on an attributed - instead of an intrinsic - relationship between behaviour on the one hand and represented contents on the other hand, can be illustrated by means of motor behaviour. If a child reaches to an object and grasps it, the extension and direction of the arm and the grasping movements of the hand and fingers have a purely functional meaning for the child himself. The movements constitute the way in which the child obtains the object. Put differently, the movements form a specific expression of a motor procedure for obtaining objects.

It is possible, however, to conceive of the motor patterns as motor representations of the distance, form and weight of the object, simply because the movements and the tension of the muscles correspond with the size, form and weight of the object. An illustrative example of the development of a motor representation of weight is provided in Bower (1974) and Mounoud and Bower (1975). The tension of the arm muscles at the onset of a grasping action can be considered the anticipatory motor representation of the weight of an object. Six month old infants grasp objects with inappropriate arm tension. The grasping force does not fit the actual (or expected) weight of the object. During the subsequent months, the child learns to adapt his arm tension to the actual weight of the object. He learns also to anticipate weight on the basis of visual characteristics of objects, such as length. It is important to note, however, that the motor programmes have a purely functional meaning from the viewpoint of the child himself. They have a representational function from the viewpoint of a theory of representation (i.e. a set of rules that is able to assign one external property or another to the set of possible motor patterns).

A second important question concerns the way in which the various types and levels of representation take a specific behavioural form. That is, how do we distinguish a representation from a presentation or from its functional, instrumental (procedural) conditions. In Piaget's and Moore and Meltzoff's approach, consciousness is a crucial criterion. When the subject knows that a behaviour refers to something, the behaviour is a form of representing. The problem with this criterion, however, is that knowledge and consciousness rarely take the form of an explicit 'knowing that' or 'consciousness of'. The difference between presentations, representations and procedural conditions is that they form classes of actions, behaviours or operations that follow different rule systems. Knowledge and awareness are descriptive terms from a - naive or sophisticated - psychological meta-language that rarely refer to their prototypical meaning. It is very difficult - if not impossible - to decide whether an imitative action is an instance of presentation, representation or involuntary imitative resonance, as long as only this sole action is taken into account. It is the place of the action in a variety of actions, motives and consequences that enables us to determine its nature.

Piaget has given an example of a sixteen month old child who tries to open a matchbox (Flavell, 1963; p. 120). At first, the trial is unsuccessful, but then the child seems to produce a motor representation of the opening of the box by slowly opening and closing the mouth. The opening and closing of the mouth can be viewed as a representation of the opening of the box if the behaviours at issue are interpreted by a system of rules that assigns a 'real world event. to a relevant subset of components of these behaviours. If we claim that the opening and closing of the mouth has a representational function, we should be able to prove that the opening and closing belong to a 'family' of behaviours whose properties are fully mapable onto the rules of the interpretation system. We have met this problem before, namely when we asked whether a single utterance, 'Two plus two equals four', could be regarded as the expression of a mathematical competence (see Chapter 9).

If we start from the previous notes on the nature of representation, the following remarks on Moore and Meltzoff's claims regarding early imitation can be made. Imitation by two and three week old children - provided that it *is* imitation - should be conceived of as involuntary imitation which can be compared more reliably with mere physical resonance than with imitation in the psychological sense of the word. Such a form of imitation requires a rather complex procedural apparatus that is able to 'translate' visual into motor information. This apparatus could be assigned a representational value if one employs a theory of representation according to which the works of clocks are considered representations of time and running cars representations of the road system. I do not say that such an interpretation is unacceptable, yet it deviates considerably from the colloquial meaning of 'representation'. The claim that the facial gestures of the older child are the expression of mental acts of representation by imitation makes sense only if the child himself is able to recognize that his imitation is a reference to the facial expression he is trying to imitate. But the only evidence we have for assuming that the child knows that his imitations refer to the imitated object is the imitation itself. It would require a detailed investigation of the totality of the child's imitative behaviour in order to decide whether its variability allows us to distinguish behavioural rules that correspond with the distinction between involuntary imitation, imitative presentation and representation, and the level of procedural conditions. The claim that 'the infant realizes that he looks like the other and the other looks like him' does not - and cannot - refer to some conscious episode of realizing, but should refer to some specific form of rule-governed imitative behaviour.

With regard to Piaget's claim about deferred imitation (imitation of something actually absent) I would raise doubts about the certitude with which deferred imitation is still called imitation. It is clear that deferred imitation is not possible without the preceding stages of imitative development sketched at the beginning of this section, but it is neither theoretically nor empirically clear that deferred imitation is imitation; that is to say, that deferred imitation requires the recall of a preceding mental image of what is going to be imitated. It is quite plausible that the procedural plan of the deferred imitation belongs to the level of functional conditions and that 'deferred imitation' is not the consequence of conscious representation, but simply (external) conscious representation (although it is doubtful whether this form is an example either of representation or of presentation).

10.2 FROM PRE-LINGUISTIC TO LINGUISTIC REPRESENTATION

In discussing the role of cognition in language development, Moore and Meltzoff state that many developmental psychologists accept a Piagetian position with respect to the necessity of cognitive precursors to language development. Below, I shall present the premises which, according to Moore and Meltzoff, are widely accepted, and then present my own criticism of the assumptions and make suggestions for revision. The three premises relate to symbolization, object permanence, and the expression of spatial, causal, and temporal relationships by infants.

The first premise holds that:

> Words and sentences have a symbolic relationship to objects and events in the world. Therefore, the infant must understand the way in which words can stand for (symbolize) objects and events in order to use language. This capacity for symbolic representation is linked to imitative development, according to Piaget. Therefore, the onset of meaningful speech should be related to imitative development.

Moore and Meltzoff have here an implicit conception of a subject, on the one hand, who uses words and sentences, and on the other a conception of a world that consists of objects and events. I find it difficult to accept their conception, which is at the very least an uncritical throwback to an old philosophical problem, namely 'In which sense can one say that the world consists of facts, objects, events and so forth?' My own view is that the world can be said to consist of objects and events only in terms of systems that 'describe' or organize the world in terms of objects and events or that 'describe' and act upon the world in such ways that 'object' and 'event' constitute descriptively adequate concepts for specifying them. I therefore suggest the following alternative to the first premise: words and sentences have a symbolizing or exemplifying relationship to ways of organizing the world in terms of objects and events. Therefore, in order to comprehend or to use language, the infant must understand the way in which words can stand for (symbolize and exemplify) ways of organizing the world in terms of objects and events.

The first problem that arises with this reformulation concerns the actual ways for organizing the world in terms of objects and events. Most probably, the supra-modal representational system or underlying computational language is such a way of organizing. What the child has to do, then, is to map linguistic symbols upon the 'symbols' used by the supra-modal system. The difficulty lies in the fact that the supra-modal system is not a representational system from the point of view of the child himself, but a conditional, procedural structure which enables him to carry out all kinds of activities. Is organizing the world in terms of objects and events one of the activities that are made possible by this underlying procedural structure? Let us look at the available evidence in order to answer this question.

In the second part of the book we have discussed the way in which the infant constructs a sensory representation of the world (which is a re-presentation from the psychologist's and a presentation from the child's point of view). The properties of this (re-)presentation consisted of a high level of organization and transformation imposed on the complex proximal stimulus. The infant perceives the world in such a way that we can safely assume that the object of his perceptual acts is a distal world that can be adequately described in terms of three-dimensionality, time and constancy, objects, events and so forth, provided that a language of objects, events and so forth is employed. We have seen, however, that we should not identify the act with its object or the object with its description. Perceiving a world that can be described in terms of objects and events is not identical with describing it in these terms and neither does it imply the presence of the description or its underlying 'theory' in the perceiver. The concepts of 'object' and 'event' are descriptively adequate with regard to the organizational properties of the infant's perceptual presentation of the world, but they should not be identified with constituent symbols of his internal representation (whatever this representation may be).

There is a second way, however, for organizing the world in terms of objects and events, namely the use of a simple object language. The world that is the object of such language can be adequately described in terms of 'object' and 'event', though the way in which a simple object language constitutes a world consisting of objects and events differs entirely from the way in which perception constitutes such a world. That is, the instrumental or procedural conditions underlying perception and object language might – and probably do – not show any degree of community (this matter will be discussed further).

If it is true that the use of words and sentences is one particular way of organizing the world in terms of objects and events, it is meaningless or tautological to claim that 'the infant must understand the way in which words can stand for (symbolize) objects and events in order to comprehend or to use language'.

If the expression 'in order' implies that the infant's understanding of that relationship must precede the emergence of language,
the claim is meaningless because using words and sentences is
(a particular) understanding of how words and sentences relate
to objects and events.

In their second premise, Moore and Meltzoff state that:

> In order to talk about objects and events not perceptually
> present, the infant is required to conceive of the continued
> existence of absent objects. Piaget has postulated that the
> capacity for understanding that objects continue to exist while
> they are out of sight - object permanence, as he (Piaget) calls
> it - develops through a series of qualitatively different stages
> over the first two years of life. Presumably, the potential
> referents of an infant's words should partially depend on the
> stage he has reached in developing the concept of object
> permanence.

In contradistinction to the introductory claims of the second
premise, I think that permanence is a property of objects which
is totally irrelevant to the possibility of speaking about them.
Such phenomena as a flame, a fist, a bolt of lightning or a noise
exist for only a very limited time. Although they are impermanent, we are talking about them at this actual moment. The same
holds for events such as an itch or a pain whose existence is
totally dependent on their being sensed. But, one might say,
these things are not objects or events at all; they are feelings,
casual phenomena, and so forth. This objection would imply
that before the child has a conception of the continued existence
of objects, he might in principle be able to talk about 'objects'
in the sense of egocentric feelings and casual phenomena, but
nevertheless he would be able to talk. (The whole question,
however, is a purely speculative issue since the beginning of
intelligible speech occurs after the acquisition of object permanence according to Piagetian criteria. Naturally, the order of
acquisition tells nothing about the nature of an eventual conditional relationship between acquired abilities.)

One might object to the previous arguments by stating that
if the infant were to talk about 'objects' as impermanent
entities, there would be an insurmountable difference between
the referents of the adult sentences and the child's interpretations of these referents, i.e. the child and the adult would
not be able to understand each other. We shall see, however,
that such a 'misunderstanding' is not problematic so much as
developmentally highly relevant.

We may conclude that the introductory claim of the second
premise either is analytically true or deals with something
different, namely 'symbol permanence'. The claim is analytically
true if one interprets it as follows. Talking about entities as
objects means, among others, that one talks about these entities
as permanent. This requires that the speaker is able to conceive

of the continued existence of objects when they are absent. It is highly probable that permanence is not solely acquired in the context of language use, but this is different from saying that language per se requires object permanence.

According to the second interpretation of the introductory statement of the second premise the child might be unable to imagine or to represent in a sensori-motor or linguistic way any object out of his sight or sensory field in general. Consequently, the content of the child's linguistic messages would be entirely determined by objects and events that are actually present and observable; that is, the child lacks an ability we might call 'symbol permanence'. It is clear that 'symbol permanence' and 'object permanence' are entirely different concepts.

The third of Moore and Meltzoff's premises states that:

> Words in sentences may express spatial, causal, and temporal relationships between persons and objects. Again, Piaget has postulated that these concepts develop over the first two years of life. Thus, the infant's ability to express or understand sentences involving these concepts should be limited by his stage in the development of these concepts.

Rephrased, the premise presumably means something like the following: the infant's sensori-motor understanding of sentences with words such as 'in front of', 'under', 'do', 'make', 'before', etc., are limited by the ways in which the child 'represents' space, action and time in a sensori-motor way.

It is clear that the actions and perceptions of a pre-linguistic child can be described in terms of a mastery of the spatial, causal and temporal properties of the world, i.e. that the object of perception and action is a world adequately describable in terms of such concepts. This is not to say, however, that perception, action and, later on, language, constitute the object-and-event world in the same way. Bower, for instance, has shown that there is a considerable difference between 'in' as a perceptual relationship (expressed in terms of a perceptual coding language, for instance) and 'in' as a relationship between objects involved in purposeful action. In a context of action, 'in' means to put something in a container, looking for an object in a container, taking the object out and so forth. According to Bower (1974) infants under six months of age lack such an actional concept of 'in'. The perceptual 'concept' of 'in' is expressed by the ability to pay attention to internal details, i.e. form or pattern elements embedded in an external boundary. We have seen that this ability has been acquired at a very early age, especially when the observed objects are moving. In summary, the instrumental and procedural conditions of the perceptual and the actional 'in' are different, although the perceptual 'in' is one of the conditions necessary for the acquisition of the actional 'in' (which does not mean that the first is somehow translated into the latter). The same conclusion holds for the instrumental and procedural structure underlying the use of the linguistic 'in', although it is clear that the perceptual and actional 'in' form a necessary condition for the acquisition of the linguistic concept. The fact that the meta-descriptive concept 'in' applies to the worlds revealed by the subject's perception, action and language, does not imply that the subject possesses a supra-modal concept 'in', unless the assignment of such a concept is analytically equal to stating that the subject is able to perceive, act with and speak about 'in'-relations.

Moore and Meltzoff give an example of the implications of their third premise, as follows: 'A child will not understand or produce the sentence, "John hit the ball," before differentiating the concepts of "past" and "present" and the concepts of "agent", "action", and "object"' (p. 159). It is not clear what 'before' means here: does the differentiation of the concepts precede the understanding and production of the sentence? If this were the case, the child would have to differentiate the concepts in terms of a representational system different from language, i.e. the sensori-motor representational system. During the process of language acquisition the child would have to employ the premise that the linguistic representational system has the same properties as has the sensori-motor representational system, insofar as such conceptual distinctions as 'past', 'present', 'action', 'agent', and 'object' are concerned. The problem is, however, that the perceptual, actional and, partly, also the linguistic system are representational systems only from a meta-point of view, i.e. from the point of view of a psychologist who is able to compare the model of perceptual and actional worlds with a model of the subject's 'objective' environment, i.e. the environment described in terms of scientifically accepted language (which may be quite close to the unreflexive language of the subject anyhow). For the subject himself, perception and action - and partly language - are forms in which the world is presented (seen, acted upon, changed, etc.). The procedural conditions that underlie the various presentational forms are system-specific. In section 6.1 we have seen that the process of perception can be described formally in terms of a surface-deep-structure relationship, although its actual content and structure differ entirely from the linguistic surface and deep structures, apart from a limited number of abstract, structural meta-similarities. It is quite plausible, therefore, that the functional apparatus underlying perception and the one underlying language are completely different.

It is not because the perceptual and the actional system enables the child to behave in ways that can be described as 'being the agent of an action' or 'employing tools' that the system must contain concepts of action and tools in the form of underlying units of meaning. The way in which competent action expresses concepts as 'action', 'agent' or 'tool' may be compared with the way in which a work of art – a painting, for instance – expresses complex underlying ideas. The classic joke representing this case is the one about the art critic decribing in glowing terms the deep and subtle ideas that have been expressed by an artist's painting, whereas on the other hand the artist maintains that he only wanted to paint two dark blue squares on a brown surface. That the painting expresses a number of ideas, concepts or feelings does not necessarily imply that these ideas, concepts or feelings played a role in the process of making the painting. What the painting expresses is solely a matter of a relationship between the painting and a (reliable) system of interpreting and giving meaning to the painting.

If language is one particular way, besides perception and action, for dealing with a world describable in terms of 'action', 'agent' and so forth, then there is no psychological difference between the acquisition of language and learning how to deal linguistically with a world of actions, objects and so forth. This is not to say, however, that the acquisition of language has nothing to do with perception or action. On the contrary, the acquisition of language requires that a new system – language – is mapped upon already existing ones – perception and action – such that language can be related to perception and language and vice versa. Such a mapping, however, is not a translation of perceptual and actional into linguistic 'concepts', as far as these concepts are identified with 'symbols' of an underlying representational system, a supra-modal format for instance.

After clarifying what they conceive of as the basic premises of a Piagetian approach to language acquisition, Moore and Meltzoff sketch the basic characteristics of their neo-Piagetian approach, which are, first, that 'the infant must develop a conception of language as a communicative system. The nature of this conception will be a function of his level of cognitive development' (p. 159); and, secondly, that 'the infant should treat language as an "object of thought" before it becomes an "instrument of thought" ' (p. 159). Consequently, 'one major task for the infant is to discover that these "sentences" (uttered by the adult) have a meaning (message) and that they are uttered with the intent to communicate it' (p. 160).

It is difficult to maintain that, for a function to be fulfilled, the object fulfilling it must have a conception of that function. For instance, before language can fulfil a communicative function for the child, he must first have a conception of the fact that language is a communicative system. This is a very peculiar line of reasoning. First, it is clear that numerous – e.g. biological – functions are performed without any awareness on the part of the organism that performs such a function (assuming that 'awareness' means 'conscious knowledge of' or 'knowing that'). For instance, people eat because they are hungry or because it is lunchtime, although one of the main functions of eating is to

keep oneself alive. Second, by 'awareness' we often mean the
specific way in which actions are carried out. That is, actions
are carried out in such a way that they fulfil particular
functions. This form of awareness is based on the acquisition
of complex rules of action and not on actual conscious images
of what one is doing. It is a form of 'knowing how' and not of
'knowing that'. Third, the functions of behaviour are not only
defined with regard to the agent but also with regard to the
environment in which the agent operates. When Kohler's apes
took sticks, they did not only succeed in getting a banana
suspended from the roof of their cage, but they also created
beautiful evidence of the use of tools by non-human primates.
While obtaining bananas was a purposeful function of their
acting with sticks, the scientific evidence was not a purposeful, yet a very relevant, function of the behaviour of the apes
which explains as much as anything else the very reason why
the apes were used by the investigators.

The second statement of Moore and Meltzoff concerns how
children learn language from listening to mature speakers utter
sentences. They assume that the infant regards these sentences
as mere sequences of sound to which meaning has to be
attached. The first problem I shall try to answer is, what is
meaning with respect to the child?

I think that in Moore and Meltzoff's view, the meaning of
an utterance is its representation in terms of a system consisting
of sensori-motor concepts. Thus Moore and Meltzoff implicitly
assume that the child can be aware of a sensori-motor representation of, for example, an event, which is perceived in terms of
such concepts as agent, action, etc. The main problem now is to
determine why the child might consider the sentences spoken
by the adult as mere sound sequences and not as meaninful utterances (if the infant does not yet understand the adult's meaning).

If we believe that the child perceives events, for instance,
not as mere visual sequences but as meaningful events, then
why can't we accept that this same child perceives the adult's
utterances not as mere sound but as meaningful events
expressing 'love', 'interest', 'attraction of attention' and so
forth? That is, the adult's sentences and utterances function as
joint social events. Further, there is absolutely no reason to
believe that the infant (or most adults either, for that matter)
has a conception of duality between 'form' and 'content' (e.g.
sound and message). An experienced event – a sentence
uttered by an adult, for instance – is never a mere appearance.
It occupies a specific place in a specific chain of events. This
place is the meaning of the event, it contains aspects such as
'function', 'antecedents', 'epiphenomena' and so forth. That is,
'meaning' is an intrinsic property of almost any experienced
event. The problem, then, is not why meaning is attached to
events such as sentences spoken by the adult, but why meaning
changes, becomes more complex and socially uniform.

The same reasoning can be applied to the claim that the infant must learn that sentences are uttered with the intention of communicating messages or meaning to the listener. 'Intentionality' is a particular and important concept in our scientific and commonsense theories of behaviour. It is also exemplified by a set of specific regularities and functions of behaviour (i.e. behavioural properties that make us decide that the behaviour at issue is intentional). The learning of these rules, i.e. learning to act in a way describable by these rules, does not require a conscious representation of these rules, knowledge of a concept of 'intentionality' and so forth, so far as this representation or knowledge is different from the presence of the procedural conditions necessary to carry out the rule-governed behaviour.

In summary, the theme that has been advanced in this section concerns the meaning of behaviour, such as imitation, language use and so forth. Traditionally, the meaning of behaviour has been associated with some internal component, an unconscious representation of meaning which is materialized in the form of the actual behaviour, action or utterance. In this chapter, I have defined the meaning of behaviour as a relationship between behaviour on the one hand and a descriptive, interpretive system on the other hand. The descriptive system should be descriptively adequate with regard to the structure of behavioural events in which the described behavioural sequence is embedded. The behaviour characteristic for a particular subject is structurally limited and structurally specific. In the majority of cases, our mentalistic concepts, such as 'knowing', 'representing' or 'meaning', do not refer to mental episodes but to specific characteristics of the rule-governed-ness of behaviour.

10.3 FUNCTION AND CONTENT IN REPRESENTATIONAL SYSTEMS: FROM PHYSICAL TO LINGUISTIC TOOLS

In accordance with recent trends in semantics (see for instance Austin (1962), Searle (1969)), Moore and Meltzoff accept that sentences are 'complex speech acts, containing both a propositional or locutionary component and a performative or illocutionary component' (p. 160). According to this analysis, the child has to acquire an understanding of two separate aspects: how something can be done with a sentence (the performative aspect); and how a sentence can contain a message (the propositional or referential aspect). Each aspect has its proper cognitive precursor. For the first it is the concept of 'tool' or the schemes of tool use, enabling the child to understand how sentences can be used as tools; and for the second it is the child's early sensori-motor representational system. Moore and Meltzoff show how these two empirically separate lines of development flow together to form one new mainstream called language.

Let us first focus on the nature of the conditional relationships

between sensori-motor tool use and language development. In
explaining how tool use is the precursor to the performative
aspect of language, Moore and Meltzoff rely on the work of
Bates and her colleagues (Bates et al., 1975), who regard the
infant's initial attempts at tool use as the precursors to the
infant's use of preverbal and verbal gestures as tools. Thus,
the infant progresses from developing action structures which
underlie such activities such as the use of a stick to obtain
another object, to learning to point to an object he desires, to
learning to utter the name of an object aloud in order to obtain
it. Gestural and verbal tools will not be acquired before the
child has learned to employ physical objects as tools. Take the
example of a child sitting in his baby-chair at the table. He
wants to have a biscuit which lies outside his immediate reach.
The child can use a spoon in order to get the biscuit within
reach, he can look at his mother while at the same time pointing
to the biscuit, and, in a later stage of development, he can say
'biscuit'.

In a functional approach to cognition, having a concept 'tool'
is defined as being capable of using tools. In this respect,
using a spoon, pointing your finger and asking for a biscuit
are three different ways of tool using and, consequently, the
expression of the concept of 'tool'. The statement 'The child
possesses the concept of "tool"', however, does not add anything
significant to the statements 'He can get the biscuit by using a
spoon' or 'by pointing to it' or 'by asking for it'. The attribution
of a concept does not imply that the various forms of tool use are
characterized by one common underlying procedural or instrumental structure.

In a conceptualistic theory of cognitive development, the
various expressions of tool use are based on an underlying
concept that functions as their instrumental or procedural condition, meanwhile representing the basic content or 'meaning'
of the tool using activities. The problem with this explanation,
however, is that it provides an ad hoc explanation. It remains
unclear how much we abstract from the actual underlying conditions for tool use when we describe them in terms of one
underlying concept.

Piaget's theory provides a more specific framework for explaining the development of tool use. In this theory, the 'scheme'
is an important explanatory concept. Schemes are the result of
developmental processes governed by the interplay between
assimilation and accommodation. The infant, using the spoon to
obtain the biscuit, must have at his disposal a sensori-motor
scheme of material-tool use, which corresponds to the sensori-
motor representation of a set of motor patterns (how to handle
a tool) in accordance with a set of sensory features which function
as a sign that the motor patterns are applicable (when, for
example, is the handling of a tool useful or applicable?). As the
scheme gradually develops, its range of application widens,
that is, new objects will be assimilated to the tool scheme. For

instance, the child will see his own mother as a potential tool, i.e. he will conceive of her as a member of the class of tools which he already has at his disposal, such as spoons, sticks, boxes, chairs, and so forth. In assimilating the mother, or any other person, to the existing tool scheme, the child will use the mother exactly like he uses a material tool: for instance, he will push her hand to the biscuit. However, the reactions of the child's mother to his attempt to use her as a tool will soon result in the discovery of the special nature of the mother-as-a-tool concept. For instance, he will learn that gestures such as pointing are better ways of employing the mother-as-a-tool than using her in the same way as an inanimate object. Translated into Piagetian terms, the already existing scheme of using inanimate tools will accommodate to the requirements set forth by the new objects (for instance, animate tools, like the mother) that were assimilated by the scheme. Thus, without possessing a scheme of inanimate object tool usage, the child will never discover that, and how, animate objects – human beings – can be used as tools. Put differently, the use of inanimate tools is a conditional precursor to the use of gestural tools (which are in fact ways of using human beings as tools), and the latter will in their turn be conditional precursors to the use of verbal expressions as tools. Moreover, the effect of assimilating new kinds of objects to a scheme is that it gradually changes and gets more general.

The scheme explanation has been put forward in order to deal with the fact that activities carried out with new types of objects reflect the structure and function of already settled action forms. Our statement that the mother is assimilated to the inanimate tool scheme means that the way in which the mother is used as a tool is based on the same structure of motives, functions and effects as the way in which spoons or toys are used as tools. It is quite conceivable, however, that the emergence of the animate tool scheme is not, or is only loosely, determined by the presence of the inanimate tool scheme. Take for instance the act of pointing. Bower (1974) has suggested that the structure of reaching movements for objects within reach differs from reaching for objects well out of reach. 'Out-of-reach' reaching shows different arm and hand extensions, it is accompanied by pleading vocalizations and can be interpreted as 'indicator gestures intended to affect the behaviour of the nearby adults' (Bower, 1974, p. 92). Even if this type of behaviour is socially facilitated, i.e. carried out mostly or only when an attentive adult is around, it need not be based on an inanimate or animate tool scheme. A tool scheme requires, among other things, that the infant is able to make a choice among alternative tools, to select the most appropriate tool, that he is surprised or angry when his efforts remain unsuccessful, and so forth. It is quite plausible, however, that the out-of-reach reaching is mere reaching, whereas the adult will assimilate the reaching with his adult tool scheme, i.e. he will interpret it as the infant's attempt to draw the adult's attention in order to obtain an object that is out of reach. Because the adult makes the assimilation of the reaching with the tool scheme, the infant will soon learn that out-of-reach reaching is functional, i.e. that it can be used as a gestural tool, while the infant's own inanimate tool scheme has not served as an antecedent to this new scheme.

In general, we may start from the assumption that tools are extensions of the action potentialities of the organism. We may also assume that the earliest or most primitive forms of extension will already reflect the basic structure of potentialities on the one hand, while, on the other hand, they do not yet fulfil an adequate tool function. Sticks, for instance, are a relatively simple extension of arms and hands – they lie within the zone of proximal attention associated with the use of arms and hands – but it is quite conceivable that the earliest assimilations of sticks into actions cannot be assigned a tool function. That is, the actual tool potentialities of sticks have to be learned, irrespective of the fact that sticks are obvious extensions of the arm.

With regard to social organisms – man in particular – the social companions are as obvious an extension of the individual body as sticks are with regard to arms and hands (imitation, for instance, is one important example of what we mean by 'social extension'). The functions fulfilled by the social extensions of the organism are not yet differentiated by the time it begins to explore these extensions. In difficult situations, such as when an object is out of reach or when he is hungry, the infant will try to establish a social extension by crying, looking at the mother, touching her, or by a form of manipulation which may be directed more or less clearly to the goal the infant wants to attain. Although these first extensions are functionally diffuse, the infant will soon learn to employ them as tools, particularly because the social companions are able to interpret these extensions as intentional behaviour.

One implication of the previous arguments is that the order of acquisition of the various tool schemes depends on one's definition of the concept of 'tool'. For instance, why can't we look at the newborn baby's cry of hunger as the use of a non-verbal, gestural sign-tool? Probably because the newborn child does not have the concept of 'tool' which the ten month old infant will have. How do we know, however, that the ten month old infant has a tool concept? Probably because he has already shown us that he can use physical tools, which we assume are conceptually less complex than sing-tools. The reason why we consider cries used as tools cognitively more complex stages of tool use than spoons or sticks used as tools is that, in order to be considered a tool, a cry must be described as an indirect tool. The cry is a tool because it is a gestural instrument by means of which the mother or another person can be brought to remove unpleasant things, pick up a fallen toy and so forth. It is clear that a gestural – i.e. indirect –

tool, which consists of a two-step tool function is more complex
from the point of view of tool use than a physical, direct tool
that consists of a one-step tool function. Probably, we are
inclined to the assumption that it would be incorrect if we
ascribed a tool function to the child's gestures before having
observed that the child was capable of employing a less complex,
conditional tool function. That is, we do not accept that the
child's gestures fulfil a tool function before we have observed
that the child can use a physical object as a tool. Thus, the
stages in the development of the tool concept are not so much
empirically as analytically, i.e. conceptually, determined.
According to our definition of tools, gestures are more complex
tools than objects, and, according to our definition of development, the less always precedes the more difficult.

The second question is why the tool use of preverbal gestures
comes before the use of verbal gestures (words, utterances,
etc.) as tools. The answer is simple. In the class of gestures to
which the predicate 'gestural tool' can be ascribed, preverbal
gestures come before verbal gestures because the only property
that distinguishes the former from the latter – insofar as their
tool character is concerned – is that they emerge before the
verbal gestures. Again, the order of appearance is determined
by the logic of our labelling rules.

In summary, if we want to explain the emergence of linguistic
tool use, we should examine, first, whether the observed
developmental process reflects a conditional instead of an
accidental succession of steps, and second, whether its order
is either conceptually or empirically determined.

10.4 FUNCTION AND CONTENT IN REPRESENTATIONAL SYSTEMS: FROM PRE-LINGUISTIC TO LINGUISTIC MEANING

Moore and Meltzoff continue by examining the referential and
propositional functions of sentences, stating that the infant's
representational system serves as a functional precursor to
them. However, their assertion that 'the relationship an infant
constructs between his internal representation of an external
object and the thing itself is one of the precursors of the
linguistic notion of reference' (p. 161) is difficult to defend.

Let us first examine what might be understood by the construction of a relationship between an internal representation
and the thing itself. It is clear that such a relationship cannot
be a mental representation itself, unless we refer to the relationship between a representation of a representation and the
representation of a represented object. This kind of referential
relationship belongs to the field of meta-linguistic knowledge,
which does not precede but follows the acquisition of language.

The relationship between a representation and the thing itself
can be defined in two different ways. First, the relationship is
an intrinsic property of any representation. If 'dog' is a linguistic

representation of a dog, the 'dog' and the dog are characterized by a referential relationship, although the referential relationship is just a particular way of saying that 'dog' represents a dog. In a paper called 'The meaning of meaning', Putnam (1975) defines 'meaning' as a relationship between words and the world. Reference is an external aspect of meaning: it specifies how the word is related to the external world, not to the internal images and procedures of the language-using individual. A similar point holds for internal representations, such as iconic images. If we state that a child has an iconic image of an absent object, the referential relationship is an intrinsic, definitory aspect of the fact that the image is an 'image'. Constructing an image means constructing a referential relationship. This does not mean, however, that there are two separate acts of constructing or two components of one constructive act.

Second, the semiotic concept of 'reference' is expressed or exemplified in a variety of ways by the activities carried out by the subject. The construction of an internal image is an example of such an activity. The question as to which formal and functional behavioural properties are characteristic for images is very complicated. One possible constitutive feature of being an image is that the image carries the same information as the original object with regard to some specific purpose. It is not required that the user of the image should 'know that' the image has a referential relationship to an absent object. He should only be able to employ the image in the required way, i.e. in such a way that a meta-observer can assign the predicate 'image' to the cognitive instrument the subject is employing.

Thus, whatever reference may be, it is not required that the child needs a notion of reference in order to become so proficient in the use of symbols that his usage can be described as referential. Let us take the case of an eighteen month old child looking at pictures and naming them. Any observer of this situation will admit that the child's utterances refer to the pictures; but does the child himself need an explicit notion of reference in order to be able to name pictures? The answers to questions of this kind are crucial in cognitive developmental psychology. The core of the problem is the relationship between the way behaviour can be described by an observer and the properties of the system generating this specific behaviour. One of the basic underlying beliefs of cognitive psychology is that there is some fundamental resemblance between expressed knowledge and the way in which this knowledge is stored in the 'mind' ('the head', 'memory'). My saying 'Dogs are animals' can be described as the expression of the proposition that dogs are animals. The cognitivistic belief is that this proposition must be stored somewhere in the mind, either in abstract conceptual form or in a more direct linguistic or imagery form. The same reasoning holds for Piaget's operatory structures that underlie cognition at a particular developmental stage. According to the cognitivistic viewpoint, these structures must be represented in one form or another in the head of the child.

In Chapter 9 we discussed a similar problem: how much of the calculating takes place within the calculator? The answer to this question lies in the structure of a behavioural or cognitive theory. We have seen that a cognitive theory consists of three components: first, a competence description which provides a formal theory or description of the behaviour at issue; second, a set of behavioural expressions of the competence; and third, a procedural structure or 'machine' that generates behavioural sequences that are describable in terms of the competence theory. The most important conclusion of the discussion was that the 'syntax' of the competence theory is not isomorphic with the 'syntax' of the procedural machine.

When applied to the question of reference, the previous reasoning implies that 'referring to an object' is a theoretical property of 'having a representation of that object', while the way in which the procedural 'machine' produces images or representations is a machine-specific process which does not contain a set of reference processes in addition to representation processes. The basic question is: does the child employ a set of cognitive instruments called 'representations' in such a way that they can be adequately called 'representations', i.e. entities referring to represented contents? It is clear that the answer to this question depends entirely on empirical investigations.

Moore and Meltzoff assume that if the infant is to learn to use language meaningfully, he must first understand how it is used meaningfully by adults: 'this implies that until the infant understands those aspects of a situation to which an adult is referring in much the same way as the adult does, he will not be able to determine any systematic correspondence between adult words and their referents' (p. 161). A completely opposite point of view is taken by Lock (1982). According to Lock, it is not the child who attributes meaning - in terms of abstract relationships between concepts like agent and object, or object and possessor - to his early one- and two-word utterances, but the adult. Mothers and fathers take the young child's utterances as expressions of thoughts which make sense in their, i.e. the adult's, practical metaphysics. And it is because the child is consequently treated as if he expresses these thoughts and meanings that he will gradually learn them.

We can now examine the nature of the cognitive similarity between an infant and an adult necessary for making the learning of language possible. The knowledge of the adult consists of the ability to employ a set of rules relating the perceptual and actional to the linguistic system, e.g. to employ descriptive language, to carry out verbal directions and so forth. These rules are precisely what the infant has to learn. The required similarity between infant and adult consists of the perceptual and actional understanding of the world, that is, the world revealed through perception and action to the infant, and the adult should have the same basic properties. In the second part of this book we have seen that the basic perceptual (and actional) understanding of the world is a fairly early cognitive acquisition. We have also seen, however, that the 'syntax' of the perceptual understanding does not require categories such as 'object' or 'action', although these categories are quite suitable for describing the world as revealed by perception. The acquisition of concepts such as 'object' or 'action' at the representational level does not precede but follows the acquisition of language, since these concepts are characteristic constituents of a way of describing the world.

It is imprecise to say, as do Moore and Meltzoff, that 'many aspects of the adult's world will not be initially understood by infants and thus, infants will not be able to learn how adult discourse relates to these aspects until they acquire a similar view of the world' (p. 162). It is certainly true that the infant does not understand the way in which the adult linguistically understands the world because the infant has not yet acquired a linguistic representational system. But, on the other hand, it is conceptually impossible to separate the acquisition of a linguistic understanding of the world from the acquisition of language. The idea that language presupposes a particular conceptual understanding of the world other than the perceptual one, starts from the idea that the presence of referents is conditional to the presence of words and expressions that refer. In fact, language is a particular way of 'making' referents, provided that there is a non-linguistic - real or imaginary - world to which language is applicable.

In order to learn language, the child must, first, be able to take and keep parts of the perceptual field in focus, form and remember spatial and spatiotemporal patterns, see the world in a three-dimensional way, and so forth. Second, the child must be capable of tuning his own perceptions to the perceptions of other people, e.g. understand that other people's eye movements indicate changes in viewing directions, how direction of gaze and eye movements indicate a shareable focus of perception (see, for instance, Scaife and Bruner, 1975).

The implicit belief in the existence of a sensori-motor similarity between adult and young child is one of the basic paradigms of the parent's or caretaker's 'pedagogy of language' (see, for example, Ninio and Bruner, 1978). In playing games with children, parents and caretakers pre-structure, in a strongly regulated way, the child's discovery of the relationship between language and reality. The way parents and caretakers structure the game shows that they believe that the linguistic structuring of the world is entirely new for the child, although language may be acquired with the help of sensori-motor mechanisms as pattern formation and memory focusing on parts of the sensory environment, joining focuses and so on.

11 The development of meaning

11.1 THE GROWTH OF PRACTICAL METAPHYSICS

Every culture possesses and employs what I would like to call a practical metaphysics or natural philosophy (Russell, 1914; Goodman, 1968b; Pinxten, 1980). It is a system of knowledge about general properties of the universe; for instance, that there are things, that things have a number of specific properties, that there is time, that things change over time, that there is a specific space in which things are situated, that things can interact and cause or undergo the effects of interaction, that there are people, that people have a mind, that people act intentionally, and so forth.

If we investigate practical metaphysics, we must make a distinction between its explicit, discursive description - which is usually a matter for philosophers, anthropologists, religious thinkers and so forth - and its expression in practical and ritual action and language. For instance, if your psychology handbook got lost, you would try to find it. The seeking action will be motivated by implicit beliefs such as that the book is an object, that objects are permanent (they do not cease to exist when they are not seen or touched), that they must be somewhere in space and so forth. Presumably you will not think or act as if the book is an animate being who tries to escape from being read.

Mehan and Wood (1975) have pointed out a number of specific features of practical metaphysics. The authors employ the term 'realities' in order to refer to the fact that in most cases subjects are not aware of the rule system of their practical metaphysics but only of the kind of reality that is its product. Practical metaphysics is a coherent body of knowledge characterized by reflexivity. That is to say, the system proves and guarantees its own consistency and truth, although this consistency or truth are not of a logical nature. Practical metaphysics functions within the framework of social interaction; creating reality is a social process (see for instance Berger and Luckmann, 1966). The fact that the creation of reality, as an expression of a specific practical metaphysics, requires continuous rule-governed social action implies, among other things, that reality is fragile and permeable. This fragility can be demonstrated by means of 'breaching experiments' in which the experimenter consistently and unexpectedly breaks some very obvious social rule, inevitably producing confusion and extreme bewilderment in the subjects. The permeability of practical metaphysics implies that

258

parts or the whole of it can be changed as a result of contacts with other cultures or subcultures or of collective experiences that do not fit its basic rules.

One of the traditional aims of philosophy has been to concentrate upon problems raised in making practical metaphysics explicit. For instance, is 'object' an aspect of reality or is it a category imposed on reality by our mind; are there other minds; how can we know that there are other minds; and so forth.

An important part of practical metaphysics consists of a practical meta-psychology, i.e. a system which underlies our interacting with other people, our conception of mind, personality, intentions, etc. Meta-psychology is basic to descriptive categories such as 'behaviour', 'action', 'intention' or 'will' (meta-psychology is also termed folk psychology (Dennett, 1979) or common sense psychology (Smedslund, 1972)). Without meta-psychology, we would have to conceptualize and describe human behaviour and action in terms of physical, spatio-temporal muscular and bodily events, which is clearly descriptively inadequate compared with the objective complexity of behavioural and actional events. The meta-psychological conceptualization of behaviour constitutes a particular realm of reality, namely the mind of the behaving subject. The concept of 'intention', for instance, refers to a particular structural and observable property of action-events, but it simultaneously constitutes the subjective, internal domain in which intentions are thought to be present, i.e. the subject's mind, and which also contains other internal entities such as 'knowledge', 'feelings', etc. Practical meta-psychology is not a way of describing the mind, as it is a priori present 'in' the subject, but a way of constructing and maintaining the mind as an important and necessary dimension of experienced reality.

Smedslund (1972), following Heider (1958), enumerates a number of concepts which are fundamental to western meta-psychology, such as consciousness, perception or thinking. Actions are explained as the result of two psychological dispositions, expressed by the auxiliary verb 'can' and the verb 'try'. 'Can' results from the relationship between the difficulty of the task and the ability of the subject (for instance, his knowledge, skill or personality). 'Try' is the result of a state of 'wanting' (needs and wishes) or of a state of 'ought' or 'must'.

A number of non-western cultures have a meta-psychology that is considerably different from ours. H.A. Selby (1974, 1975) studied the folk-personality theory of the Zapotec, a traditional Mexican community. Although the Zapotec have a rich and complex lexicon of emotional and internal states, they do not assume that internal states have explanatory power with regard to understanding social relations. That is, they have no attribution theory in which social attitudes are more or less stable personality traits of the subject explaining why he or she behaves in a particular way. The Zapotec have a sociological

theory of personality traits associated with social relations.
In this connection, their folk psychology is very similar to
interactional theories in western psychology proposed by
authors like Szasz (1961) and Scheff (1966), who claim that
psychological deviance is merely a question of being successfully
called deviant by the social environment.

Lienhardt (1961) investigated the religion of the Dinka,
people who live in the central Nile basin in the southern Sudan.
Dinka religion is a complex and elaborate practical metaphysics
containing a theory of the world but also an interesting theory
of the human mind. Lienhardt states 'The Dinka have no conception which at all closely corresponds to our popular modern
conception of the "mind", as mediating, and, as it were, storing
up the experiences of the self' (p. 149). What we explain as
entities coming from or stored in our inner mental space are
conceived of by the Dinka as exteriorly acting upon the subject.
If somebody thinks about a period of time spent in Khartoum,
'it is Khartoum which is regarded as an agent, the subject which
acts, and not as with us the remembering mind which recalls
the place. The man is the object acted upon' (Lienhardt, 1961,
p. 150).

Let us now try to determine the relationship between practical
metaphysics and meta-psychology and developmental psychology
as a scientific discipline.

First, explicit knowledge of practical metaphysics may help
the developmental psychologist in finding descriptively adequate
definitions of development. That is to say, practical metaphysics
determines the basic knowledge that a child should acquire in
order to arrive at a view of the world accepted in his social
community. This knowledge or practical metaphysics is expressed
at various levels: perception, action and language. Piaget in
particular has made clear that the practical metaphysics is not
intrinsically present in the child's mind. According to Piaget,
babies are not aware of the permanence of objects, four-year-
olds think that the amount of water changes when it is poured
into a differently shaped vessel, and so forth. In this chapter
on the development of meaning, we shall examine some aspects
of the development of practical metaphysics in depth.

Second, practical metaphysics and practical meta-psychology
in particular will help us to understand the logic of child-
rearing. The way in which children are brought up reflects
profound differences between cultures. Erikson, for instance,
has provided interesting examples of the way in which childhood and culture are related and how the child-rearing practices reflect implicit conceptions about personality and the
nature of human life (Erikson, 1950). Levine (1977) has argued
that customs of infant care reflect cultural adaptations to
specific environmental pressures, such as infant mortality.
Moreover, the way in which children are treated exerts a particular influence upon the kind of cognitive contents and abilities
that may be attributed to them. Kopp et al. (1977) compared

sensori-motor development in India and the United States. Their
article shows that our concept of object permanence is highly
socially biased. The investigation of object permanence implies
that the child has to accept a considerable amount of frustration:
an interesting object is hidden, taken back and so forth. The
investigation carried out by Kopp et al. (1977) showed that
Indian mothers react totally differently to American mothers.
They tend to break off the experimental sessions much more
easily than American mothers and are much less tolerant towards
testing. Since the Indian infants could not fulfil the testing
conditions necessary to investigate the presence of an object-
permanence concept, the attribution of object permanence is
indeterminable and descriptively inadequate.

11.2 THE DEVELOPMENT OF THE OBJECT CONCEPT

In Piagetian developmental psychology, the concepts of object
identity and permanence are of considerable importance. Their
acquisition marks an essential step in the infant's growing
understanding of reality. Moore and Meltzoff (1978) state that
object identity refers to 'the concept by which an infant determines whether an object remains the same with itself throughout a transformation', i.e. to 'an object's sameness with itself . . .
not to its featural similarity to another object' (p. 163).

On the basis of visual tracking experiments, Bower and his
associates concluded that the three month old infant has no
concept of object identity. In these experiments, infants followed
moving objects with their eyes, and when the object stopped
' the infants briefly arrested their gaze on the stopped object
and then resumed tracking the path of the moving object'
(Moore and Meltzoff, 1978, p. 162). The tracking behaviour was
seen as an indicator of object identity equivalent to verbal
reports about sameness and difference given by adults (Bower,
1974, p. 197). Assuming that Bower's interpretation is right,
the tracking behaviour of the child expresses an important
property of the world revealed through the child's perception.
After the object has stopped, the child will look for a moving
object: he does not know that the stopped object implies that
the movement of the object has ceased to exist. The immobile
state of the object has no conditional value with regard to the
absence of a mobile state. If this is the 'rule' that specifies
the perceptual activities of the child in the case of moving
objects, then these activities are directed towards a 'world' to
which the property of object identity cannot be attributed. This
is not to say, however, that the infant can be attributed a
perceptually expressed, underlying 'concept' of object-non-
identity, since it is completely unclear what a non-identity
concept might contain (see further in this chapter).

The problem with which we are dealing here concerns the
semiotic value of tracking and looking behaviour and linguistic

expressions such as 'It is the same object'.

We have seen that the extra-systemic meaning of both kinds of expressions is similar: the 'world' that constitutes the object of adequate perceptual and searching acts, e.g. correct tracking or looking under the right cloth, can be described in terms of the predicate 'object identity' that holds also for the 'world' that constitutes the object of linguistic expressions such as 'It is the same object'. The intra-systemic meaning of a behavioural act is concerned with its place in a network of related acts, i.e. its place in its proper system of behaviour (various types of perception and action, simple descriptive language, and so forth). Elements from different systems have the same intra-systemic meaning if they occupy comparable places within - more or less - isomorphic structures. The formal structures - 'syntax' - of the various behavioural systems are mutually entirely different. The relationships between the systems are not based on isomorphy but on a complex structure of 'mapping rules' (see Chapter 12 for a further discussion). Consequently, tracking behaviour would express the same intra-systemic meaning as the statement 'It is the same object' only if it belongs to a network of behaviours - e.g. different tracking behaviours, patterns of looking back, grasping and so forth - which has a one-to-one relationship with the network of words and expressions to which 'same' 'different', 'object' and comparable concepts belong. It seems very improbable, however, that the behavioural and the linguistic network present the required isomorphic relationship, which implies that tracking and linguistic sameness statements cannot be attributed similar intra-systemic meanings.

None the less, it can hardly be denied that there is a significant relationship between the older infant's tracking behaviour and the statement 'It is the same object'. If the perceptual clues that define the adequacy of (correct) tracking behaviour are the same as those that define the adequacy or truth of the statement 'It is the same object', then the tracking behaviour can be conceived of as a perceptual precursor of object permanence at the symbolic or linguistic level (the same might hold for the relationship between tracking and adequate searching behaviour). That is, perceptual identity of objects constitutes one of the conditions upon which later forms of identity will be based.

We have now seen that the concept of 'object identity' corresponds with three levels of meaning, which are insufficiently separated in the majority of the developmental literature. First, at the extra-systemic level, the possession of a concept 'X' is defined as the ability to act (perceive, search, talk, etc.) in such a way that the object of the act can be adequately described with the predicate 'X' (provided that the proper descriptive system is employed). Second, at the intra-systemic level, the concept is described as a relationship between a behavioural sign (any specific kind of act) and its proper system of behavioural signs. Third, at the level of developmental antecedents, a concept is a theoretical term employed to describe a series of conditionally related developmental steps. Thus, although the statement 'The child possesses a concept of object identity' is a reliable theoretical and empirical description of the various ways in which children deal with objects, it is not a causal explanation of why the child behaves in such a way that the previous description is applicable. It is often accepted, however, that the concept is a little internal machine – a unit of meaning – that expresses itself by generating tracking and searching behaviour, linguistic statements about sameness and so forth.

The descriptive nature of 'concept' explains why the attribution of a concept to a subject does not enable us to predict when, where and why the behaviour of the subject will express the concept. Many adults, for instance, can be attributed an adequate surface concept, i.e. they are able to solve surface problems correctly. Nevertheless, they are easily misled when some minor changes are made in the problem (van Geert, 1979). If a concept were a generative structure, we would be able to predict when and where it is expressed in behaviour. In those cases where concepts are employed in an explanative instead of a descriptive way, the psychologist has to rely on a number of ad hoc variables, such as the décalage phenomenon or the resistance of particular contents to the application of a concept, in order to explain the many exceptions and experimental inconsistencies (see also Chapter 2).

In summary, the concept of 'concept' is a descriptively adequate term with regard to human behaviour if, first, it is not viewed as an algorithm that generates the behaviour it describes; and, second, if its intra- and extra- systemic limitations are accepted.

According to Moore and Meltzoff, the concept of identity plays an important role in the explanation of the acquisition of object permanence. The authors propose what they call an identity-theory of object permanence development. Initially, the infant is supposed to have a conception of an object that has no separate independent existence outside his own self; objects exist because they are sensed by the infant. If the object is out of sight, for example, it does not exist any more. The identity theory states that the concept of object permanence develops as a function of the development of object identity. In a first stage, infants 'define' identity as continued motion (or immobility) of an object. Thus, if an object is in a position of rest and then begins to move, the infant believes that he is seeing two different objects. In the second stage (between the ages of five and eight months) the infant learns that an object at rest is the same as an object in motion if the motion path and the point of rest belong to the same spatiotemporal set of places. The infant does not yet have a concept of object permanence. If a moving object disappears behind a screen it is considered to be no longer in existence. In the third stage of permanence development, the infant is able to infer that the object occluded by the screen and the object reappearing behind the screen are actually the same object. The infant makes this inference because he notices that the disappearing and the reappearing object follow the same, partially occluded trajectory.

However, long before the emergence of permanence concepts at the age of nine months, infants are able to infer the motion path of an object occluded by a screen (Bower, 1974). This can be shown by the fact that they continue their visual tracking of a moving object after it has disappeared behind a screen. The continuing visual tracking is taken as evidence of the infant's belief that the object is still moving. If the experimenter substitutes the object that disappeared behind the screen with a different object (taking care that the substitution is hidden by the screen and that the motion path is undisturbed) infants as young as five months will notice that they have been deceived. They will turn their gaze to the place where the original object disappeared. Thus, the infant knows that the reappearing object is different from the one he saw disappear. If the infant did not possess some form of object permanence, he would simply accept the vanishing of the original object and the emergence of a new one. He would not look back to the place where the first object disappeared behind the screen if he believed that visual and existential disappearance are equal.

The visual searching behaviour of the five month old infant in the case of objects disappearing behind a screen constitutes an expression of the fact that the world revealed by the child's perceptual activities can be described with the predicate 'object permanence'. That is, the visual searching behaviour of the five month old child is an expression of object permanence at the level of perceptual action.

The standard permanence test, which has been designed by Piaget, does not deal with permanence at the level of object perception. It deals with the expression of permanence at the level of manipulative action (i.e. searching for objects). Piaget has described the process of permanence development in terms of stages which are characterized by typical errors. Among the most frequently studied is the so-called stage III error (see for instance Bower, 1974 and Brainerd, 1978, for overviews). Stage III infants, who are approximately between four and six months of age, cannot recover an object which has been fully covered by a cloth or cup. The error is described as an illustration of the fact that the child believes in the impermanence of objects: invisibility equals inexistence. Bower (1974), however, suggests that the error should be explained on the basis of the manipulatory difficulty of the task. When the object is placed under a transparent cup, the stage III error will also occur. Bower believes that the child does not understand that the transparent cup and the hidden object occupy more or less identical places in space; that is, the child is unable to deal

adequately with the spatial 'in'-relation between the object
and the cup. Irrespective of which explanation of the searching
errors is correct, the searching experiments deal with a form
of object permanence that should not be equated with object
permanence during perceptual acts. It is highly probable that
perceptual and actional permanence expressions are functionally
related. This is not to say, however, that the perceptual and
the actional form constitute distinct surface expressions of a
single mental property, i.e. the permanence concept, that is
objectively and independently present in the human mind (the
conceptual structure, associative memory, the underlying
machine language of the brain, etc.).

The permanence problem refers to a classical philosophical
question which is usually associated with Berkeley, namely the
question of whether we can believe in the existence of an
independent external world, since the only information about
the world consists of casual sensory experiences. There is no
empirical way to determine whether an object that is not sensed
in one way or another is still existent. Permanence is a property
that is assigned to the experienced world on the ground of
practical motives. Consequently, a concept of permanence
should be based on a variety of experiences in addition to processes of reasoning, association, induction, and so forth. This
implies, for instance, that newborn babies could not possibly
have a concept of permanence.

If object permanence is not intrinsically present in the structure of perception, action and language, as Piaget would
believe, the subject should start with a developmental state in
which object permanence is still absent. Does the absence of
object permanence mean that the child has a concept of object
impermanence? Let us examine what such a concept might
contain.

At the linguistic level, object impermanence implies that the
subject employs a linguistic representation of a world populated
with impermanent objects, i.e. a world which is completely
dependent on his senses. According to Zinkernagel (1962) such
a belief is incompatible with a set of basic premises of meaningful
language necessary to formulate the belief. Impermanence is a
philosophical construct, based on the fact that we finally agree
on the permanence of objects at the level of practical metaphysics. It is also possible, however, that the subject believes
in a magical relationship between his own thoughts and the
existence of objects: objects come into being as soon as we think
about them, see them and so forth. It is debatable, however,
whether this form of magical, egocentric dependence of objects
provides an adequate characterization of object impermanence
in the infant. The magical belief is so complex that its expression
requires an extensive system of symbols and actions, which is
certainly absent at the beginning of permanence development.
Moreover, magical egocentric dependence is not a form of
impermanence, since the object, although created by mental acts,

exists in a realm outside the mind of the subject.

According to Piaget, the absence of a permanence concept is based on the absence of a 'dissociation between action and object' (Piaget, 1955, p. 89) and on the fact that 'action is the source of the external universe' (p. 92). That is, 'the object has to be detached from activity' (p. 91) in order to become a permanent object. If the infant touches an object, he does not perceive the object but the pressure changes and differential muscular tensions of his hand. The object is not an exteroceptive but an interoceptive (or proprioceptive) entity, i.e. it is not an object. Because of their interoceptive nature, 'objects' exist as long as the sensory stimulation lasts. The young infant's objects are not different from itches or pains, an extension of the arm, hand or leg, and so forth. It is not so much the 'permanence' as the 'object' that is absent. In Chapter 7 on attention, however, we have seen that the presence of intero- as well as exteroceptive components is an intrinsic property of perception although attention can be focused on either aspect. There is a fundamental structural difference between mere interoceptive and exteroceptive information. In the second part of this book, we have seen that exteroceptive information consists of the structural composition of the proximal stimulus, and that the senses are specifically adapted to pick up this information. As soon as we consider the infant able to perceive, we have to accept that he perceives an interoceptive as well as an exteroceptive world, however simple these worlds might be. The statement that the infant does not perceive a touched object but the resulting pressure changes in his hand is self-contradictory (which does not imply that the infant could not focus his attention upon the interoceptive component of the touching activity).

The classical experiments on object permanence were concerned with visual disappearance of objects (the object was covered with a cloth or cup or put behind a screen). It may be questioned, however, whether the gradual occlusion of an object by a screen (a real screen, a cup, a cloth, etc.) is similar to visual disappearance in the sense of 'vanishing'. In the second part of this book we have seen that visual absence differs from retinal absence. A partially occluded object is visually completely present although it is retinally only partially present, provided that the occlusion follows a number of perceptual rules, such as the law of good continuation. Michotte has shown that the optical information produced by disappearance behind a screen on the one hand and by vanishing on the other hand are entirely different. That is to say, visual presence is not only determined by retinal presence, but also by various rule-governed types of retinal absence and disappearance. If complete occlusion by a screen could be viewed as inexistence, partial occlusion would necessarily be viewed as partial existence. The latter would be incompatible, however, with the basic rules of visual object perception that are present at a fairly early age.

According to these rules, visual existence takes the form of various sorts of partial retinal absence. Since retinal disappearance occurs gradually, complete retinal absence – provided that it forms the final state of a disappearance event – should be taken as a limit form of incomplete absence. This implies that the meaning of such retinal absence would not differ from the meaning of partial retinal absence. (See, for instance, Chapter 6, the experiment with the sets of straight and curved lines (Hopkins et al. 1976). Unfortunately, the experiment was carried out with infants no younger than ten months; it is quite probable, however, that the results refer to a basic property of perception that emerges relatively early.) In summary, it is quite improbable that gradual retinal disappearance of an object would lead to the belief that the disappearing object has ceased to exist.

If the child cannot be attributed the belief in the actual vanishing of hidden objects, how, then, can we explain the typical failures presented in the object permanence experiments? Why does the infant stop looking for an object when it is hidden under a cup? The answer to this question is that the object, by being hidden, has disappeared from the present field of action of the child. Although this answer might seem trivial, it differs basically from the viewpoint that the infant believes that the object is no longer existent. One of the basic differential properties of action consists of the structure of objects and properties that are involved. In the chapter on attention, we have seen that the difference between more and less competent action lies in the objects and properties that are taken into account by the subject. The presence or absence, and appearance or disappearance of objects in the structure of the action field is based on aspects such as action-competence, memory, attention and so forth. That is, the actual presence or absence of an object should be distinguished from its presence or absence in the field of action. When I believe that an object has vanished, or that I can expect an object to appear, the object belongs to the field of my action (it is related to acts of believing, expecting, and so forth). Objects that do not belong to the actual field of action play neither a negative nor a positive role. The permanence experiments have shown that the structure of the baby's action field is still lacking a number of important properties. The ascription of a permanence or impermanence concept to these babies should be conceived of as a rather particular, metaphorical way of saying how the infant's and the adult's action competences differ with regard to one another.

The conceptual systems of the adult and the infant can be described as the ways in which their perceptual, actional and linguistic systems are used. At the extra-systemic level, the possession of a concept 'X' refers to the ability to act in such a way that a predicate 'X' is an adequate description of the world that forms the object of the actions. Practical metaphysics, if raised to the level of discursive explicitness,

provides a number of interpretive categories such as 'object',
'time', 'space', 'causality', for describing behaviour in terms
of the kind of world that forms its object. We have seen, however, that the attribution of a concept of object permanence is
a difficult issue. Although babies act as if they believe that
hidden objects are no longer existent, it is much more precise
to speak about the presence or absence of objects in the field
of action, and leave the attribution of permanence - or impermanence - beliefs to much later stages in cognitive development.

The fact that perception, action and language can be ascribed
the same world-as-object-of-their-activities, insofar as the
concept of object permanence is concerned, is not an argument
in favour of the fact that perception, action and language have
the same intra-systemic structure, i.e. that they are based on
a supra-modal network of 'concepts' which operate as small
generative units that cause the occurrence of various percepts,
actions and language-utterances. In this chapter, we have seen
that 'concepts' are descriptive instead of explanative (causal)
terms. At the extra-systemic level, the possession of a concept
'X' refers to the ability to act in such a way that the predicate
'X' is an adequate description of the object to which the activities
of the subject are intentionally related. We have seen that an
explicit form of practical metaphysics provides a number of interpretive categories - 'object', 'time', 'causality', etc. - for describing
the meaning of behaviour in terms of the world that forms its
object. We have also seen, however, that the attribution of a
concept of object permanence is a difficult issue. Although babies
act as if they believe that hidden objects are no longer existent,
it is more precise to speak about the inapplicability of the object-
predicate to the field constituted by the babies' actions and to
leave the concept of 'beliefs' to stages in development in which
the child has an elaborate symbolic and actional structure at his
disposal.

11.3 'REFERENCE' AND THE DEVELOPMENT OF WORD MEANING

According to Moore and Meltzoff (1978) infants learn language
by detecting the relationship between an adult's utterance and
its referent, i.e. the aspect of the world to which the utterance
refers. Since the infant starts with learning concrete, descriptive words or utterances, we are not faced with the problem of
'abstract' referents not immediately perceivable by the senses.
However, as Piaget, Bruner and many others have made clear,
even with concrete referents there is no such thing as a referent
which is immediately given or which imposes itself on the mind.
In the second part of this book we have seen that the perceptual
world of the infant and the adult are basically the same. If we
employ the language of practical metaphysics, we may say that
the infant as well as the adult perceives objects, events, three-
dimensional space and so forth. This does not imply, however,

that the structure of the perceived world corresponds with the
structure of the possible concrete referents, in the same way as
the sole of a shoe corresponds with its print in the sand. If I
point to a dog and say 'X', 'X' may refer to the dog, to the
temporal appearance of the dog, to its colour, to the fact that
the dog is sitting on the mat, and so forth. Any combination of
perceivable, expectable or inferable information could constitute
the referent of the sign 'X'. How can an infant know the referent
of a word before he knows the word itself if referents can be
infinitely various functions of perceivable information (see for
instance Quine, 1960)?

In order to determine how much the infant's understanding of
the world must qualitatively resemble the adult's in order to
make the learning of language possible, we shall examine the
effects of a basic difference in world view between infant and
adult. The example I shall give is merely speculative.

Assume that we found an infant who could display all the
typical signs of absent object-identity. The infant does not know
that immobility of an object is incompatible with simultaneous
mobility. In terms of adult practical metaphysics, the infant
thinks that there are actually two objects, namely the moving
and the immobile object. Is this particular infant able to learn
the name – noun or proper name – of an object? How can the
infant learn a name that refers to one object when he conceives
of two? We shall see, however, that the concept of reference is
debatable if it is considered a mental cognitive action or part of
such action. The speculative example we shall discuss concerns
the learning of the word 'ball' which the adult uses when he or
she refers to the infant's yellow ball.

What the adult and the infant see can be described in terms
of perceptual properties of possible referents. In order to avoid
unnecessary technical difficulties, I shall describe the referents
by means of letter symbols and the perceptual contents by means
of adjectives and adjectival phrases (instead of employing a
formal coding language for instance). The adult's view of the
situation can be described as follows: the referent 'OA' is characterized by the properties yellow, round, rolling at t_1, immobile
at t_2. The infant's view of the situation must be represented
in a different way. The infant sees an object 'OI', which is
yellow, round and immobile, and an object 'OM' which is yellow,
round and rolling.

If the infant has to learn the meaning of the word 'ball', having
OA as its adult referent, there has to be a resemblance between
OA and the balls that the infant sees (OI and OM). However,
this statement implies that the following premises are accepted:
firstly, that an auditive structure, a word for instance, has
only one referent, and, secondly, that the referential relationship holds at the mental level (the speaker is aware of the referential relationship).

Moore and Meltzoff (1978) assume that the child initially employs
a 'proper name theory' of meaning; that is, that the child defines

the meaning of an auditive structure such as a word in terms
of its relationship with a unique referent. For the infant 'ball'
is the name of OI, for instance (we shall assume that the first
time the infant heard the word 'ball' was when he looked at the
immobile ball). According to the proper-name theory, the infant
will be greatly confused when the adult employs 'ball' as a name
referring to the rolling ball - the infant's object OM. However,
the proper-name theory, if consistently employed, will not
imply that the infant is unable to learn the word 'ball' unless
he is capable of understanding object identity. If an auditive
structure has only one meaning, expressed by its relationship
with a unique referent, then any auditive structure to which a
different referent has been ascribed must be considered a
different word. That is, for the infant 'ball' and 'ball' will be
homonyms (see Figure 11.1)

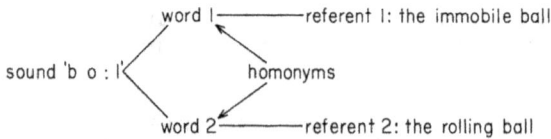

word I———————referent I: the immobile ball

sound 'b o : I   homonyms

word 2————————referent 2: the rolling ball

Figure 11.1 The relations between sound and referents for the
hypothetical infant work 'ball'

If the infant were to conceive of the ball as a new object every
time the ball reappears, his lexicon would contain an infinite
number of homonymic 'ball' words. It is clear that neither the
infant nor the adult would be able to notice the considerable
differences in the way in which they each establish referential
relationships between words and objects, since both use the
words in a way that is perfectly compatible with each other's
'theory' of meaning and referents. The adult employs a 'theory'
of generic names and referents that are members of classes,
whereas the child employs a 'theory' of homonymic proper
names. The way in which the adult uses words is describable in
terms of the infant's homonym theory, and vice versa. Learning
to use the word 'ball' in an appropriate way implies that the
infant is able to learn the conditions that govern the correct
use of the word ball. It does not matter whether these conditions are stated in terms of the infant's or of the adult's
practical metaphysics if, first, an observer - it does not matter
which one - is unable to discover the differences in the way in
which the word is used by the infant and the adult, and second,
if all the necessary conditions that govern the use of the word
can be represented in terms of the practical metaphysics of the
adult and the child. If the infant were to suffer from 'form -
blindness', he would not be able to represent one of the basic
perceptual conditions that govern the use of the word 'ball',
namely the form of balls.

Concerning the proper-name theory attributed to the child, it may be added that even the use of proto-typical proper names does not necessarily prove the existence of a unique referent that the infant would attach to them. Suppose that the child calls his dog 'Fido'. We might easily assume that the actual Fido is the unique referent of 'Fido', i.e. that 'Fido' is also a proper name to the infant. Another possibility, however, is that the infant employs 'Fido' as the name of a class of dogs characterized by the same characteristics as his Fido, the class of dogs that live in the infant's home and so forth. The fact that these classes have only one member, Fido, is a contingent and not an essential property.

The previous reasoning provides a theoretical argument against the use of the proper name theory as an explanation of the cognitive mechanisms behind the acquisition and the use of the earliest words. The predicate 'proper name' refers to a linguistic property of certain words, i.e. it refers to a linguistic category applicable in the framework of a complex and elaborate structure of language, which is characterized, for instance, by differences between 'proper' and 'generic' names, between definite and indefinite articles, etc. The proper-name quality is not a mental property of words, i.e. a property present in the mind of the speaker whenever he hears or utters the proper name. Whenever the speaker utters a proper name, he may have all kinds of accompanying representations, images or thoughts, but these do not correspond with the - explicitly linguistic - property 'proper name'. Later, we shall see that the concept of 'reference' must also be conceived of as a linguistic and not as a mental property of words and sentences.

We shall now examine some empirical findings concerning the use and the properties of the child's early vocabulary. According to Barrett (1978) early vocabularies show much more over-generalization than under-generalization, i.e. words are attached to semantic domains that are too broad rather than too small. Over-generalization is more consistent with a usage theory than with a reference theory. The child tries to discover where and how words can be used by extending the original context of the word. If the child were to be directed towards finding referential, i.e. naming, relationships, the use of the word would be much more determined by the context in which the word was heard for the first time.

A study by Gruendel (1977) shows that the growth of word meaning between the ages of twelve and twenty months is a complex process. Gruendel investigated the development of intensional and extensional meaning in two children. Intensional meaning is the 'sense' of a word as opposed to extensional meaning, which is the set of objects, properties, events and so forth to which the word descriptively applies. The children's early words had roughly two kinds of intensional meaning: one set of words had an action meaning while another set referred to perceptual form characteristics. These intensional meanings gave rise to four kinds of extensional development. One kind of word developed from specific to general. Initially, the words were used to refer to one unique object; later, their use was extended to include a class of objects. This is the kind of developmental line which might fit the proper-name hypothesis. The term 'proper name', however, refers to intensional aspects of meaning, whereas the observation that the word is used to refer to one unique object is associated with the extensional aspect of the meaning of the word. On the basis of its extension alone, a proper name cannot be distinguished from a class or generic name which for casual reasons has only one referent.

A second kind of word developed from function to form. Initially, these words were used with respect to any object that fulfilled a particular function. For instance, the word 'hat' was used to denote anything that could be put on the child's head. Later, the child learned that there are restrictions on the perceptual properties of objects that can be called 'hat'. These perceptual constraints narrow the original class of objects to which the word could be applied in a functional way.

A third kind of word develops from broad to narrow categorical use. The first time the word is used by the child, it denotes a broad class of things specified by one particular perceptual feature, e.g. four-footed. Words that belong to this kind of extensional development over-extend the adult's meaning, i.e. the child might use 'dog' for any object that possesses the perceptual property 'four-footed'. If more perceptual constraints are added, the word gradually gets its proper extensional meaning.

A fourth kind of developmental line concerns words which have different extensions in production and comprehension. It is possible that the child understands the word appropriately – that he points to a car and not to a train when he is asked, 'Where is the car?' – but gives to the same word a broader extension when he utters it himself and points to trains and other vehicles as well as to cars. Thus, the meaning of the word develops from extensionally asymmetrical to symmetrical.

To summarize, Gruendel's research makes clear that the child uses many different kinds of relationships between language and his perceptual and actional representation of the world in order to find an appropriate, i.e. socially accepted, extension of the words and expressions he has to learn.

It may be questioned, however, which psychological meaning can be attributed to the extensional and intensional meaning of the child's words. It is very tempting to identify the extensional aspect with the referents of the word and the intensional aspect with the concept that lies behind its use. In the previous chapter, we concluded that a concept is not an internal unit of meaning that expresses itself in action and language. If I say that the child has a concept 'an object that can be put on the head' expressed by the word 'hat', I am simply describing – in specifically abstract terms – the way in which the child employs the word 'hat'. I am not providing a causal or conditional explanation of the mechanism that lies behind the use of the word 'hat'.

The referential theory assumes that the child will learn the meaning of a word by trying to find out which object, property, event, etc., the word refers to. If the child knows the referent of the world - in terms of a concept - he will also know how to use the word appropriately. The problem with the previous explanation, however, is that reference forms a complex system of relationships between words and expressions on the one hand and a specific world-system on the other hand. In fact, referents are the products of the ways in which speakers employ words and expressions.

I shall try to clarify the previous statement with the aid of Frege's classical example of the morning star and the evening star. Since the age of antiquity, 'morning star' has been used to refer to a star that occurs in the easterly part of the visible pattern of stars just before sunrise. 'Evening star' has been used to refer to a stellar position in the pattern of stars visible in the evening. In more recent times, astronomers have discovered that the morning star and the evening star were distinct appearances of a planet, namely Venus. Could we say, then, that 'morning star' and 'evening star' have the same referent, namely Venus? According to Linsky (1971), however, 'morning star' refers to a specific stellar position occurring at a specific time of the day, and not to the planet Venus (see also Quine, 1953). The answer that I would prefer is that words such as 'morning star' have distinct contexts of use; each context of use constitutes its proper type of referent. That is, from the point of view of a planetarian model, 'morning star' and 'evening star' could be assigned the same referent, namely Venus. From the point of view of an observer of stellar positions and constellations, 'morning star' and 'evening star' have different referents; the terms refer to positions in different and incompatible stellar constellations.

The previous example illustrates that referents are system specific. A referent is a position or 'value' in a system of 'coordinates' or constituent variables (e.g. a planetarian model, a model of visible stellar positions, etc.). Instead of speaking about the referent of a word, we should speak about the logical extension of the word. By logical extension we mean the referent as a function of the system in which it appears.

By observing the way in which the speaker employs the word 'morning star', for instance, we should be able to infer the nature of the object of the speech act; that is, we should be able to determine which definitive system constitutes the logical extension of 'morning star'. The question of whether the speaker treats 'morning star' either as a name of a planet or as a name of a specific observable stellar position, should be determinable on the basis of a finite number of speech acts. In practice, however, the correct determination of the system that defines the

logical extension of a word employed by a speaker might be
quite difficult. When the speech of young children is concerned,
it is less important to determine the correct definitive system
than to determine the pedagogically valid definitive system. If
an infant employs a word in such a way that its logical extension
differs from the extension of the corresponding adult word, the
adult will mostly understand the word as if it did correspond
with the accepted, adult form (see for instance the discussion
on the syntax of one- and two-word sentences in the next
chapter).

The principle that the referent of a term corresponds with a
logical extension, i.e. an extension defined under a specific
definitive system, is valid also with regard to proper names.
For instance, if we assign a temporally specific predicate to a
proper name referent (e.g. 'is ill'), the referent is necessarily
determined by the temporal limits within which the predicate is
'true' or meaningful. If a temporally a-specific predicate is
assigned (e.g. 'is often ill') the logical extension with regard
to which the predicate is true should be temporally a-specific.

In summary, a referent should not be considered some external
entity whose mental reflection (e.g. the concept or image of the
entity) constitutes the mental condition to the uttering of a
referential speech act. A referent should be defined as a logical
extension, i.e. a value determined within a system of values
(e.g. the notion of 'object' within the commonsense model of the
material world).

The properties of a speech act allow us to determine which
logical extension(s) form(s) a descriptively adequate specification
of the object to which the speech act is directed. Speech acts
are directed towards various object levels e.g. the level of the
addressed object (the speaker); the level of the referred object
(the content or referent of the message); and so on. It is the
referred object that forms the referent or logical extension of
the speech act. In fact, the understanding of speech acts
requires that we are able to determine the various object levels
towards which speech acts are directed.

Since the object(s) of a speech act is (are) a particular function
of the properties of the speech act, we might conclude that the
referent (i.e. logical extension) of a word is a function of the
way in which a word is used by a speaker or a community of
speakers. The problem is, however, that there are various ways
for describing the use of a word. In developmental psychology,
two means of description play a particular role. First, use can
be specified in an intra-systemic way, i.e. the descriptive
variables depend entirely on the structural differentiations
within the described behaviour. Second, use can be specified
in an extra-systemic way. For instance, if I assimilate a one-
word sentence of an infant with the semantic structure of adult
language - e.g. the child says 'dog' and the hearer assumes that
the child refers to a dog - I employ an extra-systemic variable
to specify the use of the one-word sentence. In the next section

I shall deal with these matters in detail. We may conclude, however, that if there exists more than one way to describe the
use of a word, the word may be assigned more than one referent,
i.e. logical extension. (It is clear that this conclusion is true
only if the alternative descriptions of use are equally valid and
applicable.) Reference is not an internal psychological operation;
it is a theoretical relationship between words and worlds that
can be made explicit in the form of an actual speech act. In our
example of how an imaginary child learned the word 'ball', we
have seen that the worlds of the child and the adult were
entirely different. The referential relationship, therefore, can
be specified at the level of the child's world, of the adult's
world or at the level of any other adequate and relatively consistent model of the world. That is, words have as many
referents as there are ways to describe adequately their use.

11.4 MEANING AND USE

Alston (1967) states that 'it is a mistake to try to locate the
meaning of a word in some realm of being or another' (p. 237).
It does not matter whether this realm is the physical world
(e.g. referential theory), or the world of mental contents and
representations (e.g. ideational theory). In his 'Philosophical
Investigations', Wittgenstein (1953) advanced the idea that
words should be compared with instruments and that meaning
should be defined as the particular use made of words and
sentences.
   Most of the recent theories of language acquisition accept the
distinction made by Austin between locutionary and illocutionary
speech acts. The illocutionary aspect of language is particularly
stressed: it is shown that the meaning of the child's utterances
cannot be separated from their social instrumental function (see
for instance Greenfield and Smith, 1976, and Bruner, 1975).
In speaking and hearing, the child is not merely expressing or
interpreting the propositional content of the sentence but is
involved in the execution of a speech act. Learning language
is more than learning syntax and semantics, it means also learning the pragmatics of language, i.e. the scenarios of the different types of speech act (for a morphology of speech acts, see
Searle, 1969).
   It seems as if the distinction between locutionary and
illocutionary aspects coincides with the distinction between
meaning (as propositional content) and use (i.e. do things with
words). Meaning, however, cannot be separated from use.
Meaning is not in the head, represented in terms of concepts,
but in the use. The equation of meaning with use seems to imply
a simple, outdated behaviouristic view of language, as if meaning could be identified with a directly observable component of
verbal behaviour. The actual events that constitute verbal
behaviour, however, are meaningless unless they are interpreted

in terms of rule-following. We have seen (see section 6.1.1) that the manipulation of chess pieces should not be equated with playing chess. The manipulation of chess pieces is the expression of chess playing in that it can be interpreted in terms of the rules of chess. Accordingly, the actual manipulation of words and expressions should not be equated with meaning. The way in which words are used forms the expression of the meaning of the words in that the use can be described in terms of semantic rules. Learning the meaning of words and expressions means that the child has to learn the rules that govern their use.

Rules can be described at two levels. At the extra-systemic level, use is described in terms of its value with regard to one descriptive system or another, for instance language itself, a system of formal or technical concepts, etc. A description in terms of language itself is the most common way to specify meaning explicitly; meaning is specified in terms of paraphrases or dictionary definitions. Cognitive psychologists employ a system of technical terms, for instance terms denoting semantic features such as 'animate' or 'causative'. Although extra-systemic descriptions of meaning are perfectly adequate, they have often been ontologized in an unacceptable way by treating them as blueprints of the internal apparatus that lies behind actual verbal behaviour. Rules can be described also at the intra-systemic level. The intra-systemic description of meaning starts with the specification of the various forms or levels of use. The most general level is the level of action. Language itself can be the level at which the action is carried out, language may fulfil an instrumental role in a non-linguistic action, and so forth. Apart from a morphology of contexts and forms of use we should also try to establish rules that determine whether or not words and expressions have been used in an adequate way. Adequacy does not mean that what the speaker says is right or that his questions and orders are successful. It means that the speaking should 'make sense' within the general context of its proper (speech) acts (describing, telling a story, questioning, etc.). The logical extension of words, which we discussed in the previous section, can be considered one particular form of adequacy conditions in general, namely the form that the adequacy conditions take when we conceive of speech acts from the viewpoint of reference. Adequacy conditions in general, and logical extensions in particular, are formal constructs. Their psychological forms consist of the rules and procedures that are followed by the subject in order to build up an adequate speech act.

The morphology of speech acts, the adequacy and the procedural rules form three different ways for describing meaning at the intra-systemic level. The intra-systemic explanation of meaning is not concerned with the extra-systemic value of a word or sign; it deals only with the question of how to generate meaningful speech acts. That is, it has a purely procedural, 'syntactic' character.

Theories on the development of meaning are empirically competitive only if they occur at the same descriptive level (i.e.
either extra- or intra-systemic). I shall discuss an example in
order to illustrate this point. Suppose that we show a basket
with twelve apples to a child and ask how many apples there
are. The act that the child has to carry out can be described
in an extra-systemic way, for instance by referring to terms
such as 'number', 'one, two . . . twelve', 'more', 'less', etc.
The child can be attributed a number concept if he acts in such
a way that the term 'number' is descriptively adequate. Piaget's
famous investigations on the development of the number concept
have shown that superficial criteria, such as the ability to
count, often lead to a premature attribution of the number
concept to children. Piaget introduced new descriptive terms,
such as the concept of 'quotité' in order to describe the stage
at which children are able to count, while they do not yet know
that equal numbers express equal quantities ('Here are twelve
and there are twelve, but here are more'). The number concept
offers an adequate extra-systemic description of the rules
expressed in the behaviour of children, but it should not be
identified with a mysterious substance in the child's head.

The child's counting action can be described in an intra-
systemic way, namely at the level of a morphology of speech
acts, of adequacy rules and procedures. The speech act required
from the child can be specified as a descriptive mapping of the
vocabulary of natural numbers onto a perceptually represented
part of the world, namely the basket with twelve apples. The
adequacy rules describe, first, which natural number term(s)
are adequate with regard to the given situation, and second,
which situational information must be employed in order to
determine the adequacy of the permitted speech acts. The most
adequate descriptive term, 'twelve', is also the correct one, but
there are a number of situations in which other descriptive
terms, such as 'eleven' or 'twenty' are acceptable, for instance
when the child is not allowed to count properly or when the
child is still learning the meaning of the number terms. In
order to describe the situational information that determines
the adequacy of the number terms we may refer to the procedural rules, i.e. the rules that determine how to arrive at
an adequate number specification, in other words how the child
must find out how many apples there are. The procedural rules
require that, first, a reference class has to be chosen (i.e.
the things, properties, etc., that one wants to count); second,
a system of numbers has to be selected and then mapped upon
the reference class so that a number value (specifying how
many objects, events, or features there are) will result. If one
were to choose a very primitive system of numbers containing
exclusively words such as 'none', 'one', and 'many', a different
number value would result than if one were to choose a more
complex system containing an infinite number of number-denoting
words (e.g. our own system of natural numbers). Each number

system may in principle have its own mapping rules. The
common system of natural numbers can be applied to sets of
objects if these objects (more precisely, the perceptual representations of these objects) are ordered in a finite set and then
related on a one-to-one basis to the ordered set of natural
numbers. Put more concretely: if you want to apply the number
system to a perceptual image of a basket containing twelve
apples, you have to choose a reference set (the apples) and
then relate the objects in the reference set on a one-to-one
basis to the set of natural numbers, i.e. you have to count
them, one apple corresponding to only one number. The last
number will be the value of the reference set in terms of the
number variable (i.e. 'twelve'). It is obvious that there are
many ways in which these procedures can be carried out. The
child may point with his finger and count aloud, he may draw a
dot for each apple, and so forth. An electronic counting machine
would employ a binary number system, and 'translate' its outcome into a specific pattern of lighting dots that form the number
sign of twelve.

11.5 LEVELS OF COGNITION

In the previous section we have seen that there are various
ways for describing and explaining meaning, namely extra-
systemic versus intra-systemic specification (a morphology of
speech acts, adequacy conditions and procedures). A comparable
methodology can be followed in the case of cognition in general.
I shall try to illustrate this point by means of a classical problem of cognitive psychology, namely the relationship between
cognition and language. The well-known Piagetian point of view
is that cognition precedes language - that language expresses
what cognition can understand. The linguistic-relativistic point
of view is that language precedes cognition: cognition can understand what language can express. Bruner's position is intermediary: language - or more precisely, symbolic representation
- is a very powerful cognitive instrument that, if mastered
sufficiently, enables cognition to reach a new and higher level
of representation.
　　Comparable viewpoints can be found in the discussion between
'surface' and 'depth' theories of cognitive structure. According
to computational (Fodor, 1975) and 'mentalese' theory (Pylyshyn,
1973, 1978) the various representational systems are only super-
ficially different since every system defines its meanings by
virtue of an underlying abstract or 'computational' system (the
machine language of the brain). Surface theorists, such as
Kosslyn (1978) and philosophers such as Sellars and Goodman
claim that the various representational systems, language and
perception, for instance, are fundamentally different. Meaning
is expressed in terms of system-specific rules which are not
based on any underlying computational system. The relationships

between systems are explained by means of translation, transformation or mapping rules (see Figure 11.2).

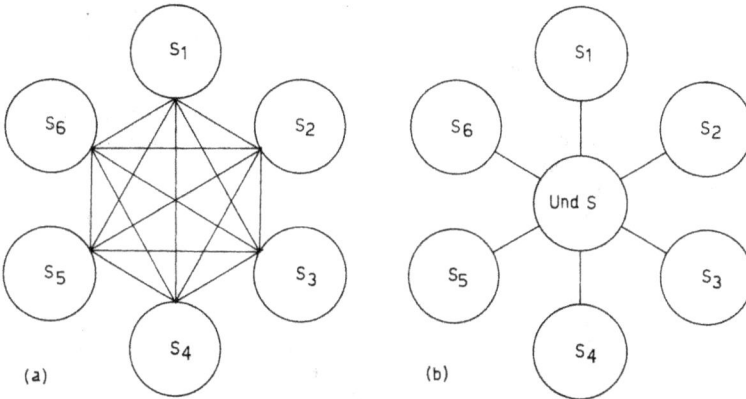

Figure 11.2 Six representational systems connected either by
means of direct links (a) or by means of indirect links via an
underlying system (b). Although (b) looks much simpler than
(a), the difference might be superficial and misleading (see
also Figure 11.1)

Anderson (1978) has tried to prove that the difference between
'depth' and 'surface' theories is meaningless because in the
interpretation of empirical data it makes no difference which one
you employ. As to the present state of empirical evidence,
Anderson's claim is probably valid. On the other hand, it does
not solve the problems associated with the conceptual analysis
of depth and surface theories. Do the theories function at
distinct levels of analysis or description (e.g. the inter-systemic
versus the extra-systemic level), or do they function at
identical levels of description (e.g. the level of the machine-
language description)? The answer to the previous questions will
determine the positions that the depth and surface theories will
take in the future discussion of cognition and cognitive development.

The depth theories of cognition are often, if not always, based
on an extra-systemic description of cognitive behaviour. We
have seen that the extra-systemic description leads to specifications in terms of 'concepts' which are derived from the system
employed to describe the behaviour at issue. The basic advantage of extra-systemic descriptions is that they wipe out the
differences between various systems, e.g. languages, perception, motor action, and show that different types of behaviour
can be conceived of as the expression of identical descriptive
predicates. The main disadvantage of the extra-systemic
approach has been mentioned before, namely that the conceptual

description is easily identified with the internal apparatus, i.e.
the machine that generates the described behaviour.

In order to make clear how I view the relationship between
language and cognition and the nature of cognition in general.
I have to go back to the example of the pocket calculator (see
Chapter 9). We have seen that the description of the behaviour
of the pocket calculator requires three levels: first, the level
of a formal competence description; second, the level of behavioural expressions of this competence; and third, an apparatus
or structure of procedures that generates the behaviour
describable in terms of the competence. It would be a mistake
to conceive of the internal procedural structure as a system of
internally stored mathematical meanings attached to the signs
that appear on the screen of the calculator.

The previous description applies also to human cognition.
Human cognition is characterized, first by a set of competences,
second by the expression of these competences, and third by
a procedural system that generates the expressions of competences. We have seen that human competences can be described
according to two different principles, namely the principles of
extra- and intra-systemic description. If we follow the extra-
systemic principle, we try to map various types of cognitive
behaviour onto one descriptive system, such as logic or practical metaphysics. If we follow the intra-systemic principle,
we start with local and limited structures of cognitive behaviour
and then, if necessary, try to find common procedural properties.

A descriptively adequate model of the basic cognitive competences should contain extra-systemic as well as intra-systemic
aspects. The extra-systemic aspects result from a mapping of
behavioural formats onto the system of practical meta-physics,
the system of logic (or any other formalization of what are
considered the 'laws of thought') and the system of action (which
Dennett has called 'intentional systems theory'). These three
systems constitute the fundamentals of our definition of cognition, namely the ability to understand the fundamental properties of reality, the ability to think properly and the ability to
act. It should be noted, however, that no a priori definition of
reality, proper thinking and acting is intended. These definitions must be inferred from the historical, social and cultural
context of the subject whose cognitive system and development
we investigate and discuss.

At the extra-systemic level, the problem of the relationship
between language and cognition obtains a particular meaning.
The question is whether our definitions of, for instance 'time',
'causality' or 'object', are descriptively applicable to behaviour
that lacks a linguistic dimension, viz. perception and sensori-
motor action. Put differently, can the object of a sensori-motor
or perceptual act be adequately assigned a property as 'causality'
or 'time', considering the usual definitions of these concepts?
If we state, as Piaget did, that cognition precedes language, we
mean that language is never conditional to the expression of

whatever fundamental cognitive concept (i.e. there is no fundamental concept that could find its expression only in language). Reformulated in this way, the relationship between language and cognition is a partly theoretical, partly empirical question which at present has no satisfactory answer.

With regard to the question on the depth-versus-surface explanation of cognition, the extra-systemic description makes it clear that the concept of an 'underlying' system or language should be conceived of in a very metaphorical way. The fact that a linguistic as well as a perceptual or sensori-motor behavioural format can be considered an expression of an identical predicate, e.g. 'object', does not imply that the machine language which underlies each of the formats should be isomorphic or identical on this point. The example of the pocket-calculator showed that different procedural principles were able to generate expressions of identical mathematical concepts or operations. The surface model of cognition, on the other hand, is faced with the difficult question of why different procedural systems are able to generate expressions of identical descriptive predicates (basic cognitive 'concepts').

In fact, the surface model is a particular elaboration of the intra-systemic approach to cognition. The general question that the intra-systemic approach has to solve concerns the minimal number of generative systems necessary for explaining the various forms of cognitive behaviour. In linguistics, the transformational generative approach has been quite successful in finding intra-systemic generative models of language. We may assume, therefore, that language is one of the basic cognitive competences at the intra-systemic level of description. Further, we may expect that it will be possible to write a generative grammar for perception, that is, a system that generates topological structures which characterize perceptual contents in a formal way (see Chapter 6 in particular). The motor system is probably the third and final basic cogn competence for which it will be possible to write a sort of generative grammar.

It is clear that the basic competences refer to components of actual behaviour. Most of the actions that people execute consist of perceptual, linguistic and motor components that are closely intertwined. In more technical terms, we may state that the basic competences can be mapped upon each other. Language can be mapped upon perception, for instance. That is, speakers are able to describe perceived events or to recognize described objects or properties. The mutual mappings are rule-governed: the basic cognitive competences are not only characterized by an intra-systemic 'grammar' but also by inter-systemic mapping rules. The latter kind of rules explain, among others, why structurally different behavioural formats (language use, motion, perception, sensori-motor action and so forth) can be assigned identical objects, i.e. they explain why their objects can be described in terms of identical predicates.

In the intra-systemic model of cognition, there is no separate competence called 'cognition' alongside the basic competences of language, perception and motion. If cognition is defined as the sum of the intra- and inter-systemic rules, the conditional relationship between cognition and language is purely conceptual. If cognition is defined as the sum of the inter-systemic or mapping rules alone, its structure will depend on the complexity and properties of the systems it has to connect. Bantu languages, for instance, have a system of six or more genders that is much more complex than the corresponding Indo-European system of three genders, namely masculine, feminine and neuter (Lyons, 1968). Consequently, the cognitive rules that will map the Bantu gender system onto perceptual representations, for instance, will be much more complex than the Indo-European system.

One of the arguments that militate against the surface model of cognition consists of the fact that, at a very early state of development, the child possesses a remarkable level of integration between the various perceptual and motor systems (in accordance with the surface model, one might expect a significant lack of integration). Early integration occurs also with mammals other than man (see, for instance, Davenport and Rogers, 1970). According to Bower (1979), the various senses are equivalent with regard to spatial information (i.e. it does not matter whether infants see a distance or whether they hear it, for instance by means of a sonar device). Does the latter fact require an underlying supra-modal representation of space? Let us first try to answer this question in a theoretical way. We have seen that the process of sensory integration implies that the perception of a Euclidean space, for instance, means that the object of the child's various spatiotemporal activities can be described as a Euclidean space, which does not imply that an internal supra-modal representation of a Euclidean space is required. 'Perceiving a Euclidean space' is an extra-systemic characterization of a variety of perceptual acts. The problem, however, is to find an intra- or inter-systemic explanation of the fact that different kinds of behaviour have identical extra-systemic properties. In the second part of this book, we have seen that the extra-systemic equivalence between perceptual acts depends on the way in which various types of proximal stimuli are provided with a deep structure, i.e. a system of internal relationships between the topological constituents. The equivalence between a visual and an auditive presentation of a place depends on the existence of transformational connections between them. Extra-systemic equivalence is not based on internal isomorphy of intra-systemic grammars (of vision, audition, etc.); it is based on the rules that describe how to map one intra-systemic structure onto one of another type.

Let us now see whether we can find empirical evidence for the fact that sensory integration does not require either a system of common underlying representations or strict intra-systemic isomorphy.

Sensory and motor deprivation experiments (e.g. Held, 1965; Held and Hein, 1963; Hirsch and Spinelli, 1970; Blakemore, 1974) indicate that experience with sensory and motor environmental information is necessary in order to maintain the functionality of the corresponding representational systems. Held and Hein conducted an experiment with pairs of kittens, in which one actively moving kitten was connected to another kitten that was kept in a small gondola. The connection was made in such a way that the locomotion of the free kitten was transmitted to the gondola kitten. Thus, the gondola kitten had more or less the same visual environmental stimulation as the freely moving kitten, although it lacked the motor information associated with the stimuli (see Figure 11.3). When the kittens were not in the gondola, they were kept in the dark and could move about freely.

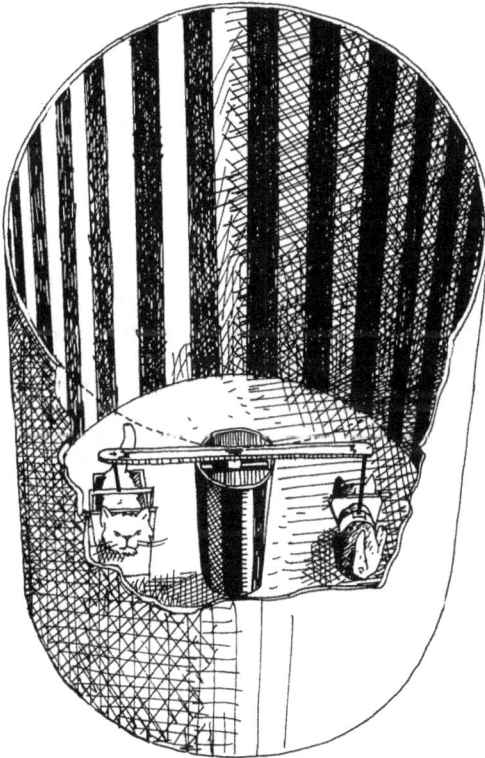

Figure 11.3 A view through the apparatus used in Held and Hein's experiment on plasticity in sensori-motor systems

The result of the experiment was that after an average of about thirty hours in the gondola, the kitten did not show appropriate spatial behaviour, e.g. visual cliff behaviour. Held and Hein concluded that adequate spatial behaviour is possible only if sensory information about space is related to active motor information. It is important to note that the gondola kittens were not completely paralysed: they could move their heads and obtain a rudimentary form of motion disparity information. But more important, since they were born and reared in the dark and after each gondola trip were returned to unlighted cages with their mother and litter mates, they could move freely in an environment with tactile, auditory and gustatory spatial information. The gondola kittens did not lack sensori-motor integration reflecting the properties of space in general, but sensori-motor integration reflecting the properties of visual space (i.e. they were unable to map motor patterns onto visual presentations of space).

Experiments by Gibson and Walk (1960) have shown, however, that kittens as young as four weeks – which is the earliest age that a kitten can move about with any facility – show appropriate avoidance of the deep side of the visual cliff. That is, kittens which are so young that they lack sufficient motor experience show adequate behaviour with regard to visual space. The apparent contradiction between the experiment of Held and Hein on the one hand and Gibson and Walk on the other hand, shows that, although the mapping rules between the visual and the motor system are probably innate in one form or another, prolonged experience with inconsistent information is able to alter the structure or functioning of the mapping rules. That is, the relationships between various cognitive systems is characterized by plasticity.

Plasticity is an argument against a depth theory which claims that the meaning of presentations in a surface system, as vision or audition, depends on their relationships with concepts – or any other meaningful essence – of a universal, underlying system. The sensori-motor system of the gondola kitten is partially integrated: there are interconnections between auditory, olfactory and visual presentations of space and between auditory, olfactory and motor presentations of space, but not between visual and motor presentations. This situation can easily be represented in the form of surface connections (see Figure 11.4). It is impossible, however, to represent this situation in terms of depth connections (i.e. the presentational formats are connected via one underlying system): either the visual system is connected with all the other systems or it is connected with none.

Although Held and Hein's findings cast doubt upon a strong version of the cognitive depth theory which claims that all surface systems are based on one common underlying system, it remains unclear how deep or superficial the connections between the various systems ought to be. We have seen, for instance,

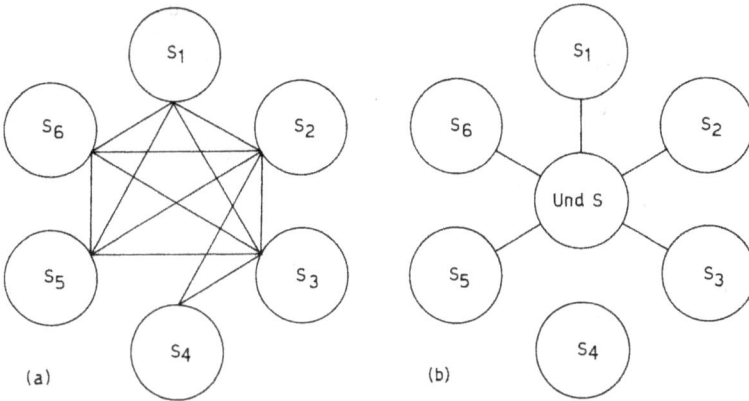

Figure 11.4 Plasticity experiments have shown that sensori-
motor representational systems can be partially unconnected.
It is possible to explain this situation by means of the direct
link model (a) but not by means of the underlying systems
model (b)

that the various sensory modalities might have a number of
common processing principles, due to the fact that all forms of
sensory stimulation are characterized by topological-spatial
forms of variability. The 'distance' between the representational
systems depends on the number of common properties: the more
properties one system has in common with another one, the
less complex their inter-systemic mapping rules will be. Although
the various perceptual and motor systems are based on distinct
underlying 'machines', i.e. neurological structures, their
activities can be described in terms of a common formal competence description which employs concepts such as 'clustering',
'computing' and so forth (see Chapter 6). It is quite conceivable, therefore, that the underlying 'machines' are at least
partly procedurally identical, such that innate integration as
well as plasticity is possible.

11.6 CONCEPTS AND PROCEDURES

Depth models conceive of cognition as a supra-representational
system comprising abstract representations and concepts that
underlie all other kinds of representations and concepts that
meaning and the relations between them. The argument for
introducing a supra-representational depth system is of a
strategic nature. A person who has five representational systems
at his disposal - e.g. perceptual, imagistic, pictorial, English
and French - needs twenty translation systems since each
representational system should be relatable to the remaining

four (see Figure 11.2). However, the second diagram only
seems to be more simple. We know nothing about the complexity
that would be required for introducing a common representational format to act as mediator. From Fodor's analysis of the
relationship between computational and natural language
(Fodor, 1975), we know that one representational system
capable of representing everything that can be represented
in five different representational systems must be of incredible
complexity. Therefore, it is not a priori clear that the second
model is more efficient, or even different from, the first or
'surface' model. Moreover, in the previous section we have
seen that the depth model is incompatible with the evidence on
sensori-motor plasticity.

In the previous chapters I have sketched a model of the
cognitive system based on a distinction between intra- and
extra-systemic descriptions of cognition. The intra-systemic
description distinguishes three levels, one of which contains
the machine procedures that generate the behaviour, while
another contains formal competence descriptions. In the section
on the object concept (section 11.2), I defined having a concept 'X' as the ability to act in such a way that the object of
the act can be characterized by means of the predicate 'X'. In
the present section I shall explore some of the procedural
aspects of concepts.

The following example may be useful in elucidating the meaning of 'concept' in relation to representational systems and
procedures. The example concerns a piece of music, say the
'Gymnopédies', a composition for piano by Eric Satie. The
'Gymnopédies' can exist in many different forms. It can take the
form of a structure of vibrations in the air; the form of actually
heard, consciously experienced music; of a black plastic disc
on which a specific pattern has been pressed; of a plastic tape
covered with an arrangement of particles of metallic oxide; of
a piece of ruled paper covered with black dots; of a motor
programme in a pianist's head; of a set of finger movements
carried out by the pianist; of a structural description by a
musicologist; and so forth. Although each of the previous forms
is a specific 'presentation' of the 'Gymnopédies', none of them
is the 'Gymnopédies' itself. The 'Gymnopédies' can be considered
the structure or logical content, common to all the presentations.
However, what is common to all the presentations? They have an
extra-systemic descriptive predicate in common, namely the
predicate 'Gymnopédies', which can be assigned to each of the
presentations by a competent observer. This predicate belongs
to a particular descriptive system, namely the set of names of
existing musical pieces.

The fact that the various presentations have one descriptive
predicate in common says nothing about their eventual internal
similarity or isomorphy. The isomorphy or similarity refers to
the properties that the presentational forms might have in
common because they are all presentations of the 'Gymnopédies'.

In fact, isomorphy, if understood as complete or direct correspondence between form-properties, is either inexistent or superficial and arbitrary (e.g. the relationship between pitch and the place of the notes on the music paper). Isomorphy is an inadequate criterion for explaining why different presentations have the same meaning. It is technically more appropriate to connect the question of corresponding meaning to the existence of transformational rules which describe how a presentational format of one type can be transformed into a presentational format of another type. These rules do not function at the level of the actual presentations but at the level of the systems to which these presentations belong. Transformational rules are of an abstract, formally descriptive character. In practice, they take the form of procedures executed by a 'machine' or any other form of apparatus. We need a record player to transform the uneven pattern on the black disc into a pattern of vibrations in the air; a human ear and brain to 'translate' the vibrations into heard, experienced music; the ability to write and read notes to translate the heard music into a pattern of dots on music paper; and so forth. The statement that the distinct presentations present the same content, namely Satie's 'Gymnopédies', means that for any presentation there exists a procedure such that the result of applying the procedure to the presentation results in a presentation belonging to another presentational system. The transformational relationship explains why the extra-systemic term 'Gymnopédies' is applicable to a set of presentations.

Starting from the previous example, we can make a general statement on the conceptual or 'logical' conditions of theories of mental (re-)presentation. First, conceptual priority must be given to the intra-systemic syntax of the various presentational systems, i.e. the rules that generate system-specific presentations (perceptual images, internal images, English sentences and so forth). In Part II we discussed some aspects of the intra-systemic syntax of perception. Transformational generative grammar has provided models of intra-systemic syntaxes of language, although it should be noted that these syntaxes should contain more than the traditionally 'syntactic' elements of language, such as 'noun', 'verb', 'phrase' or 'sentence'. The intra-systemic syntax forms the basis of the inter-systemic syntax, i.e. the inter-systemic mapping rules which transform a specific presentation into one (or many or none) of another type. Finally, the inter- and intra-systemic syntaxes explain the descriptive – or functional – equivalence of presentations with regard to extra-systemic predicates. These predicates specify a particular, although 'additional', property of the subject's mind, namely a property which is usually called a 'concept'.

Presentation and representation are words with different connotations. If we say that a specific perceptual image is a presentation of the concept of 'chair' we actually mean that the descriptive predicate chair is descriptively adequate with regard to the perceptual image (we have seen in Part II, however, that the descriptive adequacy of predicates can be very problematical when perception is concerned). If we consider the perceptual image from a representational point of view, we refer to its relationship with corresponding presentations from different systems (language, for instance).

The logical structure of (re-)presentation has some definite implications for our understanding of 'understanding'. According to the widespread, often implicit conceptual model of understanding, subjects understand symbolic structures by translating them into (a structure of) underlying concepts. We have seen, however, that a concept is an extra-systemic property of (re-)presentation: there is no place in the head where the concepts are stored, separated from the storage of perceptual or linguistic structures. Primarily, understanding means that a symbolic structure has an intra-systemic form or 'value' for the subject. (I hear a sentence as an intra-systemic linguistic structure, not as a purely acoustic phenomenon which I have to decode). Understanding can be completed, if necessary, by exploring the inter-systemic value of the symbolic structure, e.g. by recalling a perceptual image or by translating it into a form with which I am more accustomed. Inter-systemic translation, however, is a possible though not necessary completion of understanding and not understanding itself.

It is important to note that the conceptual or logical structure of a theory of (re-)presentational systems should not be equated with a model of their development. This problem will be dealt with in the next chapter. Let us first explore the further psychological consequences of the theory of (re-)presentation by means of an example. It concerns the relationship between perceptual and motor knowledge of spatial relations and the learning of spatial-relations words.

In the chapters on perceptual development we have seen that by the age of one year the object of a child's perceptual actions consisted of a world describable in terms of Cartesian three-dimensional space, constancy of objects and object-properties and so forth. The child shows also a considerable sensori-motor mastery of the structure of space. He can efficiently map perceptual presentations of spatial properties and relations between objects onto movements and actions in space. The processes and rules of mapping the perceptual onto the motor system will be defined as sensori-motor cognition.

Language contains a number of words which can be employed in extra-systemic descriptions of the child's sensori-motor spatial competence. If we observe a one year old child we can say that his behaviour expresses an adequate understanding of spatial relationships expressed in descriptive prepositions such as 'in', 'under', 'on' and so forth (the child is able to put things into boxes or under clothes, to find things that are hidden behind a screen, etc.).

What kind of role do these extra-systemic descriptive devices play with regard to the structure of sensori-motor cognition? Is sensori-motor cognition organized as a set of underlying concepts 'in', 'on', 'under', etc.? The problem is that our colloquial spatial prepositions are not the only way to describe adequately and reliably the child's spatial behaviour. It is also possible to describe the child's spatial behaviour in terms of a non-Euclidean topology, of an extremely simple spatial lexicon containing the descriptive terms 'here' and 'there', of non-Indo-European vocabularies of spatial terms and so forth (with regard to the problem of spatial vocabularies, see Pinxten 1975, 1980). It would be a mistake to identify anyone of these descriptive devices with an isomorphic picture of the underlying apparatus of sensori-motor cognition, i.e. the 'machine' that generates the behaviour describable as sensori-motor mastery of a number of spatial relations.

If we state that the child's sensori-motor actions express concepts such as 'in', 'under' and 'on', we mean something quite different than if we state that the infant's sensori-linguistic actions express the concepts 'in', 'under' and 'on'. In the first case, we mean that the child is able to execute actions which can be described as a mastery of 'in'-, 'under'- or 'on'-relations if one employs the system of common spatial prepositions. In the case of sensori-linguistic cognition, the presence of 'in-', 'under-' or 'on-' concepts means that the child knows how to employ spatial prepositions in an adequate way, e.g. by describing spatial relations, carrying out verbal orders that contain spatial prepositions and so forth.

Bower, for instance, has provided a number of illustrations of the fact that the lack of mastery of sensori-motor concepts of spatial relations explains a great deal of the effects observed during object-permanence experiments. Five month old children will no longer look for an object when it is hidden under an opaque cup. The same effect arises, however, when the object is hidden under a transparent cup. The infant lacks sensori-motor understanding of spatial inclusion, i.e. he is unable to organize his sensori-motor actions in such a way that the object will become accessible to him. Infants under nine months have difficulties in understanding 'on'-relations. When a small object is put on a larger one and when they both have a relatively extensive contact surface (a matchbox on a book, for instance), the infants will have great difficulties in retrieving the smaller object, since they do not seem to understand that it is still separable from the larger one (see Bower, 1974).

It will be clear that the procedures mapping the motor onto the perceptual system will differ from the procedures mapping the linguistic onto the perceptual system, although both kinds of procedures can be described by the same extra-systemic predicate, e.g. 'in-', 'under-' or 'on-' concepts. The procedural difference is due to the fact that the intra-systemic structure of the motor and the linguistic system are basically different.

The explanation of how an 'in-visual-motor'-concept, for instance, contributes to the acquisition of an 'in-visual-linguistic' -concept constitutes a basic problem for developmental psychology. The 'in-visual-motor' concept implies, for instance, that the child is able to put objects in containers, and that he is able to get them out. Let us call this kind of ability the intensional meaning of the visual-motor concept 'in'. In addition to the intensional meaning, the child should also master the extensional meaning of the 'in'-concept. That is, the child must be able to determine to which pairs of objects the 'in'-relationship is applicable. If a child is able to put blocks in boxes, and on the other hand, tries to get the block in the table-top or in the floor, we cannot conclude that he really possesses the visual-motor 'in'-concept.

Eve Clark (1972, 1973a, 1973b, 1974) conducted a number of experiments in which she investigated how children acquire the meaning of the words 'on', 'under' and 'in'. Clark showed that children employ specific strategies to find out what these spatial prepositions mean. If children are asked to put a block in a box, they immediately assume that the question put by the experimenter refers to a place relationship between the objects. Eighteen month old children do not know the exact meaning of the spatial prepositions but apply a meaning which corresponds with the most natural or 'canonical' relationship holding between the given objects. In the case of a block and a box, the child will put the block in the box, regardless of whether he is asked to put the block in, on, under or beside the box.

The western child lives in a world that is almost entirely man-made and materially very complex. Objects are designed to fulfil specific place relations. Boxes and baskets are made to contain discrete objects; bottles and beakers are made to put liquid in: tables are made to put objects on; chairs are made to put people on, etc. In learning to put things on, in and under specific objects, the child learns the spatial relations functions of the objects he meets in his daily world. He learns 'official' or canonical functions (e.g. tables are made to put dishes, toys and books on), and he also learns 'unofficial' or non-canonical functions (e.g. you can crawl under the table if you want to hide from someone). This kind of practical knowledge constitutes the system of sensori-motor 'concepts' of space. The child is able to recognize objects such as tables, beakers and boxes, and he is able to use them for such particular purposes as putting things under or on them.

According to Gibson (1979) we might say that objects are characterized by specific, perceptually revealed spatial 'affordances'. For instance, a horizontal, supported, plain surface 'affords' to put things on it; while a hollow, attainable space 'affords' to put things in it . . . Polyvalent objects are characterized by an ambiguous 'affordance': the object looks like a box, i.e. something to put things in, but it also looks like a table, i.e. something to put things on. The ambiguity of the

object can be taken away by giving it a non-ambiguous name
(either 'box' or 'table'). If the child has to locate something in
relation to a polyvalent object, he will select a location that fits
the functional interpretation attributed to the object. If it is
called a box, the child will put something in it, if it is called
a table the child will put something on it, regardless of the
adult meaning of the preposition employed in the verbal order
(see Hoogenraad et al., 1978).

The system of sensori-motor concepts of spatial relationships
is quite complex. It consists of pairs of objects for which a
particular spatial relationship holds, e.g. table and dish (dishes
are put on tables in such a way that the 'open' side of the
dishes is accessible), table and chair (the seat of the chair
should be under the table), and so forth. The nature of the
spatial relationship is determined by the kind of objects for
which it holds. Being 'in' a bed differs from being 'in' a box,
'in' the cupboard or 'in' your hand. These objects constitute
different systems of possible (functional or canonical) places.
Different knowledge of functions and sensori-motor programmes
are required to get something 'in' a bed, 'in' a cupboard or
'in' a box. The sensori-motor system of spatial relations is
much more complex than the linguistic system of spatial relations
that is used to describe it. It may be stated that the linguistic
system imposes a simple symbolic 'lattice' upon the complex
system of sensori-motor spatial relationships between objects.
The child's task is to find out how the linguistic system can be
mapped upon the perceptual and the sensori-motor presentation
of space.

In an investigation of the development of spatial prepositions
in one child, the present writer observed that spatial prepositions are acquired in three stages (Van Geert, 1975). During
the first stage, prepositions are used in a correct way, although
their frequency is relatively small. From the observations it is
clear that the child employs spatial prepositions in a conventionalized way. The second stage is much more interesting. The
frequency of the spatial prepositions increases and the child
starts to make a number of typical mistakes which suggest that
he is trying to develop a rule for the use of 'in', 'on', etc.
Typical expressions were 'in the telephone' (i.e. with), 'in the
belly' (i.e. round or on), 'in the table' (i.e. on), 'in the floor'
(i.e. on) 'in the pillow' (i.e. on), 'in the window' (i.e. through),
'in my legs' (i.e. on). In a considerable number of expressions,
'in' has taken the place occupied by 'on' during the first stage.
In general 'in' refers to a relationship between a place and a
set of places which can be either two- or three-dimensional.
Some observations, however, are difficult to explain in terms of
a simple rule ('in my legs', for instance). At the third stage,
the typical, creative errors disappear and the child employs the
prepositions according to their correct rules and exceptions.

I shall now discuss some formal properties of the perceptual-
linguistic mapping rules that are concerned in the use of spatial

prepositions. In general, these rules determine which mappings of linguistic onto perceptual presentations – and vice versa – are adequate or 'acceptable'. Previously we have called these rules, which are of the intra-systemic type, the 'conditions of adequacy'. The perceptual conditions of adequacy are necessary conditional components of a great number of speech acts, but they should never be identified with the sufficient conditions nor with the meaning of the verbal messages. The conditions of adequacy are the theoretical or logical expression of the inter-systemic procedures that regulate the relationship between language and perception. Consequently, they also provide a formal characterization of a developmental final state, namely the ability to map linguistic onto perceptual presentations of spatial relations between objects.

The most general level of conditions of adequacy with regard to spatial prepositions consists of a typology and a grammar of actions in which linguistic reference to spatial relations is meaningful. Although a discussion of this grammar and typology falls outside the scope of this chapter, it is important to note that, by making the perceptual conditions of adequacy subordinate to a framework of (speech) actions, an implicit and untenable stimulus-response model of language is avoided. If we would only look to the perceptual conditions of speech we would fall into a model in which the conditions serve as stimuli and the linguistic utterances as responses. The conditions of adequacy determine whether a speech act that contains a reference to spatial relations between objects is either adequate or not, that is, whether the speech act is performed according to the rules of the game, whether the speaker follows an expectable strategy, and so forth. We shall discuss this issue in section 12.3 where we shall introduce the notion of linguistic reflexivity.

The perceptual conditions of adequacy which I shall discuss here are concerned in a simple, descriptive speech act without further reference to its particular goal or underlying intention (which are aspects that have to be dealt with at the level of the speech-act grammar). My aim is simply to illustrate some properties of perceptual adequacy conditions in the field of spatial prepositions and to discuss some of their developmental consequences. The conditions of adequacy which are at issue here take the form of pairs consisting of a set of topological properties of perceptual presentations on the one hand and a set of simple descriptive speech acts which are considered adequate or meaningful on the other hand.

Although the topological form of place relations between objects can be infinitely variable (e.g. with regard to size, distance, form of the objects, etc.) we are able to distinguish some general aspects. In the chapter on perception and perceptual development (see Chapter 3) we introduced the notion of a place system. Forms and patterns were defined as sets of joint and ordered places in a specific place system. Figure 11.5

shows a collection of place systems and place sets. Although the variety of systems and sets is quite extensive, we may distinguish a number of topological properties that seem quite important with regard to the use of spatial prepositions. These properties are, first, community (set A has n places in common with set B), second, contiguity (n places of A and B are contiguous) and, third, non-community and non-contiguity. The reason why the sets A and B are taken into consideration by the speaker should not be sought at the level of the perceptual conditions of adequacy but at the level of the speech act (which I will not discuss here). It is important to note that community and contiguity are not intrinsically basic perceptual properties of place sets. They are important because we have observed that they belong to the basic conditions of adequacy with regard to spatial prepositions.

Community and contiguity - and the absence of these properties - constitute symmetrical topological relationships between place sets. In principle, they could be employed as conditions of adequacy for three simple symmetrical spatial prepositions, i.e. 'have common places', 'are contiguous' and 'have no common places - are not contiguous'. Indo-European languages, such as English and Dutch, have a much more complicated vocabulary of spatial prepositions, i.e. they contain many more prepositions than three, and, second, most of these prepositions express asymmetrical relationships. Nevertheless, the simple topological distinctions denoted by 'community' and 'contiguity' are conditions of adequacy for three 'generic', largely asymmetrical spatial prepositions 'on', 'in' and 'beside'. Community, either complete or not, is a condition of adequacy for the generic preposition 'in', contiguity is a condition for the generic 'on', whereas the absence of community and contiguity is a condition for the generic 'beside'. The illustrations in Figure 11.5 show that community and contiguity are general topological properties of place sets and that the use of spatial prepositions is not determined by properties such as three- or two-dimensionality or relative size.

Before starting a further examination of spatial prepositions, I want to discuss an important, conditional aspect of statements about spatial relationships, namely the choice of the referent. Since most spatial prepositions refer to asymmetrical relations, it is necessary to make a distinction between a referent- and a subject-set. Although it is possible to provide a number of - mostly marginal - perceptual criteria for distinguishing the referent - from the subject-set (see for instance Clark et al., 1973), the perceptual adequacy rules deal only with the adequacy of spatial-relations statements and not with the choice of the referent or the subject. In order to explain why set A is chosen as the referent- and B as the subject-set, we should go back to the basic level of adequacy conditions, namely the level of the speech act. At this level, the intentions and the interest of the speaker are defined, the possible topics of

PLACE RELATIONS

	1.1. Community	1.2. Contiguity	1.3. Non Community/ Non Contiguity
1. FIRST-ORDER PLACE SYSTEM	1.1.1. A∩B≠0 1.1.2. B⊂A	1.2.1. A⊄B =1 1.2.2. A⊄B = 2	1.3.1. A∩B=0 , A⊄B=0
	2.1. First-order community	2.2. First-order contiguity	2.3. First-order non-com- munity/non-contiguity
2. SECOND-ORDER PLACE SYSTEM *first-order place sets*	2.1.1. A∩B≠0; ∃b:b⊄(3e)=2	2.2.1. A⊄B=1;∃a:a⊄(3e)≟1; ∃b: b⊄(3e)≟1	2.3.1. see 1.3.1.
	2.1.2. A∩B≠0, ∃ b:b⊄(3e) =1	2.2.2. A⊄B⋝1;∃a:a⊄(3e)≟0 ∃b:b⊄(3e)≟0	2.3.2. Orientation added
	2.1.3. B⊂A (see 1.1.2.)	2.2.3. A⊄B ⋝1,∃b:b⊄(1e)≟0	
		b⊄(1e) = 2 b⊄(1e)=1 b⊄(1e) =0	

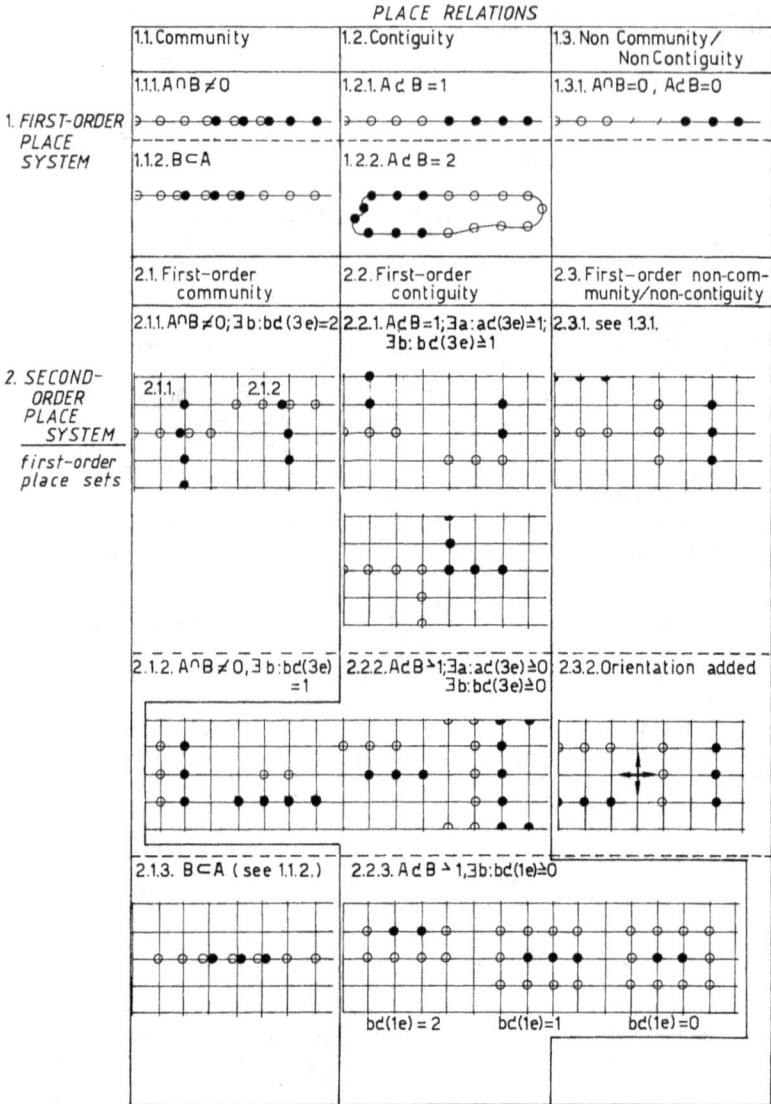

Figure 11.5 A summary of topological relations between place sets (contiguity, community, and non-contiguity/non-community) that are relevant with regard to the use of spatial prepositions. Three place sets are important: A (white circles), B (black circles), and the set of empty places(e) (Empty places are places neither occupied by A nor by B.)
Section 4 contains some examples of relations between three-

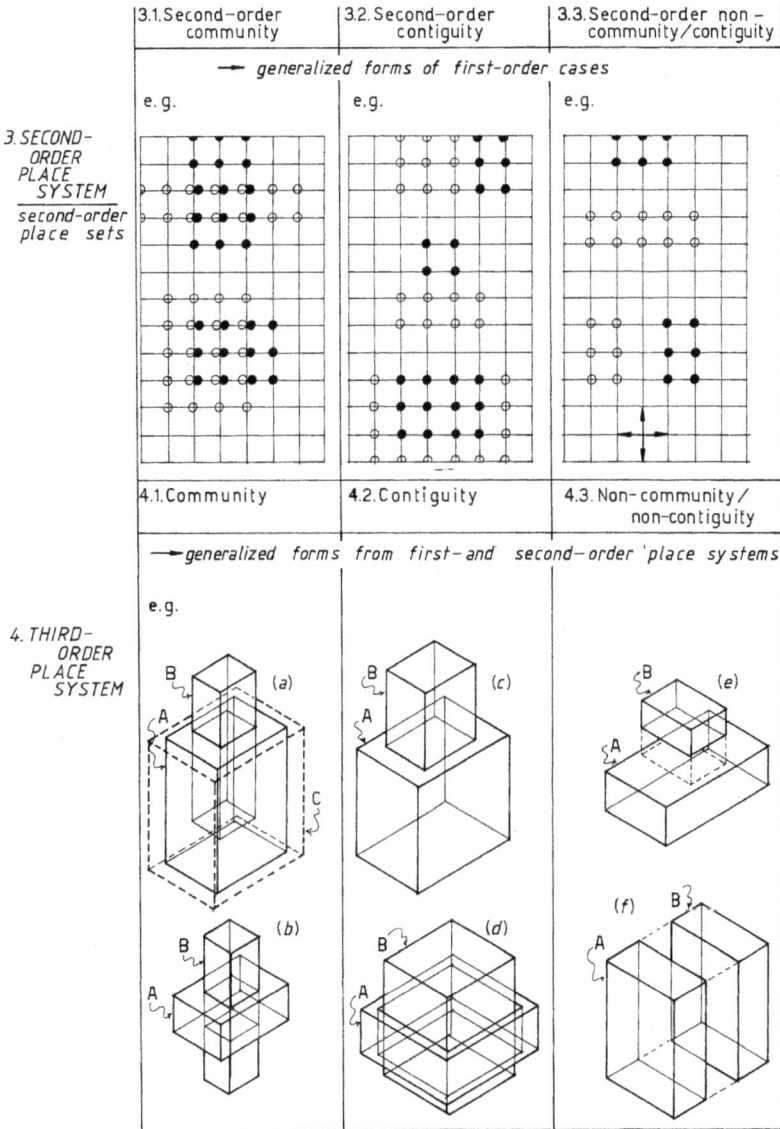

3.1.Second–order community	3.2. Second–order contiguity	3.3. Second–order non – community/contiguity

→ *generalized forms of first-order cases*

| e. g. | e.g. | e.g. |

3. SECOND-ORDER PLACE SYSTEM
second-order place sets

4.1.Community	4.2.Contiguity	4.3. Non-community/ non-contiguity

→*generalized forms from first–and second–order 'place systems*

e.g.

4. THIRD-ORDER PLACE SYSTEM

(a) (b) (c) (d) (e) (f)

dimensional place sets. (a) is a generalized form of 1.1.1.: B
and A have a number of common places. Community is an
adequacy condition for 'in'. The direction of the 'in' relation
depends on a number of additional criteria. In practice, set A
will consist of a place set circumscribed by a container (C; see
also (d)). (b) is a generalized form of 2.1.1. 'A in B', 'B in A'
and 'B through A' are acceptable descriptions of the place

relations between A and B. If the variable 'fixed spatial
orientation' is added to the set of adequacy conditions, the
spatial relation between A and B is described by 'B on A'.
(c) is a generalization of 2.2.3. A and B are characterized by
a set of contiguous places: 'A is around B'. B and the place set
circumscribed by A have a number of common places (a generalization of 2.2.3.): 'B in A' or 'B through A' (see also (b)). If
fixed spatial orientation is added to the set of adequacy conditions. 'B(A) is above (under) A(B)' in (e), and 'B(A) is
besides A(B)' in (f). The set of adequacy conditions in this
Figure is incomplete. In order to deal with spatial prepositions
in a more general way, fourth-order place sets (space and
time) should be included. Languages differ with regard to the
way in which they select conditions of adequacy for their
proper sets of spatial prepositions

statements are selected, and so forth.
   Figure 11.5 provides an overview of the topological properties
that complete the conditions of adequacy. In the contiguity
column, for instance, we see that the introduction of the
distinction between complete and incomplete contiguity coincides
with the distinction between 'on' and 'round'. In some cases,
complete contiguity 'degenerates' to a form of community, i.e.
to a condition for 'in'. In the community column, the distinction
between complete and incomplete does not constitute a conditional
difference with regard to the spatial prepositions. In English,
as well as in Dutch, for instance, it does not make a difference
whether the subject-set is either completely or only partly
included in the referent-set. The introduction of orientation in
the place system (which has been discussed in section 5.2) has
considerable consequences for the non-contiguous non-community
column. The space around the referent-set is divided into sub-
spaces that correspond with distinctions between 'under' and
'above' (or 'over'), 'left' and 'right', and so forth. Finally, the
introduction of temporal order permits us to regulate the distinction between 'in' and 'out' or 'to' and 'from'.
   Conditions of adequacy for spatial prepositions are not only
determined by topological properties of perceptual presentations,
but also by particular contexts of use (e.g. 'in London', 'at
Bath'). These particular context rules vary from language to
language.
   The form and content of the adequacy rules illustrate a
previously made point, namely that the inter-systemic rules, i.e.
the adequacy or mapping rules, and the intra-systemic rules,
i.e. the grammar of language or perception, should not be
mixed up. Because of their extra-systemic equivalence with
regard to the applicability of spatial relations terms, the perceptual and the linguistic system might be attributed a structure
of underlying spatial relations concepts. We have seen, however,
that the adequacy rules consist of a limited and specific selection
of the topological properties that determine perceptual presen-

tations. Contiguity and community, for instance, are basic topological features with regard to the applicability of the generic 'in' and 'on', but they are not the basic features of perceptual presentations per se.

The differences which hold with regard to the intra- and inter-systemic rules hold also at the level of the distinct inter-systemic rules. A spatial preposition, such as 'in' or 'on', refers to a large number of possible spatial relationships between place sets (there are many places 'in' a box or 'in' a cupboard). Motor actions, on the other hand, are always directed towards the specific place of objects. Further, motor actions require a temporal organization, which is only an optional feature in the case of spatial prepositions. Motor actions are determined by a number of spatial properties of objects, e.g. openness or closed-ness, size, distance, etc., which are largely irrelevant with regard to the applicability of spatial prepositions. In summary, the fact that spatial prepositions are applicable to motor actions does not imply that the language of spatial relations and the system of motor action in space have a common underlying struc-ture. The relationship between language and motor action is based on the existing mapping rules between language and perception on the one hand and perception and motor action on the other hand.

Finally, the conditions of adequacy can be conceived of as logical specifications of perceptual distinctions that the speaker should be able to make, e.g. the distinction between community and contiguity. The previous perceptual abilities specify final stages of perceptual development that should be achieved in order to make the learning of spatial prepositions possible. That is, children should be able to make a distinction between common and contiguous place sets, if the proceeding acquisition of spatial prepositions requires them to do so. This is different from saying, however, that the distinction between topological community and contiguity should have been made at the non-linguistic level - for instance at the level of action - before the child was able to learn the linguistic meaning of 'in' and 'on'.

The idea of a fundamental structural difference between cognitive sub-systems (language, motor action, perception, etc.) seems incompatible with a widely accepted premise, namely that the acquisition of new systems - language, for instance - is based on a pre-structuring at the level of already existing structures - for instance perception, motor action and social interaction. In the next chapter I shall focus on the development of syntax in the light of the previous problem.

12 Cognitive aspects of the development of syntax

12.1 LANGUAGE AND ACTION

Since Chomsky's reflections on the nature of grammar developmental psychologists have acquired a new view on the learning of language. They have discovered that language is based on a solid, underlying, formal structure of rules. Without these rules language is simply not possible. Although each linguistic utterance forms an expression of these rules, the rules themselves remain implicit and covert: they will never be seen, heard or shown directly. The problem which arose together with this new view on language concerned the possibilities and ways for learning the underlying structure. Chomsky's critique of Skinner's 'Verbal Behaviour' supported the assumption that the existing behaviouristic and learning theoretical approaches could not offer an adequate explanation. In accordance with his basic rationalist view, Chomsky developed the theory of the 'language acquisition device', i.e. the theory that grammar is an innate heritage of each human being. In general, however, resistance to the behaviouristic past was not so strong that the majority of developmental psychologists could be brought to accept Chomsky's nativistic solution (see, for instance, Chomsky, 1979 for reflections and comments on these problems).

The problem of the acquisition of the complex, covert rule structure of language came closer to a solution after Fillmore's influential essay on the case-grammatical basis of language (Fillmore, 1968). Case grammar seemed to offer a link with Piaget's theory of cognitive development. For Piaget, the basis of cognition is action. A linguistic theory such as that of Fillmore's which explains a parallelism between syntax and the structure of action created excellent opportunities for a Piagetian interpretation of linguistic development. An alternative case grammar, put forward by Anderson (1971), which is much closer to perception, i.e. topology, than to action, has never been successful among developmental psychologists, probably because it did not fit the widespread 'metaphysics of action' which is clearly predominant in cognitive psychology.

In his comprehensive book on the first stages in language development, Roger Brown puts forward the assumption that:

> The first sentences express the construction of reality which is the terminal achievement of sensori-motor intelligence. What has been acquired on the plane of motor intelligence (the

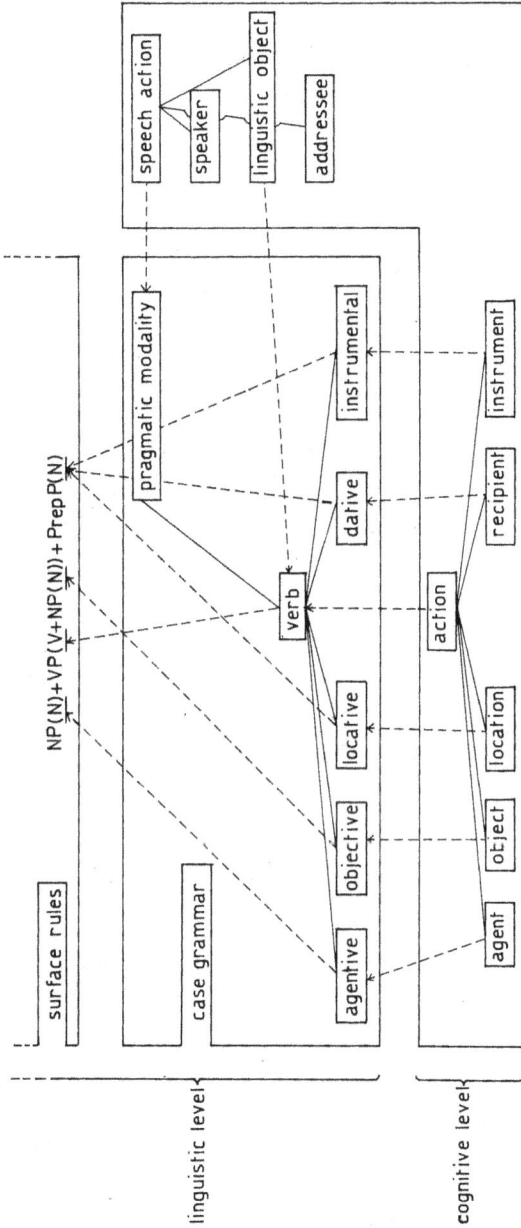

Figure 12.1 A representation of Bruner's view on the relationship between cognition and grammar (based on Bruner, 1975). At the cognitive level, knowledge of the structure of action is employed to carry out successful speech actions. Knowledge of action components underlies a basic linguistic structure, namely case grammar. Case grammar underlies the linguistic surface rules upon which the actual production and understanding of language is based. In the diagram, connections in full line indicate intra-level dependencies between concepts or case-grammatical categories. Dotted lines indicate extra-level dependencies

permanence of form and substance of immediate objects and
the structure of immediate space and time) does not need to
be formed all over again on the plane of representation.
Representation starts with just those meanings that are most
available to it, propositions about action-schemas involving
agents and objects, assertions of non-existence, recurrence,
location and so on (Brown, 1973, p. 200).

Jerome Bruner states that 'a concept of agent-action-object-
recipient at the pre-linguistic level aids the child in grasping
the linguistic meaning of appropriately ordered utterances
involving such case categories as agentive, action, object,
indirect object and so forth' (Bruner, 1975, p. 17). (For
comparable points of view, see Greenfield et al., 1972; Sinclair-
De Zwart, 1973; Cromer, 1974, 1976.) See Figure 12.1.
The previous quotations clearly refer to a conceptual transfer
theory. Concepts, acquired at a lower, i.e. sensori-motor level,
are raised to a higher level, i.e. language. In order to explain
and compare some of the cognitive models of language acquisition
we may rely on a simple geomorphological metaphor. The sensori-
motor conceptual system forms a landscape with hills and valleys.
The language used in the child's environment can be compared
with a constant rain that falls on the land. During the first year
of life, the water disappears into the soil, although it already
prepares the basis for the later hydrographical structure, i.e.
language. When the child is around eighteen months old, we see
that some of the water collects in small pools and lakes formed by
the relief of the landscape. These small pools can be compared
with the child's first word-classes whose meaning is based on
the general sensori-motor concepts. When the rain is continuous,
small pools flow together to form bigger lakes and rivers which
mask the original form of the sensori-motor landscape. The
assumption that the basic structure of the sensori-motor landscape is preserved in the structure of grammar (the hydrographical structure of the landscape) has been put forward in
papers by McNeill (1974), Sinclair-De Zwart (1973), Bruner
(1975) and others.
Adherents to the Piagetian viewpoint will explain the forces
that form the sensori-motor landscape in terms of assimilation
and accommodation. Bruner, however, believes that the environment, the child's caretakers in particular, have an important
function in shaping sensori-motor cognition. The mother's interaction and play with the child is responsible for a structuring
of the sensori-motor landscape in the direction of the main
structures of language (see Bruner, 1975; Ninio and Bruner,
1978; Ratner and Bruner, 1978).
The following is an example of mother-infant play studied by
Ratner and Bruner (1978). Mother and child play a game with a
clown that can be withdrawn inside a cloth cone and then made
to re-appear. The game appears when the child is five months
old and lasts until he is one year and two months. At this time,

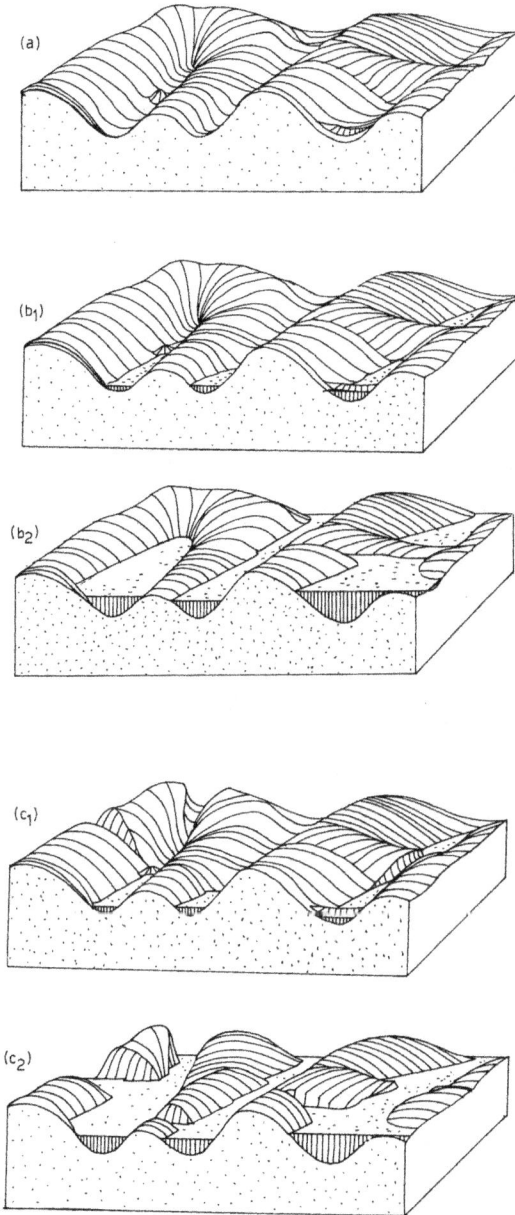

Figure 12.2 The landscape metaphor of cognitive and linguistic development. (a) represents the cognitive, pre-linguistic land-

scape. Its relief has been formed by the basic forces of cognitive development (assimilation and accommodation, for instance). (b_1) and (b_2) represent changes in the landscape caused by the appearance of language, according to the cognitivistic view. Language, represented by the water, is shaped according to the main forms of the cognitive landscape. At later stages, language may hide parts of the original cognitive relief, although the deep structure of language remains to be determined by the structure of cognition. (c_1) and (c_2) represent the emergence of language according to the interactionist view. The water – i.e. language – has exerted a marked influence upon the cognitive landscape.

the child has achieved complete insight into the structure of the game and loses his interest in it. Careful examination of video-recordings showed that the mother took great pains to give a clear and stable structure to the clown-and-cone-game, always in connection with what the child could understand at that moment. Further, the mother constantly tried to keep the child's attention and was particularly focused on the structural 'breaks' in the game, i.e. the transitions between the structural constituents. The game consisted of ten different constituents which were marked by specific vocalizations by the mother and were kept separate by short pauses. At the age of seven months, the child had discovered the structure of the game, which was illustrated by the fact that the child's smiling responses no longer appeared at any arbitrary moment – they acquired a clearly anticipating function. At the age of eleven months, the child was able to play the game himself and to accompany the constituents of the game with appropriate vocalizations. The development of the clown game illustrates a variety of aspects which, according to Bruner, are essential to the shaping of language and cognition. The mother, who knows the basic constituents of action, tries to make them as explicit as possible for the child and provides them with appropriate linguistic labels. Her efforts are directed towards enabling the child to carry out the actions independently; that is, she tries to convey her knowledge of action and its mapping upon language to the child.

In contrast with the view that cognition shapes language, Schlesinger (1971) proposed a model in which language and cognition interact. This view corresponds quite well to our language metaphor. Water always tries to find its own way down. If it is offered the space to stream freely, it will soon change the landscape drastically, it will wear out new valleys and alter the original relief. Put differently, the process of acquisition starts with the basic forms of sensori-motor cognition, after which the fixed forms of language exert their own influences upon the further shaping of cognition.

Although the landscape metaphor serves to structure a number of theories on the development of language, it may be questioned whether the cognitive transfer theory on which it is based is tenable. It is quite doubtful, for instance, whether Piaget, to which most of the previous theories refer, would agree with the idea of a transfer of concepts to higher - or at least differ- ent - levels of cognitive structure.

Piaget has advanced the idea that the infant conceptualizes the world in the form of action: the world consists of 'suckable', 'graspable', 'viewable' or 'pushable' things, according to the kind of action scheme applicable. Action is the level at which the child's world is presented. In the previous chapters I stated that, in order to act in a competent way, the child had to establish relationships between perceptual presentation and motor action. Motor schemes can be applied only when the child knows under which circumstances they are applicable. The child most know, for instance, which kind of perceptual information constitutes the conditions of adequacy for his various action schemes. The child does not think or reason 'internally': his acting is his thinking and reasoning. Knowledge is expressed by the 'logic', regularity and functionality of the child's actions.

The conceptual apparatus of the sensori-motor infant consists of the structure of the infant's presentational systems, namely perception and motor action. We have seen that the child's 'con- cepts' are extra-systemic descriptions of his abilities. For instance, if the child is able to track moving objects, to look back when the object has been changed during its way behind a screen, to look for the object at appropriate places after it has been hidden, we may say that the object of his actions is some- thing which has thing- or 'object'-properties.

In the previous chapter we have seen that the applicability of spatial relations concepts to the child's spatial acting and perceiving, does not imply that the 'syntax' of motor action or perception of space is based on structural units that correspond with these concepts, i.e. it does not imply that the syntax of action or perception has a direct isomorphic relationship with the structure of attributed concepts. If the foregoing is true, the conceptual transfer theory, which seems to underlie much of the current reasoning about cognition and language, becomes rather problematic. It remains true, for instance, that adequate spatial perception is a necessary condition for learning the structure of spatial prepositions, but it should not be inferred that the structure of the (early) spatial prepositions is a kind of linguistic 'translation' of the available perceptual or sensori- motor spatial relations concepts.

According to Piaget, sensori-motor concepts are acted out, they are not internally represented (the stage of beginning internal representations marks the end of the sensori-motor stage). Sensori-motor concepts are particular, regulated ways of acting upon the environment. By the end of the sensori- motor stage, the child has become a fully competent actor able to cope with all the practical, i.e. sensori-motor, problems with which he may be confronted. The neonate, however, possesses only very limited actional abilities. Piaget sees no reason to believe that the neonate's actions express a distinction between subject and object. The making of such a distinction, which evolves through a process of assimilation and accommodation, does not imply that the child should have a sort of inner consciousness or representation of a distinction between himself and the world. 'Distinguishing between subject and object' is an adequate, though extra-systemic characterization of the complexity and structure of the child's actions. This is not to say, however, that the subject-object distinction does not exist in the mind of the child but only in the mind of the investigator. The subject-object distinction is indeed a property of the child's mind, but we should reckon with the fact that the child's mind is his actions.

At the end of the sensori-motor period the child has become a competent actor. That is, his actions can be described as structures composed of functional units or constituents. These constituents - 'agent', 'action', 'goal', etc. - are necessary components of any 'well-formed' action. Their actual content, i.e. which action is carried out, which is its goal, etc., is taken from a stock of possible actions, goals, tools and so forth. It would be a conceptual mistake, however, if these constituents were identified with representational units which in one way or another are independent of actual acting and therefore, at least in principle, translatable into other presentational forms, language for instance.

In his book on the construction of reality in the young child, Piaget (1937) states explicitly that all the problems of trying to differentiate agent, action and object with which the child was coping during the sensori-motor stage, come back and have to be resolved when the child attains the level of (Piagetian) representation, i.e. at the onset of the pre-operational stage. Representation can take the form of symbolic play, imagery, imitation or drawing, but the most important form of it is language. The acquisition of sensori-motor abilities has brought the child to a level of sensori-motor equilibrium which forms the platform from which he will learn to cope with the problem of interiorization of action and representation. The mechanisms that helped the child to discover the basic sensori-motor 'concepts', i.e. that helped him to attain the fundamental sensori-motor skills and knowledge - assimilation, accommodation, the tendency towards equilibrium, etc. - will now be employed in the process of acquiring the basic pre-operational abilities.

For Piaget, representation arises directly from sensori-motor action. In one of Piaget's observations, a child 'represents' the opening and closing of a matchbox by opening and closing her mouth. The sensori-motor presentation of the matchbox consists of the action patterns involved in recognizing boxes, manipulating them and so forth. The opening and closing of the mouth can be described as a sensori-motor representation because its basic function lies in the topological resemblance between the mouth and the box. Language, however, is a very peculiar way of representing. Its basic property is that it does not apply the principle of topological resemblance. Its structure is intra-systemically linguistic and its representational function with regard to perception follows from the mapping rules between language and perception. Yet language is clearly assimilated to the structure of sensori-motor action. This assimilation means that the structure and function of early linguistic utterances can be entirely described and explained in terms of sensori-motor action properties, and, second, that the child will initially use his sensori-motor 'techniques' in order to discover the primary rules of the language game. In such a conception, there is no place for the conceptual transfer theory. The sensori-motor child does not possess a separate level of agent, action or object concepts (these will occur later, if they occur at all). Moreover, the sensori-motor child will not be able to transfer an abstract underlying scheme to an entirely new realm of pre-sentation (i.e. language).

One of the basic motives for claiming that the onset of language indicates a step into a structurally new field of cognition can be found in the concepts 'meaning' and 'reference'. Basically, language is regarded as a system of representation, a system of symbols which refer to objects, properties or states of affairs that lie outside the system. Perception and action, on the other hand, are considered neither symbolic nor referential. Consequently, the learning language requires the discovery of meaning and reference.

In this book, we have advanced a different conception of language. Language, like perception and action, is primarily a presentational system, which, thanks to the existence of mapping rules, can also fulfil representational functions. We have seen that reference is not a mental operation – or mental property – which occurs during language production or understanding. Reference should be viewed as a theoretical characterization of a relationship between properly formed linguistic presentations and 'worlds' of various types. Reference and meaning are theoretical-linguistic terms for expressing the presentational and representational functionality of language, although these concepts do not have any causal, conditional or generative relationship with the actual processes of language use. Adequate language use finds its generative explanation in the intra- and inter-systemic rules of language, e.g. the conditions of adequacy and the procedures of sentence formation which find their abstract description in syntax.

The idea that the learning of syntax is based on the child's ability to act and perceive competently is a widely accepted and valuable working hypothesis. Even if one would claim – as Chomsky or McNeill originally did – that language acquisition is based on innate grammatical knowledge, the ability to employ this knowledge in a competent way is still required. It may be questioned, however, which specific function and meaning should be assigned to the child's ability to act competently. Cognitive transfer theory starts from the relationship between grammatical constituents of sentences (noun phrase, verb phrase, subordinate noun phrase, etc.), grammatical functions (subject, verb, object, etc.) and conceptual constituents of action (agent, action, patient or object). Second, the child's ability to act competently is explained on the basis of concepts – agent, action, patient or object – that have been acquired during the sensori-motor stage. Consequently, the acquisition of syntax should not be an insurmountable problem for the child, since he is provided with a basic representational structure – the concepts of action – that prefigures the structure of syntax.

Unlike cognitive transfer theorists, I believe that the conceptual structure of action should neither be sought in our head nor in reality. The conceptual structure of action is an aspect of our practical metaphysics. It is a basic experiential fact that distinct presentational forms – perceptions, motor actions and linguistic expressions – can have the same 'logical' content. A particular event can be perceived, carried out or described in a sentence. What then, are the immanent constituents of the event that explain why it can take distinct forms? The foregoing question, which is a typical metaphysical question, asks for a linguistic description, i.e. a description of the basic and general constituents of events. Language, then, will also offer the key to answering this question. Linguistic practice employs a limited number of prototypical forms for describing events. These forms consist of two, three or four linguistic constituents: noun + verb; noun + verb + noun, noun + verb + noun + noun; or noun + verb + noun + preposition + noun. According to the 'law-of-reference', which is also basic to our practical metaphysics, the constituents of the signifier – the descriptive sentence – correspond with the constituents of the signified – the described event. Linguistic constituents are not free: they occupy specific positions in the sentence and possess specific surface properties. Positions and syntactic properties are mapped upon specific properties of the signified: the first noun phrase in the sentence, for instance, cannot be mapped upon any arbitrary aspect of the perceptually or actionally presented event. Thus, the mapping rules of language introduce particular structural distinctions in perceptual and actional presentations of events. These distinctions correspond with the concepts of agent, action, object and so on. The structure introduced by a perceptual, i.e. topological, specification of an event is entirely distinct from the linguistically introduced structure (see Chapter 6). Nevertheless, our practical metaphysics accepts an inherent structure of events which is entirely based on the syntactic structure of descriptive sentences. (In the next Chapter, we shall investigate whether or not the syntactic structure of sentences is derived from the inherent structure of events.) If actions – which are particular forms of events – can be described as agent-action-object structures, the child's ability to act competently can be 'explained' by stating that the action concepts are represented in the cognitive structure of the child. Although the previous explanation is not directly wrong, its meaning remains entirely metaphorical and limited to the scope of practical metaphysical explanations of the child's mind.

If we start from the basic competences that the child possesses at the onset of language, we must conclude that the learning of language is a practical problem. Surely, language possesses a very particular practical problem, since even its most simple products are describable in terms of a complex, formal rule system, i.e. syntax. The learning of language is a linguistic problem if – and only if – it is stated in linguistic terms. The child himself, however, looks at language 'from underneath', i.e. from the level of practical action. In the first stages of language learning, the child will employ his practical skills in order to acquire the particular mode of behaviour whose basic nature is characterized in terms of formal linguistic constituents and rules which fall completely beyond the dimensions of practical action. The child should learn how to use words in such a way that this use can be reliably and adequately described with concepts such as 'reference', syntactic structure', 'meaning' and so forth. These concepts give theoretical specifications of what will be acquired but not of how the process of acquisition proceeds.

Psycholinguists, however, are used to assigning a formal linguistic interpretation to any linguistic activity of the child. A child knows how, when and why to say 'milk', for instance. Technically spoken, the child is able to establish a referential relationship between 'milk' and milk (e.g. when he wants to have some milk). In order to employ 'milk' on the appropriate occasions, however, the child does not need to acquire a notion of 'reference' which precedes or accompanies the merely practical knowledge of how and when to use 'milk'. If a child utters a two-word sentence, for instance, the sentence is almost automatically interpreted in terms of an 'equivalent' adult sentence with an explicit syntactic structure, e.g. a subject-verb-object structure. The investigator may then wonder how and why the child acquired his covert knowledge of subject-verb-object structure which is so clearly expressed in his two-word sentence. This, however, is a completely wrong statement of the problem. The fact that a primitive two-word structure can be translated into an 'equivalent' adult sentence is an expression of the adult's linguistic abilities, not of the child's. This problem will be discussed in the next sections.

Let us now try to recapitulate the problem of the relationship between action and language. At the onset, the learning of language is a practical problem which will be solved with the practical action skills acquired in the pre-linguistic stage. Clearly, these skills have been acquired in social, 'tutorial' interaction, for instance with the mother. As the learning of the practical linguistic rules proceeds, the genuinely linguistic aspect of the rules will differentiate gradually. This will lead to a new level of action and presentation - language - which can no longer be described in terms of practical action but requires a formal syntactic, semantic and pragmatic descriptive framework.

At any stage in the developmental process, the acquisition of language is specified by four parameters. The first kind of parameter consists of the specific limitations and possibilities associated with the actual state of the child's emerging linguistic competence, i.e. the zones of proximal attention and proximal development. The second parameter consists of the properties and peculiarities of the non-linguistic systems - perception, motor action, various conceptual domains - upon which language should be mapped. The third parameter consists of the language addressed to the child, i.e. the source from which the child will get the building blocks for his own language. Language offers a number of surface differentiations that the child might try to employ with regard to possible differentiations in depth; i.e. relationships between linguistic constituents, relationships between language and domains upon which it can be mapped. The fourth parameter consists of the 'tutorial' interactions with the child, i.e. the way in which language is taught by parents, peers and so forth.

12.2 PERCEPTUAL AND SYNTACTIC STRUCTURES

During the nineteenth century, linguists were primarily interested in the 'vertical' approach to language. Language was understood by means of its diachrony, i.e. its history and evolution. At the beginning of the twentieth century, de Saussure started to change the focus of linguistics. Language should no longer be understood on the basis of its diachrony. The basic property of language is its horizontal structure or 'synchrony', i.e. the structure of relationships between linguistic constituents. The study of language development forms a belated reflection on this discussion. During the first decades of the twentieth century, the acquisition of language was viewed in the perspective of natural history. Otto Jespersen (1922), for instance, engaged in the problem of the creation of language. He believed that groups of children who were for some reason or another left to themselves in uninhabited regions were responsible for the creation of new languages. His hypothesis was supported by an observation made by Hale that the variety of languages in a territory is proportional to the richness of the natural food resources, the appropriateness of the climate, and so forth. Jespersen, and linguists such as Stumpf (1901) and Morse-Nice (1925), were also interested in a peculiar phenomenon called 'Eigenartige Sprache', i.e. idiosyncratic languages created by children without reference to

the language of the environment (see also Blumenthal, 1970).
The occurrence of self-made languages was found an interesting phenomenon because it was assumed that a self-made
language would reflect some of the properties that language
would have had during the first stages of its phylogenesis.
At the beginning of the 1960s, transformational linguistics
provided a new and powerful instrument for the study of
language development. It was accepted that every linguistic
utterance, however simple, is the expression of an underlying
grammar. Chomsky was one of the most extreme advocates of
this view. The syntactic simplicity of early linguistic forms is
only on the surface. In reality every linguistic utterance is
embedded in the underlying system of basic syntax. At present,
developmental psycholinguists have turned to Piaget. They
believe that the early linguistic utterances are embedded in the
structure of basic cognitive concepts. As far as the synchronic
structure of early language is concerned, however, the cognitive
viewpoint is not basically distinct from Chomsky's point of view,
since the relevant underlying conceptual structures are more or
less direct prefigurations of the fundamental syntactic constituents.

In the previous section, I have tried to show that the learning
of language, particularly during the first stages, is a practical
problem solved with the aid of practical action skills. At the end
of the section, I distinguished four parameters which determine
the course of language learning. One of these parameters consisted of the properties of the language addressed to the child.
Another parameter consisted of the teaching efforts of the child's
parents or mates. It is clear that these two parameters provide
the model that the child has to copy. In this sense, the child's
linguistic utterances are always embedded in the structure of
mature language. Although the way in which the child's
language is embedded in the structure of mature language is
perfectly clear to mature speakers, the child himself may have
great difficulties in distinguishing and profiting from this
embedding. The meaning of examples or remarks is clear to
someone who knows what the examples exemplify and what the
remarks refer to, but they might be quite unclear to someone
who has to learn an exemplified rule, for instance. There are
two other parameters, the child's actual linguistic competence
and the properties of the systems upon which language is
mapped, that might explain whether, why and how the examples,
indications or remarks function with regard to the child. In
the present section, I shall give a purely formal and artificial
treatment of the relation between emerging language and the
non-linguistic systems upon which it is mapped. The treatment
is artificial in that it abstracts from the remaining parameters
of language learning. My aim is to show that this particular
approach to the ontogenetic diachrony of language might
elucidate the nature of the successive synchronic relations that
characterize the development of language.

The non-linguistic system we shall deal with is the system of sensori-motor presentation. Thus far, we have worked either with the perceptual or with the motor system of presentation. It is possible to construe a compound system consisting of the perceptual and the motor system and their inter-systemic mapping rules. This 'super system' - which is a purely formal construction - is characterized by topological principles of presentation taken from perception, in connection with structures of attention and events that are associated with motor action. The sensori-motor system of presentation will be able to generate spatiotemporal sets, spatiotemporal relations between sets, sets with focal and peripheral domains, and so forth. The internal structure of a sensori-motor presented world must be viewed as a very complex heterarchy of similarities and differences. The possible contents of the world - describable as 'objects', 'actions', 'events', etc. - are characterized by an infinite number of properties, which implies that they can be classified according to an infinite number of classificatory principles.

The problem I shall discuss concerns the relationship between the sensori-motor system and the set of possible languages that can be mapped upon it. I shall not deal with meaning or reference but confine myself to the procedural basis of these linguistic functions, namely the inter-systemic mapping rules. The problem will be discussed in the form of a particular kind of game. The goal of this game is to discover rules according to which 'signal systems' - i.e. languages - can be constructed which are characterized by consistent mapping relations with the sensori-motor system. In fact, the game is never finished since the complexity of the signal systems can be infinitely increased. One particular constraint should be taken into account, therefore, namely the limited competences of the future user of the signal system. Let us assume that the signals have an acoustic form produced by a single channel. A channel itself is a human being, who is characterized by a limited memory, a limited language production time and so forth. In our mapping game, the properties of language performance will limit and probably direct the principles of language competence (the rules of the system).

The first and most obvious move that can be made is to map one signal onto an arbitrary sensori-motor presentation, i.e. an arbitrary topological set (subset, relation between sets, collection of sets, etc.). This first move will result in a structurally very simple set of signals (let us call them 'words'). Each word is mapped upon one specific topological set belonging to the sensori-motor presentation system. The number and 'meaning' of the words is not intrinsically limited. The set of words, i.e. the language, has a very simple intra-systemic structure. Its communicative units, i.e. the sentences, consist of one word:

$$S = A; \ B; \ C; \ D; \dots$$

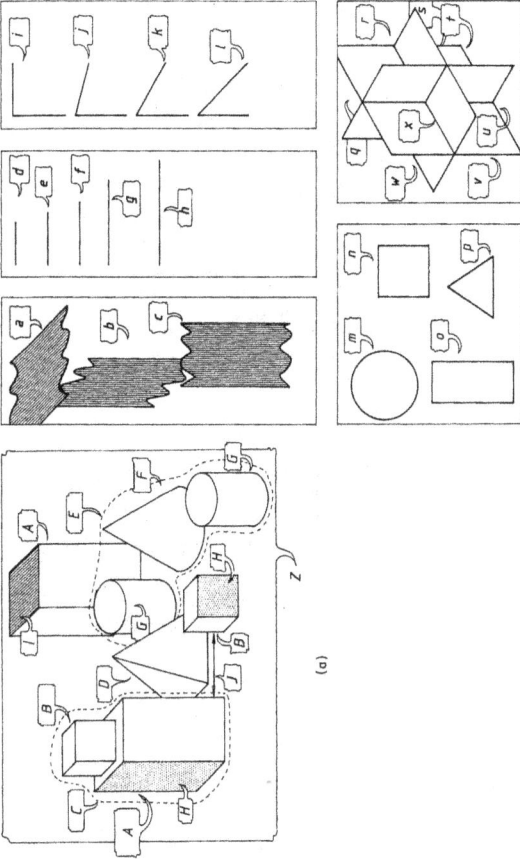

Figure 12.3 The structure of mapping relations associated with a nominative and an additive syntax. (a) represents a world inhabited by geometrical objects. The set of depicted mappings between words (letters) and topological objects is far from exhaustive. Some words are mapped onto collections of objects (Z,E and C); others are mapped onto single objects (A,D,F,G,); onto parts of objects (H,I); onto spatial relations between objects (J); and finally onto objects in different positions (B,K). The relationship between, for instance, G,F and G on the one hand and E on the other hand is analytical. (b) represents a possible atomistic mapping of words onto atomistic constituents of the geometrical object world (planes, lengths, angles, forms and spatial positions). It is unclear, however, how atomistic the atomistic constituents should be

We shall call the rule system of the language a 'nominative syntax'.

The starting principle of the language is that the topological extension of the sets upon which words are mapped is completely free. Words can be mapped upon extensive spatiotemporal sets (we would call them 'objects'), upon any particular part of such a set, upon a spatiotemporal path, upon a collection of sets, upon past or future sets, and so forth. The basic disadvantage of this simple language is that it will soon contain an immense number of words which will exceed the memory capacities of the language user. Moreover, the mapping relations between words and topological sets show a considerable amount of overlap (see Figure 12.3). This implies that any spatiotemporal set can be mapped upon a variety of one-word sentences. Such a collection of sentences may be distinguished from a collection of sentences mapped upon unrelated topological sets. The distinction between these collections of sentences can be mapped upon the rules of language itself. For that purpose, we introduce an entirely new syntactic principle, namely a morphological index that indicates whether or not words are mapped upon related topological sets. The morphological index might consist of variable intervals between words, intonation patterns or suffixes that are attached to each word:

$$S = (A.B.C.D) \text{ intonation pattern}$$
$$S = (Aa).(Ba).(Ca).(Da)$$
etc.

The introduction of this new syntactic principle marks the second move in our mapping game. The language is now characterized by an 'additive syntax' which is able to generate 'many-words' sentences.

An additive syntax does not alter the disadvantages of a nominative syntax, namely the immense vocabulary and the overlap between topological extensions (i.e. between the 'meaning' of the words). Let us illustrate this problem by means of a 'Michottean' world, inhabited by differently coloured and textured blocks which are either simple or composite and which display all kinds of actions (singular actions, place changes, simple and complex interactions, etc.). Every topological set that can be isolated in a perceptual or actional way can be mapped upon a different word. There is a word for 'a green block pushing a red block', 'a black composite block pushing a green block', 'a green block on a pushing path', 'the top of a red block', etc., etc. If we build up an immense lexicon we are able to map a sentence – i.e. one word – upon any possible state of affairs. (It is taken for granted that the topological sets upon which our words are mapped are characterized by some sort of abstraction; otherwise, we would need a different word for each new appearance of a set.) Our additive syntax allows us to map a 'many-word sentence' upon a specific state of affairs, e.g. a green block pushing a red block (see Figure 12.3 for the structure of mapping relations). It is clear that our sentence will have an analytic structure (word A implies words B, C, D..., B implies C, D..., etc.). Analytic sentences are mostly redundant and uninformative. This disadvantage stimulates us to make a third move in the game, namely the mapping of the structure of attention upon the sentence. Identical topological sets can be subject to different attentional structures, i.e. they can be perceived according to different attentional programmes (see Chapter 7). In principle, the temporal structure of an attentional process could be mapped directly upon the temporal structure of words in the additive sentence, provided that we have a word that corresponds with each new focus. That is, the succession of foci is mapped upon word order in the sentence. Word order is an example of morphological indexation. Instead of word order, we might have chosen another form of morphological indexation, order affixes, for instance. If word order is applied, the position of a word in a sentence becomes a part of the 'meaning' of this word, i.e. it determines the attentional aspect upon which it is mapped. It is important to note, however, that a direct mapping of an attention programme upon the sentence will result in a very complex structure, simply because the attentional process consists of a multitude of changing foci, proximal and peripheral zones. In order to overcome this difficulty, the sentence should be mapped upon a 'logical' function of the attention process. We might try to reduce the process of focal shifts to a relation between the most stable focus and its proximal zone (the most stable focus will be the one that occurs most frequently during an attentional programme, for instance).

The principle of free topological extension implies that the majority of our sentences will contain analytic relationships (see Figure 12.3). Our sentences are informative in that they are able to express different attention structures. In order to reduce the immense number of words in our lexicon, we should decrease the number of analytic word-families. This will be the fourth move in our mapping game. We decide to map words upon mutually exclusive topological sets (see Figure 12.3). This will result in synthetic instead of analytic sentences. Total mutual exclusiveness, however, will lead to a sort of 'atomistic' language which has some considerable disadvantages. First, it is unclear upon which level of topological specificity our words should be mapped. That is, what are the mutually exclusive 'features' that can be considered the building blocks of topological sets? Second, the lexicon will be reduced at the cost of considerably increasing sentence length. Any topological set to which we want to refer is represented in terms of a great number of elementary feature-words. Third, composite topological sets not only differ in the elementary sets they contain, but also in the relationships between the elementary sets. Unless any possible position of an elementary set were to be mapped upon a different word – which would lead again to an immense lexicon – a sentence would not only contain feature words but also a number of lexical indications about the relationships between the words. These lexical indications have a purely linguistic origin. They do not refer to relationships between 'things' but to relationships between words. Assume that we have a sentence containing the words 'a behind-situation', 'an A-situation' and 'a B-situation'. The sentence is ambiguous unless we specify the positions of A and B in the behind-situation. The relationships between words can be indicated by means of morphological indexation, word order for instance.

If there are many elementary feature-words in a sentence, the relations between words in the sentence might become very complex, which implies that word order alone will not be appropriate. This difficulty can be solved by decreasing the number of elementary feature words, i.e. words mapped upon mutually exclusive sets, and by re-introducing a number of words that will have an analytic relation with a number of elementary feature words. This is the fifth move in our mapping game. The result will be a language that profits from the advantages of both the analytic and synthetic additive syntax.

Before continuing the mapping game, I want to draw attention to a fundamental characteristic of the syntactic principles that have been constructed. The mapping game should have made clear that the principles of syntax, given that they are developed in connection with the presentational principles of the sensori-motor system, may not be identified with a 'copy' of these principles. Syntax is an independent system of rules, designed to make the mapping of linear, successive word structures upon sensori-motor presentations possible. Syntax itself might provide a new model or 'metaphysics' of the world. The imaginary user of a synthetic additive language will probably employ an atomistic metaphysics. To him, 'features' will be real things, whereas 'objects' will be viewed as constructions.

The next move we shall make in the mapping game is of considerable importance. If we take an arbitrary topological set, we will see that it can be altered by means of a variety of 'moduli'. The set can be either the focus or the periphery of attention; it can be repeated spatially and/or temporally; it can take different spatial or temporal (quantitative) extensions; it can be characterized by various modalities, for instance time of occurrence with regard to the actual presentation of the sentence; it can differ with regard to the environment in which it occurs, and so forth. In a nominative syntax, we would be obliged to introduce a new word for each modulus of a topological set. In an additive syntax, we might map a particular word upon the moduli themselves (e.g. a size word, a time-of-occurrence word, etc.). Sentences might contain 'ordinary' set words in addition to modulus words. Instead of modulus words, we might employ morphological modulus indexations. Sentences would have the following basic structure:

$$S = \{[(A^m)(..)]^m[...]^m\}m$$

(Morphological indexes referring to moduli are attached at the word, constituent and sentence level.) In order to transform a basic into a surface structure, the morphological indexes must be attached to the words in a correct way. The next move in the mapping game consists of finding an appropriate method of morpheme attachment. The most obvious possibility is that any modulus morpheme can be attached to any word. It is probable, however, that this will result in very complex morpho-syntactic rules at the word level. Nevertheless, it is possible to construct a syntactic language upon the principle of non-selective morphological indexation. Nitinat, a language discussed in Whorf's article on grammatical categories (Whorf, 1937; in Carroll, 1956), is an example of such a language.

The problem of complexity at the word level could be solved by introducing a new principle, namely selective morphological indexation. This will be our eighth move in the mapping game. Selective morphological indexation implies that the sentence is assigned a structure of index-specific positions. For instance, position 1 is associated with morpheme m_1, position 2 with m_2, and so forth (these positions do not necessarily correspond with word order). Selective morphological indexation has considerable implications for the structure of the sentence. Whereas an additive sentence can have an unlimited length and complexity, the new type of sentence is based on an a priori structure of index-specific positions. This structure can be optional: $'A.m_1'$, $'B.m_2'$, $'A.m_1-B.m_2'$, and so forth, are all acceptable sentences. The principle of selective indexation appears most efficient, however, if the structure is not optional but obligatory. That is, a sentence has an obligatory $'A.m_1-B.m_2-C.m_3'$ structure (for instance). It may be questioned however, whether and how a sentence with an obligatory deep structure can be transformed into a surface structure with variable length and number of words. If the structure is freely extended – for instance $'A.m_1-K.m_1-X.m_1-B.m_2\ L.m_2-Y.m_2-C.m_3-M.m_3-Z.m_3$ ...' – the resulting sentence would be incompatible with the principle of selective indexation.

The problem of sentence extension can be solved by introducing the recursivity principle. Let $'A.m_1-B.m_2-C.m_3'$ be an obligatory sentence structure. From the principle of free topological extension, it follows that an arbitrary topological set can be mapped upon a word as well as a sentence or any other combination of words. Consequently, A, B and C can be replaced by a sentence which is mapped upon the $A-,B$ and C sets:

$$A.m_1-B.m_2-C.m_3 = (K.m_1-L.m_2-M.m_3).m_1-(R.m_1-S.m_2-T.m_3)$$
$$.m_2-(X.m_1-Y.m_2-Z.m_3).m_3$$

The foregoing rule is only a rudimentary and probably not very efficient form of syntactic recursivity. Nevertheless, it illustrates some of the problems that will have to be solved (e.g. how to transform a $(L.m_2).m_1$ deep structure into a surface structure).

Thus far, selective morphological indexation has had no consequences for the lexicon. In principle, any word may occur at any obligatory position in the sentence. Our ninth move will consist of the application of the selective indexation principle to the lexicon. The lexicon will be divided into various types of words. Each type will correspond to one morphological position in the sentence. If the sentence has an underlying A-B-C structure, the lexicon will be divided into A, B and C words. A lexical division might facilitate the production of sentences in that the selection of words is quantitatively simplified.

It may be questioned whether the division of the lexicon is either arbitrary or based on inherent properties of the topological sets associated with the words that belong to the various word-classes. For instance, is there a property which is common to all topological sets associated with A words, and which is absent in the B and C sets? Is there any intrinsic classification of topological sets into A, B and C types? The answer to this question depends on the content which is represented by the A, B and C morphemes. For this purpose, I shall discuss this question in the light of familiar languages, such as English or Dutch, which are characterized by lexical and syntactic morphological indexation.

In English or Dutch, sentences may have the following structure:

Noun phrase (determiner + noun) + verb phrase ((auxiliary + verb) + noun phrase (determiner + noun)) + prepositional phrase (preposition + noun phrase (determiner + noun))

'Noun', 'verb', 'preposition', 'adverb', 'adjective' are lexical types that correspond with specific morphological slots in the sentence. The verb, for instance, takes morphemes of tense, aspect and modality, whereas the noun takes the number morpheme. Adverb and adjective are characterized by a 'dependency' morpheme, i.e. their position in the sentence can depend on the presence of nouns or verbs (the foregoing should not be considered an exhaustive characterization of the various syntactic categories).

In contrast to this purely formal view of the nature of grammatical categories, the cognitive-semantic view starts from a notional view, i.e. nouns are considered names for objects, persons and animals, verbs are names for actions, and so forth. More precisely, objects, persons, actions, etc., are primary categories of (subject-mediated) reality, while grammatical categories such as 'noun' or 'verb' are secondary, i.e. 'inferred'. Clearly, the mere identification of formal with notional categories is untenable: 'speed' or 'truth', for instance, are not names for objects or 'things'. Nevertheless, all things and persons are named by means of nouns. Although it is unclear whether the majority of nouns refers to objects and things (persons, etc.) it may be stated that things and persons constitute the prototypical content of nouns.

Although I do not deny that things, persons, actions and so forth represent extra-linguistic categories, I do wonder, however, whether this classification is based on the logic of sensori-motor presentation. In the previous chapters, I have tried to show that the distinction between objects, actions, properties, etc., is not a descriptively adequate intra-systemic characterization of the structure of perceptual and motor presentation. The syntax of perceptual presentation, for instance, is utterly dissimilar from the system of notional categories. This is not to say, however, that concepts such as 'object' or 'action' would not provide an adequate extra-systemic characterization of perception and motor action.

If our mapping game has resulted in a correct analysis of the formal nature of grammatical categories, why is it, then, that formal categories do correspond with - prototypical - notional categories? During the discussion of the mapping game, we have seen that topological sets can be modulated by a number of moduli, e.g. time of occurrence, number, size, repetition, etc. These moduli could be mapped upon morphological indexes. The morphological indexes would be divided among index-specific positions in the sentence. These positions correspond with a classification of words in the lexicon ('noun', 'verb', etc.). In order to answer the question as to whether nouns and verbs are based on 'natural categories' such as objects and actions, I shall discuss the effect of tense indexation on the meaning of the indexed words.

Let 'tense' ('t') be a modulus that marks the distinction between various times of occurrence of a topological set with regard to the time of utterance of a word or sentence (namely 'past', 'present' and 'future'). Let V be a word belonging to a lexical category 'v' that is characterized by tense-indexation. That is, V occurs at the tense-indexed position in a sentence. N is a word belonging to the category 'n', which does not take tense-indexation. If V is t-indexed, V is mapped upon a topological set T_V with a determinate t-modulation. If t is 'past tense', for instance, T_V should have occurred in the past, reckoning from the moment that V was uttered. T_N - which is mapped upon N - is not t-modulated, simply because N does not take t-indexation. That is, N can be mapped upon any possible t-modulus of T_N, past, present and future. Put differently, if N is not t-indexed, the t-modulus of T_N (i.e the topological set mapped upon N) consists of the 'sum' of the various tense-values, i.e. past + present + future. T_N is not t-modulated, or better, T_N is not t-determinate.

Let $S(t)$ be a tense-indexed sentence-symbol mapped upon a

set T_S. If A and B are lexical items that can be mapped upon T_S, $S(t)$ can be rewritten as follows:

$$S(t) => (A + B)(t)$$

If the syntax associated with S starts from selective morphological indexation and lexical categorization, the rewriting proceeds in the following way:

$$(A + B)(t) => N(A) + V(B)^t$$

Since A as well as B can be mapped upon T_S and $V(B)$ is tense-indexed, whereas $N(A)$ isn't, $T_{V(B)}$ must be a subset of $T_{N(A)}$:

$$T_{V(B)} \cdot {}^{(t_k)} \text{ is a subset of: } T_{V(A)} \cdot {}^{(t_k, t_1, t_m)}$$

In summary, if Vs are tense-indexed and Ns are not, V is always mapped upon a subset of T_N, i.e. the set upon which N is mapped. The 'mapping' of V is a subset of the 'mapping' of N, provided that N and V occur in the same sentence.

By applying noun- and verb-categorization to the lexicon, we create two different ontological types, namely referents that are not t-determinate, i.e. 'permanent' and referents that are t-determinate, i.e. referents with a transitory nature which are always parts or aspects of 'permanent' referents. Consequently, 'permanent' sets, i.e. sets that are relatively permanent and durable in comparison with human action, are considered prototypical examples of nouns, whereas transitory sets are considered prototypical examples of verbs.

A relation between two sets is an example of a set which is less extensive than any of the sets that are related (see Figure 12.3). Words that are mapped upon relation-sets should be particularly suited for tense-indexation, i.e. V-categorization. Transitive verbs are tense-indexed relation-words, while prepositions are relation-words that are not tense-indexed. Let us first discuss the transitive verbs.

Sentences with transitive verbs have a hierarchic syntactic structure: the verb takes the number index of the subject and not of the object, the object can be deleted whereas the subject cannot, etc. Formal syntactic hierarchy is mapped upon a particular property of tense-modulated topological sets. In Figure 12.4 two spatiotemporal place-sets are related because they are characterized by connected paths (the figure is a diagram of a simple Michottean pushing situation). We see that the distributional formula (see Chapters 6 on form perception) of path m equals the formula of path k but not that of path n. Michotte described this particular property of related spatio-temporal paths with the term 'ampliation': m is a derivative of k. We might also say that the set a - to which k belongs - is the origin of m. The hierarchical structure of the sentence

that refers to the relation between a and b expresses the fact
that the origin of m lies in a and not in b. In general, the
hierarchic structure of the sentence is based on the conditional
and non-symmetric relationship between topological sets.

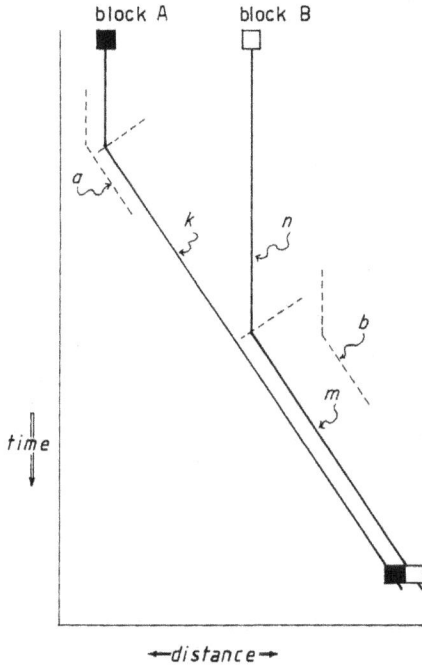

Figure 12.4 A spatiotemporal place diagram of a Michottean
pushing situation. Subset m of b has the same place formula
as subset k of a

The next modulus function that will be discussed is the
inclusion modulus. Any set can be modulated by treating it as a
subset of a more extensive set (i.e. there is no a priori upper
bound to sets). Set inclusion can be mapped upon a morphological
index that we shall call the 'dependency'- or d-index. The d-index
expresses that the extension of a set, T_i, is specified in terms
of another set, T_j. If a set is not d-determinate, its extension
is specified without explicit reference to another set.

If D is a word related to the d-indexed position, its occurrence
in the sentence depends on the presence of a non-d-indexed
word (e.g. '$N + D$' is an acceptable sentence, whereas 'D' or
'$D + D$' isn't).

The influence of d-indexation on the topological extension of
words is of particular importance. If a set is mapped upon a d-
indexed word, the set itself must be made d-modulated, i.e. its

extension has to be defined in terms of another set (e.g. D is mapped upon T_D if and only if T_D is defined in terms of another topological set, T_I). Adjectives and adverbs are typical examples of d-indexed words. They refer to properties, not because 'property' is an intrinsic aspect of reality but because 'properties' are sets that are defined in terms of other sets.

Tense is a particular form of d-indexation. If a word occurs at a t-indexed place in the sentence, it should be mapped upon a subset of the set that corresponds with the non-t-indexed word. Consequently, the presence of a verb in the sentence depends on the presence of a noun. The subject-predicate distinction refers to the fact that the basic structure of a sentence consists of a combination of a d-indexed and a non-d-indexed position.

Prepositions constitute a remarkable syntactic category. First, they belong clearly to the class of d-indexed words, and, second, they express relations between non-d-indexed words (nouns). If we examine the topological sets upon which prepositions are mapped, we may wonder why prepositions are not replaced by verbs or nouns.

Spatial prepositions, for instance, can be easily t-indexed, i.e. transformed into a verb. On the other hand, they might be transformed into names of spatial states of affairs, e.g. vertical or horizontal proximity. If A and B are participants of a 'vertical proximity' situation ('A is above B', for instance), the following imaginary sentence might be constructed:

N(vertical proximity situation) + A.(d-indexed) + B.(d-indexed).

Such a sentence form, which is compatible with the mapping rules that have been worked out thus far, introduces a number of particular difficulties. First, we would need a corresponding D-word for any A or B in the lexicon (i.e. for any possible participant of a spatial relation situation). Second, we would need a morphological index for expressing the hierarchical difference between A and B (the hierarchical distinction would not occur if the spatial axis along which A and B are situated would be characterized by a relative direction – see section 5.2 on orientation perception). The previous difficulties can be solved by putting the spatial-situation word in the d-indexed position:

$N(A)$ + $N(B)$ + D (vertical proximity situation).(d-indexed)

The hierarchical relationship between A and B can be expressed by means of simple morphological indexes, word order, for instance.

Although the present discussion of the relationship between the formal properties of language and the system of sensorimotor presentation is sketchy and highly incomplete, it might

help us to understand some aspects of the historical and individual genesis of language. In the light of our general problem,
I shall confine myself to the ontogenesis of language. I start
from the idea that the mapping game simulates an important
aspect of the learning of language and of syntax in particular.
It should be taken into account, however, that actual language
learning takes place against the background of an already
elaborated language, the child's mother tongue, which is taught
by mature speakers. Nevertheless, a great deal of the underlying rules of language cannot be perceived or taught directly,
because knowledge of the rules is conditional to perceiving the
surface forms of language as an expression of these rules.
Therefore, the child has to reconstruct the syntactic categories
and rules of his mother tongue himself (i.e. the child has to
acquire the ability to produce linguistic forms that are describable in terms of these categories and rules). It is not incon-
ceivable that the emerging syntax will pass through the stages
described in the mapping game.

With regard to the construction of the lexicon, a basic difference exists between the (imaginary) player of the mapping game
and the language learning child. Whereas the player created
his words himself, the child will borrow his words, expressions
and morphological forms from the mother tongue. Consequently,
the child's utterances will be interpretable in terms of mature
syntactic categories, even if the child's proper 'syntax' (i.e.
his position in the mapping game) has an entirely different
structure. The child's one- and two-word sentences probably
reflect a simple additive syntax without modulus elements and
their corresponding morphological indexation. Nevertheless, the
sentences will be composed of words that belong to definite
categories in the mature language (noun, verb, adjective, etc.).
This will give rise to the assumption that the child has either
an innate or a cognitively-based knowledge of the basic properties of syntax and the corresponding semantic functions (subject-
predicate; subject, verb, object; etc.). In the next section,
we shall explore the interpretation and explanation of one- and
two-word sentences in the light of the previous discussion of
the relationship between language and the system of sensori-
motor presentation.

12.3 THE INTERPRETATION OF ONE- AND TWO-WORD UTTERANCES

Most people will set the beginning of 'real' language development
at the age of eighteen months. The main distinction with the
preceding (babbling) stage is that the adult will be able to
recognize the sounds uttered by the child as 'words'. The
sounds as well as the way in which they are used begin to
resemble the words and expressions of mature language. From
now on, the child is accepted as an active member of the linguis-

tic community (he no longer speaks a 'different' language).

Roman Jakobson (1968) described a particular way in which the linguistic 'adoption' of the child may take place. Jakobson was a proponent of linguistic feature theory, according to which the sounds of a language consist of a specific set of distinctive acoustic features. The more sounds differ in featural composition, the easier they can be discriminated, and the smaller will be the chance to confuse them in an attempt to produce or imitate such a sound. The easiest word one can produce is a word consisting of phonemes characterized by maximal distance with respect to featural composition. Words like 'ba', 'pa' or 'ta' fulfil this requirement, which implies that they will constitute the universal set of firstly uttered words. The former had already been discussed by Wilhelm Preyer, in a book written in 1881. Preyer called these words the 'Ursilben'.

Jakobson observed that a great number of languages, without regard to their degree of linguistic familiarity, have borrowed the nursery-room words for the caretakers from the universal stock of 'Ursilben'. Consequently, parents or caretakers believe that 'mother' ('grandmother' or whoever takes care of the child) is the first word uttered by the child. The explanation given to this fact is that the bond between mother and child is so close that the child will first of all learn the word that refers to his mother. According to Jakobson, however, the folk-psychological explanation is a myth, although a psychologically and developmentally very functional one.

In general, the words learned by the child in the first stage (which is not really the first stage) are neither the shortest or the easiest ones, nor do they necessarily refer to concrete, material objects. The child will learn words that are associated with objects, functions, situations, needs and properties that are important in his daily life (Brown, 1958). A frequently used class of words refers to relations, like 'more' (Bloom, 1973).

Although the one-word sentence seems to be the most simple structure possible, students of linguistic and cognitive development have advanced a variety of theories on the underlying or deep structure of the one-word sentence. A classical theory (Stevenson, 1893 in Dore, 1975; McCarthy, 1954) views the one-word sentence as a holophrase, that is to say, a complex content expressed by one word. Stevenson (in Dore, 1975) has stated that the infant's one-word sentences are equivalent to whole sentences. If the child says 'milk' he is not simply referring to the white liquid known as milk. In fact, he expresses a complex content such as 'I want you to give me some of that milk now'. Jespersen (1922) does not agree with this viewpoint. If somebody is clapping his hands, for instance, the clapping expresses the same content as does the sentence 'I find the preceding performance of . . . splendid'. Nevertheless, the clapping will not be recognized as a holophrase.

In fact, it is absolutely unclear which kind of content is expressed or represented in the holophrase and which kind of representational or expressive function would be required to describe the relationship between the holophrase and its referent in an adequate way. Does the holophrase represent a linguistic, a conceptual or a perceptual (sensori-motor) structure, or an objective state of affairs in the real world? Must the content expressed in the holophrase be present 'in the head' of the speaker?

Transformational developmental linguists have argued that the holophrase is a 'one-word transformation' of a complex, basically complete grammatical deep structure (see McNeill, 1970, for instance). Conceptual hypotheses, such as the assumption that the holophrase represents situations in terms of agent-action-object structures have been put forward by several authors. According to Bloom (1973), however, one-word sentences do not express complex, articulated contents. The following observation illustrates her point. David, aged eighteen months (van Geert, 1975) is watching a photo of a man with bare feet, a child sitting on his knee, beside a palm tree in a pot. David says - I give a literal translation of the Dutch sentence - 'Foot.Lady.Tree. Wash'. By comparing the observation with others that have been made at the same time, we may infer something of the meaning expressed by these four one-word sentences, i.e. we can interpret them in terms of adult words or sentences. 'Foot' is ordinarily used to refer to a foot or feet. David uses 'Lady' to refer to women and men without beards. 'Tree' refers to trees and large plants. Finally, 'Wash' refers not only to washing situations but also to bare parts of the body, naked persons, etc. The four one-word sentences refer to recognizable and discriminable parts of the photo, i.e. they represent a number of attention shifts.

Dore's criticism of the holophrase controversy is that it represents a theoretical stalemate: there are as many arguments against as there are arguments in favour of the conflicting viewpoints (Dore, 1975). Actually, the previous theories start from a wrong level of analysis, namely the sentence. In studying the emergence of language, the most relevant level of analysis is the speech act. By uttering a one-word sentence, the child is carrying out a speech act, i.e. he wants to convey information about something, change a state of affairs, etc., by using a particular kind of instrument, namely the one-word sentence. Much of the underlying meaning of the sentence is determined by the speech-act aspect (such as the component 'I want to have' in the sentence 'Milk'). Menyuk and Bernholtz's study (1969) on intonation patterns in one-word sentences shows that the child makes a distinction between intonation patterns (e.g. declarative versus questioning patterns). The latter finding led Menyuk (1971) to represent one-word sentences as the expression of two underlying morphemes, namely a word and an intonation morpheme (see Figure 12.5 for an overview).

However much the performative aspect (as opposed to the propositional aspect and expressed by the intonation morpheme) accounts for the underlying meaning of the one-word sentence, it remains to be questioned whether the propositional aspect, expressed by the word morpheme, can be attributed a complex underlying structure. That is, is the meaning or referent of the one-word sentence a structure of constituents or is it an unstructured whole. The previous question, however, requires a determinate definition of 'meaning' or 'reference'. We have seen that in the cognitive approach meaning and reference are defined as psychological processes or phenomena, i.e. components that play a substantive role in the process of language production and understanding.

Stevenson (1893)	propositional intention ⟶ I want milk reference ⟶ utterance ⟶ 'milk'
Jespersen (1922)	situation ⟶ S motive ⟶ utterance ⟶ 'milk'
McNeill (1970)	deep structure ＼ S NP VP NP one-word- I want (owl) transformation ⟶ utterance ⟶ 'milk'
Bloom (1973)	conceptual structure ⟶ agent + action + object selective reference ⟶ utterance ⟶ 'milk'
Menyuk and Bernholtz (1969)	utterance containing two structural constituents ⟶ intonation word 'milk'
Dore (1975)	speech act containing two structural constituents ⟶ speech act intention uttered word 'milk'

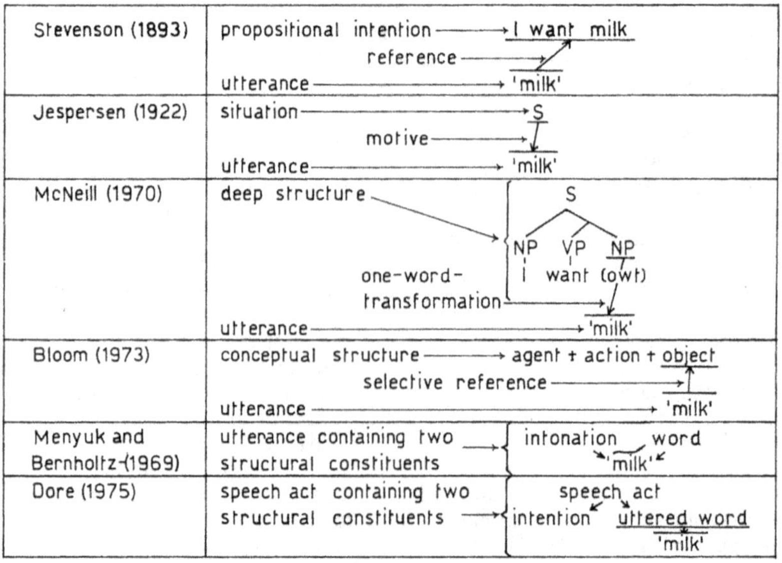

Figure 12.5 Various views on the nature of one-word sentences. Stevenson and McNeill represent two versions of the holophrase theory, according to which the one-word sentence refers to a complex meaning expressed by means of a complete sentence in mature language

In section 11.3 I stated that reference is a relationship between a presentational form (a sentence, a sign, a perceptual image, a picture, etc.) and an aspect of a world to which this presentational form is applicable. Although these worlds are the objects of presentational (and many other) actions, they are always 'outside' and never 'in' the head of the subject. The psychological processes behind the production and understanding of language consist of decisions and constructions based on rules of usage (extra-systemic rules) and form (intra-systemic rules). A specific referential relationship is a property that can be assigned to any sentence or expression that has been used and formed appropriately. If we say that the one-word sentence 'Milk', for instance, refers to the child's wish to get some milk, we actually mean that the speech act 'Milk' can be interpreted as a sign that is referentially related to the wish to drink some milk in a world containing psychological states such as intentions, wants, needs and so forth. The one-word sentence itself does not determine with which kind of worlds it maintains referential relationships (e.g. the world that is the object of perception, the world construed on the basis of our practical metaphysics, the world that is the object of scientific description and explanation, and so forth). Although many referential relationships can be discerned, not all of them are equally fruitful and descriptively adequate.

In summary, the question of whether or not a one-word sentence refers to or represents a complex underlying content depends entirely on the properties of the model that is used to describe the one-word speech-act (i.e. what are the properties of the world in which the speech act is carried out, what is the role of the child in this world, and so on). It is perfectly acceptable, for instance, to apply a framework of intentions, wants, needs and comparable concepts to human action and to conceive of the one-word sentence as the expression of a proposition, e.g. 'I want you to give me some milk'. It should never be implied, however, that the proposition has been present in the mind of the child and that it has played either a causal or a conditional role in the production of the sentence. The description of a one-word sentence as a want of milk, for instance, is adequate as long as the (propositional) form of the underlying want is not ontologized.

The production of a one-word sentence is an instance of rational and functional behaviour. Transformational linguists have defined this rationality in terms of an underlying deep structure. The deep structure is not viewed as a model of the actual process of sentence production; it describes the linguistic knowledge on which the production process is based.

The basic characteristic of the transformationalist approach is that it assigns a set of negative surface properties to the one-word sentence, i.e. it describes a number of absent constituents. The method according to which deep structures are assigned to one-word sentences consists of a comparison between the child's sentence and a 'mature' sentence that is considered semantically and functionally equivalent. If the one-word sentence 'Milk' can be reliably interpreted as the expression of a want for milk, the 'mature' equivalent sentence would be 'I want some milk'. Then, the one-word sentence is assigned an absent nominal constituent 'I' and an absent verbal constituent 'want'. However, the corresponding 'mature' sentence voices a certain linguistic praxis rather than a cognitive theory. That is to say, 'I want milk' is considered the natural and obvious linguistic expression of a situation in which somebody wants to have some milk. If the interpreter were to speak a language which had a particular word for the content expressed in 'I want some milk' - 'Iwame', for instance - he would not feel the need to view the one-word sentence as the expression of a multi-predicate structure. On the other hand, we might also state that 'Milk' is the one-word transformation of the underlying structure 'At this particular moment, the person denoted by "I" is in a state of believing that he feels the need to obtain an unspecified amount of liquid. The liquid has a white colour and is now kept in the refrigerator. The person who should give the liquid to the speaker, etc., etc.'. In summary, it is impossible to determine the number and nature of the negative surface properties attributable to the one-word sentence, simply because there are various equally valid ways of describing the content that the child wants to express by means of the sentence. For that reason, the deep-structure representation cannot provide a literal description of the knowledge expressed by the one-word sentence (the form and constituents of this knowledge should not be identified with the form and constituents of the deep structure). Never-theless, the deep structure does represent an important functional variable, namely the interpretation of the meaning of the one-word sentence by the linguistic community (the child's caretakers, for instance).

In contrast with the linguistic approach, the behaviouristic approach tries to explain the occurrence and function of one-word sentences on the basis of external, 'public' variables. The production of the sentence is based on conditional antecedents and will have consequences (verbal replies, giving milk, etc.) that will affect its future production and use. Primarily, the one-word sentence could be conceived of as a response to a preceding stimulus. In practice, however, the situational antecedents of one-word sentences are always rich collections of possible stimuli, which implies that each situational antecedent would evoke a whole series of one-word sentences. Instead of 'stimuli', we should speak about conditions of adequacy, i.e. situational, 'public' variables that determine which utterances are adequate and which are not. 'Adequacy' does not necessarily mean that the utterance has been materially successful; it is the reverse of 'nonsense'. If the child says 'Milk', he might get some milk, a verbal reply, a coercive refusal, an explanation of the reasons why he can't have some milk, and so forth. The various forms of material or verbal effects constitute the consequences of the one-word sentence that will determine its further use.

The antecedents and consequents of the child's utterances can be described as formal structures. The conditions of adequacy, for instance, consist (partly) of the inter-systemic mapping rules, i.e. the rules that determine the relations between language and sensori-motor or perceptual presentation. The verbal consequents of the one-word sentence can be formalized by means of the linguistic theory discussed previously. Deep structure descriptions of one-word sentences can be considered models of the interpretations of these sentences made by caretakers, for instance. The models can be employed to predict the nature and form of the verbal replies to one-word sentences.

The third approach we shall discuss is the cognitive one. The utterance of a one-word sentence is conceived of as the overt part of a much more complex covert cognitive process. Some cognitive theories are comparable to linguistic theory in that they assume that the one-word sentence expresses an underlying structure of concepts or semantic relationships based on the structure of action (see Ingram, 1971; Bruner, 1975; Sinclair-de Zwart, 1973; McNeill, 1974; Bowerman, 1974; Schlesinger, 1974; Greenfield and Smith, 1976). In the previous sections, I argued that the production of one-word sentences is an expression of the child's ability to act competently. This ability can be described as the understanding that actions are characterized by components such as agent, the action itself, the object, the goal, the intention, etc. However, it is wrong to assume that these components form a kind of 'sentence', for instance 'Agent A + Action B + Object C + Goal D . . .', in an underlying conceptual language of thought.

The cognitive approach has dealt also with the pragmatic aspects of early sentence production. It is now generally accepted that the sentence can no longer be the level of analysis on which theories and explanations of sentence production should be based. The production of a one-word sentence should be viewed as a speech act: speaking is a particular form of action. It is clear that the latter theory of language requires a theory of action, for instance a critical typology of acts. In general, investigators confine themselves to rather obvious typologies that reflect primarily the commonsense classification of (speech) acts - 'requests', 'orders', 'statements', etc. Like the deep-structure description, the description of the pragmatic components of one-word sentences provides a model of the interpretations made by the linguistic community, e.g. the child's caretakers. Accordingly, the pragmatic theory of one-word sentences provides the opportunity to understand and predict the possible reactions of the caretakers to the linguistic productions of the child.

The cognitive theory, however, is not limited to a conceptual explanation of the one-word sentence. I shall briefly sketch a functional-cognitive approach, which is based on a notion that has been introduced by ethnomethodology, namely 'reflexivity' (see Mehan and Wood, 1975). 'Reflexivity' implies that the uttering of the one-word sentence is an act of defining how the situation in which it is uttered ought to be seen or experienced. By saying 'Milk' with a begging intonation, the situation in which the utterance occurs is defined as a begging-for-milk situation. This is entirely different from behaviouristic or conceptual-cognitive approaches to the one-word speech-act. In both approaches, the fundamentally reflexive, 'defining' nature of the speech act is not discerned.

VIRTUAL
ANTECEDENT   ANTECEDENTS   CONDITIONS

Communicative intention	Psychological state, memory, imagery, attention	Actual situation	Knowledge of linguistic rules, lexicon, mapping rules, action forms	Material and social possibilities of action
		Perceptual presentation		
		Conditions of adequacy		

One-Word Sentence

| Direct verbal and non-verbal replies, indirect effects | Cognitive: reflexive relation between one-word sentence and antecedent; feedback function effect on conditional knowledge of language, action |

CONSEQUENTS

| | Social : maintaining social contact and interaction |

| Knowledge of speech and action content of one-word sentence | Situational: changing the situation in accordance with communicative intention |

| Knowledge of general action and language structures | FUNCTIONS |

CONDITIONS

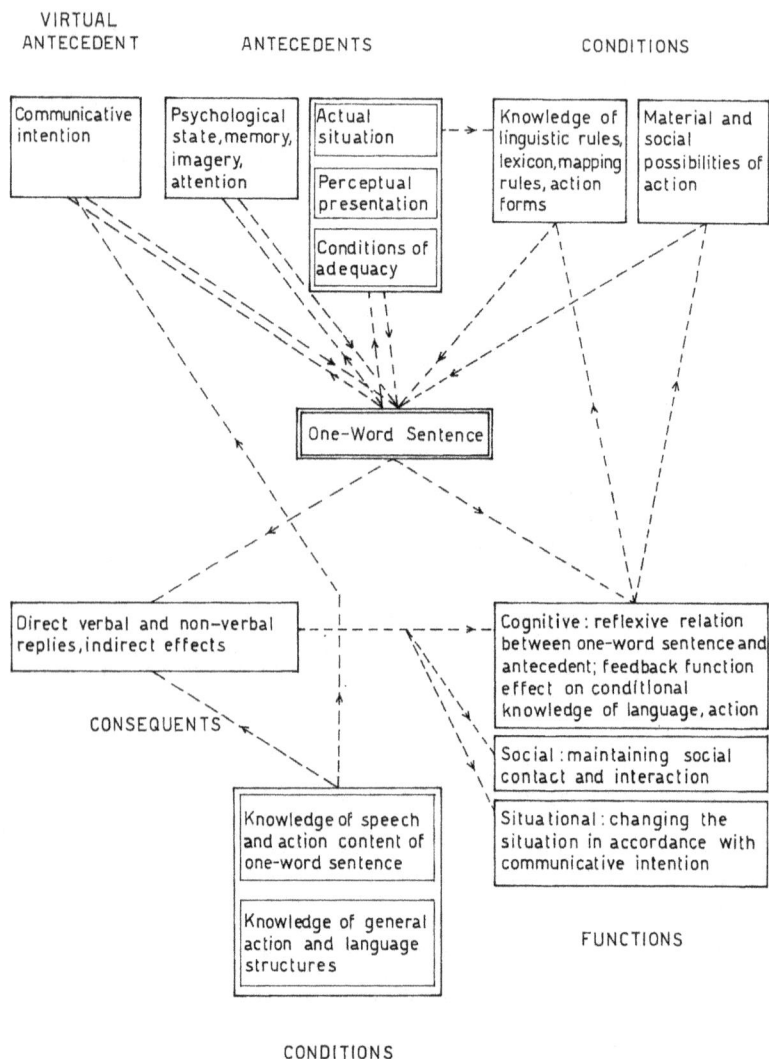

Figure 12.6 A conceptual network representing the various theoretical and empirical levels for explaining the one-word sentence. The one-word sentence is viewed as a pivotal point in a structure consisting of antecedents, conditions, consequents and functions. The virtual antecedent – the communicative intention – may be considered a 'translation' of the real antecedents, based on the conditions underlying the consequents (e.g. the linguistic intuition of the replying adult). The components of the network are characterized by a diversity of

relationships. The functions of the one-word sentence, for
instance, are based on the direct and indirect consequents; in
their turn they affect the conditions that determine the production of one-word sentences

Previously, we have seen that the perceptual or sensori-
motor presentation of a situation is linguistically ambiguous, i.e.
that it can be mapped upon a variety of (one-word) sentences.
The notion of reflexivity subscribes to this basic ambiguity and
views the actual speech act as the solution of it. In producing
a one-word sentence, S, the subject 'declares' that he wishes
to understand the present situation as an instance of S. Perceptual presentations express the perceptual, whereas linguistic
presentations express the linguistic understanding of the situation in which they are produced and whose sense they define.
The use of a one-word sentence in a specific situation implies
that the situation is mapped upon the 'history' of this particular
one-word sentence as well as on its current use.

The concept of reflexivity is closely related to the idea that
the child's actions constitute the world in which they are performed (see Chapter 3 on perceptual development). Moreover,
reflexivity is compatible with Piaget's concept of adaptation
(assimilation and accommodation). The situation or event in
which the one-word speech-act is produced is assimilated to the
history of the sentence, e.g. its adequacy conditions and
specific forms of use.

Figure 12.6 summarizes the previous discussion. The one-
word sentence – and all its successors during the further
course of development – is viewed as a pivotal point in a network
of conditions, antecedents, consequents and functions. Although
one's theoretical basis – i.e. behaviouristic, cognitive, functionalistic – will determine the relative importance of the variables
involved, any descriptive or explanative statement about the
one-word sentence should start from this conceptual network
(which does not imply that I claim that it is complete in its
current state). The conceptual network has a definitory function, i.e. it defines the nature of a one-word speech-act in a
developmental perspective. Moreover, the specific topic that one
wants to discuss – e.g. pragmatic consequences versus inter-
systemic mapping rules – determines which theoretical variables
will be assigned either a peripheral or a central role. A peripheral role in a developmental (micro- or macro-) theory, however, should not be identified with a peripheral function in a
developmental process.

I shall now discuss a number of speech acts adopted from a
biographical study of the language development of my son,
David (see Van Geert, 1975). My first topic is the word 'Dodo'
which is the ordinary Flemish baby-word for 'Good night' or
'Sleep well'. Although I have focused on the one-word sentence
thus far, the observations that I shall discuss do not consist
solely of one-word sentences. In fact, David never showed a

pure one-word stage (which is the rule rather than the exception). David's sentences consisted either of 'Dodo' or 'Dodo +
word'.

In distinguishing a two-word sentence from two successive
one-word sentences I relied on my perception of pauses and
intonation (many one-word sentences show an intonation
pattern equal to that of an entire two-word sentence). In fact,
the present observations, although they have been carried out
as objectively as possible, are 'subjective' reports in that they
consist of mappings of David's speech acts upon my adult
linguistic intuition. Finally, the classification of a speech act
as a two-word sentence, for instance, is based on the observer's knowledge of word boundaries. The interpretation is not
– or only moderately – determined by an adequate definition of
the word category. The applicability of the word category to
the earliest speech acts of children is usually not questioned:
it is sufficient that the observer is able to assimilate the
speech acts to his own linguistic knowledge. The dodo observations are enumerated in Table 12.1.

Table 12.1 Observations on the use of 'Dodo' ('Sleep well').
Age expressed in months and days

19,14   dodo zoontje, beestje, dodo poesje
         (dodo-son, pet, dodo-pussy)
         David utters the sentence when putting the kitten
         back in its sleeping box

19,17   dodo
         D closes sleeping box of the kitten (sleeping box is an
         ordinary cardboard box with a piece of cloth in it)

19,17   dodo
         Uttered when closing another cardboard box

19,17   dodo
         Uttered when closing a cupboard door

19,20   dodo poessie (2x)
         (dodo pussy)
         D's father says 'The kitten is waking up'. D. is sitting
         in a rocking chair, starts rocking the chair and says
         'Dodo poessie'

19,20   dodo papa
         (dodo daddy)
         D lies in his bed, his father comes to look at him,
         D. says 'Dodo daddy'

19,21   dodo Pinky (Pinky is the name of the hamster)

> D. is watching Pinky sleeping in a corner of its cage.
> D. says 'Dodo Pinky'

20,1   dodo papa
       D's father closes the window of the living room; it is
       not time to go to bed, neither does D sleep in the living
       room

20,1   dodo konijn
       (dodo rabbit)
       D closes the door of the rabbit cage, accompanying it
       by saying 'Dodo rabbit' (there is one rabbit in the cage)

20,1   dodo Pier (Pier is the name of the dog)
       D says 'dodo Pier' while closing the door of the cowshed
       in which the dog ordinarily sleeps. Actually, the dog is
       lying outside the shed, which is very clearly visible
       to D

Even from a superficial view it is clear that the situational antecedent of 'Dodo' is fairly complex. It is doubtful whether the use of dodo can be explained on the basis of a simple stimulus. The cognitive-conceptual explanation would presumably imply that the child has discovered a common content or concept in the various situations in which 'Dodo' is used. Unfortunately, it is not quite clear which underlying concept will be powerful enough to represent the common aspect of the many different situations. Normally, 'Dodo' is used as an introduction to sleeping - it is a kind of send-off when David's father or mother are leaving the bedroom. On the other hand, 'Dodo' is used also as a description of something or somebody who is sleeping; it accompanies the closing of windows, cupboards and cardboard boxes and finally of spaces that are specifically intended for sleeping (the rabbit-hutch, the cow-shed where the dog sleeps, etc.); 'Dodo' can be used as a send-off without explicit reference to sleeping ('Dodo rabbit'); and, finally, it is used as a reply to the announcement that the kitten is waking up. The latter observation is interesting because the verbal 'Dodo' is completed by a non-verbal reaction. David, who is sitting in a rocking chair, hears his father say that the kitten is waking up. David immediately starts rocking, saying 'Dodo pussy' twice. Rocking is the standard accompaniment to a frequently sung nursery-rhyme.

In summary, I doubt whether there is one common concept that underlies the use of 'Dodo' in the distinct situations. Instead, I assume that there is one common situation which underlies the use of 'Dodo', namely the bed-time routine. The bed-time routine consists of the following procedure. David, in pyjamas, on his father's or mother's arm, is carried to the bedroom. Then, the windows and curtains are closed. David is put in his bed, 'Dodo' is said for the first time. David's father or mother are leaving the bedroom and say 'Dodo' while closing the door, leaving David in the dark. 'Dodo' is also used as a question, announcing the bed-time routine or after David has taken a nap. Any of the situations in Table 12.1 resembles either the whole or a part of the bed-time routine. The bed-time routine constitutes the condition of adequacy for 'Dodo', that is, 'Dodo' is mapped upon the routine, including a number of significant modulus-functions, such as a sub-routine (closing the door, for instance), a significant participating object (a bed), and so forth.

Although there are no theoretical or empirical arguments against the claim that the child possesses a concept or concept-structure of the bed-time routine, I think that its effects would be misleading. The conceptual explanation implies that the sentences are the expression of a single underlying unit of meaning, i.e. that the concept (structure) constitutes the content of the sentence. The fact that the bed-time routine constitutes the condition of adequacy of 'Dodo' does not imply that it is the conceptual content of 'Dodo'.

Let us now examine what the child actually does when he says 'Dodo' or uses it in a sentence. Although the condition of adequacy of 'Dodo' consists of any situation that resembles the bed-time routine or a significant modulus-function of it, saying 'Dodo' should not be considered the overt expression of the (covert) recognition of the required resemblance. Actually, the number of situations that resemble the bed-time routine and its modulus functions is quite high (e.g. all closing situations, each time David sees the rabbit-hutch or the sleeping place of the dog, etc.). It should be questioned, then, why the recognition of resemblance and the corresponding use of 'Dodo' does not occur much more frequently. However, in this section, we have seen that a speech act is a reflexive action, i.e. an act by means of which the speaker provides a specific definition of the situation to which the sentence refers. Although many situations might be defined as 'bed-time' situations, only a few of them should be taken into consideration. David makes a bed-time situation from any appropriate uninterpreted situation if - and only if - the making is meaningful, if it serves a particular purpose, and so forth.

The second example I want to discuss concerns the meaning of early sentences. Like reference, meaning cannot be considered an internal cognitive operation. 'To mean' is a kind of action or operation that is categorically different from actions expressed by verbs such as 'to write', 'to drink', 'to walk', etc. The same holds for understanding. 'To understand something' denotes a specific disposition of a subject towards words, sentences, objects, events, etc. It cannot be equated with actions such as 'to speak internally' or 'to solve a problem'. The concept of meaning refers to a collection of functions, for instance the way in which words or expressions are used, the adequacy conditions (mapping rules), diverse relations between words and expressions and the possible worlds with regard to

which they can be used, and so on. Not meaning and understanding itself, but the various ways of using words,
expressions, symbols, etc., can be considered cognitive
operations.

The idea that meaning is a mental content that will be attached
to a sign during the process of speaking or understanding is
presumably based on the fact that signs have a material form.
The material form, however, should not be identified with the
sign itself. Something is a sign if - and only if - it is defined
as a specific position in a sign system, i.e. a system characterized by intra- and inter-systemic rules. A word is like a piece
from a - very complex - jigsaw puzzle. Understanding the word
means that there is a slot in the puzzle into which the piece will
fit. If a sign is not defined as a semiotic function but as a mere
material form, it is no longer a sign (i.e. it is only the material
carrier of the sign). 'Meaning' and 'understanding' mean that
the way in which signs are used is an exemplification of the
sign function (the place in the sign system). If a speaker or
listener does not understand a sign (a word, for instance), they
are unable to perceive it as a sign function, i.e. their use is
limited to the material form of the sign.

The question of the meaning of one- and two-word sentences
must be answered by specifying how these sentences are used.
Unfortunately, the problem of specifying how sentences are
used is very problematic, since it can be solved in so many
different ways. I shall give an example of a sentence employed
by David at the age of twenty months and thirteen days. David
and I are standing on top of a vault which is the floor of a barn.
Because of the barrel-shaped form of the vault, the central
part lies somewhat higher than the parts that touch the walls.
David says 'Put val', which can be literally translated as 'Hole
(put) fall (val)'. Since David is standing safely next to his
father on the slightly arched vault, there is absolutely no danger
that he will fall into the lower part near the wall.

The question about the meaning of this sentence can be
answered in two ways. The first way is the one which functions
in normal social interaction with the child. The meaning of 'Put
val' equals the meaning of the maximally simple equivalent adult
sentence. Since 'Put val' was not intonationally marked as a
question or as a request, it must be viewed as a descriptive
phrase. Given the situation in which 'Put val' is uttered, the
simplest adult paraphrase is not 'I fall into that hole', but 'I
might fall into that hole' or 'That is a hole and holes are things
into which one could fall'.

The previous, spontaneous interpretation of the meaning of
'Put val' allows the adult to extend the sentence (semantic as
well as syntactic extension), and to provide the child with a
model of a more developed sentence that fits the given situation.
The adult ascribes an articulated communicative intention to the
child and then provides him with a model of how the intention
can be appropriately expressed.

The second way to answer the question about meaning consists of determining the conditions of adequacy that govern the use of 'Put val'. There are various kinds of conditions of adequacy. The first kind is purely linguistic. In many cases, the antecedents of linguistic expressions are other linguistic expressions (in conversation, for instance). The rules that determine whether linguistic expressions are adequate replies to other expressions are very complex. Actually, they consist of the entire grammar of the language (semantics, syntax, pragmatics, etc.). The second kind of adequacy conditions is 'private', such as in expressions like 'I think that . . .', 'I know that . . .' (which is not to say that 'private' conditions shouldn't have to be learned on the basis of 'public' conditions). In this chapter, I shall confine myself to the non-linguistic 'public' conditions of adequacy, i.e. the observable situational features that allow any competent observer to judge the adequacy of a speech act executed by a subject.

Table 12.2 Observations made on the use of 'put' (pit, hole) (age expressed in months and days)

19,10	put
	(hole)
	D points to a flat layer of sand in the pig-sty and says 'Hole'

19,12	put
	D is sitting with his father in the sandbox. D's father gathers some sand, without digging a hole, and makes a mountain out of it. David says 'put'

19,27	put hee?
	(hole isn't it?)
	D is looking into a bucket filled with white sand, standing on the pavement

22,11	kijken put
	(look hole)
	D hears the water running through the waste-pipes under the sink. D tries to look through a hole in the wall through which he can probably see the water running. He says 'Look hole'

29,06	zal niet putten (shall not hole)
	(David makes a verb from the noun 'Put')
	D, sitting on his heels next to a deep but rather small hole in the ground, says 'Shall not hole'

Table 12.3 Observations made on the use of 'val' (fall) (age expressed in months and days)

18,10   val
        (fall)
        D's father pushes accidentally against a chair which
        is thereby slightly thrown out of balance. David says
        'Fall'. Then, the chair recovers its balance

18,13   val
        D sits on the edge of his chair, slides down smoothly
        and lands on his bottom, saying 'Fall'

20,03   kom-val
        (come fall)
        A nut drops out of the coat pocket of D's father.
        D takes the nut, saying 'Come'. Then he goes to his
        father, hands him the nut and says 'Fall'

20,10   auto val
        (car fall)
        D is playing with a toy car at the table. The car falls
        down. D looks at the floor where the toy car lies and
        says 'Car fall'

Before proceeding to the analysis of the 'Put val' (Hole fall) sentence, I should say a few more things about the notion of 'adequacy'. First, 'adequacy' does not imply 'truth' (in the case of descriptive sentences) or 'success' (in the case of requests, orders, etc.). Adequacy is the opposite of 'nonsense'. In order to assign a truth or a success function, the speech act should answer the criterion of adequacy: nonsense can be neither right nor false. Second, 'adequacy' is a very flexible criterion. The adequacy assigned to a speech act will depend largely on the level of rationality one has attributed to the speaker (this is particularly important in the case of infants who are in the first stages of language development). The third remark concerns the importance of 'public' conditions of adequacy with regard to language learning. This point has been forward by Wittgenstein and further discussed by Von Slagle (1974). Every word or expression, however much it refers to covert unobservable properties, such as someone's thoughts and feelings, must be based on publicly observable conditions of adequacy; if not, the word or expression cannot be learned.

In order to determine the meaning of 'put val' via the conditions of adequacy. I shall discuss a number of observations made on the use of 'put' (hole) and 'val' (fall) (Tables 12.2 and 12.3).

In the supposition that the daily observations have resulted in a fairly representative set of 'Put'- and 'Val'-sentences, we may infer the conditions of adequacy by comparing the various situations in which the words have been used.

'Put' (hole) is clearly not used in the way a mature speaker would do, i.e. as a nominal reference to a hole in the ground, in the wall, etc. For David, every situation that either resembles the digging-a-hole-in-the-sand-of-the-sandbox situation or that contains a constitutive aspect could serve as a condition of adequacy to 'put'. The word can be used with regard to a bucketful of sand, sand on the pavement, a heap of sand, a hole dug in the ground, and a horizontal hole in the wall. David's 'hole' does not only refer to pits but also to heaps, i.e. it refers to a situation in which a topological unevenness occurs. Further, it not only refers to the topological unevenness itself, but also to constitutive aspects of the act of creating a topological unevenness (e.g. sand). The observation made at the age of twenty-nine months and six days provides an interesting example of syntactic creativity. If 'zal' (shall) in 'Zal niet putten' (shall not hole) is used appropriately, the sentence means something like 'I shall not fall into that hole' (I shall not step into that hole, etc.). In Dutch, 'putten' means 'to draw (water)'. In its concrete meaning, the verb is rarely used. David's 'putten' is a neologism. Presumably, it is based on the application of the modulus function associated with the verb category to the 'hole' situation (i.e. the tense- or modality-modulus). David projects his relationship to the hole in the ground in a possible future. In his descriptive sentence, he employs a new verbal constituent, inferred from a familiar noun.

The analysis of the 'val' (fall) observations shows that David employs 'fall' in situations that either resemble or contain a constitutive aspect of the falling situation: the introduction to falling, the falling movement, the result of the falling, etc. The basic feature of the falling situation seems to be the fact that an object changes its position in a set of vertical levels.

In order to specify the meaning of the sentence 'Put val', we should first combine the conditions of adequacy of 'put' and 'val'. The conditions of adequacy of 'put' are fulfilled in that David and his father are standing on a vault characterized by a specific kind of topological unevenness. The conditions of adequacy of 'val' (fall) are determined by a modulus function (tense, modality): the fall situation is potential, not actual. In 'mature' Dutch (English, etc.), modulation corresponds with selective morphological indexation in the sentence (see section 12.2). If 'val' (fall) is based on a tense- (modality-) modulated condition, it would take a verb form. Since there are no indications that David's language (at the time of the 'Put val' observation) shows selective morphological indexation, we are not allowed to apply verb and noun categorization to 'val' (fall) and 'put' (hole). It will be very difficult, therefore, to 'translate' the sentence into a definite proposition. The fact that the meaning of 'Put val' is difficult to describe, provided that we start from the conditions of adequacy, is not a disadvantage of the method we have employed. On the contrary, the fact that the meaning of early sentences is relatively indeterminate if – and only if – 'mature' language is used as a standard, is one of the fundamental properties of the first stages of language acquisition.

The previous discussion makes it clear that there is no sufficient basis for syntactic categorization of the words employed in the early stages of language acquisition. Syntactic categorization consists of ascribing a syntactic category, such as noun, verb, adjective, etc. to the child's words. The assumption of reliable and meaningful categorizability is one of the major underpinnings for the models of child language production which were published during the early 1970s. In adult language, the categories of noun, verb, adjective, and so forth stand for specific surface characteristics of words in sentences. A noun, for instance, occupies different places in the sentence than the verb, the conjugations applicable to verbs do not apply to nouns, etc. Nothing of the former is the case in early sentences of children. Words do not show conjugations which would mark them as verbs or plural forms which would mark them as nouns. Thus, it may be questioned which kind of indications might be used in order to categorize the child's lexical items as nouns, verbs, adjectives, etc.

Bloom (1970) applies the following method. Any of the child's words which has a noun status in adult language is assigned the noun category. All the other words are categorized according to their combinations with the noun class. A word is classified in the verb category if it occurs previous to a noun that has a direct object-relation to the verb. If a word follows a noun, it is classified as a verb if it bears a predicative relationship to the noun. A word is put in the adjective class if it has an attributive relationship to the noun and occurs previous to the latter. The basic point in Bloom's categorization method is the assignment of the noun category, which is done in the form of a bold assimilation of the child's lexical items to those of the adult.

Schaerlaeckens, in her study of the grammar of two-word sentences (1973) states that a word can be called a noun if it refers to a person or an object, a verb if it refers to an action and a qualifier (a generic class containing proto-adjectives and adverbs) if it refers to a quality or a modality.

Schaerlaeckens's as well as Bloom's method do not lead to a representation of the child's linguistic intuition (whatever that may be). They are based on an assimilation of the child's to the adult language, which is the normal and pragmatically relevant way of interpreting the child's utterances. The question answered by the previous methods of categorization is: how far does the child's language anticipate the language of the adult. This question has a linguistic value in that it points to a structural relationship between adult and child language if both are described in terms of the same categorical constituents. The pedagogical value of categorization is that it provides a

formal specification of the intuitions of the caretakers in the
matter of meaning and structure of early sentences.

The psychologically explanative value of the previous categorization methods is doubtful, simply because the required
syntactic surface properties are still lacking in one- and two-
word sentences. Schaerlaeckens's proposal, for instance, is based
on a correspondence between semantic (cognitive) and syntactic
categories (e.g. object, person, etc., and noun, action and
verb). In the previous chapter, however, we have seen that
the semantic prototypes of syntactic categories are a posteriori,
i.e. they result from the introduction of modulus functions and
the corresponding morphological indexes. Certainly, the concepts of 'object', 'person', 'action', etc., are descriptively
applicable to the sensori-motor world of the child. Nevertheless,
they do not correspond with the intra-systemic distinctions and
structural principles that represent the 'grammar' of sensori-
motor presentation.

On the other hand, it is highly plausible that children are able
to apply diverse modulations to the spatiotemporal sets that constitute the conditions of adequacy of their words (see the 'Put
val' example). Since any form of modulation is applicable to any
arbitrary spatiotemporal set, any word from the child's lexicon
could take any possible categorical form. ('A' is a verb if it is
t-indexed, it is an adjective/adverb if it is d-indexed and not
t-indexed, etc.) Consequently, a priori categorization of words
is impossible. In order to determine the actual categorical value
of a word (e.g. in sentence S_1, A is a noun, in S_2, A is a verb,
etc.), the word either should be marked by an overt morphological index or should be mapped upon a specifically modulated
spatiotemporal set (condition of adequacy).

Since productive overt morphological indexation is lacking
during the one- and the two-word stage, we should rely on the
modulation of the conditions of adequacy upon which the
sentence rests. The problem is, however, that the majority of
sentences do not allow a reliable interpretation of the underlying
modulation. Dependency and tense modulation, for instance, is
mostly indeterminable. Certainly, if one starts from the
correspondency hypothesis and interprets the child's words in
terms of their correspondence with adult words, the difficulty
will not arise. If one relies solely on the information based on
the use of words and sentences by the child, modulation and
corresponding categorization turn out to be indeterminable. In
my own study of two-word sentences (see van Geert, 1975) I
found that the absolute majority of two-word sentences are
semantically and syntactically ambiguous; more precisely, that
each sentence could be interpreted in a variety of ways.

The problem of semantic categorization has been discussed in
section 12.1 on the relationship between language and action.
Do two-word sentences express relations between agent and
action, agent and object, object and property, and so on?
Although the evidence in favour of semantic categorizability

seems overwhelming, the previous sections have raised doubts
on the explanative adequacy of the semantic categories.
Take for instance the observations in Table 12.4.

Table 12.4 Examples of word-order reversal in two-word
sentences (age expressed in months and days)

21,27   melk poes-poes melk
        (milk puss-puss milk)
        D is squatting beside the cat's dish in which there is
        some milk left. The cat is absent. D says 'Milk puss'.
        Then the cat comes walking along and starts lapping
        the milk. Then D says 'Puss milk'

22,06   pijn poessie, poessie melk, melk poessie
        D gets the kitten put into his hands. The sharp claws
        of the kitten seem to prick his hands. David says
        'Pain pussy' and gives it back to his father, saying
        'Pussy milk'. His father answers, 'I will give some
        milk to the kitten'. He puts the kitten back and pours
        some milk in the dish. Then the kitten starts lapping
        and David sits down on his heels beside the kitten and
        says 'Milk pussy'

In observation 21,27, 'Milk pussy' is easily interpreted as the
expression of either a directive or a possessive relationship
between kitten and milk, whereas 'Pussy milk' appears to represent the expression of a relationship between agent and object.
In observation 22,06, 'Pain pussy' refers to a relationship
between an agent and an effect of an action ('pain'); 'Pussy
milk' is a request, milk is its direct and pussy its indirect
object; 'Milk pussy' expresses a relationship between an agent
(pussy) and an object (milk). In fact, I have made the previous
interpretation spontaneously when I replied to 'Pussy milk' with
'I shall give some milk to the kitten'. My reply can be conceived
of as a linguistic expansion of David's two-word sentence.
    Semantic categorization is a methodological principle that
occurs in almost any study of early grammar and semantics.
Although it is perfectly appropriate from a pedagogical point of
view, it is a debatable method if viewed as a form of psychological
explanation. We are not at all certain that our adult, language-
mediated intuition is applicable to the child's sentences.
    Let us first assume that children do express semantic relation-
ships between agent, action and object. We can never be sure,
however, about the actual semantic relation expressed in a given
sentence. In observation 21,27, in Table 12.4, for instance,
'milk' as well as 'pussy' can be interpreted as an action ('Drinking milk', 'Walking to the milk', 'Drinking like a cat', etc.), an
object or a property. The only reason to reject the alternative
interpretations is that they do not correspond with the adult

meaning and conditional extension of the words at issue.

Let us now assume that the child does not express the present semantic relations in his sentences. Is this assumption tenable? If the child does not express semantic relations, what, then, is the content of his sentences? It is quite plausible that the one- and two-word stages correspond with a relatively early stage in the mapping game, discussed in section 12.2. If so, the mapping relationships between 'Milk puss' and the perceptual presentation of the situation - the cat drinking milk - is quite diversified. 'Puss' could be mapped upon the entire situation (a situation in which a cat is involved is mapped upon 'cat', 'puss', etc.), whereas 'milk' could be mapped upon a subset of the situation (or vice versa). On the other hand, 'milk' as well as 'puss' could be mapped upon the entire situation, that is, the drinking event serves as the condition of adequacy for 'milk' as well as 'puss'. Although various mapping relationships are possible and functional, none of them corresponds with the distinction between 'agent' and 'object'.

In summary, the attribution of underlying semantic categories depends on the complexity of the surface grammar and the corresponding mapping rules. If the latter are insufficiently complex and diversified, semantic categories as agent and action do not correspond with valid intra-systemic properties of the linguistic system at issue. However, semantic categories constitute a descriptively adequate extra-systemic description of early language production, in that they provide a technical specification of the adult's intuitions concerning the meanings expressed by the child. These intuitions are important, since they exemplify the verbal and non-verbal reactions of the adult to the speech acts of the child. Put differently, cognitive theories of language development are descriptions of interpretational habits, not of underlying processes and contents of memory. These theories show how behaviour can be made explicable when it is mapped on - i.e. assimilated to - various non-behavioural systems, such as logic, commonsense metaphysics and adult language.

13 Mind, model and reality

13.1 Mind and reality: a distinction on a Moebius plane

In the previous chapter we have seen that the understanding of
the child's first sentences and the dynamics of their development requires a preliminary reflection on the nature of our
psychological understanding in general, and in particular on
the various ways to get hold of the child's developing mind.
The concept of mind, however, is very complex. According to
the socially accepted view, the mind is a covert, internal world
that contains a specific model of the public, external word and
that offers an internal working space to the subject. In the
present book, I have employed a different concept of mind.
The mind and the public world are not two different worlds: in
fact, they coincide; that is, they belong to the same epistemological category. This category is the interpreted, 'subjective'
world, the world made by the various activities, attitudes,
concepts, etc., of the social and cultural group.

Naturally, I do not intend to say that there is no world outside human subjectivity. What matters, however, is the question:
In which kind of world are we living? My answer is that we live
in a (socially) constructed world. Second, the acceptance that
our living space is a social construct does not imply that it is
arbitrary. Certainly, there is some sort of arbitrariness in the
kind of questions we ask ourselves and the goals we want to
attain. The answers we find, and the successes in attaining our
goals, however, are not arbitrary. Objective and empirical
knowledge is constituted by means of questions and goals that
are 'externally' determinable; i.e. they are determinable on the
grounds of definite forms of action (experiments, teaching,
constructive activities, etc.) that are repeatable and teachable.

The basic difference between the mind and the public world
is that, although they must be considered forms of the world
interpreted, they differ in locus. The public world is the world
interpreted with the community, culture or society as its ground
of reference, whereas the mind is the way in which a specific
individual shares the public world. The baby, for instance,
shares the public world in a very particular way. His action
forms are very limited, his presentation of the world occurs by
means of the perceptual system and a rudimentary, reflex-
based system of motor action. His relations to the public world
consists of the protecting and supporting activities of older
people. The baby is ascribed a rudimentary understanding of the

way in which adults conceive of the world. That is, the baby is assumed to take part in the world shared by all other people. Development can be viewed as the further growth into the public world, starting from the rudimentary participation at the beginning of life.

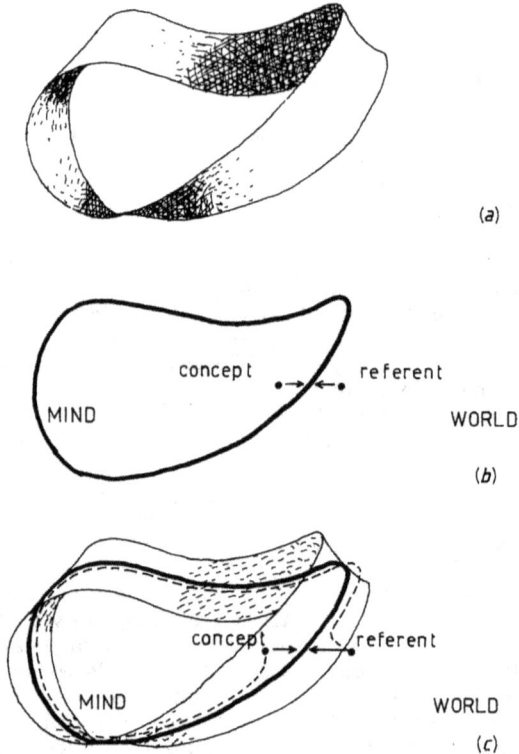

Figure 13.1 A geometrical analogue of the dualistic and the monistic model of the mind-world distinction. In (b), the mind is represented by the inner, whereas the world is represented by the outer, domain of a closed curve. It is impossible to relate an internal element (a concept, image, etc.) with an external element (a referent, an object, etc.) without crossing the boundary between mind and world. In (c), the curve is drawn onto a Moebius-plane (see (a)). If one follows the dotted line, it is possible to connect internal and external elements without ever crossing the curved line (although this seems illogical from a two-dimensional point of view)

In the classical dualistic theories - mind versus world - a mental event or property (a perceptual image, a concept) and its referent in the world (the perceived object, a class of objects, a property, etc.) are viewed as two opposite points; one lies inside, whereas the other lies outside a closed curve that represents the mental domain. In order to connect both points, one has to cross the boundary between the inner and the outer domain, i.e. the inner and the outer domain are qualitatively different (see Figure 13.1).

In the monistic theory, which I prefer, the curve that marks the boundary between the inner and outer world is only seemingly closed. The closed curve of Figure 13.1 should be viewed as a flat projection of a curve on a Moebius plane. Consequently, the curve does not separate two domains: with an open curve, there is only one domain. (A Moebius ring can be made with a strip of paper; turn one end 180 degrees and glue the ends together; the result will be a ring with only one side.) In the Moebius model (more precisely, the Moebius metaphor), an image and its referent still occupy opposite points. The opposite, however, is only apparent: if you start at one point and follow the curve, you will end at the other point without having crossed the boundary. From a two-dimensional point of view, the transition seems illogical and inexplicable. The Moebius metaphor shows, however, that the two-dimensional view is wrong, not the transition.

Let us now apply the metaphor to the mind–reality distinction. We might state that the difference between the inner and the outer world – mind and reality – is only 'local' and not fundamental: both are the object of our experience, actions, knowledge, etc. In an extremely 'naive' ontology – for instance the epistemology of the neonate, provided that we believe Piaget on this point – the distinction between subject and object, i.e. inner and outer world, is not yet made. In a less naive ontology, the subject-object distinction goes together with a form of naive realism. The internal world is viewed as a complete and correct reflection of the properties of the outer world. Probably, some form of conceptual realism is the most adequate ontology a subject can have. Concepts – such as the object and causality concept – are related to adequate ways of acting, to clusters of skills that have to be acquired through a process of constant adaptation. Because these concepts are ways to act upon the world – to speak or theorize about the world, to plan actions, etc. – they easily become 'ontologized', i.e. viewed as the inherent properties of the outer world. Just because concepts are ways to constitute the world, it is very difficult to show that there are many others possible (see for instance the discussion on the agent-action-object concepts; it turned out to be very difficult to prove that other ways exist to describe action in an adequate way).

A nominalistic and constructivist ontology results from a reflection on conceptual realism. The subject arrives at the conclusion either that the outer world is fundamentally unknowable, or that reality consists of particulars upon which contingent conceptual categories have been imposed.

The Moebius-metaphor marks the next step in the construction of an ontology. 'Subject' and 'object' - 'mind' and 'reality' - are considered necessary categories, although the distinction between them is not fundamental. They belong to the same ontological field. Subject and object are categories of our experience, they are the components of our actions, and so on. Although the transition from the subject domain may be long and complex - see for instance the steps between the proximal and the distal stimulus in perception - there is no fundamental boundary or qualitative difference between both domains. A boundary occurs only if we want to relate the internal and the external domain in a direct, straightforward way; for instance if we want to know the referential relationship between a word and an object, a perceptual image and its distal cause, etc. In the previous chapter we discussed the relation between linguistic categories on the one hand and the world on the other hand. If we want to know the referential relationship between, for instance, the noun category and the world, we are committed to one of the dual ontologies. Either we stick to a form of conceptual realism and accept that the noun category reflects an ontological class - the class of things, objects, persons, etc. - or we accept that the noun category is a linguistic construct that shapes our view of the world. We have seen, however, that there is another way to understand the relation between the world and linguistic classes. Starting from the position of the subject, we are able to provide a topological description of his perception. Then, we try to discover how language can be mapped upon the topological presentation. This enables us to track the complex relation between perceptual and linguistic presentation. This relation is formal or conditional, not referential.

Our monism is an epistemological monism: it is not a theory of how the world is; it is a theory of how our knowledge of the world is or should be (but on the other hand, if we are able to say something true or valid about our knowledge of the world, we should also be able to say something true or valid about other aspects of reality; an epistemology is never a mere epistemology, it has always definite ontological traits). Moreover, our monism is a conceptual monism. The world, which is the collection of possible subjects and objects, is always revealed in a specific way, which is only one out of many possible ways. Nevertheless, we should never employ two different, i.e. incompatible ways of description together (e.g. a language of matter and a language of mind). This will lead to classical, unsolvable problems, such as the mind-body problem, the ontological status of linguistic categories, and so on.

Let us now look at the concept of behaviour. Traditionally, 'behaviour' is viewed as the external part of our psychological processes. Usually, behaviour is identified with the physical, whereas our thoughts, feelings, etc., are identified with the mental aspect of reality. This dualistic theory has led to a mis-

understanding of the nature of behaviour, which resulted,
among other things, in the introduction of an internal cognitive
domain which contains the meanings expressed in overt
behaviour. The covert cognitive domain is considered basically
different from the overt domain of behaviour. The dualistic
theory, which clearly lies behind this conception, is epistemo-
logically undesirable.

If behaviour is described as a mere physical event, it is not
behaviour. A bodily event is an instance of behaviour if it is
conceived as a specific part of a system of behaviours.
Basically, behaviour is not different from a sign. Just like a
material form is considered a sign if it belongs to a system of
signs, a physical event is an instance of behaviour if it belongs
to a system of behaviours. Significance is an aspect of the sign
itself; it is not a content in some underlying immaterial substrate. Significance is the structure of intra- and extra-
systemic relationships of a sign, i.e. between the sign and
other members of the sign system and between the sign and
extra-systemic fields of application. Accordingly, the significance
of behaviour is a property of behaviour itself and not of an
underlying mental format. We might conclude that a theory of
behaviour should take the form of a semiology, and that its
methods and problems are not basically different from those of
linguistics or semiotics in general.

13.2 MODELS OF BEHAVIOUR

13.2.1 *Horizontal models*
The first way of understanding behaviour consists of investigating its 'public' antecedents and consequents. The external, i.e.
public antecedents function as criteria of adequacy of the
behaviour. The consequents or effects of behaviour are
important because they will affect its further use and eventual
changes.

The explanation of behaviour on the basis of its antecedents
and consequents is the basic issue of the behaviouristic programme. Recent accounts of behaviourism no longer discard the
notion of internal, non-public behavioural phenomena, such as
inner speech, imagery, etc. They explain them by pointing out
their public, i.e. manipulatable causes (see for instance Skinner,
1974; Waller, 1977; and Mapel, 1977, for a discussion of some
conceptual issues in behaviourism). Further, the behaviouristic
approach does not need to stick to its classical stimulus-response
concepts in which the response is considered an automatic,
inevitable consequence of the presence of a stimulus. The
stimulus must be viewed as the description of the external conditions which function as criteria of adequacy for a behavioural
form (action, speech act, etc.). The behaviour itself should be
interpreted only metaphorically as an inevitable 'response' to the
stimulus. Moreover, the concepts 'stimulus' and 'response'

should not be viewed as the interpretation-free descriptions of the causes, consequents and properties of a behavioural form. Description implies an interpretation within the framework of a descriptive system.

According to the behaviouristic tradition, the ground-form of psychological phenomena consists of a relationship between public antecedents (remote and direct antecedents), the behaviour based on them, and the contingent effects and consequences of the behaviour. The behaviourist does not investigate the covert part of the process. The reason for this is not that he believes either that the internal processes are inexistent or that they cannot be uncovered. The fact that the subject is conceived as a black box is not an empirical but a conceptual question. Behaviourism is a theory that operates with structural relationships between antecedents, behaviours and consequents. Everything that cannot be expressed in one of these terms does not belong to the theory and would otherwise introduce conceptually incompatible elements. If it is possible to define empirically traceable inner speech in terms of an antecedent, a behaviour or a consequent, the inner-speech episode would become an acceptable variable of a behaviouristic description.

The second horizontal approach to behaviour is the information processing theory (the predicate 'horizontal' is assigned more or less arbitrarily; it expresses a form of family-relationship between various theories and the existence of a 'topological' distinction from others).

The basic form of behaviour consists of a set of input functions, a set of processes and operations onto the input functions and a resulting set of output functions. The success of information processing explanations depends on the Turing criterion: to what extent is a specific behavioural predicate – e.g. behaviour X – applicable to a given output of an information processing automaton. That is, does the output of a process mimic a specific form of behaviour, e.g. problem solving, anticipating future events, etc. The problem attached to the resemblance (Turing) criterion is, first, that output resemblance does not necessarily imply process resemblance and, second, that 'resemblance' is a system-specific criterion. Resemblance is always concerned with essential or constitutive features. As a result, resemblance always reflects a certain theory about the nature of the resembling objects. It is quite probable, for instance, that one of the basic aspects of problem solving consists of a correct identification of the problem type (e.g. a complex mathematical problem disguised as a simple concrete problem). It is also probable that the identification of the problem type implies that the subject will anticipate a specific solution and then will try to find evidence that should support his intuition (see for instance Van Geert, 1979). If we were to limit the problem-solving to the process that takes place after the problem type has been identified, an eventual simulation of this process might be highly misleading, not only with regard to the real internal problem-solving processes but also with regard to the nature of human problem-solving itself.

The third horizontal way of explaining behaviour is perpendicular to the previous ones, in that it can be considered a semiology of behaviour (more precisely, a semiology of a much more complex type than the previous ones). This theory, which we shall call the structural theory, deals with the underlying properties of the synchronical systems of behaviour, as contrasted with the behaviouristic approach which is primarily interested in a diachrony of behaviour, i.e. its antecedents and consequents, its long-term history, etc. Famous examples of a structural approach to cognition are provided by Chomsky and Piaget.

Structural theories are competence theories. In Piaget's theory, for instance, the ascription of a formal operational system to a subject neither implies that every cognitive process of the subject should be an expression of formal operational principles, nor that the model describes the properties of the underlying 'machine'. The differences between a competence and a process model have been explained in Chapter 3 (see Figure 13.2).

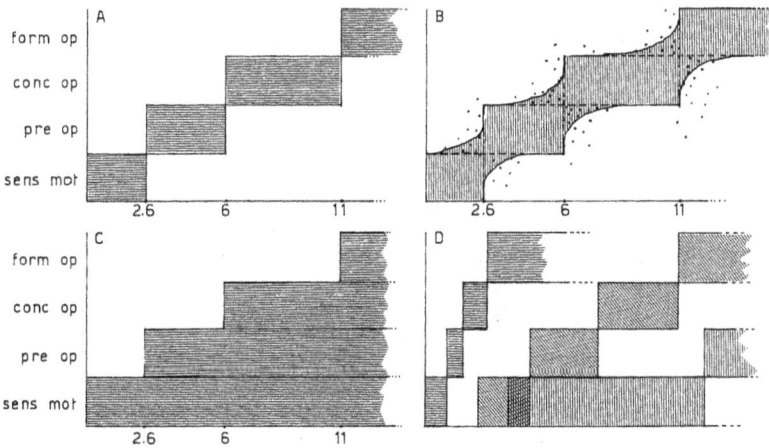

Figure 13.2 Four alternative Piagetian stage models. Model A represents an ideal, theoretical line of development with sharply distinguished developmental stages. Model B is more like the actual Piagetian models. Although the stages are clearly discernible, they are contaminated by the occurrence of 'décalages', i.e. forms of behaviour that do not correspond with the actual developmental level of the subject. Model C represents a competence version of the stage theory. Although the most advanced thought processes of the subject occur at the highest actual level of development, behaviours based on lower levels of development remain present. Model D is based on the assumption

that the achievement of higher developmental levels is limited
to specific domains or cognitive contents (i.e. some are more
complex than others). Consequently, the developmental speed
of various cognitive domains may show considerable differences

In the previous chapters we have discussed the attribution
of beliefs, i.e. the description and explanation of behaviour in
terms of underlying, covert beliefs, such as object permanence,
conservation of mass, etc. We have seen that the belief itself
should not be present 'in the head' of the believer, that is, if
'belief' is defined as a propositional content and not as a mere
functional condition to certain forms of behaviour.

The previous reasoning holds also with regard to the structural descriptions of behaviour in general (for instance the
formal operational logic that describes the cognitive competence
of children older than eleven years). The structural description
specifies the interconnections between various types of behaviour, starting from a particular descriptive viewpoint (e.g.
behaviour conceived as the possible expression of a logic). The
structural description specifies the underlying competence,
that is, it provides a definition of the behaviour in question.

The surface properties of the structural description, a logic,
for instance, have no direct consequences with regard to the
surface properties of the 'machine' that produces the behaviour.
In fact, the underlying 'machine' does not even produce
'behaviour', i.e. behaviour qua expression of an underlying
structural description; it produces the data base to which
descriptive predicates can be assigned.

The structural theory starts from a specific theory of
expression, which has been discussed, among others, in Nelson
Goodman's book on the 'Languages of Art' (1968a). The theory
states that an expressive form, expressing a certain content,
should not need to contain the expressed content in some literal,
material or mental form. Expressing a certain content means that
the content can be predicatively assigned to a certain form, that
is, the form should possess those formal properties that make
the assignment of the content adequate. This is not to say,
however, that the expressive content is merely a contingent
property of an expressive form. On the contrary, the content
is an essential property, because it defines the form qua
expressive form (that is, the form is an expressive form only in
relation to the assignment of a content, otherwise the form would
be a mere material particular). Second, the assignment of a content is descriptively adequate only if the form in question belongs
to a set of forms to which the set of content-assigning rules is
applicable. The assignment of a logico-structural form, for
instance, requires that the behavioural form in question belongs
to a set of behavioural forms to which the entire logical structure
is sufficiently applicable. When behaviour is concerned, set
membership means that the behavioural forms should have a
common origin (e.g. one particular subject; a set of subjects who

have one variable in common, such as age; etc.).

Why couldn't we state, however, that the beliefs or formal rule systems expressed by the child's behaviour are actually present in the form of unconscious representations in the mind of the subject? Since Freud, the introduction of the unconscious has been the standard solution to the problem of expression in human behaviour. Actually, the theory of the unconscious seems to conceive of mental contents as whales: the whale can be at the water surface - the conscious level - or he can dive and get out of sight, i.e. go to the unconscious level. Whether the whale is either at or under the surface of the water, it remains the same whale. That is, regardless of whether a mental content is conscious or unconscious, it remains the same content. Unfortunately, this cannot be true. For any inventive attributor, a subject's behaviour can be viewed as the expression of an infinite number of beliefs (e.g. that Napoleon is not your grand-father, that Darius the Great probably had no more than ten fingers, and so on). In order to solve this problem, we might state that the unconscious contains a number of core beliefs, comparable with the axioms of a mathematical system. There are no logical criteria, however, that could enable the system to decide which beliefs should be the core beliefs, i.e. the stock of core beliefs might change continuously.

I would like to propose another solution to the problem of the infinite number of beliefs. The propositional form is a property of the description of a belief. The belief itself can be expressed in many possible ways; in the form of verbal statements, a series of actions, dispositions to action, 'machine' properties of the believing subject, etc. The problem of conscious versus unconscious representation of beliefs resolves itself into the distance between the representation of the belief by the 'attri-butor' on the one hand on the 'believer' on the other hand. If the number of steps necessary to transform the one into the other representation is relatively small - for instance when the belief is expressed in the form of verbal statements - we shall say that the belief is expressed at the conscious level. If the number of steps is relatively extensive - which occurs frequently when psychoanalytic contents are concerned - we shall state that the belief is represented at the unconscious level.

Structural theories of development seem more closely related to specific ontologies than do behaviouristic or information processing theories. In the first part of this book we have seen that a theory of development starts from a definition of a final state from which the set of possible preceding states can be deductively inferred. Development itself, however, starts at the initial and stops at the final state. The dynamics of the process are causal and conditional and only rarely teleological. The developmental goals that the subject or his parents and teachers have in view rarely correspond with the final-state description of current developmental theories. Moreover, developmental goals function as motives to action and not as blueprints of the entire developmental process.

Why is it, then, that the causal and conditional processes – assimilation and accommodation, for instance – cease to exert their developmental influence as soon as the theoretically defined stage is attained? Where does this remarkable submission of causality to theory come from?

The essence of the developmental dynamics lies in the fact that each non-final way of structuring, understanding or 'making' the world will reveal aspects of this world with which it cannot yet deal appropriately and that will force the structuring system into a particular direction. Now, every theory of development operates with a model of the relationship between a world-making system – a subject, a logical structure, etc. – and a world based on a particular way of world-making. It is obvious that the psychologist will describe the world that constitutes the developing space of the subject on the basis of a system of world-making that he considers true, descriptively adequate, sufficiently sophisticated, etc. It is also obvious that the conception of the world that the psychologist considers the most 'true', will also be the one that constitutes the model of the final state of (cognitive) development. Consequently, as soon as the subject has achieved an understanding of the world that coincides with the psychologist's understanding, the discrepancies between the subject's world-making system and the world in which this system operates will have ceased to exist, since the world in which the subject functions is shaped according to the principles that the subject has now acquired. Put differently, the empirical discrepancy between the subject's system of world-making and the world will no longer exist as soon as the subject has attained the theoretically defined final state of development.

An interesting application of the previous point can be found in Riegel's assumption that there is a fifth stage in cognitive development, namely the stage of dialectical operations (Riegel, 1973). Such an assumption must be based on the conviction that the final understanding of the world requires a dialectical logic. In accordance with this conception of the world, the highest level of cognitive functioning that can be attained consists of such a dialectical understanding. In fact, the distinction between Riegel's and Piaget's theory lies at the level of ontology or metaphysics, not at the level of an empirical discussion, i.e. it is a reflection of the discussion between a dialectical versus a non-dialectical ontology (see Figure 13.3)

13.2.2 *Vertical Models*

The vertical explanation of behaviour is most clearly represented by 'folk' or 'naive' psychology, and in the works of Hampshire (1959), Bruner (1975, 1979) and Leont'ev (1977, 1979). One of the basic concepts of the vertical models is the concept of intention. Having intentions and executing intentional acts is what distinguishes the human or the mental from the non-mental, the material or the mechanical.

In natural language, words like 'want', 'need', 'will', 'expect', 'try' and so on, refer to the intentional modality of human events. The meaning of these terms might be quite problematical, however. This is nicely expressed in one of Wittgenstein's aphoristic statements (number 621 of the 'Philosophical Investigations'): 'When "I raise my arm", my arm goes up. And the problem arises: What is left over if I subtract the fact that my arm goes up from the fact that I raise my arm? (Are the kinesthetic sensations my willing?)'

'Intention' combines with 'motive', 'goal', 'aim', etc., in a family of concepts. The concepts refer to the fact that behaviour is more than the spatiotemporal contingency of events in causal, conditional or associative series. The basic scenario of human behaviour is action, i.e. an event characterized by specific intentions, motives, goals, etc. For this reason, Piaget's developmental theory contains a vertical dimension in that it stresses the importance of action with regard to the development of cognitive structures and operations. On the other hand, Piaget has never been as explicit as Bruner or Leont'ev, for instance, as far as the functions and properties of intentions, motives, etc., are concerned.

The second property of the vertical approach to behaviour, besides the importance assigned to action and intention, consists of the fact that the human mind is relatively open and permeable. The mind, which is the place where intentions reside and plans of action are formed, is a private domain. Its privacy decreases drastically, however, as soon as the subject starts to act. Thoughts and intentions cannot be read as long as the subject remains silent and passive, but as soon as he starts to talk, manipulate things, etc., the intentions associated with the actions become directly observable. Pretending, on the other hand, is an art that has to be learned: it is an intended breach of the rules of normal behaviour, i.e. behaviour that is always communicative in the sense of 'common' or 'public'.

The third property of the vertical approach is that the subject is conceived as a unity. This property is expressed, for instance, by the fact that the behaviour of the subject is considered relatively coherent (habits), that each subject is characterized by a definite identity, that the subject has a specific character and personality, and so on. The unity of the subject is based on the primacy of action and the roles of agent and object. If the agent, for instance, was not an existential unity, the action might be based on a variety of - possibly incompatible - intentions. That is, there would be as many actions as intentions. If the subject were to be identified with the agent of an action, the subject would have only one intention. In order to deal with the undeniable multiplicity shown by various kinds of behaviour, a theory of subject levels has to be introduced, e.g. the level of automatic versus intended actions, conscious versus unconscious intentions, etc.

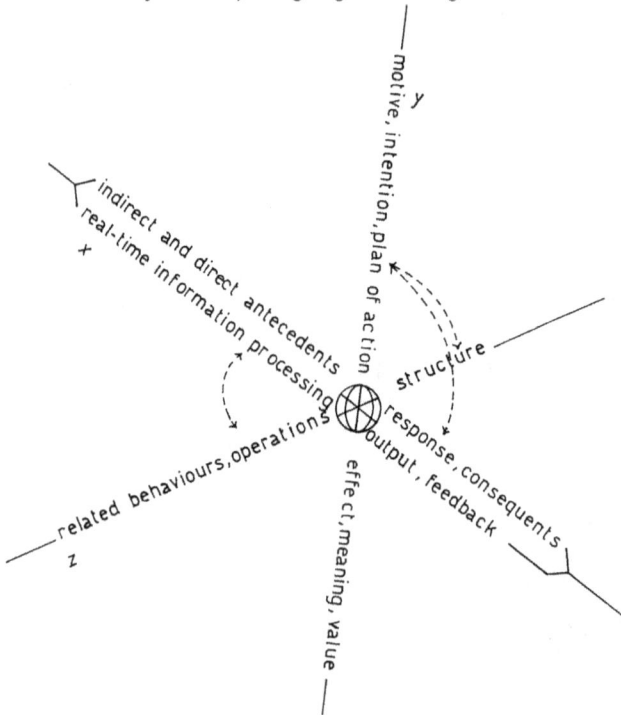

Figure 13.3 An elastic explanation space. Instances of
behaviour (circle in the middle) are considered pivotal points in
various explanatory networks. On the x axis, behaviour is
defined as a response to a set of antecedents and as the starting point to a number of consequents (behaviouristic model);
according to information-processing models, behaviour is defined
as the output of information processes. On the z axis, behaviour
is defined as a member of a set of structurally equivalent or
compatible behaviours (structural models). On the y axis,
behaviour is considered the product of motives and intentions,
giving rise to meaningful or valuable effects (intentional model).
The various dimensions can be mapped onto each other

It might be questioned whether Gibson's recent theory of
direct perception (Gibson, 1979) represents a vertical explanation
of behaviour. Gibson denies the existence of internal cognitive
processes. Objects, causality, intentions are not conceptual
categories, they are not inferred on the basis of meaningless
sense data: they are directly perceived. Gibson seems to bring
us back to some sort of 'naive' realism that fits the realism of
naive or folk psychology (see Figure 13.3).

13.2.3 An 'elastic' explanation space
The vertical and horizontal models of behaviour constitute an
explanation space which has a number of interesting properties.

First, the theories in the space are empirically equivalent. That is, decisions about the empirical value of the theories cannot be based on a Popperian criterion of empirical falsification, since each theory should be viewed as a definition of a domain or style of explanation. It is meaningless to say, for instance, that behaviourism is unable to explain the course of covert thought processes, and, thus, that it is an empirically weak theory. The concept of covert thought processes does not belong to the domain of behaviouristic discourse. The empirical variables that correspond with this concept will be dealt with by typically behaviouristic concepts that do not necessarily correspond with the cognitive concept of covert thought processes. Behaviourism might be blamed for not being able to deal with the empirical variables associated with the concept of covert thought processes; on principle, it cannot be blamed for not being able to deal with the theoretical concept itself. We have also seen that, if the falsification criterion does not apply, additional empirical criteria might be introduced, for instance the criterion of descriptive adequacy or the coherence of the empirical mapping rules. The concept of intention, for instance, does not belong to the vocabulary of behaviourism. It might be questioned whether this concept shouldn't be introduced in order to describe some typical property of human behaviour. That is, for the sake of descriptive adequacy, 'intention' could be introduced in the behaviouristic vocabulary. Its meaning, however, will be based on the principles of the behaviouristic semantics.

Second, every theory in the space should be provided with a set of complete and determinable mapping rules, however private the referents of their concepts might be. Although we can never see a covert event – an internal image, for instance – we should be able to determine a number of overt properties with which it is associated. The distinction between 'private' and 'public' phenomena has no fundamental influence on the quality of the empirical mapping rules. In folk psychology, for instance, the concept of intention has relatively simple mapping rules (see Heider, 1958 and Defares and De Haan, 1962). The mapping rules associated with the concepts of stimulus and response, on the other hand, might be very complex and difficult to apply.

The third and most important property of the explanation space is that it has an 'elastic' form. The space could shrink or stretch in various ways, various parts of the space can be mapped onto each other, and so forth (see Figure 13.3).

Let us now view which topological shifts are possible within the explanation space. First, the vertical and the horizontal theories can be mapped onto each other. This is what happens in 'naive' or 'folk' psychology, for instance. Intentions, goals, plans of action, are seen as distinct components of an internal process. The agent starts with a representation of the goal he wants to attain, then a plan of action is constructed, the action is carried out according to the plan, the effects are evaluated, etc.

Galperin's (1980) approach to the nature and development of
cognitive processes is possibly a rather behaviouristic variant
of the mapping of a vertical onto a horizontal theory. His
particular stress on the material basis of psychological phenomena,
the role played by the orientation base in action, etc., is
compatible with a fundamentally behaviouristic approach (by
'behaviouristic' I do not mean American behaviourism, but any
theory that views behaviour as a structure of public or material
antecedents and consequents). The vertical theory has also
been mapped on the information processing paradigm. In Miller,
Galanter and Pribram's approach, for instance, actions are
considered collections of qualitatively distinct steps of information processing (see for instante the TOTE unit, in Miller
et al., 1960). It may be questioned whether or not Dennett's
view on the nature and function of 'folk' psychology presents
the fundamental characteristics of a structural theory. According
to Dennett (1979), 'folk' psychology is a kind of logical or
symbolical behaviourism; that is, its concepts refer to complex
properties of collections of behaviour.

Second, horizontal theories can be mapped onto one another.
Information processing, for instance, might be viewed as a
structure of internal stimulus-response series. D. Berlyne's
book on structure and direction in thinking provides an example
of this approach (Berlyne, 1965). Structural models could be
mapped onto information processing models. That is, the description of a competence will become the description of a process.
This problem has occurred with Chomsky's generative description of sentence structure (see Chapter 6). The generative
model resembles a step-by-step process of sentence production,
while the transformations rules seem to describe the necessary
and minimal steps between various surface forms of semantically
equivalent sentences.

The relation between a logical competence description and
the structure of underlying processes (e.g. actual logical
thinking) is one of the basic problems of 'psycho-logic'. Experiments have shown, however, that a model of logical competence
does not correspond with the collection of real-time processes
that constitute the logical performance (see Osherson, 1975).

It may be questioned whether or not a thorough study of
logical performance could lead to a competence model that coincides with a description of the deepest performance - i.e.
process - levels. I personally believe that the distinction
between competence and process theories is fundamental. Whereas the former is a semiology of behaviour, the latter provides
a model of real-time processes independent of what the products
of the processes - the behaviour - actually express. It is considered a matter of principle that any competence could be
expressed by more than one process form (the semiology of
behaviour does not deal with the physics of the process).

The structural model can also be mapped on behaviouristic
models. A structural theory, then, is considered a classification

system employed by the investigator. The system has no implications with regard to the subject. Gagné's account of the
conservation phenomenon is an example of this approach (see
Gagné, 1968). The concept of conservation represents the fact
that the investigator has classified various skills - conservation
of mass, conservation of length, etc. - under one common term.
There is no implication whatsoever that these skills should have
a number of class-specific and class-uniform properties. Since
structural theories describe a competence and not its corresponding performance, it may be questioned whether or not all
structural theories are implicitly behaviouristic. A competence
description, however, is more than a mere description or classification of behaviour; it defines the nature of behaviour. The
various conservation skills, for instance, are not just a number
of separate skills put together for encyclopedic or taxonomic
purposes. For the structural theorist, conservation is a fundamental property of what he conceives of as cognition; it does
not matter whether the ability to conserve is based on a number
of relatively independent skills. The introduction of the conservation concept in a theory of human cognition is not justified
by the existence of common process properties. It is based on
theoretical reflections on the components of a cognitive system.
The justification of the concepts should be found in the criterion
of descriptive adequacy (see the first part of this book).

In summary, the explanation space functions as an algorithm
that can be employed to generate or compare theories on psychological phenomena. The space should be viewed as a 'synthetic
a priori', that is, it specifies the conceptual circumscription
of the set of possible psychological phenomena. In principle,
the various theories are empirically equivalent. In practice,
however, the empirical value of a theory depends on the functions it is asked to fulfil, the problems it is asked to solve, etc.
For this reason, it is quite difficult to predict which kind of
theory will finally survive, whether or not the explanation will
be changed in the future, or whether the distinct theories will
become mere notational variants.

13.3 THE LOCUS OF DEVELOPMENT

At first sight, the question about the locus of development
seems to have an obvious answer. Development takes place
within the subject, in the form of bodily and mental growth.

In the present book, I have tried to demonstrate the theoretical nature of psychological phenomena. If we look at a subject
from an existential point of view, we consider him a mere particular, having no determinate discursive or semantic values. If
viewed within the framework of a psychological theory, a subject
is defined as a specific value in a structure of variables. These
variables have a definitory function, they define the logical
intension, i.e. the meaning, of the subject concept. We have

seen that these variables ('perception', 'logical thinking', 'grammatical language', etc.), can be conceived of as final states, that is, they represent the final term of a theoretical developmental process. This process can be deductively inferred, starting from the properties of the final state.

If a specific structure of variables constitutes the discursive basis on which the subject concept is defined, it will also constitute the locus of development for the subject.

In Part I, we have seen that the subject – his knowledge, skills, cognitive rule systems, motives, etc. – are determined by the social and cultural framework in which he lives. That is, the definitory variables that determine the content of the subject-concept are culturally and socially specific. From this, it follows that theories that are applied to a subject should be descriptively adequate. In the previous section, we have seen that there are various ways to define the variables that are constitutive with regard to the subject concept (e.g. vertical versus horizontal definitions of behaviour).

Development can now be defined as the journey through a specific logical or conceptual space, i.e. the space constituted by the variables that define the subject concept. These variables are characterized by a number of specific developmental values that extend between the initial- and the final-state value.

The space of variables is a purely theoretical construction. In its technical form, it consists of a discursive developmental theory. The space of variables takes a concrete form in the structure of culture or society, the symbol systems, the forms of action, and so on. I shall discuss two aspects of social organization that illustrate this point.

First, society actively assigns a specific value or meaning to any of its members at any of their possible social and developmental positions. The neonate, for instance, is not just somebody who lacks almost everything that would make him a mature member of society (the neonate is mainly passive, he is not capable of locomotion, he does not speak, it is unclear how much he perceives, etc.). Nevertheless, the neonate is welcomed as a particular member of the community. He is viewed as a person who possesses an internal mental world. He is given a name, which reflects his individuality as well as his membership of a particular family, social group, culture, nation, religious community, etc. Mostly, the introduction of a new member into society is based on ritual precepts that contain the basic components of social identity. Clearly, cultures differ as to the way in which they adopt newborn members. The average number of children and the risk of infant mortality might affect the intensity of the social assimilation of the neonate, for instance.

At any stage in the development of the child, definite interpretations are made of the child's actual competences. In the chapter on the one- and two-word sentences, for instance, we

have seen that mature speakers automatically impose their model
of speech – the existence of articulated communicative intentions
in the speaker, for instance – upon the earliest forms of speech
produced by the infant. In general, any form of behaviour and
performance of the child is mapped onto models of mature competences. That is the social group pursues an active policy of
assimilation with regard to all its members.

Second, society is characterized by a specific ecological structure that passively reflects the abstract space of variables that
defines the subect concept. Society is characterized by a number
of age-specific action forms (but also by forms that are sex-
group specific, social-class specific, etc.). In present western
culture, children do not take part in the process of labour.
Children go to school, they have to learn, they acquire knowledge and skills that will be useful to collective productivity as
soon as the children have attained the appropriate age. Infants
do not have to learn, that is, they are not submitted to forms of
explicit teaching. The distinctive mode of action for the infant
is play. Playing, learning and working are three action forms
that occupy a central role in the developmental theory of Leont'ev
(1977, 1979). His theory is a characteristic vertical theory; it
deals with human action, its characteristic forms and motives.

Descriptively adequate theories of development reflect the
basic aspects of the socio-cultural ecology. Theories of cognitive development, for instance, reflect, among other things,
the properties of the educational system. That is not to say
that a developmental theory should be isomorphic with the
educational philosophy of a given society. However much the
educational system directly affects the behaviour and skills of
the subject, the developmental theory itself is not necessarily
a copy of the educational goals and methods. Piaget's theory,
for instance, distinguishes a number of developmental steps
that are not recognized in that capacity by parents or teachers,
unless they have heard about Piaget's theory. Nevertheless,
if the theory is descriptively adequate, it should bear a definite
relationship with relevant social institutions such as the schooling system or the philosophy and practice of child rearing. The
particular importance of logical and scientific thinking, for
instance, is reflected in the structure of the schooling system as
well as in Piaget's developmental stages.

The problem of human development is subordinate to the problem of human identity in general. Identity is the position occupied
in a system of defining variables; it is not a component of the
human body or brain, it is not an information processing programme or a series of regularities in behaviour. The system of
variables is comparable with a morphological-taxonomical system,
such as the system of plant classification. There are various
criteria of classification: internal morphology, external morphology, function, external resemblance to other forms,
isomorphy with existing systems of classification, etc. (see for
instance the Linnaean system or the various non-scientific and

non-western systems of plant classification). Once a classification
system has been chosen, the identity of a specific plant is determined by its position in the system which, in its turn, is based
on a number of objective properties of the plant. That is,
identity is not an arbitrary property, although the system of
defining variables might reflect a certain degree of arbitrariness.

The current epistemological status of psychology is quite
complex. On the one hand, psychology has a 'Linnaean' deep
structure, that is, it is involved in the construction of taxonomic
morphologies and confronted with the inherent plurality of human
identity. This has resulted in a number of - probably only
apparently - conflicting theories that cannot be compared on the
basis of system-specific empirical data.

On the other hand, psychology has a surface structure which
is strongly influenced by a number of disciplines that have a
different epistemological status, such as the natural sciences,
logic and linguistics. I think that, at present, psychology would
profit most from a close relationship with the epistemological
principles of linguistics and logic, more than with the natural
sciences which have influenced psychology particularly during
the first half of the century.

Developmental psychology on the one hand and theoretical
psychology on the other hand will probably occupy an important
position in the future development of psychology in general,
the former because it deals with the dynamics of change and the
determination of possible goals and final states, the latter
because it might be able to uncover the epistemological ambiguity
that characterizes psychology at present.

Bibliography

Abramovitch, R. (1977), Children's recognition of situational aspects of facial expression, 'Child Development', 48, 459-63.

Acredolo, L.P. (1978), Development of spatial orientation in infancy, 'Developmental Psychology', 14(3), 224-34.

Aiken, L.S., and Williams, T.M. (1973), A developmental study of schematic concept formation, 'Developmental Psychology', 8, 162-7.

Allen, T.W., Walker, K., Symonds, L., and Marcell, M. (1977), Intrasensory and intersensory perception of temporal sequences during infancy, 'Developmental Psychology', 13(3), 225-9.

Alston, W.P. (1967), 'Meaning', in P. Edwards, (ed.), 'The Encyclopedia of Philosophy', New York, Macmillan, London, Collier-Macmillan, 233-41.

Anderson, J.M. (1971), 'The Grammar of Case', Cambridge University Press.

Anderson, J.R. (1978), Arguments concerning representations for mental imagery, 'Psychological Review', 85, 4, 249-77.

Ariès, P. (1962), 'Centuries of Childhood. A Social History of Family Life', New York, Vintage Books.

Arnheim, R. (1970), 'Visual Thinking', London, Faber & Faber.

Aronson, E., and Rosenbloom, S. (1971), Space perception in early infancy: perception within a common auditory-visual space, 'Science', 172, 1,161-3.

Ashby, W.R. (1952), 'Design for a Brain', London, Chapman & Hall.

Ashton, R. (1976), Infant state and stimulation, 'Developmental Psychology', 12(6), 569-70.

Austin, J.L. (1962), 'How to do things with words', Oxford University Press.

Ball, W., and Tronick, E. (1971), Infants' responses to impending collision, 'Science', 171, 818-20.

Balter, L., and Fogarty, J. (1971), Intra- and intersensory matching by nursery school children, 'Perceptual and Motor Skills', 33, 467-72.

Barrett, M.D. (1978), Lexical development and overextension in child language, 'Journal of Child Language', 5, 205-79.

Bartholomeus, B. (1973), Voice identification by nursery school children, 'Canadian Journal of Psychology', 27, 464-72.

Bartley, S.H. (1969), 'Principles of Perception', New York, Harper & Row.

Bates, E., Camaioni, L., and Volterra, V. (1975), The acquisition of performatives prior to speech, 'Merrill-Palmer Quarterly', 21, 205-66.

Beck, J. (1967), Perceptual grouping produced by line-figures, 'Perception and Psychophysics', 2, 491-5.

Beck, J. (1972), Similarity grouping and peripheral discriminability under uncertainty, 'American Journal of Psychology', 85, 1-20.

Bemner, J.G. (1978), Egocentric versus allocentric spatial coding in nine month old infants: factors influencing the choice of code, 'Developmental Psychology', 14(4), 346-55.

Berger, P.L., and Luckmann, T. (1966), 'The Social Construction of Reality', Harmondsworth, Penguin Books.

Bergman, T., Haith, M.M., and Mann, L. (1971), Development of eye contact and facial scanning in infants, paper presented at the meeting of the Society for Research in Child Development; Minneapolis, April, 1971.

Berlin, B. and Kay, P. (1969), 'Basic Color Terms', Berkeley and Los Angeles, University of California Press.

Berlyne, D.E. (1960), 'Conflict, Arousal and Curiosity', New York, McGraw-Hill.

Berlyne, D.D. (1965), 'Structure and Direction in Thinking', New York, John Wiley.

Berman, P.W. (1976), Young children's use of the frame of reference in construction of the horizontal, vertical and oblique, 'Child Development', 47(1), 259-63.

Berman, P.W., and Colab, P. (1975), Children's reconstruction of the horizontal, vertical and oblique in the absence of a rectangular frame, 'Developmental Psychology', 11(1), 117.

Berman, P.W., and Cunningham, J.G. (1977), Development of ability to discriminate orientation: learning to use the frame of reference, 'Developmental Psychology', 13(5), 545-6.

Berman, P.W., Cunningham, J.G., and Harkulich, J. (1974), Construction of the horizontal, vertical and oblique by very young children: failure to find the 'oblique effect', 'Child Development', 45, 474-8.

Berry, J.W., and Dasen, P.R. (1974), 'Culture and Cognition: Readings in Cross-Cultural Psychology', London, Methuen.

Bierwisch, M. (1970), Semantics, in J. Lyons (ed.), 'New Horizons in Linguistics', Harmondsworth, Penguin, 166-84.

Black, M. (1972), How do pictures represent?, in E.H. Gombrich, J. Hochberg and M. Black, 'Art, Perception and Reality', Baltimore, Johns Hopkins University Press, 95-130.

Blakemore, C. (1974), Developmental factors in the formation of feature extracting neurons, in F.O. Schmitt and F.G. Worden (eds), 'The Neurosciences Third Study Program', Cambridge (Mass.), MIT press; 105-13.

Bloom, L. (1970), 'Language Development: Form and Function in Emerging Grammars', Cambridge (Mass.), MIT Press.

Bloom, L. (1973), 'One Word at a Time', Den Haag, Mouton.

Blumenthal, A.L. (1970), 'Language and Psychology', New York, Wiley.

Bornstein, M.H. (1975), Qualities of color vision in infancy, 'Journal of Experimental Child Psychology', 19, 401-19.

Bornstein, M.H. (1976a), Infants are trichromats, 'Journal of Experimental Child Psychology', 21, 425-45.

Bornstein, M.H. (1976b), Infants' recognition memory for hue, 'Developmental Psychology', 12, 185-91.

Bornstein, M.H. (1978), Visual behavior of the young human infant: relationships between chromatic and spatial perception and the activity of underlying brain mechanisms, 'Journal of Experimental Child Psychology', 26, 174-92.

Bornstein, M.H., Kessen, W., and Weiskopf, S. (1976), Color vision and hue categorizations in young human infants, 'Journal of Experimental Psychology', 21, 115-29.

Bower, T.G.R. (1966), The visual world of infants, 'Scientific American', 215(5), 80-92.

Bower, T.G.R. (1971), The object in the world of the infant, 'Scientific American'. 225(4), 30-8.

Bower, T.G.R. (1974), 'Development in Infancy', San Francisco, Freeman.

Bower, T.G.R. (1977a), Comment on Yonas et al. Development of sensitivity to information for impending collision, 'Perception and Psychophysics', 21(3), 281-2.

Bower, T.G.R. (1977b), 'A Primer of Infant Development', San Francisco, Freeman.

Bower, T.G.R. (1979), The origins of meaning in perceptual development, in A.D. Pick (ed.), 'Perception and its Development: A Tribute to E.J. Gibson', New York, Erlbaum, 183-97.

Bower, T.G.R., Broughton, J.M., and Moore, M.K. (1970a), The coordination of visual and tactual input in infants, 'Perception and Psychophysics', 8, 51-3.

Bower, T.G.R., Broughton, J.M., and Moore, M.K. (1970b), Infant responses to approaching objects: an indicator of response to distal variables, 'Perception and Psychophysics', 9, 193-7.

Bower, T.G.R., and Wishart, J.G. (1973), see Bower, 1974, 118-9.

Bowerman, M.F. (1974), Discussion summary: development of concepts underlying language, in R.L. Schiefelbusch and L.L. Lloyd (eds), 'Language Perspectives: Acquisition, Retardation and Intervention', London, University Park Press, 191-209.

Boyle, J.P., and Hull, R.H. (1976), Electromyographic responses in infants after auditory stimulation, 'Perceptual and Motor Skills', 42, 721-2.

Brainerd, C.J. (1978), 'Piaget's Theory of Intelligence', Englewood Cliffs (New Jersey), Prentice Hall.

Brennan, W.M., Ames, E.M. and Moore, R.W. (1966), Age differences in infants' attention to patterns of different complexities, 'Science', 151, 354-6.

Brittain, L.W. (1976), The effect of background shape on the ability of children to copy geometric forms, 'Child Development', 47, 1179-81.

Brown, R. (1958), How shall a thing be called, reprinted in Brown, R. (1970), 'Psycholinguistics', New York, Free Press.

Brown, R. (1973), 'A First Language: the Early Stages', London, George Allen & Unwin.

Bruner, J.S. (1964), The course of cognitive growth, 'American Psychologist', 19(1), 1-15.

Bruner, J.S. (1966), On cognitive growth: II, in J.S. Bruner, R.R. Olver and P.M. Greenfield, 'Studies in Cognitive Growth', New York, Wiley, 30-67.

Bruner, J.S. (1975), The ontogenesis of speech acts, 'Journal of Child Language', 2, 1-19.

Bruner, J.S. (1979), The organization of action and the nature of adult-infant transaction, paper presented at the meeting on the Organization of Action, Paris, 1979.

Bruner, J.S., Olver, R.R. and Greenfield, P.M. (1966), 'Studies in Cognitive Growth' New York, Wiley.

Bruner, J.S., and Sherwood, V. (1976), Peekaboo and the learning of rule structures, in J.S. Bruner, A. Jolly and K. Silva (eds), 'Play: its role in Evolution and Development', Harmondsworth, Penguin.

Bryant, P.E. (1974), 'Perception and Understanding in Young Children: an Experimental Approach', London, Methuen.

Bryant, P.E., Jones, P., Claxton, V., and Perkins, G.M. (1972), Recognition of shapes across modalities by infants, 'Nature', 240, 303-4.

Bryant, P.E., and Raz, I. (1975), Visual and tactual perception of shape by young children, 'Developmental Psychology', 11(4), 525-6.

Burnham, D.K., and Day, R.H. (1979), Detection of color in rotating objects by infants and its generalization over changes in velocity, 'Journal of Experimental Child Psychology', 28, 191-204.

Bushnell, I.W.R. (1979), Modification of the externality effect in young infants, 'Journal of Experimental Child Psychology', 28, 211-29.

Butterworth, G., and Castillo, M. (1976), Coordination of auditory and visual space in newborn human infants, 'Perception', 5, 155-60.

Cabe, P.A. (1976), Transfer of discrimination from solid objects to pictures by pigeons: a list of theoretical models of pictorial perception, 'Perception and Psychophysics', 29(6), 545-60.

Cairns, E., and Coll, P. (1977), The role of visual imagery in visual, tactual and cross-modal matching, 'British Journal of Psychology', 68(2), 213-4.

Campbell, R.N. (1979), Cognitive development and child language, in P. Fletcher and M. Garman (eds), 'Language Acquisition', Cambridge University Press, 419-34.

Carey, S., and Diamond, R. (1977), From piecemeal to configurational representation of faces, 'Science', 195, 312-14.

Caron, R.F., and Caron, A.J. (1969), Degree of stimulus complexity and habituation of visual fixation in infants, 'Psychonomic Science', 14, 78-9.

Caron, A.J., Caron, R.F., Caldwell, R.C., and Weiss, S.J. (1973), Infant perception of the structural properties of the face, 'Developmental Psychology', 9(3), 385-99.

Caron, A.J., Caron, R.F., and Carlson, V.R. (1978), Do infants see objects or retinal images? Shape constancy revisited, 'Infant Behavior and Development', 1, 229-43.

Caron, A.J., Caron, R.F., and Carlson, V.R. (1979a). Infant perception of
the invariant shape of objects varying in slant, 'Child Development', 50,
716-21.

Caron, R.F., Caron, A.J., Carlson, V.R., and Cobb, L.S. (1979b),
Perception of shape-at-a-slant in the young infant, 'Bulletin of the Psychonomic Society', 13, 105-7.

Caron, A.J., Caron, R.F., Minichiello, M.D., Weiss, S.J., and Friedman,
S.L. (1977), Constraints on the use of the familiarization-novelty method in
the assessment of infant discrimination, 'Child Development', 48, 747-62.

Carpenter, D.L. (1979), Development of depth perception mediated by motion
parallax in unidimensional projections of rotation in depth, 'Journal of
Experimental Child Psychology', 28, 280-99.

Carroll, J.B. (1956), 'Language, Thought and Reality: Selected Papers of
Benjamin Lee Whorf', New York, Wiley.

Carterette, E.C., and Friedman, M. (eds) (1974), 'Handbook of Perception'
(vol. I), New York, Academic Press.

Casey, M.B. (1979), Color versus form discrimination learning in 1-year-old
infants, 'Developmental Psychology', 15(3), 341-3.

Chang, H.W., and Trehub, S.E. (1977a), Auditory processing of relational
information by young infants, 'Journal of Experimental Child Psychology',
24, 324-31.

Chang, H.W., and Trehub, S.E. (1977b), Infants' perception of temporal
grouping in auditory patterns, 'Child Development', 48, 1666-70.

Chipman, S.F., and Mendelson, M.J. (1975), The development of sensitivity
to visual structure, 'Journal of Experimental Child Psychology', 20, 411-29.

Chomsky, N. (1957), 'Syntactic Structures', Den Haag, Mouton.

Chomsky, N. (1979), 'Language and Responsibility: based on conversations
with Mitsou Ronat', Hassocks, Sussex, Harvester.

Chomsky, N., and Halle, M. (1968), 'The Sound Pattern of English', New York,
Harper and Row.

Christensen, S., Dubignon, J., and Campbell, D. (1976), Variations in intra-
oral stimulation and nutritive sucking, 'Child Development', 47(2), 539-42.

Cicourel, A.V. (1973), 'Cognitive Sociology, Language and Meaning in Social
Interaction', Harmondsworth, Penguin Books.

Clark, E.V. (1972), On the child's acquisition of antonyms in two semantic
fields, 'Journal of Verbal Learning and Verbal Behaviour', 11, 750-8.

Clark, E.V. (1973a), Non-linguistic strategies and the acquisition of word
meaning, 'Cognition', 2, 161-82.

Clark, E.V. (1973b), What's in a word? On the child's acquisition of semantics
in his first language, in T.E. Moore (ed.), 'Cognitive Development and the
Acquisition of Language', New York, Academic Press, 65-110.

Clark, E.V. (1974), Some aspects of the conceptual basis for first language
acquisition, in R.L. Schiefelbusch and L.L. Lloyd (eds), 'Language Perspectives: Acquisition, Retardation and Intervention', London, University
Park Press, 105-28.

Clark, H., Carpenter, P.A. and Just, M.A. (1973), On the meeting of semantics
and perception, in W.G. Chase, 'Visual Information Processing', New York,
Academic Press, 311-18.

Cohen, L.B., DeLoache, J.S., and Pearl, R.A. (1977), An examination of
interference effects in infants' memory of faces, 'Child Development', 48,
88-97.

Cohen, L.B., DeLoache, J.S., and Rissman, M.W. (1975), The effect of visual
complexity on infant visual attention and habituation, 'Child Development',
46(3), 611-17.

Cohen, L.B. and Strauss, M.S. (1979), Concept acquisition in the human
infant, 'Child Development', 50, 419-24.

Cohen, W. (1957), Spatial and textural characteristics of the Ganzfeld, 'American Journal of Psychology', 70, 403-10.

Cole, M., and Bruner, J.S. (1971), Cultural differences and inferences about
psychological processes, 'American Psychologist', 26, 867-76.

Cole, M., Gay, J., Glick, J., and Sharp, D. (1971), 'The Cultural Context of

Learning and Thinking', London, Methuen.

Cook, M., Field, J., and Griffiths, K. (1978), The perception of solid form in early infancy, 'Child Development', 49, 866-9.

Cornell, E.H. (1974), Infant discrimination of photographs of faces following redundant presentations, 'Journal of Experimental Child Psychology', 18(1), 98-106.

Cornell, E.H. (1975), Infants' visual attention to pattern arrangements and orientation, 'Child Development', 46, 229-32.

Cornell, E.H., and Strauss, M.S. (1973), Infants' responsiveness to compounds of habituated visual stimuli, 'Developmental Psychology', 9, 73-8.

Cox, M.V. (1978), Spatial depth relationships in young children's drawings, 'Journal of Experimental Child Psychology', 26, 551-4.

Crassini, B., and Broerse, J. (1980), Auditory-visual integration in neonates: a signal detection analysis, 'Journal of Experimental Child Psychology', 29, 144-55.

Cromer, R.F. (1974), The development of language and cognition: the cognition hypothesis, in B. Foss (ed.), 'New Perspectives in Child Development', Harmondsworth, Penguin, 184-252.

Cromer, R.F. (1976), Developmental strategies for language, in V. Hamilton and M.D. Vernon (eds), 'The Development of Cognitive Processes', London-New York, Academic Press, 305-58.

Cronin, V. (1973), Cross-modal and intra-modal visual and tactual matching in young children, 'Developmental Psychology', 8, 336-40.

Crook, C.K., and Lipsitt, L.P. (1976), Neonatal nutritive sucking effects of taste stimulation upon sucking rhythm and heart rate, 'Child Development', 12, 518-22.

Cross, J.F., Cross, J., and Daly, J. (1971), Sex, race, age and beauty as factors in recognition of faces, 'Perception and Psychophysics', 10, 393-6.

Dasen, P.R. (1972), Cross-cultural Piagetian research: a summary, 'Journal of Cross-Cultural Psychology', 3, 23-39.

Davenport, R.K., and Rogers, C.M. (1970), Intermodal equivalence of stimuli in Apes, 'Science', 168, 277-80.

Davidson, D. (1963), Actions, reasons and causes, 'Journal of Philosophy', 60, 685-700.

Davidson, P.W., Cambardella, P., Stenerson, S., and Carney, G. (1974), Influence of age and tasks memory demand on matching shapes within and across vision and touch, 'Perceptual and Motor Skills', 39, 187-94.

Day, R.J., and McKenzie, B.E. (1973), Perceptual shape constancy in early infancy, 'Perception', 2, 315-20.

Day, R.H., and McKenzie, B.E. (1977), Constancies in the perceptual world of the infant, in W. Epstein (ed.), 'Stability and Constancy in Visual Perception: Mechanisms and Processes', New York, Wiley.

Defares, P.B., and De Haan, D. (1962), The perception of movement modalities in static form changes, 'Acta Psychologica', 20, 210-23.

Degelman, D., and Rosinsky, R. (1979), Motion parallax and children's distance perception, 'Developmental Psychology', 15(2), 147-52.

De Groot, A.D. (1961), 'Methodologie', Den Haag, Mouton.

DeLoache, J.S. (1976), Rate of habituation and visual memory in infants, 'Child Development', 47(1), 145-64.

Dennett, D.C. (1978), 'Brainstorms', Brighton, Sussex, Harvester Press.

Dennett, D.C. (1979), Three kinds of intentional psychology, paper presented at the Conference on Knowledge and Representation, Wassenaar, The Netherlands, March, 1979.

Deregowski, J.B. (1976), Implicit shape constancy as a factor in pictorial perception, 'British Journal of Psychology', 67, 23-30.

De Saussure, F. (1974), 'Course in General Linguistics', Glasgow, Collins.

Deutsch, D. (1975), Musical illusions, 'Scientific American', 223(4), 92-104.

Diamond, R., and Carey, S. (1977), Developmental changes in the representation of faces, 'Journal of Experimental Child Psychology', 23, 1-22.

Dirks, J., and Gibson, E. (1977), Infants' perception of similarity between live people and their photographs, 'Child Development', 48(1), 124-30.

Dore, J. (1975), Holophrases, speech acts and language universals, 'Journal of Child Language', 2, 21-40.

Douglas, M. (1970), 'Natural Symbols', New York, Random House.

Dowling, W.J. (1978), Scale and contour: two components of a theory of memory for melodies, 'Psychological Review', 85(4), 341-54.

Dworetzki, K. (1939), Le test de Rorschach et l'évolution de la perception, Étude expérimentale, 'Archives de Psychologie', 27, 233-96.

Eilers, R.E., Gavin, W., and Wilson, W.R. (1979), Linguistic experience and phonemic perception in infancy: a crosslinguistic study, 'Child Development', 50, 14-8.

Eimas, P.D. (1975), Auditory and phonetic coding of the cues for speech: discrimination of the r-l-distinction by young infants, 'Perception and Psychophysics', 18(5), 341-7.

Elkind, D., Koglar, R., and Go, E. (1964), Studies in perceptual development II: Part-whole perception, 'Child Development', 35, 81-90.

Ellis, H.D. (1975), Recognizing faces, 'British Journal of Psychology', 66(4), 409-26.

Ellis, H.D., Sheperd, J., and Bruce, A. (1973), The effects of age and sex upon adolescents' recognition of faces, 'Journal of Genetic Psychology', 123, 173-4.

Erikson, E.H. (1950), 'Childhood and Society', New York, Norton.

Fagan, J.F. III (1972), Infants' recognition memory for faces, 'Journal of Experimental Child Psychology', 14, 453-76.

Fagan, J.F. III (1976), Infants' recognition of invariant features of faces, 'Child Development', 47(3), 627-38.

Fagan, J.F. III (1977), Infant recognition memory: studies in forgetting, 'Child Development', 48(1), 67-78.

Fantz, R.L. (1961), The origin of form perception, 'Scientific American', 204, 66-72.

Fantz, R.L., and Fagan, J.F. III (1976), Visual attention to size and number of pattern details by terms and preterm infants during the first six months, 'Child Development', 47(1), 3-18.

Fantz, R.L., Fagan, J.F. III, and Miranda, S.B. (1975), Early visual selectivity, in L.B. Cohen and P. Salapatek (eds), 'Infant Perception: from Sensation to Cognition' (vol. I), New York, Academic Press, 249-347.

Fantz, R.L., and Miranda, S.B. (1975), Newborn infant attention to form of contour, 'Child Development', 46(1), 224-8.

Field, J. (1976a), Relation of young infants' reaching behavior to stimulus distance and solidity, 'Developmental Psychology', 47, 444-8.

Field, J. (1976b), The adjustment of reaching behavior to object distance in early infancy, 'Child Development', 47, 304-8.

Field, J. (1977), Coordination of vision and prehension in young infants, 'Child Development', 48(1), 97-103.

Field, J., Muir, D., Pilon, R., Sinclair, M., and Dodwell, P. (1980), Infants' orientation to lateral sounds from birth to three months, 'Child Development', 51, 295-8.

Field, T.M. (1979), Visual and cardiac responses to animate and inanimate faces by young term and preterm infants, 'Child Development', 50, 188-94.

Field, T.M., Dempsey, J.R., Hatch, J., Ting, G., and Clifton, R.K. (1979), Cardiac and behavioral responses to repeated tactile and auditory stimulation by preterm and term neonates, 'Developmental Psychology', 15(4), 406-16.

Fillmore, C.J. (1968), The case for case, in E. Bach and R.T. Harms (eds); 'Universals in Linguistic Theory', New York, Holt, Rinehart and Winston, 1-88.

Firth, Y. (1971), Why do children reverse letters?, 'British Journal of Psychology', 62, 459-68.

Flavell, J.H. (1963), The Developmental Psychology of Jean Piaget', London, Van Nostrand.

Flavell, J.H. (1977), 'Cognitive Development', Englewood Cliffs (New Jersey), Prentice Hall.

Fodor, J.A. (1975), 'The Language of Thought', New York, Thomas Y. Crowell.

Fodor, J.A., Garret, M.F., and Brill, S.C. (1975), Pi Ka Pu: the perception of speech sounds by pre-linguistic infants, 'Perception and Psychophysics', 18(2), 74-8.

Ford, M.P. (1973), Imagery and verbalization as mediators in tactual-visual information processing, 'Perceptual and Motor Skills', 36, 815-22.

Foucault, M. (1970), 'The Order of Things. An Archeology of the Human Sciences', London, Tavistock.

Franks, A., and Berg, W.K. (1975), Effects of visual complexity and sex of infant in the conjugate reinforcement paradigm, 'Developmental Psychology', 11, 338-89.

Frederickson, W.T., and Brown, J.W. (1975), Posture as a determinant of visual behaviour in newborns, 'Child Development', 46(2), 579-82.

Freeman, N., Eiser, C., and Sayers, J. (1977), Children's strategies in producing three-dimensional relationships on a two-dimensional surface, 'Journal of Experimental Child Psychology', 23, 305-14.

Friedlander, B.Z. (1970), Receptive language development in infancy: issues and problems, 'Merrill-Palmer Quarterly', 16, 7-51.

Friedman, S. (1972), Newborn's visual attention to repeated exposure of redundant versus 'novel' targets, 'Perception and Psychophysics', 12, 291-4

Friedman, S., Bruno, L.A., and Vietze, P. (1974), Newborn habituation to visual stimuli: a sex difference in novelty detection, 'Journal of Experimental Child Psychology', 18, 242-51.

Gagné, R.M. (1968), Contributions of learning to human development, 'Psychological Review', 75(3), 177-91.

Gaines, R. (1972), Variables of color perception in young children, 'Journal of Experimental Child Psychology', 14, 196-218.

Gaines, R. (1973), Matrices and pattern detection by young children, 'Developmental Psychology', 9, 143-50.

Gaines, R. (1977), Developmental assessment of pattern detection in matrices, 'Child Development', 48(2), 445-51.

Gaines, R., and Little, A.C. (1975), Developmental color perception, 'Journal of Experimental Child Psychology', 20, 465-86.

Galperin, P.J. (1980), 'Zu Grundfragen der Psychologie', Köln, Pahl'Rugenstein.

Garvey, C. (1977), 'Play', London, Fontana, Open Books.

Gibson, E.J. (1969), 'Principles of Perceptual Learning and Development', New York, Appleton-Century-Crofts.

Gibson, E.J., Owsley, C.J., and Johnston, J. (1978), Perception of invariants by five month old infants: differentiation of two types of motion, 'Developmental Psychology', 14(4), 407-15.

Gibson, E.J., and Walk, R.D. (1960), The visual cliff, 'Scientific American', 202, 64-71.

Gibson, J.J. (1950), 'The Perception of the Visual World', Boston, Houghton, Mifflin.

Gibson, J.J. (1966), 'The Senses Considered as Perceptual Systems', Boston, Houghton Mifflin.

Gibson, J.J. (1979), 'The Ecological Approach to Visual Perception', Boston, Houghton Mifflin.

Girton, M.R. (1979), Infants' attention to intra-stimulus motion, 'Journal of Experimental Child Psychology', 28, 416-23.

Glass, D.C., Neulinger, J., and Brim, O.G. (1974), Value and chroma discriminations of young children and adults, 'Child Development', 45(3), 812-14.

Gobar, A. (1968), 'Philosophic Foundations of Genetic Psychology and Gestalt Psychology', De Haag, Nijhoff.

Gogel, W.C. (1961), Convergence as a cue to absolute distance, 'The Journal of Psychology', 52, 287-301.

Goldstein, A.G. (1975), Recognition of inverted photographs of faces by children and adults, 'Journal of Genetic Psychology', 127, 109-24.

Golinkoff, R.M. (1975), Semantic development in infants: the concepts of agent and recipient, 'Merrill-Palmer Quarterly', 21(3), 181-93.

Golinkoff, R.M., and Kerr, J.L. (1978), Infants' perception of semantically defined action role changes in filmed events, 'Merrill-Palmer Quarterly', 24(1).

Goodenough, J.J. (1976), The nature of intelligent behavior: questions raised by cross-cultural studies, in L.B. Resnick (ed.), 'The Nature of Intelligence',

Hillsdale (New Jersey), Erlbaum; 169-88.

Goodman, N. (1960), The way the world is, 'The Review of Metaphysics', 15 (1), 48-56.

Goodman, N. (1968a), 'Languages of Art: an Approach to a Theory of Symbols', Indianapolis, Bobbs-Merrill.

Goodman, N. (1968b), The Structure of Appearance', Dordrecht, Reidel.

Goodman, N. (1978), 'Ways of Worldmaking', Hassocks (Sussex), Harvester.

Gordon, F.R., and Yonas, A. (1976), Sensitivity to binocular depth information in infants, 'Journal of Experimental Child Psychology', 22, 313-22.

Goren, C.C., Sarty, M., and Wu, P.Y.K. (1975), Visual following and pattern discrimination of face-like stimuli by newborn infants, 'Pediatrics', 56, 644-49.

Gottfried, A.W., Rose, S.A., and Bridger, W.H. (1977), Cross-modal transfer in human infants, 'Child Development', 48(1), 118-23.

Gottfried, A.W., Rose, S.A., and Bridger, W.H. (1978), Effects of visual, haptic and manipulatory experiences on infant's visual recognition memory of objects, 'Developmental Psychology', 14(3), 305-12.

Greenberg, D.D., and Blue, S.Z. (1977), The visual preference technique in infancy: effect of number of stimuli upon experimental outcome, 'Child Development', 48(1), 131-7.

Greenberg, D.D., and Weizmann, F. (1971), The measurement of visual attention in infants: a comparison of two methodologies, 'Journal of Experimental Child Psychology', 11, 234-43.

Greene, J. (1972), 'Psycholinguistics', Harmondsworth, Penguin.

Greenfield, P.M. (1966), On culture and conservation, in J.S. Bruner, R.R. Olver and P.M. Greenfield (eds), 'Studies in Cognitive Growth', New York-London, Wiley, 225-256.

Greenfield, P.M., Nelson, K., and Saltzman, E. (1972), The development of rulebound strategies for manipulating seriated cups: a parallel between action and grammar, 'Cognitive Psychology', 3, 291-310.

Greenfield, P.M., and Smith, J.H. (1976), 'Language beyond Syntax: the development of Semantic Structure', New York, Academic Press.

Gregg, C., Clifton, R.K., and Marshall, H. (1976), A possible explanation for the frequent failure to find cardiac orienting in the newborn infant, 'Developmental Psychology', 12(1), 75.

Gregor, A.J., and McPherson, D.A. (1965), A study of susceptibility to geometric illusions among cultural subgroups of Australian aborigines, 'Psychologia Africana', 11, 1-13.

Gregory, R.L. (1966), 'Eye and Brain', London, Weidenfeld & Nicholson.

Gruendel, J.M. (1977), Referential extension in early language development, 'Child Development', 48, 1567-76.

Gyr, J.W., Willey, D.G., Gordon, D., Bram, S., and Davis, S. (1973), Children's attention to mathematically ordered transforming stimuli, 'Perceptual and Motor Skills', 36, 463-75.

Gyr, J.W., Willey, R., Gordon, D., and Kubo, R.H. (1974), Do mathematical group invariants characterize the perceptual schema of younger and older children?, 'Human Development', 17, 176-86.

Haaf, R.A. (1974), Complexity and facial resemblance as determinants of response to face-like stimuli by 5- and 10-week old infants, 'Journal of Experimental Child Psychology', 18, 480-7.

Haaf, R.A. (1977), Visual response to complex facelike patterns by 15- and 20-week-old infants, 'Developmental Psychology', 13(1), 77-8.

Haaf, R.A., and Bell, R.Q. (1967), A facial dimension in visual discrimination by human infants, 'Child Development', 38, 893-9.

Haaf, R.A., and Brown, C. (1976), Infants' response to facelike patterns: developmental changes between ten and fifteen weeks of age, 'Journal of Experimental Child Psychology', 22, 155-60.

Haber, R.N., and Hershenson, M. (1974), 'The Psychology of Visual Perception', London-New York, Holt, Rinehart & Winston.

Hagen, M.A. (1974), Picture perception: toward a theoretical model, 'Psychological Bulletin', 81, 471-97.

Hagen, M.A. (1976), Development of the ability to perceive and produce the pictorial depth cue of overlapping, 'Perceptual and Motor Skills', 42, 1007-14.

Hagen, M.A. (ed.) (1980), 'The Perception of Pictures', vols I and II, New York, Academic Press.

Hagen, M.A. and Jones, R.K. (1978), Differential patterns of preference for modified linear perspective in children and adults, 'Journal of Experimental Child Psychology', 26, 205-15.

Hamel, B.R. (1974), Piaget's Zahlbegriff bei Kindern in ersten Schuljahr, 'Zeitschrift für Entwicklungspsychologie und Pädagogische Psychologie', 6, 99-108.

Hamel, B.R., and Riksen, B.O.M. (1973), Identity, reversibility verbal rule instruction and conservation, 'Developmental Psychology', 9, 66-72.

Hampshire, S. (1959), 'Thought and Action', Viking Press edn. 1969, New York, Viking Press.

Hanson, N.R. (1958), 'Patterns of Discovery', Cambridge University Press.

Harris, L.J., and Allen, T.W. (1974), Role of object constancy in the perception of object orientation, 'Human Development', 17, 187-200.

Harris, L., and Schaller, M.J. (1971), Form and its orientation: re-examination of a child's eye view, 'American Journal of Psychology', 84, 218-34.

Harris, P.L. and Van Geert, P. (1979), De ontwikkeling van de perceptie, in W. Koops and J.J. van der Werff, 'Overzicht van de Ontwikkelings-psychologie', Groningen, Wolters-Noordhoff, 91-119.

Hartlep, K.L., and Forsyth, G.A. (1977), Infants' discrimination of moving and stationary objects, 'Perceptual and Motor Skills', 45, 27-33.

Heider, F. (1958), 'The Psychology of Interpersonal Relations', New York, Wiley.

Heider, F., and Simmel, M. (1944), An experimental study of apparent behavior, 'American Journal of Psychology', 57, 243-59.

Held, R. (1965), Plasticity in sensory-motor systems, 'Scientific American', 213(5), 84-94.

Held, R., and Hein, A.V. (1958), Adaptation of disarranged hand-eye-coordination contingent upon reafferent stimulation, 'Perceptual and Motor Skills', 8, 87-90.

Held, R., and Hein, A. (1963), Movement-produced stimulation in the development of visually guided behavior, 'Journal of Comparative and Physiological Psychology', 56(5), 872-6.

Henle, M. (1942), An experimental investigation of past experience as a determinant of form perception, 'Journal of Experimental Psychology', 30, 1-22.

Hess, V.L., and Pick, A.D. (1974), Discrimination of schematic faces by nursery school children, 'Child Development', 45, 1151-4.

Hirsch, H., and Spinelli, D.N. (1970), Distribution of receptive field orientation: modifications contingent on conditions of visual experience, 'Science', 168, 869-71.

Hochberg, J., and Brooks, V. (1962), Pictorial recognition as an unlearned ability: a study of one child's performance, 'American Journal of Psychology', 75, 624-8.

Hock, H.S., and Hilton, T. (1979), Spatial coding and oblique discrimination by children, 'Journal of Experimental Child Psychology', 27, 96-104.

Hoogenraad, R., Grieve, R., Baldwin, P., and Campbell, R.N. (1978), Comprehension as an interactive process, in R.N. Campbell and P.T. Smith (eds), 'Recent Advances in the Psychology of Language: Language Development and Mother-Child-Interaction', London, Plenum Press.

Hopkins, J.R., Kagan, J., Brachfeld, S., Hans, S., and Linn, S. (1976), Infant responsivity to curvature, 'Child Development', 4, 1,166-71.

Hubel, D.H. (1963), The visual cortex of the brain, 'Scientific American', 209, 54-62.

Hubel, D.H., and Wiesel, T.N. (1962), Receptive fields, binocular interaction and functional architecture in the cat's visual cortex, 'Journal of Physiology', 160, 106-54.

Hubel, D.H., and Wiesel, T.N. (1965), Receptive fields and functional architecture in two non-striate visual areas (18 and 19) of the cat, 'Journal of

Neurophysiology', 28, 229-89.

Hubel, D.H., and Wiesel, T.N. (1968), Receptive fields and functional architecture of monkey striate cortex, 'Journal of Physiology', 195, 215-43.

Hudson, W. (1967), The study of the problem of pictorial perception among unacculturated groups, 'International Journal of Psychology', 2, 90-107.

Imberty, M. (1969) 'L'Acquisition des structures tonales chez l'enfant', Paris, Klincksieck.

Ingram, D. (1971), Transitivity in child language, 'Language', 47, 888-910.

Irvine, J.M. (1978), Wolof 'magical thinking'. Culture and conservation revisited, 'Journal of Cross-Cultural Psychology', 9(3), 300-16.

Jackson, J.P. (1973), Development of visual and tactual processing of visually presented shapes, 'Developmental Psychology', 8, 46-50.

Jacobson, S.W. (1979), Matching behavior in the young infant, 'Child Development', 50, 425-30.

Jahoda, G. (1966), Genetic illusions and environment: a study in Ghana, 'British Journal of Psychology', 57, 193-9.

Jahoda, G., and McGurk, H. (1974a), Development of pictorial depth perception: cross-cultural replications, 'Child Development', 45, 1042-7.

Jahoda, G., and McGurk, H. (1974b), Pictorial depth perception: a developmental study, 'British Journal of Psychology', 65, 141-50.

Jahoda, G., and Stacey, B. (1970), Susceptibility to geometric illusions according to culture and professional training, 'Perception and Psychophysics', 7, 179-84.

Jakobson, R. (1968), 'Child Language Aphasia and Phonological Universals', Den Haag, Mouton.

Jespersen, O. (1922, reprinted 1959), 'Language: its Nature, Development and Origin', London, Allen & Unwin.

Jessen, B.L., and Kaess, D.W. (1973), Effects of training on intersensory communication by three- and five-year-olds, 'Journal of Genetic Psychology', 123, 115-22.

Johansson, G. (1950), 'Configuration in Event Perception', Uppsala, Almkvist & Wiksell.

Johansson, G. (1964), Perception of motion and changing form, 'Scandinavian Journal of Psychology', 5(3), 181-208.

Johansson, G. (1973), Visual perception of biological motion and a model for its analysis, 'Perception and Psychophysics', 14, 201-11.

Johansson, G. (1974), Vector analysis in visual perception of rolling motion, 'Psychologische Forschung', 36, 311-19.

Johansson, G. (1976), Spatiotemporal differentiation and integration in visual motion perception: an experimental and theoretical analysis of calculus-like functions, 'Psychological Research', 38(4), 379-93.

Johansson, G. (1977), Studies on visual perception of locomotion, 'Perception', 6(4), 365-76.

Johnson, D., and Brody, N. (1977), Visual habituation, sensorimotor development and tempo of play in one-year-old infants, 'Child Development', 48(1), 315-19.

Jones, B. (1975), Spatial perception of the blind, 'British Journal of Psychology', 66, 461-72.

Jones-Molfese, V. (1975), Preference of infants for regular and distorted facial stimuli. 'Child Development', 46, 1005-9.

Jones-Molfese, V.J. (1977), Responses of neonates to colored stimuli, 'Child Development', 48, 1092-5.

Julesz, B. (1975), Experiments in the visual perception of texture, 'Scientific American', 232(4), 34-43.

Juszyk, P.W. (1977), Perception of syllable-final stop consonants by two-month-old infants, 'Perception and Psychophysics', 21(5), 450-4.

Juszyk, P.W., Cutting, J.E., Ford, C.F., and Smith, L.B. (1977), Categorical perception of non-speech sounds by 2-month-old infants, 'Perception and Psychophysics', 21, 50-4.

Kaess, D.W. (1970), Difference between identifying of real shape and perspective shape, 'Journal of Experimental Psychology', 83, 465-71.

Kaess, D.W. (1971), Methodological study of form constancy development, 'Journal of Experimental Child Psychology', 12, 27-34.

Kaess, D.W. (1974), Effect of distance and size of standard object on the development of shape constancy, 'Journal of Experimental Psychology', 102, 17-21.

Kalveram, K.T., and Ritter, M. (1979), The formation of reference systems in visual motion perception, 'Psychological Research', 41, 397-405.

Karmel, B.Z. (1974), Contour effects and pattern preferences in infants: a reply to Greenberg and O'Donnell, 'Child Development', 45, 196-9.

Karmel, B.Z., and Maisel, E.B. (1975), A neuronal model for infant visual attention, in L.B. Cohen and P. Salapatek (eds), 'Infant Perception: from Sensation to Cognition, vol. I, New York, Academic Press, 78-131.

Karmiloff-Smith, A., and Inhelder, B. (1975), If you want to get ahead, get a theory, 'Cognition', 3(3), 195-212.

Kaufmann, L. (1974), 'Sight and Mind', Oxford University Press.

Kendler, H.H., and Kendler, T.S. (1970), Developmental processes in discrimination learning, 'Human Development', 13, 65-89.

Kendler, T.S. (1964), Verbalization and optional reversal shifts among Kindergarten Children, 'Journal of Verbal Learning and Verbal Behavior', 3, 428-36.

Kennedy, J.M. (1974), 'A Psychology of Picture Perception. Images and Information', San Francisco-Washington-London, Jossey Bass.

Kennedy, M., and Sheridan, C. (1972), Backwriting: a crossmodal equivalence of shape and slant as a function of age, 'Perceptual and Motor Skills', 34, 982.

Kessen, W., Salapatek, P., and Haith, M. (1972), The visual response of the human newborn to linear contour, 'Journal of Experimental Child Psychology', 13, 9-20.

Kinney, D.K., and Kagan, J. (1976), Infant attention to auditory discrepancy, 'Child Development', 47(1), 155-64.

Klahr, D., and Wallace, J.G. (1970), An information-processing analysis of some Piagetian experimental tasks, 'Cognitive Psychology', 1, 358-87.

Klapper, Z.S., and Birch, H.G. (1971), Developmental course of temporal patterning in vision and audition, 'Perceptual and Motor Skills', 132, 547-55.

Klausmeier, H.J. (1976), Conceptual development during the school years, in J.T. Levin and V.L. Allen (eds), 'Cognitive Learning in Children. Theories and Strategies', New York-London, Academic Press, 5-29.

Koenderink, J.J. and van Doorn, A.J. (1975), Invariant properties of the motion parallax field due to the movement of rigid bodies relative to an observer, 'Optica Acta', 22,9, 773-91.

Koenderink, J.J. and van Doorn, A.J. (1976a), Visual perception of rigidity of solid shape, 'Journal of Mathematical Biology', 3,79-85.

Koenderink, J.J. and van Doorn, A.J. (1976b), Geometry of binocular vision and a model for stereopsis, 'Biological Cybernetics', 21, 29-35.

Koenderink, J.J. and van Doorn, A.J. (1976c), Local structure of movement parallax of the plane, 'Journal of the Optical Society of America', 66,7, 717-23.

Koenderink, J.J. and van Doorn, A.J. (1976d), The singularities of the visual mapping, 'Biological Cybernetics', 24, 51-9.

Koenderink, J.J. and van Doorn, A.J. (1977), How an ambulant observer can construct a model of the environment from the geometrical structure of the visual inflow, in G. Hanske and E. Butenandt (eds), 'Kybernetik 1977', Munich, Oldenburg, 224-47.

Koenderink, J.J. and van Doorn, A.J. (1979a), The structure of two-dimensional scalar fields with applications to vision, 'Biological Cybernetics', 33, 151-8.

Koenderink, J.J. and van Doorn, A.J. (1979b), The internal representation of solid shape with respect to vision, 'Biological Cybernetics', 32, 211-6.

Koenderink, J.J. and van Doorn, A.J. (1980), Photometric invariants related to solid shape, 'Optica Acta', 27,7, 981-96.

Kopp, C.B., Khoka, E.W., and Sigman, M. (1977), A comparison of sensorimotor development among infants in India and the United States, 'Journal of Cross-Cultural Psychology', 8(4), 435-52.

Kosslyn, S.M. (1978), On the ontological status of visual mental images, in
D.L. Waltz (ed.), 'TINLAP-2', University of Illinois at Urbana-Champaign,
167-79.
Kremenitzer, J.P., Vaughan, H.G., Kurtzberg, D., and Dowling, K. (1979),
Smooth-pursuit eye movements in the newborn infant, 'Child Development',
50, 442-8.
Kuhlman, E.S., and Wolking, W.D. (1972), Development of within and cross-
modal matching ability in the auditory and visual sense modalities, 'Develop-
mental Psychology', 7, 365.
La Barbara, J.D., Izard, C.E., Vietze, P., and Parisi, S.A. (1976), Four-
and six-month-old infants' visual responses to joy, anger and neutral
expressions, 'Child Development', 47(2), 535-8.
Labov, W. (1970), The logic of non-standard English, in F. Williams (ed.),
'Language and Poverty', Chicago, Markham Press, p. 153-89.
Lakatos, I. (1970), Falsification and the growth of knowledge, in I. Lakatos
and A. Musgrave (eds), 'Criticism and the Growth of Knowledge', Cambridge
University Press, 91-196.
Lasky, R.E. (1974), The ability of six-year-olds, eight-year-olds and adults
to abstract visual patterns, 'Child Development', 45, 626-32.
Lawson, K.R. (1980), Spatial and temporal congruity and auditory-visual
integration in infants, 'Developmental Psychology', 16(3), 185-92.
Leavitt, L.A., Brown, J.W., Morse, P.A., and Graham, F.K. (1976), Cardiac
orienting and auditory discrimination in six-week-old infants, 'Developmental
Psychology', 12, 514-23.
Leech, G. (1974), 'Semantics', Harmondsworth, Penguin.
Leeuwenberg, E.L.J. (1969), Quantitative specification of information in
sequential patterns, 'Psychological Review', 76, 216-20.
Leeuwenberg, E.L.J. (1971), A perceptual coding language for visual and
auditory patterns, 'American Journal of Psychology', 84, 307-49.
Leeuwenberg, E.L.J. (1978), Quantification of certain visual pattern proper-
ties: salience, transparency and similarity, in E.L.J. Leeuwenberg and
H.F.J.M. Buffart (eds), 'Formal Theories of Visual Perception', New York,
Wiley; 277-98.
Leont'ev, A.N. (1977), 'Probleme der Entwicklung des Psychischen', Kronberg,
Athenäum.
Leont'ev, A.N. (1979), 'Tätigkeit, Bewusstsein, Persönlichkeit', Berlin, Volk
and Wissen.
Leslie, A.M. (1982) Discursive representation in infancy, in B. de Gelder
(ed.), 'Knowledge and Representation', London, Routledge & Kegan
Paul, 80-93.
Lesser, H. (1974), Children's unusual responses to observed movement,
'Journal of Genetic Psychology', 125, 201-6.
Lesser, H. (1977), The growth of perceived causality in children, 'Journal
of Genetic Psychology', 128, 145-52.
Lester, B.M. (1975), Cardiac habituation of the orienting response to an
auditory signal in infants of varying nutritional status, 'Developmental
Psychology', 11, 432.
Levine, R.A. (1977), Child rearing as cultural adaptation, in P.H. Leiderman,
S.R. Tulkin and A. Rosenfeld (eds), 'Culture and Infancy: Variations in the
Human Experience', New York, Academic Press, 15-28.
Lévi-Strauss, C. (1966), 'The Savage Mind', University of Chicago Press.
Lewis, T.L., Maurer, D., and Kay, D. (1978), Newborns' central vision:
whole or hole?, 'Journal of Experimental Child Psychology', 26, 193-203.
Lienhardt, G. (1961), 'Divinity and Experience: The Religion of the Dinka',
Oxford, Clarendon Press.
Linsky, L. (1971), Reference and referents, in D.D. Steinberg and L.A.
Jakobovits (eds), 'Semantics. An Interdisciplinary Reader in Philosophy,
Linguistics and Psychology', Cambridge University Press, 76-85.
Lock, A. (1982), The early stages of communicative and linguistic develop-
ment underlying processes, in B. de Gelder (ed.), 'Knowledge and
Representation', London, Routledge & Kegan Paul, 94-110.

Lord, C. (1974), The perception of eye contact in children and adults, 'Child Development', 45, 1,113-17.

Lyons, J. (1968), 'Introduction to Theoretical Linguistics', Cambridge University Press.

Lyons-Ruth, K. (1977), Bimodal perception in infancy: response to auditory-visual incongruity, 'Child Development', 48, 820-7.

McCall, R.B. and Kagan, J. (1970), Individual differences in the infant's distribution of attention to stimulus discrepancy, 'Developmental Psychology', 2, 90-8.

McCall, R.B., Kennedy, C.B., and Appelbaum, M.I. (1977b), Magnitude of discrepancy and the distribution of attention in infants, 'Child Development', 48(2), 772-85.

McCall, R.B., Kennedy, C.B., and Dodds, C. (1977a), The interfering effect of distracting stimuli on the infant's memory, 'Child Development', 48, 78-87.

McCarthy, D. (1954), Language development in children, in L. Carmichael (ed.), 'Manual of Child Psychology', New York, Wiley, 477-581.

Maccoby, M., and Modiano, N. (1966), On culture and equivalence, I. in J.S. Bruner, R.R. Olver and P.M. Greenfield (eds), 'Studies in Cognitive Growth', New York, Wiley, 257-69.

McGarvil, S.L., and Karmel, B.Z. (1976), A neural activity interpretation of luminance effects on infant pattern preferences, 'Journal of Experimental Child Psychology', 22, 363-74.

McGurk, H. (1974), Visual perception in young infants, in B.M. Foss (ed.), 'New Perspectives in Child Development', Harmondsworth, Penguin, 11-52.

McGurk, H. and Jahoda, G. (1974), The development of pictorial depth perception: the role of figural elevation, 'British Journal of Psychology', 65, 367-76.

McGurk, H., and Lewis, T.L. (1974), Space perception in early infancy, 'Science', 186, 649-50.

McGurk, H., Turnure, C., and Creighton, S.J. (1977), Auditory-visual coordination in neonates, 'Child Development', 48, 138-43.

McKenzie, B.E., and Day, R.H. (1972), Object distance as a determinant of visual fixation in early infancy, 'Science', 178, 1,108-10.

McKenzie, B.E., and Day, R.H. (1976), Infant's attention to stationary and moving objects at different distances, 'Australian Journal of Psychology', 28, 45-51.

McKenzie, B.E., Tootell, H.E., and Day, R.H. (1980), Development of visual size constancy during the first year of human infancy, 'Developmental Psychology', 16(3), 163-74.

McNeill, D. (1970), 'The Acquisition of Language: the Study of Developmental Psycholinguistics', New York, Harper & Row.

McNeill, D. (1974), 'Semiotic Extension', unpublished paper.

McWorth, N.H., and Otto, D.A. (1970), Habituation of the visual orienting response in young children, 'Perception and Psychophysics', 7, 173-8.

Mak, P. (1981), 'Een muzikaal patroonperceptiemodel en de ontwikkelings-psychologische implikaties ervan', Groningen, Instituut voor Ontwikkelings-psychologie.

Mann, I. (1964), 'The Development of the Human Eye', London, British Medical Association.

Mann, V.A., Diamond, R., and Carey, S. (1979), Development of voice recognition: parallels with face recognition, 'Journal of Experimental Child Psychology', 27, 153-65.

Mapel, B.M. (1977), Philosophical criticisms of behaviorism, an analysis, 'Behaviorism', 5(1), 17-32.

Maurer, D., and Lewis, T.L. (1979), Peripheral discrimination by three-month-old infants, 'Child Development', 50, 276-9.

Maurer, D., and Salapatek, P. (1976), Developmental changes in the scanning of faces by young infants, 'Child Development', 47, 523-7.

Mead, G.H. (1934), 'Mind, Self and Society', University of Chicago Press.

Mehan, H., and Wood, H. (1975), 'The Reality of Ethnomethodology', London, Wiley.

Mehler, J. (1963), Some effects of grammatical transformation on the recall of English sentences, 'Journal of Verbal Learning and Verbal Behavior', 2, 346-51.

Mehler, J., and Bever, T.G. (1967), Cognitive capacity of very young children, 'Science', 162, 141-2.

Mendelson, M.D., and Haith, M.M. (1975), The relation between non-nutritive sucking and visual information processing in the human newborn, 'Child Development', 46(4), 1025-9.

Menyuk, P. (1971), 'The Acquisition and Development of Language', Cambridge (Mass.), MIT Press.

Menyuk, P., and Bernholtz, N. (1969), Prosodic features and children's language production, 'Res. Lab. of Electronics Quart. Progress Reports', 93.

Metzger, W. (1966), 'Allgemeine Psychologie, I', Göttingen, Verlag für Psychologie.

Michotte, A. (1946), 'La Perception de la causalité', Leuven, Editions de l'Institut Supérieur de Philosophie.

Michotte, A. (1962), 'Causalité, permanence et réalité phénoménales', Leuven, Presses Universitaires de Louvain.

Milewski, A.E. (1976), Infants' discrimination of internal and external pattern elements, 'Journal of Experimental Child Psychology', 22(2), 229-46.

Milewski, A.E. (1979), Visual discrimination and detection of configurational invariance in 3-month-old infants, 'Development Psychology', 15(4), 357-63.

Milewski, A.E., and Siqueland, E.R. (1975), Discrimination of color- and pattern-novelty in one month old infants, 'Journal of Experimental Child Psychology', 19, 122-36.

Millar, S. (1972), The development of visual and kinesthetic judgments of distance, 'British Journal of Psychology', 63, 271-82.

Millar, S. (1972b), Effects of interpolated tasks on latency and accuracy of intra-modal and cross-modal shape recognition by children, 'Journal of Experimental Psychology', 96, 170-5.

Millar, S. (1975), Effects of input-conditions on intra-modal and cross-modal visual and kinesthetic matches by children, 'Journal of Experimental Child Psychology', 19, 63-78.

Miller, D.J., Ryan, E.B., Short, E.J., Ries, P.G., McGuire, M.D., and Culler, M.P. (1977a), Relationship between early habituation and later cognitive performance in infancy, 'Child Development', 48(2), 658-61.

Miller, D.J., Sinnott, J.P., Short, E.J., and Harris, H.A. (1977b), Individual differences in habituation rates and object-concept performance, 'Child Development', 47(2), 528-31.

Miller, G.A. (1967), Psycholinguistic approaches to the study of communication, in D.L. Arm (ed.), 'Journeys in science', University of Mexico Press, 22-73.

Miller, G.A., Galanter, E.H. and Pribram, H.H. (1960), 'Plans and the Structure of Behavior', New York, Holt.

Miller, G.A., and McKean, A. (1964), A chronometric study of some relations between sentences, 'Quarterly Journal of Experimental Psychology', 16, 297-308.

Miller, L.K. (1975), Effects of auditory stimulation upon non-nutritive sucking by premature infants, 'Perceptual and Motor Skills', 40, 879-85.

Miranda, S.B. (1970), Visual abilities and pattern preferences of premature infants and full term neonates, 'Journal of Experimental Child Psychology', 10, 189-205.

Miranda, S.B., and Fantz, R.L. (1971), Distribution of visual attention of newborn infants among patterns varying in size and number of details, 'Proceedings of the American Psychological Association', Washington DC.

Moerk, E.L. (1975), Piaget's research as applied to the explanation of language development, 'Merrill-Palmer Quarterly', 21(3), 151-69.

Moffitt, A.R. (1973), Intensity discrimination and cardiac reaction in young infants, 'Developmental Psychology', 8, 357-9.

Moore, M.K., and Meltzoff, A.N. (1978), Object permanence, imitation and language development: toward a neo-Piagetian perspective, in F.D. Minnifie and L.L. Lloyd (ed), 'Communicative and Cognitive Abilities. Early Behavioral

Assessment', London, University Park Press, 151-84.

Morehead, D.M., and Morehead, A. (1974), From signal to sign: a Piagetian view of thought and language during the first two years, in R.L. Schiefelbusch and L.L. Lloyd (eds), 'Language Perspectives: Acquisition, Retardation and Intervention', London, University Park Press, 153-90.

Morse-Nice (1925), see Blumenthal (1970).

Mounoud, P., and Bower, T.G.R. (1975), Conservation of weight in infants, 'Cognition', 3(1), 29-40.

Muir, D., and Field, J. (1979), Newborn infants orient to sounds, 'Child Development', 50, 431-6.

Mundy-Castle, A.C. (1966), Pictorial depth perception in Ghanaian children, 'International Journal of Psychology', 1, 290-300.

Munsinger, H., and Banks, M.S. (1974), Pupillometry as a measure of visual sensitivity among infants, young children and adults, 'Developmental Psychology', 10(5), 677-82.

Murch, G.M. (1973), 'Visual and Auditory Perception', New York, Bobbs-Merrill.

Neisser, U. (1967), 'Cognitive Psychology', New York, Appleton-Century-Crofts.

Neisser, U. (1976), 'Cognition and Reality. Principles and Implications of Cognitive Psychology', San Francisco, Freeman.

Ninio, A., and Bruner, J.S. (1978), The achievement and antecedents of labelling, 'Journal of Child Language', 5, 1-15.

Northman, O.E., and Northcross-Black, R. (1976), An examination of errors in children's visual and haptic-tactual memory for variation in forms, 'Journal of Genetic Psychology', 126, 161-6.

Noton, D., and Stark, L. (1971), Eye movements and visual perception, 'Scientific American', 224, 34-43.

Olson, D.R. (1970), 'Cognitive Development. The Child's Acquisition of Diagonality', New York, Academic Press.

Olson, R.K. (1975), Children's sensitivity to pictorial depth information, 'Perception and Psychophysics', 17(1), 59-64.

Olson, R.K., and Boswell, S. (1976), Pictorial depth sensitivity in two-year-old children, 'Child Development', 47(4), 1175-8.

Olson, R.K., Pearl, M., Mayfield, N., and Millar, D. (1976), Sensitivity to pictorial shape perspective in five-year-old children and adults, 'Perception and Psychophysics', 20(3), 173-8.

Olum, V. (1956), Developmental differences in the perception of causality, 'American Journal of Psychology', 69, 417-23.

Olum, V. (1958), Developmental differences in the perception of causality under conditions of specific instructions, 'Vita Humana', 1, 191-203.

Osherson, D. (1975), Logic and models of logical thinking, in R.J. Falmagne (ed.), 'Reasoning Representation and Process', Hillsdale (New Jersey), Erlbaum, 81-91.

Papalia, D.E. (1972), The status of several conservation abilities across the life-span, 'Human Development', 15, 229-43.

Papousek, H. (1969), Individual variability in learned responses in human infants, in R.J. Robinson (ed.), 'Brain and Early Behaviour', London, Academic, 251-63.

Phillips, W.A., Hobbs, S.B., and Pratt, F.R. (1978), Intellectual realism in children's drawing of cubes, 'Cognition', 6, 15-33.

Piaget, J. (1927), La causalité chez l'enfant, 'British Journal of Psychology', 18, 276-301.

Piaget, J. (1937), 'La Construction du réèl chez l'enfant', Neuchâtel, Delachaux et Nièstlé, English translation: Piaget, J. (1955); 'The Construction of Reality in the Child', London, Routledge & Kegan Paul.

Piaget, J. (1959), Le rôle de la notion d'équilibre dans l'explication en psychologie, 'Acta Psychologica', 15, 51-62.

Piaget, J. (1968), Quantification, conservation and nativism, 'Science', 162, 976-81.

Piaget, J. (1972), Intellectual evolution from adolescence to adulthood, 'Human

Development', 15, 1-12.

Piaget, J. and Inhelder, B. (1956), 'The Child's Conception of Space', New York, Norton.

Pinxten, H. (1975), 'Bijdrage tot de studie van het wereldbeeld van de mens', doctoral dissertation, Ghent, RUG.

Pinxten, H. (1980), 'Anthropology of Space', Ghent, Communication and Cognition.

Pipp, S.L., and Haith, M.M. (1977), Infant visual scanning of two- and three-dimensional forms, 'Child Development', 48, 1640-4.

Pirenne, M. (1970), 'Optics, painting and photography', Cambridge University Press.

Pirenne, M. (1975), Vision and art, in E.C. Carterette and M. Friedman (eds), 'Handbook of Perception, Volume V', New York, Academic Press, 433-90.

Polanyi, M. (1967), 'The Tacit Dimension', New York, Anchor Books/Doubleday.

Poresky, R.H. (1976), Screening infants to clarify research results, 'Perceptual and Motor Skills', 43, 1,305-6.

Porges, S.W., Arnold, W.R., and Forbes, E.J. (1973), Heart rate variability: an index of attentional responsivity in human newborns. 'Developmental Psychology', 8, 85-92.

Posnansky, C.J., and Neumann, P.G. (1976), The abstraction of visual prototypes by children, 'Journal of Experimental Child Psychology', 21, 367-79.

Prechtl, H.F.R. (1965), Problems of behavioral studies in the newborn infant, in D.S. Lehrman, R.A. Hinde and E. Shaw (eds), 'Advances in the Study of Behavior', New York, Academic Press, 75-99.

Preyer, W. (1881), 'Die Seele des Kindes', Leipzig, Grieben.

Pribram, K. (1977a), Holonomy and structure in the organization of perception, in J.M. Nicholas (ed.), 'Images, Perception and Knowledge', Dordrecht, Reidel, 155-83.

Pribram, K. (1977b), 'Languages of the Brain', Belmont, Brooks/Cole.

Pribram, K. (1979), Holographic Memory (Karl Pribram interviewed by Daniel Goleman), 'Psychology today', February, 71-84.

Price, J.R. (1978), Conservation studies in Papua New Guinea: a review, 'International Journal of Psychology', 13(1), 1-24.

Price-Williams, D., Gordon, W., and Ramirez, M. (1969), Skill and conservation: a study of pottery-making children, 'Developmental Psychology', 1, 769.

Putnam, H. (1975), The meaning of meaning, in H. Putnam, 'Mind, Language and Reality. Philosophical papers, II', Cambridge University Press, 215-71.

Pylyshyn, Z.W. (1973), What the mind's eye tells the mind's brain: a critique of mental imagery, 'Psychological Bulletin', 80, 1-24.

Pylyshyn, Z.W. (1978), What has language to do with perception? Some speculations on the *lingus mentis,* in D.L. Waltz (ed.), 'TINLAP-2', University of Illinois at Urbana-Champaign, 172-9.

Quine, W.V. O. (1953), The problem of meaning in linguistics, in W.V.O. Quine, 'From a logical point of view', Harvard University Press, 47-64.

Quine, W.V.O. (1960), 'Word and Object', Cambridge (Mass.), MIT Press.

Ratner, N.K, and Bruner, J.S. (1978), Games, social exchange and the acquisition of language, 'Journal of Child Language', 5(3), 391-401.

Reichardt, J. (1971), 'The Computer in Art', London, Studio Vista; New York, Van Nostrand Reinhold.

Restle, F. (1979), Coding theory of the perception of motion configurations, 'Psychological Review', 86(1), 1-24.

Richards, W., and Miller, J.F. (1969), Convergence as a cue to depth, 'Perception and Psychophysics', 5, 317-20.

Riegel, K.F. (1973), Dialectic operations. The final period of cognitive development, 'Human Development', 16, 346-70.

Rieser, I., Yonas, A., and Wikner, C. (1976), Radial localization of odors by human newborns, 'Child Development', 47(3), 856-9.

Robinson, J.O. (1972), 'The psychology of visual illusion', London, Hutchinson.

Rock, I. (1974), The perception of disoriented figures, in 'Psychology in Progress: Readings from Scientific American', San Francisco, Freeman, 108-15.

Rock, I., and Harris, C.S. (1967), Vision and Touch, 'Scientific American', 225, 96-104.

Rock, I., and Leafman, R.S. (1963), An experimental analysis of visual symmetry, 'Acta Psychologica', 21, 171-83.

Roederer, J.G. (1975), 'Introduction to the Physics and Psychophysics of Music', New York, Springer Verlag.

Rosch, E.H. (1973), On the internal structure of perceptual and semantic categories, in T.E. Moore (ed.), 'Cognitive Development and the Acquisition of Language', New York, Academic Press, 111-44.

Rose, S., Katz, P.A., Birke, M., and Rossman, E. (1977), Visual following in newborns: role of figure-ground contrast and configurational detail, 'Perceptual and Motor Skills', 45, 515-22.

Rose, S.A. (1977), Infants' transfer of response between two-dimensional and three-dimensional stimuli, 'Child Development', 48, 1,086-91.

Rose, S.A., Blank, M.S., and Bridger, W.H. (1972), Intermodal and intra-modal retention of visual and tactual information in young children, 'Developmental Psychology', 6, 483-6.

Rose, S.A., Schmidt, K., and Bridger, W.H. (1976), Cardiac and behavioral responsivity to tactile stimulation in premature and full-term infants, 'Developmental Psychology', 12(4), 311-20.

Rosinsky, R.R., and Levine, N.P. (1976), Texture gradient effectiveness in the perception of surface slant, 'Journal of Experimental Child Psychology', 21, 261-71.

Ruff, H.A. (1976), Developmental changes in the infant's attention to pattern detail, 'Perceptual and Motor Skills', 43(2), 351-8.

Ruff, H.A. (1978), Infant recognition of the invariant form of objects, 'Child Development', 49, 293-306.

Ruff, H.A., and Birch, H.G. (1974), Infant visual fixation: effect of concentricity, curvilinearity and number of directions, 'Journal of Experimental Child Psychology', 17(3), 460-73.

Ruff, H.A., and Turkewitz, G. (1975), Developmental changes in the effectiveness of stimulus intensity on infant visual attention, 'Developmental Psychology', 11(6), 705-10.

Russell, B. (1914), 'Our Knowledge of the External World', London, Allen & Unwin.

Ryle, G. (1949), 'The Concept of Mind', London, Hutchinson.

Salapatek, P. (1975), Pattern perception in early infancy, in L.B. Cohen and P. Salapatek (eds), 'Infant Perception: From Sensation to Cognition' (vol. I), New York, Academic Press, 133-249.

Salapatek, P., and Kessen, W. (1973), Prolonged investigation of a plane geometric triangle by the human newborn, 'Journal of Experimental Child Psychology, 15, 22-9.

Sameroff, A.J., Cashmore, I.F., and Dykes, A.C. (1973), Heart deceleration during visual fixation in human newborns, 'Developmental Psychology', 8, 117-19.

Savin, H.B., and Perchonok, E. (1965), Grammatical structure and the immediate recall of English sentences, 'Journal of Verbal Learning and Verbal Behavior', 4, 348-53.

Scaife, M., and Bruner, J.S. (1975), The capacity for joint visual attention in the infant, 'Nature', 253 (5489), 265-6.

Schaerlaeckens, A.M. (1973), 'The Two-Word Sentence in Child Language Development', Den Haag, Mouton.

Schaller, M.J., and Dziadosz, G.M. (1976), Developmental changes in foveal tachistoscopic recognition between prereading and reading children, 'Developmental Psychology', 11, 921.

Schank, R. (1982), Depths of Knowledge', in B. de Gelder (ed.) 'Knowledge and Representation', London, Routledge & Kegan Paul, 170-93. 1979.

Scheff, T.J. (1966), 'Being Mentally Ill: a sociological theory', Chicago, Aldine.

Schlesinger, I.M. (1971), Production of utterances and language acquisition, in D.I. Slobin (ed.), 'The Ontogenesis of Grammar: a Theoretical Symposium', New York, Academic Press, 63-101.

Schlesinger, I.M. (1974), Relational concepts underlying language, in R.L. Schiefelbusch and L.L. Lloyd (eds), 'Language Perspectives. Acquisition, Retardation and Intervention', London, University Park Press, 129-51.

Schumann (1900), see Boring, E.G. (1942), 'Sensation and Perception in the History of Experimental Psychology', New York, Appleton-Century-Crofts.

Schwartz, S.P. (1977), 'Naming, Necessity and Natural Kinds', Ithaca, Cornell University Press.

Searle, J.R. (1969), 'Speech Acts: An Essay in the Philosophy of Language', Cambridge University Press.

Segall, M.H., Campbell, D.T., and Herskovits, M.J. (1963), Cultural differences in the perception of geometrical illusions, 'Science', 139, 769-71.

Selby, H.A. (1974), 'Zapotec Deviance: The Convergence of Folk and Modern Sociology', Austin, University of Texas Press.

Selby, H.A. (1975), Semantics and causality in the study of deviance, in M. Blount and B.G. Sanches (eds), 'Sociocultural Dimensions of Language Use', New York, Academic Press, 11-24.

Selfridge, O.G. (1959), Pandemonium: a paradigm for learning, reprinted in P.C. Dodwell, 'Perceptual Learning and Adaptation', Harmondsworth, Penguin, 465-78.

Sellars, W. (1967), 'Science and Metaphysics: variations on Kantian themes', London, Routledge & Kegan Paul.

Sigman, M. and Parmelee, A.H. (1974), Visual preferences of four-month-old premature and full term infants, 'Child Development', 45, 959-65.

Sinclair, A. (1979), personal communication.

Sinclair-De Zwart, H. (1973), Language acquisition and cognitive development, in T.E. Moore (ed.), 'Cognitive Development and the Acquisition of Language', New York, Academic Press, 9-25.

Sinnott, J.D. (1975), Everyday thinking and Piagetian operativity in adults, 'Human Development', 18, 430-3.

Siqueland, E.R., and Lippsitt, L.P. (1966), Conditioned head turnings in human newborns, 'Journal of Experimental Child Psychology', 3, 356-76.

Skinner, B.F. (1974), 'About Behaviorism', New York, Knopf.

Slater, A.M., and Findlay, J.M. (1975a), The corneal reflection technique and the visual preference method: sources of error, 'Journal of Experimental Child Psychology', 20, 240-7.

Slater, A.M., and Findlay, J.M. (1975b), Binocular fixation in the newborn baby, 'Journal of Experimental Child Psychology', 20, 248-73.

Slater, A.M., and Sykes, M. (1977), Newborn infants' visual responses to square waves gratings, 'Child Development', 48(2), 545-54.

Smedslund, J. (1972), 'Becoming a psychologist', New York, Halstead Press; Oslo, Universitetsforlaget.

Smedslund, J. (1977), Piaget's psychology in theory and practice. 'British Journal of Educational Psychology', 47, 1-6.

Smedslund, J. (1978), Bandura's theory of self-efficacy: a set of commonsense theorems, 'Scandinavian Journal of Psychology', 19, 1-14.

Smith, E.E., Shoben, E.J., and Ripps, L.J. (1974), Structure and process in semantic memory: a featural model for semantic decisions, 'Psychological Bulletin', 81(3), 214-41.

Spectorman, A.R., Shulman, T., and Ernhart, C.B. (1977), The influence of concept and orientation training on letter discrimination, 'Journal of Genetic Psychology', 127, 153-4.

Spelke, E.S. (1979), Perceiving bimodally specified events in infancy, 'Developmental Psychology', 15(6), 626-36.

Sroufe, L.A. (1977), Wariness of strangers and the study of infant development, 'Child Development', 48, 731-46.

Stein, N.L., and Mandler, J.M. (1974), Children's recognition of reversals of geometric figures, 'Child Development', 45, 604-15.

Steinberg, B.M., and Dunn, L.A. (1976), Conservation competence and performance in Chiapas, 'Human Development', 19, 14-25.

Stern, C., and Stern, W. (1907), 'Die Kindersprache', Leipzig, Johan Ambrosius Barth.

Stevenson, A. (1893), The speech of children, 'Science', 21, 118-20.

Strauss, S., Danziger, D., and Ramati, T. (1977), University students understanding of non-conservation: implications for structural reversion?, 'Developmental Psychology', 13, 359-63.

Stumpf (1901), see Blumenthal, 1970.

Swoboda, P.J., Morse, P.A., and Leavitt, L.A. (1976), Continuous vowel discrimination in normal and at risk infants, 'Child Development', 47(2), 459-65.

Szasz, T.S. (1961), 'The Myth of Mental Illness', New York, Hoeber-Harper.

Thayer, S. (1977), Children's detection of on-face and off-face gazes, 'Developmental Psychology', 13(6), 673-4.

Thompson, G.B. (1975), Discrimination of mirror image shapes by young children, 'Journal of Experimental Psychology', 19, 165-76.

Tiedemann, D. (1782), Observations on the development of the mental faculties of children, in A. Bar-Adon and W.F. Leopold (eds) (1971), 'Child Language', Englewood Cliffs (New Jersey), Prentice-Hall, 13-17.

Tolkmitt, F.J., and Brindley, R. (1977), Auditory perception of spatiotemporal patterns, 'American Journal of Psychology', 90(1), 73-83.

Trabasso, T. (1975), Representation, memory and reasoning: how do we make transitive inferences, in A.D. Pick (ed.) 'Minnesota Symposium on Child Psychology', (vol. 9), University of Minneapolis Press, 135-72.

Trehub, S.E. (1973), Infants' sensitivity to vowel and tonal contrast, 'Developmental Psychology', 9, 91-6.

Trehub, S.E. (1975), The problem of state in infant speech discrimination studies, 'Developmental Psychology', 11, 116.

Trehub, S.E. (1976), 'The discrimination of foreign speech contrasts by infants and adults', Child Development, 47(2), 466-72.

Tronick, E., and Clanton, C. (1971), Infant looking patterns, 'Vision Research', 11, 1479-86.

Turkewitz, G., Birch, H.G., and Cooper, K.K. (1972), Responsiveness to simple and complex auditory stimuli in the human newborn, 'Developmental Psychobiology', 5, 7-19.

Van den Berg, J.H. (1960), 'Het menselijk lichaam. Een metabletisch onderzoek', Nijkerk, Callenbach.

Van Geert, P. (1975), 'Taalontwikkeling in het licht van kognitie en perceptie', doctoral dissertation, Gent, Rijksuniversiteit.

Van Geert, P. (1979), De ontwikkeling van het begrijpen, in W. Koops and J.J. van der Werff (eds), 'Overzicht van de Ontwikkelingspsychologie', Groningen, Wolters-Noordhoff, 163-93.

Vaught, G.M., Pittman, M.D. and Rooding, P.A. (1975), Haptic-visual form identification in children aged 4 through 13, 'Perceptual and Motor Skills', 40, 305-6.

Vogel, J.M. (1977), The development of recognition memory for the left-right orientation of pictures, 'Child Development', 48, 1,532-43.

Vogel, J.M. (1979), The influence of verbal descriptions versus orientation codes on kindergartners' memory for the orientation of pictures, 'Child Development', 50, 239-42.

Von Senden, M. (1932), 'Raum- und Gestaltauffassung bei operierten blindgeborenen', Leipzig, Barth.

Von Slagle, U. (1974), 'Language, Thought and Perception. A Proposed Theory of Meaning', Den Haag, Mouton.

Vurpillot, E. (1974), Les débuts de la construction de l'espace chez l'enfant, in 'Symposium de l'Association de Psychologie Scientifique de langue Française, "De l'espace corporel à l'espace écologique"', Paris, Presses Universitaires de France.

Vurpillot, E. (1976a), Development of identification of objects, in V. Hamilton and M.D. Vernon (eds), 'The Development of Cognitive Processes', New York, Academic Press, 191-237.

Vurpillot, E. (1976b), 'The Visual World of the Child', London, Allen & Unwin.

Vurpillot, E. (1978), De waarneming van sociale objekten door baby's, in F.J. Mönks and P.G. Heymans (eds), 'Communicatie en Interactie bij het jonge kind', Nijmegen, Dekker en van de Vegt; 1-15.

Vygotsky, L.S. (1978), 'Mind in Society: The Development of Higher Psychological Processes', M. Cole, V. John-Steiner, S. Scribner and E. Souberman (eds), Cambridge, Mass., Harvard University Press.

Walk, R.D. (1968), Monocular compared to binocular depth perception in human infants, 'Science', 162, 473-5.

Waller, B. (1977), Chomsky, Wittgenstein and the behaviorist perspective on language, 'Behaviorism', 5(1), 43-59.

Walters, C.P., and Walk, R.D. (1974), Visual placing by human infants, 'Journal of Experimental Child Psychology', 18, 34-40.

Wason, P.C., and Johnson-Laird, P.N. (1972), 'Psychology of Reasoning: Structure and Content', Cambridge (Mass.), Harvard University Press.

Watson, J.S. (1968), Conservation: an S-R analysis, in I.E. Sigel and F.H. Hooper (eds), 'Logical Thinking in Children', New York, Holt, Rinehart and Winston, 447-60.

Watson, J.S., Hayes, L.A., Vietze, P., and Becker, J. (1979), Discriminative infant smiling to orientations of talking faces of mother and stranger, 'Journal of Experimental Child Psychology', 28, 92-9.

Watzlawick, P., Beavin, J.H., and Jackson, D.D. (1967), 'Pragmatics of Human Communication', New York, Norton.

Weizmann, F., Cohen, L.B., and Pratt, R.J. (1971), Novelty, familiarity and the development of infant attention, 'Developmental Psychology', 4, 149-54.

Welch, J. (1974), Infants' visual attention to varying degrees of novelty, 'Child Development', 45, 344-50.

Wertheimer, M. (1923), Untersuchungen zur Lehre von der Gestalt, 'Psychologische Forschung', 4, 301-50.

Wertheimer, M. (1961), Psychomotor coordination of auditory and visual space at birth, 'Science', 134, 65.

Wertsch, J.V. (1979), From social interaction to higher psychological processes. A clarification and application of Vygotsky's theory, 'Human Development', 22, 1-22.

Whorf, B.L. (1937), Grammatical Categories, 'Language', 21, 1-11,1945; reprinted in Carroll, J.B. (1956), 'Language, Thought and Reality', 87-101, Cambridge, Mass., MIT Press.

Wilcox, B.M. (1969), Visual preference of human infants for representations of the human face, 'Journal of Experimental Child Psychology', 7, 10-20.

Williams, L., and Golenski, J. (1978), Infant speech sound discrimination: the effects of contingent versus noncontingent stimulus presentation, 'Child Development', 49, 213-17.

Williams, T.M., and Aiken, L.S. (1975), Auditory pattern classification: continuity of prototype use with development, 'Developmental Psychology', 10, 715-23.

Williams, T.M., and Aiken, L.S. (1977), Development of pattern-classification: auditory-visual equivalence in the use of prototypes, 'Developmental Psychology', 13(3), 198-204.

Williams, T.M., Fryer, M.L., and Aiken, L.S. (1977), Development of visual pattern classification in pre-school children: prototypes and distinctive features, 'Developmental Psychology', 13(6), 577-84.

Williamson, A.M., and McKenzie, B.E. (1979), Children's discrimination of oblique lines, 'Journal of Experimental Child Psychology', 27, 533-43.

Winters, J.J., and Baldwin, D. (1971), Development of two- and three-dimensional size constancy under restricted cue conditions, 'Journal of Experimental Psychology', 88, 113-18.

Wittgenstein, L. (1953), 'Philosophical Investigations', Oxford, Basil Blackwell & Mott.

Wohlwill, J.F. (1960), Developmental studies of perception, 'Psychological Bulletin', 57, 249-88.

Wohlwill, J.F. (1971), Effect of correlated visual and tactual feedback on auditory pattern learning at different age levels, 'Journal of Experimental Child Psychology', 11, 213-28.

Wormith, S.J., Pankhurst, D., and Moffit, A.R. (1975), Frequency discrimination by young infants, 'Child Development', 46(1), 272-9.

Wright, P.B. (1978), The training of Socrates, 'Inquiry', 19, 91-8.

Yarbus, A.L. (1967), 'Eye movements and vision', New York, Plenum Press.

Yonas, A., Bechtold, A.G., Frankel, D., Gordon, F.R., McRoberts, G., Norcia, A., and Sternfels, S. (1977), Development of sensitivity to information for impending collision, 'Perception and Psychophysics', 21(2), 97-104.

Yonas, A., Cleaves, W.T., and Pettersen, L. (1978), Development of sensitivity to pictorial depth, 'Science', 200, 77-9.

Yonas, A., and Hagen, M.A. (1973), Effects on static and motion parallax depth information on perception of size in children and adults, 'Journal of Experimental Child Psychology', 15, 254-65.

Yonas, A., Oberg, C., and Norcia, A. (1978), Development of sensitivity to binocular information for the approach of an object, 'Developmental Psychology', 14(2), 147-52.

Young-Browne, G., Rosenfeld, H.M., and Horowitz, F.D. (1977), Infant discrimination of facial expression, 'Child Development', 48, 555-62.

Zenatti, A. (1969), Le développement génétique de la perception musicale, 'Monographies Francaises de Psychologie', 17.

Zinkernagel, P. (1962), 'Conditions for Description', London, Routledge & Kegan Paul.

Subject index

accommodation, 198-9, 225, 251f, 300, 302

act, 60; object and domain, 212; perceptual, 95-6, 127

action, 256-7; and causality perception, 156; and conceptualization of world, 303f; constituents, 156-7, 303f; and investigation of perceptual development, 54, 180; and object of perception, 45; and practical metapsychology, 259; as precursor to language, 156; see also language development; one-and-two-word sentence

adaptation, 198-9

additive syntax, 312; see also syntax and perception

adequacy conditions, 276, 292, 294, 296, 303, 305, 326f, 332; and context, 296; public character, 334f

affordances, 290-1

agent, 247, 256; see also action constituents

algorithm, 198

allocentric space, 104; see also space; spatial

ambiguous figures, 172

Ames room, 45

ampliation, 156, 318; see also causality perception

analysis of stimulus variation, 41

analytic sentence, 313

antecedents of speech acts, 345; see also speech acts

applicability of developmental models and statements, 20f, 27; empirical, 6, 15

aspect (linguistic), 316

assimilation, 198-9, 225, 251f, 300, 302

attention, 182f; components of, 182f; and dynamics of perceptual development, 182f; and object space, 187; and selectivity, 182; social aspects, 194-5; tropisms, 53; see also focus; periphery; selective attention; zone of proximal attention

attention shift and programmes, 190f; see also programme

auditory cues of space, 83

auditory pattern (development of), 151, 157; see also music; speech; temporal pattern

auditory space, 62

auditory tropistic programme, 195

auditory-visual integration, 65

babbling stage, 321

behaviour, concept of, 344-5; and semiology, 345

behaviour, models of, 345; behaviouristic, 345f, 353; common sense, 350; competence theory, 347; cybernetic, 6; elastic explanation space, 352f; horizontal, 345f; horizontal mapping, 354; information processing theory, 346, 354; and practical metapsychology, 259; structural theory, 347; structural-behaviourist mapping, 354-5; vertical, 350f; vertical-horizontal mapping, 353f

behaviourism, 214

belief attribution, 348

bimodally specified events, 69

bimodally specified objects, 70

binocular cues, 89, 92

binocular disparity, 81-2, 92, 127

breaching experiments, 258

calculation as mental act, 229ff; theory of, 230, 232

calculator, electronic, 229ff; Pascal, 231f

carrier programme, 197

Cartesian coordinate system, see coordinate system

case grammar, 298; and action-structure, 298

categorical perception, 160

causality concept, 154

causality perception, 150, 153; and causality concept, 154; developmental experiments, 154f; and syntax, 318-19

central projection system, 79f, 88-90

classificatory level, 12

clever Hans effect, 51

closure, 173

clown-and-cone game, 302

Name index

Abramovitch, R., 178
Acredolo, L.P., 104
Aiken, L.S., 160-9
Allen, T.W., 70, 101, 161
Alston, W.P., 275
Ames, E.M., 162
Anderson, J.M., 298
Anderson, J.R., 279
Appelbaum, M.I., 54
Ariès, P., 4-5, 25-6
Arnold, W.R., 53
Aronson, E., 65, 77
Ashby, W.R., 6
Ashton, R., 51
Austin, J.L., 250, 275

Baldwin, D., 124
Baldwin, P., 291
Ball, W., 84
Balter, L., 71
Banks, M.S., 53
Barrett, M.D., 271
Bartholomeus, B., 158
Bartley, S.H., 141
Bates, E., 251
Bechthold, A.G., 85
Beck, J., 96
Becker, J., 54
Bell, R.Q., 176
Bemner, J.G., 104
Berg, W.K., 53
Berger, P.L., 23, 258
Bergman, T., 176
Berkeley, 49, 79-80, 265
Berlin, B., 21
Berlyne, D.E., 182, 354
Berman, P.W., 103
Bernholtz, N., 323
Berry, J.W., 20
Bierwisch, M., 22
Birch, H.G., 61, 73, 167
Birke, M., 151, 163
Black, M., 240
Blakemore, C., 283
Blank, M.S., 71-2
Bloom, L., 322-3, 337
Blue, S.Z., 52
Blumenthal, A.L., 309
Bornstein, M.H., 163, 165, 167, 180

Boswell, S., 91
Bower, T.G.R., 37, 51, 53-4, 57,
  59, 61, 74, 77, 84-6, 92, 116, 119,
  120-2, 151, 196, 241, 246, 252, 261,
  282, 289
Bowerman, M., 167, 238, 327
Boyle, J.P., 53
Brachfeld, S., 168-9, 267
Brainerd, C.J., 8, 214-15, 222-3
Bram, S., 152
Brennan, W.M., 162
Brentano, F., 60
Bridger, W.H., 70-2, 203
Brill, S.C., 158
Brimm, O.G., 163
Brindley, R., 58
Brittain, L.W., 103
Brody, N., 52
Broerse, J., 61, 197
Brooks, V., 90
Broughton, J.M., 74, 84
Brown, C., 176
Brown, J.W., 51, 53
Brown, R., 51, 213, 298, 300, 322
Bruce, A., 177
Bruner, J.S., 4, 19-20, 24-5, 55,
  214, 226, 257, 268, 275, 299-300,
  302, 327, 350-1
Bruno, L.A., 163, 176, 203
Bryant, D.E., 70-2, 104, 214
Burnham, D.K., 151-2
Bushnell, I.W.R., 151
Butterworth, G., 61

Cabe, P.A., 168
Cairns, E., 73
Caldwell, R.C., 176
Camaioni, L., 251
Cambardella, P., 73
Campbell, D., 53
Campbell, D.T., 126
Campbell, R.N., 238, 291
Carey, S., 158-9, 177
Carlson, V.R., 121
Carney, G., 73
Caron, A.J., 53, 121, 176
Caron, R.F., 53, 121, 176
Carpenter, P.A., 293
Carroll, J.B., 315

For Product Safety Concerns and Information please contact our EU
representative GPSR@taylorandfrancis.com
Taylor & Francis Verlag GmbH, Kaufingerstraße 24, 80331 München, Germany

www.ingramcontent.com/pod-product-compliance
Lightning Source LLC
Chambersburg PA
CBHW070538270326
41926CB00013B/2142